American Religious Traditions

American Religious Traditions

The Shaping of Religion in the United States
with CD-ROM

Richard E. Wentz

Fortress Press
MINNEAPOLIS

AMERICAN RELIGIOUS TRADITIONS
The Shaping of Religion in the United States with CD-ROM

This book is a full-scale revision and updating of the author's earlier work, *Religion in the New World: The Shaping of Religious Traditions in the United States,* published by Fortress Press in 1990.

Cover art: Menorah © Photodisc, Inc. *Baptism* © Anna Belle Lee Washington / SuperStock; used by permission. *San Diego Mission* by Josephine Joy is used by permission of the Smithsonian American Art Museum (transfer from the Museum of Modern Art).
Cover and interior design: Beth Wright

"The Gift Outright" by Robert Frost from *The Poetry of Robert Frost,* edited by Edward Connery Latham and Jonathan Cape, is copyright 1936 by Robert Frost, © 1964 by Lesley Frost Ballantine, © 1969 by Henry Holt and Co. Reprinted by permission of Henry Holt and company, LLC, the Estate of Robert Frost, and the Random House Group, U.K.
Excerpt from "Choruses from 'The Rock'" in *Collected Poems 1909–1962* by T. S. Eliot, © 1936 Harcourt, Inc., © 1963, 1964 T. S. Eliot, is reprinted by permission of Harcourt, Inc., and Faber & Faber Ltd.

ISBN 0-8006-3616-3

The paper used in this publication meets the minimum requirements of American National Standard for Information Sciences — Permanence of Paper for Printed Library Materials, ANSI Z329.48-1984.

Manufactured in Canada

4   5   6   7   8   9   10

For Cynthia

Contents

A gallery of illustrations follows page 186.

Preface

This is a book about American religious traditions. Traditions are identifiable ways of expressing how human beings set about organizing their thoughts and actions about what it means to exist. Traditions include ideas, commitments, customs, manners, and celebrations of life in its complexity. Traditions help us to understand and to portray the inconsistencies and disharmonies of existence.

Although not all of our religious activity is confined to traditions, most of our festivals, private assumptions, and experiences take place in relationship to an existing tradition. The point is that religious traditions exist and those of us who study religious activity must know something about them. A tradition is never a closed system, but a collective memory—a way of perceiving existence. Perception includes perspectives (tendencies, attitudes) as well as actions that may be either conscious and deliberate or unpremeditated (often idiosyncratic). Even the most rational or pragmatic of us draws upon tradition to assist in the living of our days beyond the laboratory, the academic conference, or the marketplace. Each of us is expected to be a mensch, who must respond to failure and the need for love and care. Unless we allow ourselves to be reduced to what we know as researchers, executives, or attorneys, we realize that we exist in circumstances that are always more than what we know of them. To be at home with a spouse, three children, and a border collie requires an imaginative grasp of life that cannot be controlled by our individual genius.

Like life itself, traditions are both organism and artifact. *Artifacts* are the things we do and make, our contributions to the arts of discovery and problem-solving. *Organism* refers to the way life grows as the result of intentional thoughts and actions as well as serendipitous consequences quite beyond expectation. A tradition is never static. The traditionalist may hope to make it so, but both her motivations and the outcome of her efforts bear witness to the dynamic quality of tradition. It can never be "the same" because what we ask of it and our implementation of its insights and practices will be shaped by a particular moment in the human journey.

Religion is often thought of as the sacred—the affirmation of an experience or commitment to an event, place, or person who becomes the center of existence. The sacred becomes a point of reference. The Fourth of July and what we now refer to as "9/11" are sacred moments in relation to which we Americans organize our sense of time and our programs of meaningful action. However, religion is not the sacred; rather it represents the way we hold the sacred in dynamic (dialectical) tension with the everydayness (what Martin Heidegger called the *Alltäglichkeit*) of existence. The sacred may inform and organize everydayness, but the quotidian can never be identified with it. Everydayness includes chaos, disorder, and disharmony. Religion provides the ideas and actions that enable us to maintain the significance of the sacred in circumstances that deny it. To use Mircea Eliade's familiar terms, religion is the *dialectic* of the sacred and profane. If religion were limited to the sacred, it would be contrary to the manner in which human beings have expressed it throughout history. The evidence of history, in both past and present (social) contexts, suggests that religion is the way human beings petition and juggle the sacred in the profane world of pain, suffering, joy, depression, success, failure, and sheer invariability. Therefore, we may expect to observe religion anywhere, anytime.

In this book we shall concentrate on those religious traditions that have been important to the cultural shaping of the United States of America. There will be many religious phenomena not tended to in this volume. However, I will assume that those religious traditions discussed are a significant and continually present element in our religious life. Whatever else we may study, we should not ignore them because they are historical frames of religious reference. They contain the stories by means of which people maintain the dialectic of the sacred and the profane. The categories of religious expression referred to later in chapter 1 may be used to investigate ideas and practices that exist outside of and complementary to the traditions studied in this book. These categories form what may be called a method of study; however, they should not be construed as a methodology—a devotion to method that frequently leaves little room for alternative modes of reflection.

Finally, it must be said that any method used in the study of religion should lead us to learn something about what it means to be human. When, for example, we turn to the description of a religion like the Lutheran tradition, we should ask: What very human issues, such as those with which I myself must contend, are encountered in Lutheranism? What do I learn about being human by struggling to understand this tradition? If I learn little or nothing, I probably have not really encountered the tradition, and my study is little more than the collation of information.

Obviously, this book need not be used exclusively according to its chapters—Tuesday: chapter 1; Thursday: chapter 2; etc. The students and the professor may decide to use themes or questions that require reading across chapters. They may ask, for example, what is the comparative value of the verbal expressions of all traditions directly related to the Reformation? Students are also encouraged to assemble a glossary of terms encountered in their reading. Do not rely on dictionary definitions, but instead fashion definitions from reading and understanding the terms as they appear in context.

My colleague, Moses N. Moore, has kept me grounded in historical particularity, with his careful study of uncharacteristic African American religion. My wife and colleague, Cynthia Carsten Wentz, has contributed her laudable critical skills and her study of Native American traditions. And, of course, the more recent works of Mark Noll, Jon Butler, Robert Orsi, David D. Hall, and Leigh Schmidt have helped to reorganize my thinking about the uncharacteristic nature of religion in America. Yet my long-standing interest in the Mercersburg Movement served as a basis for questioning consensual models of understanding. It remains impossible for me, however, to ignore the "lived religion" of the traditions, the denominations, and religious thought. Sooner or later, she who thinks about religion must find a story, a frame of reference, for her ideas. I have become fascinated by festivals and images. I have begun to think of our Lady of Guadalupe as "Mother of the Americas," and she is present in a shrine in my backyard. But theology keeps me honest and remains an important element in my religious imagination and practice. And I think that the prevailing American religion that exists in complementary fashion to the traditions, and to civil religion, is no longer a *Protestant* ideology. As a lived religion it can be found among Roman Catholic, Jews, humanists, and, increasingly, Muslims.

This volume, which is the second edition of my earlier work, *Religion in the New World,* incorporates substantial revisions and updates in all chapters, particularly heavy reworking of material on the contemporary American religious scene, and the addition of a CD-ROM. The latter includes not only the full text of the book, chapter summaries, and reflection questions, but also links to a wealth of exciting and important web-based texts, graphics, and bibliographies. All of this, I hope, will deepen and enhance the student's encounter with the living traditions of American religious life.

Part 1

The Age of Transmission and Reformation

In the first part of this book we attempt to understand religious traditions that had their origins in continental Europe and the British Isles. These traditions emerged out of the struggle to assert new ideas and to reclaim those that had been presumably neglected over centuries of history. Beginning in perhaps the fourteenth century, scholars and other persons of intellectual vision sought to discover the great ideas, practices, and achievements of the European past. These searches and discoveries found expression in art, literature, philosophy, and religion. The early part of this great discovery was dubbed the Renaissance, separating it from the sixteenth-century endeavor to affirm Christian insights that were considered lost during the centuries of Catholic history.

However, we must remember that the Renaissance was as important to religious history as was the Reformation of the sixteenth century. The European "discovery" and colonization of the western hemisphere coincided with the time in which Renaissance ideas were intermingling with the conflicting notions of Christianity in circulation as a result of the Reformation. Few of the ideas, practices, and institutions of the renascence and reform of the Christian world had yet taken any final shape. They were formed in the course of the settlement of the North American continent. They came to America with the people who were the agents of European colonization— either as authorized colonizers or as refugees. Ideas and practices generated in Europe and the British Isles were fashioned into unique religious traditions in the American setting. And, of course, when we explore Native American traditions, we must note that our religious traditions were shaped not only by Europe by also by the existence of ideas and practices active on this continent from times coincident to the beginnings of Christianity.

As we embark on the study of American religious traditions, we must first arrive at an understanding of how religion is studied in the academic world. We must examine the special forms of thought and communication that are part of religious expression. We must re-think the nature of such categories as myth and legend, and be certain that we realize that religious ideas and practices are never confined to religious institutions and official doctrinal pronouncements. Once we open our minds to the many ways of thinking about religion, we shall be prepared to investigate those traditions transmitted to America from Europe and shaped in the particular circumstances of the Colonial and early National Periods of our history.

Note: Traditions such as Judaism and Eastern Orthodox Christianity will be discussed in part 2 because the presence of representatives of these traditions was minimal in the periods under discussion in part 1.

chapter 1

The Study of Religion

During the fall of 1985, I spent a sabbatical semester in Japan. I was interested in learning something about the beliefs, ideas, images, and ritual life of the Japanese people. Perhaps you will think this pursuit is a strange thing for an Americanist to do. After all, I have spent much of my professional life studying what is called "religion in America" and "American religion," and I am directing this book toward an understanding of religion in the United States. However, I wanted to gain some perspective from another culture, another history, another place with religious traditions. Japan is a fascinating land, with marvelously hospitable people. But, of course, they are human beings like the rest of us. They eat and sleep, eliminate waste, engage in sexual relationships, get angry, give birth, and die. They long for peace and they make war—just like the rest of us.

There are two sets of issues that interest me as a scholar of religion. One set comprises those things that people believe, think, and do that are often ignored by official representatives and spokespersons for conventional religious traditions like Christianity, Buddhism, and Islam. Such concerns come under the heading of "folk religion." Japan has a long history of folk religion, and scholars have been studying it for a long time. I went to Japan to study folk religion because I wanted to learn how to study folk religion in the United States.

The other issue that occupies my thinking and tempers my reading is that there are often beliefs, ideas, images, and practices that are closely associated with a nation, a people. In other words, sometimes just being a Russian or an American is like belonging to or following a religious tradition, like Judaism or Christianity. Early in the twentieth century British journalist G. K. Chesterton called America the "nation with the soul of a church." And there is little doubt that Americans attach religious significance to the land and its destiny. I knew that the history of Japan was based on a story about the descent of the emperor and his people from Amaterasu-Omikami, the holy daughter of the sun. I wanted to find out how the sense of peoplehood in Japan expresses itself religiously in society and its culture.

I discovered many things in Japan. It is a land of contemplation. Through the centuries there has marched a long procession of pilgrims—poets and thinkers in search of the soul of existence. In beautiful words and ideas they have celebrated the order and meaning of life. Some of these thinkers have identified themselves with known religious traditions like Buddhism, Confucianism, or Taoism. However, these imported traditions have quickly developed a distinctly Japanese character. Today we may hear of the Kyoto school of Buddhist philosophy. And a student of Zen Buddhism quickly learns that, in spite of the Chinese heritage to which Zen is indebted, it is a Japanese form of Buddhism. To observe Japanese culture is to discover that what human beings call religion can be a very contemplative, philosophical, or aesthetic affair. Their religious life takes expression in what we recognize today as a very secular and techno-corporate society.

I saw a tiny, very old Shinto shrine on the grounds of the Sapporo Brewery in Hokkaido. In fields and mountainsides throughout Japan I saw *torri*, gates leading into the sacred precincts of a local shrine. And at the great shrines like Ise, Atsuta in Nagoya, Meiji in Tokyo, or Shiogama on the northern coast of Honshu, I saw hundreds of people making offerings, saying prayers, and receiving special readings of their individual futures. There is not much conscious thought or study given to such practices; people just do them. These actions, too, are part of what we are accustomed to calling religion.

Japan is a land of festivals. There are solemn occasions that take focus at the Shinto shrines or Buddhist temples. But there are also times of great festivity when people feast, dance, parade, and drink great quantities of *sake*. The great festival of the dead, *Bon,* celebrated in August with prayer, fires, feasting, and games, is an occasion that plays an important role in the religious life of Japan. There is such diversity in Japan. Yet all these things may be called religion.

I think of the United States and remember the Memorial Days of my childhood and youth. I once had to deliver a five-minute address at a ceremony held in a cemetery near my home. We marched together with bands playing "Onward, Christian Soldiers," "The Battle Hymn of the Republic," and "The Stars and Stripes Forever." And after the prayers and the hymns and addresses, we went home for a special feast. Memorial Day, like Thanksgiving and the Fourth of July, was an important religious occasion.

On a visit to a Jewish synagogue in the Williamsburg section of Brooklyn, one may observe a curious excitement over the interpretation of texts and a solemn recitation of prayers that reach back into the hearts of people whose voices have been silent for centuries. One can visit a pentecostal assembly in an auditorium in any American city and observe the jerking movements and hear the groans and cries of people overwhelmed in ecstasy by the Holy Spirit. These pentecostals are a variety of Christian people. One can walk into the precincts of the Cathedral of St. John the Divine or St. Patrick's Cathedral in Manhattan or the Cathedral of Saints Peter and Paul, also known as the National Cathedral in Washington, and find an uplifting silence that dissolves all anxieties and burning desires. Visits to such places as the National Cathedral have been known to demonstrate, even to children from religiously indifferent families, that life is awesomely more than it seems to be. Cathedrals are also places in which to observe or participate in very dignified and stately ceremonies that are nothing like the routine activities of our daily life and work. These sacred precincts and their practices belong to all of the people of the nation in addition to their special significance to many who would call themselves Christian.

On the Hopi mesas of north central Arizona, one may observe some of the kachina rituals. The kachinas are the sacred beings who share their spirit with the Hopi people. They are not so much gods to be worshiped as they are honored and powerful associates. When the dancers in their kachina costumes impersonate those spirits, they lose their personal identity and are transformed into kachinas. The rituals put the people in touch with the power of fertility that is fundamental to the life they celebrate. The messengers visit each house of the village, bringing a cornhusk "to be breathed upon." It contains pollen and prayer feathers. The seed corn is blessed inside the sacred kivas, Hopi ceremonial huts, and as each collector climbs the ladder to leave the kiva, he simulates sexual intercourse. Everyone in the community knows the mystery of life, its beginnings and endings. America is a place of great religious diversity.

We could continue to fill in vast murals in our depiction of the great diversity of beliefs, ideas, and practices that are part of American life, its history and culture. How is it possible that all of this may be called religion? There are those who would insist that a religion is a system of belief in a supreme being, but there are many human traditions in which the notion of a supreme being or beings is not a central issue. Accordingly, it is necessary to ask: Then what exactly is religion? Why do we give the name *religion* to such a diverse set of ideas and practices?

Toward a Definition of Religion

First of all, it is necessary to accept the fact that religion cannot be defined in terms of what we think it ought to be. After all, we all have convictions of one sort or another about such matters. A Shiite Muslim may wish to suggest that the Shiite way of practicing the traditions of Muhammad and the Qur'an is the only true religion. Therefore, to that Muslim, that particular way is the only one, and there are no others. A born-again American evangelical Christian may wish to conclude that true religion is personal acceptance of the salvation provided to the individual by the atonement of Jesus Christ and that anything else is not really religion. A skeptic may view all such matters as evidence of human ignorance or naïveté, silly superstition, a hangover from an age of credulity. All of these attitudes are evidence of a normative understanding of religion. That is, the people who make these assumptions are creating a norm for defining religion—a norm that is based on individual or group convictions and commitments.

In order to study religion, it is necessary to set aside our norms for what religion ought to be or how we define the word. We must accept the fact that religions involve many elements of the lives of human beings like ourselves who are no less and no more intelligent than the brightest or dullest among us and who have needs and relationships common to all. It is our business to understand to the best of our ability what a Buddhist is and what Buddhism means. We must be ready to understand what the religious assumptions and practices of a member of the Fellowship of Atheists really are. In our opinion or according to the norms of our own faith, the Buddhist or the atheist may be a representative of false religion or less-than-adequate religion. But they exist. Their ways of living are part of the human story. They are to be understood. No religious movement may be dismissed by calling it a cult and exiling it to the status of the inferior or the ignorant.

Once we are prepared to understand, we are ready to ask: What do all of those diverse beliefs, ideas, and practices to which we ascribe the term *religion* have in common? A definition emerges: Religion is the systematic set of expressions that reflects the ultimate order, meaning, and possible transformation of existence for a people. Let us see what it means to make such a statement. Let us begin with the phrase "set of expressions." Whatever else human beings are, they are religious. "Religion," wrote Thomas Luckmann, "is rooted in a basic anthropological fact: the transcendence of biological nature by human organisms."[1] The acorn knows no freedom, no transcendence. It matures on the oak tree and falls to the ground. In the process of decay, a "coded message" of nature may draw it into the earth where it will root itself to become a sapling, perhaps one day an oak tree. It is a biological organism, with no conscious stake in its destiny. So far as we know, there is no freedom, therefore no choice, no responsibility, for the acorn. But as human beings, we are more than biological organisms. There is a "more than" quality to our existence. We transcend—rise above—our own existence. There is an element of freedom to our being, so we also have a measure of responsibility for our lives. We must make choices, decisions; sometimes the failure to make conscious decisions introduces surprise, accident— perhaps serendipitous results—into our lives. The existence of the acorn is in this world and of this world. We, on the other hand, see what is invisible to the acorn. We reflect upon its world and our own. We are not "of a piece" as is the acorn. As William James put it in his 1895 essay, "Is Life Worth Living?" a human being lives in this world while being aware of the fact that the world may be more than it seems to be. In fact, we know that there is much that we do not sense, much that may not be accessible to our ordinary, workaday minds—no matter how intelligent or scientific those minds may be. Human beings are forced to speculate, to imagine, to intuit, and think that what we do not see, what is outside our coded sensual existence, may have an essential role to play in our lives. The only way to ignore this "more than" quality to our existence is to act as if we were acorns—an action much more detrimental to us than to acorns. The acorn does not need to integrate its existence; we do.

The word *religion* comes from the Latin *re ligare*, which means to bind together. The word came into use as a reference for those human ways of integrating existence, of expressing meaning in an integrated universe. We are creatures who must be able to perceive the world as whole, with ourselves sharing that wholeness. This is what we mean when we say that human beings are religious. In some sense it means that all of us are religious because the integration of existence is never an entirely private or individual affair. Being religious does not mean being pious or even practicing a religion.

Expressions of Religiousness

Does this mean that we can be religious in many ways, that anything and everything can become the occasion for us to express our religiousness? One answer is yes. The history of religions is the story of the many ways in which virtually everything in this world has been the focus of human religiousness in some way and at some time or another. An animal, a rock, a mountain, a hole in the earth may become sacred. In becoming sacred—holy—it serves as an occasion to make life whole.

Whatever else we may be, we are religious because of our transcendent character as human beings—our need for integration. Our religiousness expresses itself in several ways. First, it expresses itself as experience. Experience has two sides to it, the one subjective, the other objective. We are very used to limiting experience to its subjective side, in which it comes to mean something intense, private, and filled with feeling. We may ask someone, Have you ever had a religious experience? In doing so we are wondering whether that someone can point to some emotionally charged incident that was mind-altering or that disrupted ordinary consciousness, such as a vision, receiving an important message, or communication with the "spirit world," or merely the consciousness of some great warmth or inrushing presence—a sense of not being alone. Subjective experience of this kind is a common form of religious experience. It may result in a centering or reorganization of our lives. And, of course, we may not even call it religious.

But experience means something else as well. When we apply for a job, the personnel director may ask us what experience we have had. Obviously, she or he is not inquiring into our private psychology but wants to know whether we have worked with ideas and skills that are related to responsibilities we might have with her or his organization. In the same way, a person may speak or write of having experienced World War II. The reference is to having been in touch with the war in some way that the person's thoughts, ideas, and ways of doing things were affected. This reflects *objective* experience, by which we imply a "living through." That is to say, experience is not only the private, subjective, and emotional, but it is the act of "living with" someone or something in such a manner that we can discover special significance. We can experience education, Jewishness, or World War II. Often we may not be aware of this kind of experience; it may have no intense or explosive moments. But objective experience may be even more important than the subjective kind. And for many of us such "lived with" and "lived through" occasions may well be more important than the peak subjective experiences we may sometimes have. Human religiousness expresses itself in subjective and objective experience. The point is that we humans are social beings and find ultimate order and meaning through the family, the village, the nation, and participation in groups that share a common story.

As transcendent beings, our religiousness also expresses itself in images and ideas that are best described as storytelling. We live not so much in a world as in a perception of the world. The mind works with images and ideas that tell a story. The traditional words for such storytelling are myth and legend. Myths are the stories we live with that let us know who we are, where we come from, and where we are going. Myths are inescapable. Even the scientist becomes a mythmaker when telling a story of why things happen, creating images of particles and fluidity, and communicating a perception of the world that many people can live with. The perception of the world satisfies the scientist's own religious need (at least to a point) and lends hope that "things will be better" if everyone lives the story offered.

The people responsible for the emergence myths of the Hopi and the ancestors of the Jews and Christians who gave us the Genesis stories were expressing their sense of having a meaningful and ordered place in the world in which they found themselves. The only means we humans have of expressing our transcendence is through myth and story. Only if we are acorns will there be no myths. Only if human beings do not stand beyond their own organism to view it and take responsibility for it will there be no need for myths and stories.

But there is another kind of story besides myth that expresses our religiousness. We call it legend. No individual and no committee creates a legend or a myth. Both are cultural products. They emerge like the shape of the houses in which we have been living for centuries. A legend differs from a myth in that it is related to the significance of a person or an event. A legend dips into and touches history. A myth reaches into the darkness before and beyond history. It creates images of origins and images that place us in the world of time and place—history. Myth tells us who we are and helps to sustain us in our going. Myth is not a negative thing to be exorcised; it should not be confused with a misconception—an erroneous idea. It is a creative reality to be explored and nurtured. No human lives without myth.

Legend, on the other hand, is a story that tells us about the importance or the meaning of a certain happening or person. The exodus of the Jews from captivity in Egypt thousands of years ago is known to us by way of legend. That some such event occurred in Hebrew and Egyptian history is quite likely. But the event itself is not nearly so significant as the meaning it has held in Jewish—and Christian—memory. The meaning and power of whatever occurred is so much a part of the event that the only means of expressing it is through a storytelling form we call *legend*. A historian may try to find evidence to discredit the event but only does so out of a desire to get at the heart of its significance. It will still continue to be important because it furnishes images of hope necessary to human existence. As transcendent beings, we always look to a future, and in order to do so hopefully, we reach into the depths of history and tradition for the images that serve as paradigms—examples and patterns of hope. The sermons and addresses of Martin Luther King Jr., delivered at the height of the black civil rights movement, drew heavily upon images received from the legend of Exodus. The legends of Daniel Boone and Davey Crockett tell us what frontier American values were, what life on the frontier meant to people in the nineteenth century. It is difficult to separate the significance of these men from the actual circumstances of their lives because they have become legendary figures. In the same way, we carry legends of George Washington and Abraham Lincoln and speak reverently of the "founding fathers." All this storytelling activity is an expression of our religiousness, our transcendent need to express order and meaning in existence.

Another expression of our religiousness is conceptual. When it becomes necessary to think about the ultimate order and meaning of life, we develop ideas. We try to make sense of things. Our minds work at clarifying our understanding of these matters. We form concepts—ideas we can use to talk to ourselves and to others. The end result may be a set of seemingly private theories and convictions, or it may be an articulation of teachings we have knowingly received from a great teacher or tradition. All people are thinking people who must clarify and communicate ideas of how life is ordered and what it means. That thinking is an expression of our religiousness.

Our religiousness also expresses itself ethically. As Plato said, "the unexamined life is not worth living." One reason we examine our lives and try to find concepts that satisfy us is that we have some concern for the way we should live. That is, we seek a reliable pattern or set of motivations for our behavior. That is called *ethics,* and it is seldom a private affair inasmuch as we would not be much concerned about behavior if we were individual and separate atoms in the scheme of things. We would only be concerned about not hurting ourselves. Having to live with "others" (others as humans, others as animals, others as trees and water) poses the necessity of finding a way to behave—a way to live, to make life "worth living." And we must learn how and why to do certain things and not others.

Of course, there are actions we take as human beings that are not so much concerned with right behavior and right living as with our sense of participation in the ongoingness of existence. A man comes home from his construction job on a Monday evening in the fall of the year. He hurries to empty the garbage and eat the TV dinner he has shoved into the microwave. He takes off his shoes and shirt and opens his belt, letting his stomach ease out from under the edge of his T-shirt. He slides into his recliner, elevates his feet, and grabs the remote. On the table next to him is a bowl of chips, some salsa, and a can of beer. He watches the Dallas Cowboys play the Detroit Lions. This man is a ritualist, as we all are. As a transcendent being he is not simply a functioning biological organism. He has to act out some aspect of life that gives order and meaning to his life. He celebrates life. He participates in an event that expresses the beliefs and values of the world in which he works, eats, sleeps, and makes love (does anyone really *make* love?). Someone might point out that this man's ritual life is almost sacramental. The chips and beer are a means of taking into his life the sustaining values of power and winning that are being celebrated on the field.

Ritual is an expression of our religiousness. Ritual is a way of making right what is very wrong in our experience. It is the dramatization of a big picture, by means of which we are able to live with our sorrow, our sense of failure, our knowledge that we have not done as we ought to have done and have been involved in doing what we ought not to have done. When we erect white crosses bedecked with flowers by the sides of the highways, when we place colored balloons and flowers at the site where a friend was killed, we are being ritualistic—acting out some religious sense of order and meaning. Ritual usually involves some special movement or movements, a given set of words, or some special equipment, and it has a story behind it.

Another form of religious expression is the social. Quite often we express a sense of ultimate order and meaning by reference to who we are, to whom we belong, and where we are. When a Navajo speaks of himself as *Diné,* he refers to "the people." Implicit is the notion that *being* and *Navajo* are bound together. *Being Navajo* is to have a meaningful place in a special and sacred order. For the Jew there is ultimate order and meaning expressed in being Israel, the covenanted community, the people of God. In the Chinese tradition the family is a sacred and unique order of existence; even the state is an extension of it. The head of the family enjoys a status akin to priesthood. A priest is one who knows the special ways that are necessary to offer up the values and commitments of a people. Behind this concept of belongingness is the knowledge that the centers of our living—the towns, houses, mountains, streams in our world—are somehow patterned after a basic and original model that exists before and beyond history as we know it. For example, the family may be for us a holy community because it reflects the heart of what is really real. The divine is itself a family, and life is modeled after it. The social expression of religiousness is the sense of rootedness and belonging that links us to other people and special landscapes.

Thus far the discussion has focused on the way in which human religiousness works at discerning the ultimate order and meaning of existence. We have discussed the modes of religious expression, all of which are directed at the transformation of existence. If, for example, we engage in ritual, it is to distance ourselves from the ordinariness of existence, to gain some perspective from which to perceive our lives. This gaining of perspective plays a role in transforming life. Along with other modes of expression, it is transformative. A question we frequently raise is: Is it possible that the human condition can be altered? If life is more than we are able to perceive or know at any one time, then it is possible that there are other ways of perceiving it. In other words, perhaps we do not ordinarily know reality (what is real). Perhaps the mind can be transformed—become other than what it is (preferably, more than what it is)—so that it may perceive what is not ordinarily perceived.

Some people in the world assume that transformation make us one with the animals, the plants, and other people. The kachina dancer in the Hopi tradition becomes the spirit person whose mask he wears. He is transformed by dancing and ecstasy and crosses the boundaries that he ordinarily recognizes as an everyday person. The Zen monk seeks to overcome his reliance upon ordinary reason by means of *zazen* (sitting meditation) or the use of *koan* (puzzling statements). When he achieves *kensho* (a state of enlightenment or seeing one's own true nature), it is because he now perceives reality differently. He has been transformed.

Categories of Religious Expression

The six modes of religious expression may be condensed into three functional categories or forms, in keeping with a device of Joachim Wach, a sociologist of religion who defined the three primary categories of religion as theoretical, practical, and sociological.[2] The corresponding terms we shall use throughout this study are *verbal, practical,* and *social.* By the verbal expression of religiousness we refer to the use of words *to conceive and communicate* the ultimate order and meaning of existence. In other words, the verbal expression will be discerned in stories, doctrine, ideas, beliefs, and ethical systems. In the tribal or nonliterate traditions we shall expect story, especially myth, to be a fundamental means for the conception and communication of truth. The literate traditions of the religions that are not confined to tribal culture but are worldwide in scope or potential will combine oral communication (story) with written records. This literature may take the form of sacred writings (scripture) or doctrinal statements.

By the practical expression of religiousness we refer to *practice*—those things that people do, actions that are regularized in order to express the ultimate order and meaning of existence. This will ordinarily include such activities as ritual, worship, and pilgrimage.

By the social expression of religiousness we refer to the manner in which interpersonal identification or grouping itself serves as a form of ultimate order and meaning. For the Akamba of Africa, the tribe is itself an expression of sacred order. To be Akamba is to be part of a system that orders life and gives it meaning. For Judaism, the people Israel is the social expression of religion. To be Jewish is to be part of meaningful existence. For Christianity the church is a sacred social reality; it is the Body of Christ. Belonging and identity are important elements in the social expression of religiousness. This must be understood if we are to comprehend why it is that violence often breaks out between tribes, between Sikhs and Hindus, between Muslims and Christians. It is because religious significance is attached to being Sikh or Navajo. Religiousness, in other words, is expressed not only in ideas, beliefs, and practices but also in the social entity to which one belongs—an entity that is a center of sacred order and meaning. Violence and warfare occur when the sacred identity of a people is threatened.

The three forms of religious expression may function independently of each other or in combinations of two. Each form of expression may show itself in art, music, design, science, or even one's labor. After all, expressions of the ultimate order and meaning of existence go on all the time. By themselves we may call them religious expressions and let it go at that. However, when it occurs that all three forms of expression are integrated in a system that is intentional and concerned with continuity in time and space, we may speak of a religion, or a religious tradition. For example, by itself the verbal expression of our religiousness may constitute a philosophy, a school of thinking. When it combines with practices and expresses itself in a social form that promotes identity, it becomes part of a religious tradition. Regarding system, when we speak of "Buddhism," it is because there is a systematic arrangement of the religious expressions we have discussed. The set of expressions is recognizable; they fit together in such a way that we may call the system *Buddhism*. We may speak of the Navajo way as a religion or religious tradition because there is a distinctiveness about the manner in which being Navajo gives form to the entire set of religious expressions. Regarding intentionality, Buddhists must intend that all of their religious expressions shall fit together in a distinctive fashion. They intend being Buddhist by following the Buddhist way. A measure of their human identity is derived from that intention. Navajos know that they are Navajo because they understand and practice the ways of their people. They intend expressing themselves religiously by the special system of the Navajo way.

Having made a case for system and intention in the formation of religions, I now want to modify the conclusion. Sometimes it is possible to recognize the presence of all the religious expressions in a systematic and even intentional way without any acknowledgment that we are dealing with a religion. This means that it is possible for a way of life to function as a religion without being called a religion. We might call such systems quasi-religions—systems that act like religion, play the role of religion. Such systems are part of the postmodern world. Students of religion must be alert to this insight. As people who are concerned with understanding religious behavior, they must be prepared to study it wherever it occurs, in whatever form it occurs. Marxism is one of the quasi-religions of our time. Technology, in its collective link with corporate economics and politics, is another. The techno-corporate world is a religious system, even though we may be unaccustomed to calling it one.

Tradition

Two further observations are important to this introduction. First, the study of religion recognizes the importance of tradition. Tradition is a body of teaching and practice that is maintained through time. A tradition must be conserved, transmitted, and received. The contention of this work is that all human activity is based upon tradition. If we wish to become physicists, we do not walk boldly into some laboratory, impudently proclaim that we are physicists, and start proclaiming truths about the physical properties of the universe. Rather, we study *physics,* learn something of the use of the term, learn the findings of the history of physics, begin to understand what physicists have done and thought. Physics has a tradition, and we must learn from it if we wish to be physicists or have any credibility as persons who understand the physical universe. Even if we launch forth in bold and revolutionary ways (as a Newton, an Einstein, or a Heisenberg), we launch forth as people who speak for the tradition of physics, to which we owe most of our understanding.

Religion is that branch of human knowledge and behavior that has been especially aware of the significance of tradition. That is why we speak of religious traditions—Hinduism, Judaism, Christianity. Christianity is a tradition, or, more accurately, the Christian tradition is an anthology of religious traditions—Reformed, Lutheran, Wesleyan, Pentecostal, Roman Catholic, Anglican, and Orthodox. Religions recognize that in the human struggle to find ultimate order and meaning, but especially to find transformation, tradition is an important guide. Tradition is always the place to begin the search for knowledge and wisdom. It is always the testing ground where one may examine one's own insights and experience. Tradition is the conserved knowledge and understanding concerning basic questions about human life and meaning. Ralph Waldo Emerson expressed the typical American inability to comprehend the significance of tradition when he said, "The foregoing generations beheld God and nature face to face; we through their eyes. Why should not we also enjoy an original relation to the universe?"[3] Of course, we do enjoy an original relation to the universe, but it is never absolute. Our relation to the universe is always enjoyed along with the "foregoing generation." And every previous generation also enjoyed its relationship along with those who had come before. Certainly in the attempt to understand the original relation we enjoy with the universe it will be necessary to consult the conserved wisdom of the past. Tradition will be essential. Tradition is always the teacher. Although the teacher cannot teach us without our permission, it can shape our lives in ways that are often unexamined.

Second, no religious tradition exists in a vacuum. In a certain sense there is no such thing as Buddhism or Christianity. It is always a matter of studying a religion as it is expressed in the lives of a people in a given place and time. We must always be prepared to ask: Christianity when? Christianity where? The Christianity of the early centuries in North Africa or in Antioch is most definitely a different Christianity from the Christianity of Scandinavia in the nineteenth century. And the Buddhism of Japan is very different from the Buddhism of Sri Lanka, just as American evangelical Christianity is different from the Christianity of Romania. Now, of course, the advocate or representative of one form of a religion may assume that her or his particular way is the true one, the norm by which others should be judged. But the fact remains that there are many forms. Time and place make a difference in the manner in which all religiousness expresses itself. That is why historical methods are necessary to the study of religion. As one scholar, Wilfred Cantwell Smith, put it thirty years ago: "The most important single matter to remember in all this is that ultimately we have to do not with religions but with religious persons." He was pointing out the importance of history. History is people affecting the direction of their lives by their ideas, commitments, and actions. History is the human penchant for making more of the course of existence than it would take by nature. When we study religion, we study the way of perceiving and transforming the world by particular people in particular times and places. We want "to apprehend how other [people] perceive the stars and their neighbors, the making of a living, love, death, moral conflict, and all that makes human life human and life."[4]

That is why some scholars of religion will tell us there is no such thing as religion; there are only religions, they say. It is certainly true that we must always remember that we are dealing with people in time and place—with particularities. In one way of thinking, there are only Thai Buddhists, Tibetan Buddhists, Japanese Shingon Buddhists, and Pure Land Buddhists. However, like any observation, this way of thinking can lead to absurdity if it becomes an absolute principle. It would ultimately mean that in order to study Christianity, for example, we must always be satisfied with discussing the members of the Free Will Baptist Church in Mulberry Gap, Tennessee.

The fact is, there are religions (or religious traditions) and the people who are representative of them in time and place, but there is also religion. That is, many human beings want to know how and why their own perception of the world may point to a more universal way of perceiving. They try to transcend their particularities and reach for what is common to people in all times and places. Even if they cannot be totally successful, they touch the edges of more than their own particularities. Their religiousness touches a universal chord. After all, we have already seen how it is that no one lives on one's own, that we are traditional beings as well as "original . . . [in our] relation to the universe." As creatures who are societal and interpersonal beings, whose societal nature reaches through time, there is a certain commonality and universality to our existence. That is what makes it both necessary and possible to speak of religion as well as of religions.

We study religions and religion because they exist; they are a fundamental aspect of human life. The educated and intelligent person always seeks to gain some knowledge and understanding of all important elements in the human pilgrimage. Regardless of what we may think of religions and human religiousness, we are obligated to lay aside our judgments and open our minds to the thoughts and actions of millions of human beings like ourselves who have expressed themselves as Hindus, Jews, Navajos, or Copts. Our responsibility is to know and to understand.

Many social scientists beginning with Emile Durkheim have sought to demonstrate the fact that the foundation of every society and culture is religious. Religion is that which integrates and serves as the principle of coherence for the people of a particular social order. Religion is the heart of the social constructions of reality that account for human history. That is a very important reason for studying religion, and it is in keeping with our definition of religion as the systematic set of expressions that reflect the ultimate order, meaning, and possible transformations of existence for a people. It also mirrors the observation that we live not so much in a world as in a perception of the world. It is with these thoughts in mind that we turn to those perceptions, those shapes of human religiousness, that have been fundamental to the American experience.

chapter 2

Myths, Legends, and the Promised Land

There are two narrative forms in which people often express their religiousness. As explained in the previous chapter, the ideas and images that make up our perception of the world are often expressed in what have been called *myths* and *legends*.

Story

Myths and legends are basically stories. They are a narrative form of communication and expression, and as stories they transmit truth and meaning. Every story is filled with images and ideas that make it possible for us to understand our world and trust it will somehow sustain us—keep us going. Whenever we want to say something that is really important to us, we tell a story. We somehow know that a simple statement or formula, no matter how scientific, will not do.

Story is essential to the thinking process. If we wish to identify ourselves as human beings, we tell stories. We do not say, "I am a biological organism made up of 98 percent water." That would not be true. That is not who we are; that is the manner in which a physiologist might describe observations about the constituent character of the human body. If we want to talk about the great new discovery we have made as physicists or the great new marketing technique we have devised as junior executives, we tell a story—otherwise, we communicate nothing at all. One of the best forms for the conception and transmission of human knowledge and understanding is story. That is mostly because, as indicated before, we are self-transcending creatures. We are always more than a formula or analysis would make of us. We are the ones doing the measuring and the analyzing—of ourselves and others. The only form of thought and communication adequate to the task of doing justice to this "more than" is one that is somewhat open-ended and imprecise at points. That form is story.

Every story told by an individual, whether as fiction or as report, draws upon larger, public stories that are not the property or creation of a private, single individual. In other words, we all live in a story, and the story has been going on for some time. It is always an old story, and it includes others. A typical American story may include parents, grandparents, children, and friends. There may be chapters from schools and colleges, people known and long forgotten. The story may be filled with images of "founding fathers" and special wars never witnessed—perhaps holy wars fought in the name of an ideal or a hope. It is a very mysterious story. It includes images of progress and hope, failure and dream. The images in the story help to keep the individual going. They motivate, judge, and comfort. They make the person human, more than a biological organism, a robot, or something observed in a laboratory. Not only is the story mysterious; it is large. It includes the cosmos, the universe, and more. The scientist speaking of galaxies and universes creates images by telling a story, and we understand the utterance in terms of story, no matter how technical the conversation becomes.

While we humans may not be the final stage in the life-making process, we are a special, free, and responsible stage in that process. People are sacred. Even if we do not believe we are creatures of God, we probably believe that we have "certain inalienable rights." All of these beliefs are part of our story, and they emerge out of the first story of Genesis in the Hebrew Bible (the Old Testament in Christian parlance). Even the most secularized, skeptical, and nonbelieving American will find living difficult without drawing upon images and assumptions from the Genesis story. Even the way of thinking and organizing our lives in weeks, leading from periods of work to times of rest and leisure, is derived from the power of the Genesis story. It is a powerful story, a primal story.

Of course, there are other primal stories that are a part of the story of America. In a sense, America is a story of many stories. The Genesis story is important because it is central to the story of Euro-Americans, who had to make sense of their voyages and settlements in the Americas by retelling the Jewish and Christian stories (the biblical story) in relation to an unfamiliar landscape and unfamiliar people. It is no secret that Euro-American story-telling *dominated* the thinking of Americans well into the twentieth century.

We must remember that religious traditions are formed in the context of encounter and contact among people. I am forced to think about "our story/my story" as a result of meeting those for whom I must make a place in the story. Stories and traditions are always in formation. Therefore, we may observe certain images and ideas in the origin stories of Native American peoples that display a similarity with the Genesis story.

The Genesis story provides a kind of sequential order to the meaning of existence. Europeans, therefore, have been motivated by the assumption of beginnings that are active in a past, present, and future. Life moves toward an end or goal. This imaginative perspective has shaped the way we have thought about the United States as being involved in a drama of destiny.

Most Native American creation stories seem to have their beginnings in the midst of the earth as we know it, with all of its dust, winds, waters, vegetation, and curious animals. From this center these stories move outward to tell of "the first people" as a *given,* about whom it is impossible to ask, "Well, who created them?"

Myth and Legend

A primal story may be called a myth by the scholar of religion. A myth is a story that reaches into the time before time. It is a story about life and how humans in a given time and place perceive what it is like, what it means, to live in the world as they know it. As Barbara Sproul has written, "the power of a specific myth is not as important to realize as the power of myth itself. Indeed, each of the claims made by the first Genesis myth has been attacked from some quarter. What is essential to understand is that they have been challenged not by new facts, but by new attitudes toward facts; they have been challenged by new myths."[1]

Myth is inescapable. It is the story from which all the basic images, ideas, and attitudes about reality are derived. Myth is a story that creates time and place. However, as we have seen, there is another kind of story that is set within the world of time that myth creates. It shares many of the attitudes of myth, but it involves either a person or an event that actually occurred within time as we know it. This kind of story is called legend. Legend reveals what a person or event means to a people. After a legend has been told for a long period of time, it becomes difficult to sort out the so-called facts from the meaning that people have attached to them. Historians may do their best to unravel the skeins of wool that surround the lives of certain persons. There may be little doubt that they existed, but what they mean to us is a greater historical fact than whether we can separate the fact from the meaning. Events like the Alamo and the Pilgrim landing at Plymouth Rock (actually the Separatist Puritan) are of legendary significance to us. The American Revolution and the Civil War have great legendary meaning for Americans.

From the legend of the exodus emerge images of liberation, freedom from captivity, new birth, the providence of God, and the promised land. There are also the correlative images of trial and temptation, endurance in the wilderness, and divine commission. It is very difficult for a Westerner to think without reference to the images derived from the story of the exodus. The Puritans who established Massachusetts Bay Colony would have been speechless without the exodus. "Now if the Lord shall please to hear us," wrote John Winthrop, "and bring us in peace to the place we desire, then hath he ratified this Covenant and sealed our Commission [and] will expect a strict performance of the articles contained in it." Even Thomas Jefferson, in his second inaugural address, expressed it this way:

> I shall need, too, the favor of that Being in whose hands we are, who led our forefathers, as Israel of old, from their native land, and planted them in a country flowing with all the necessaries and comforts of life, who have covered our infancy with his providence, and our riper years with his wisdom and power, and to whose goodness I ask you to join with me in supplication.

African Americans make special use of the exodus story, and it is impossible to conceive many of their sermons, addresses, and songs without reference to the images of the exodus.

The Battle of Greasy Grass (Little Big Horn, 1876) and the Wounded Knee Massacre (1890) are events filled with powerful symbolic memory for Native Americans, especially the Lakota people. Their dream of earth that would be restored to its original harmony remains rooted by legend in those events that serve as the basis for survival. Sitting Bull, Black Elk, and Wowoka are figures whose lives are legendary symbols of struggle and hope. They reflect the religious imagination of the early inhabitants of North America, as they sought to understand the invasive presence of white Europeans, for whom this land waited to be *possessed* by the refugees of a broken world across the great waters.

Myths and legends are forms of story that are very important to the study of religion. Long before America was "discovered" by European explorers in the fifteenth and sixteenth centuries, it was already a promised land in the minds of European people. There is an ancient Irish story, called the Legend of St. Brendan, recounted in manuscripts from the mid-tenth century that may be copies of even earlier versions. It is very likely that the legend itself had been in existence for several centuries before the manuscript. It is the story of an Irish monk, Brendan of Ardfert. Another monk had told him of a visit to a land in the West, a Land Promised to the Saints, where an angel told them they were on the soil of the early paradise, where humans had dwelt before the fall.[2] Brendan decided to make the voyage himself, and he chose fourteen monks to accompany him. Together they built a *curragh*—a short, wide boat with wicker sides and ribs, covered with cowhide.

Brendan and his monks first set sail about the time of the summer solstice and made their way across the Atlantic in search of the promised land. After forty days of sailing they came to rest on a rocky island where they were given food and shelter for several days. They landed on another island and finally settled for a time on a smaller island that, after it stirred underfoot, Brendan acknowledged to be a whale named Jasconius. The voyage continued to numerous fabulous islands, with pure-white sheep of extraordinary size and talking birds. They had been gone from home for a year. On one island they discovered a community of Irish monks who had lived there since the days of St. Patrick. There were dangerous encounters with other whales and storms. Strange islands with crystal columns, others with giant blacksmiths working at forges and tossing burning slag at the voyagers—these are a few of the many marvels they happened upon before finally coming to the land of promise. For forty days they pushed into the country until they stood on the bank of a great river and were met by a young man who ordered them to turn back. Brendan and his monks had wandered for seven years. His pilgrimage was complete. The land of promise that had been revealed to him would be shown to his successors, in an age when they would need liberation from bondage and tribulation.

The voyage of St. Brendan is a legend. It bears little resemblance to an attempt at journalistic reporting or a modern chronicle of events, such as a war or an earthquake. It is very likely that early writers and reporters seldom separated "facts" from their meaning, as we often try to do. Of course, few facts ever exist without interpretation. Facts are selected because they mean something, serve someone's agenda. "July 4, 1776" is not a raw datum; it is a fact with its meaning attached by way of a principle of selection. What is the importance of the story of St. Brendan, with its curious expeditions into lands and experience often more exotic than *Alice's Adventures in Wonderland* and *Through the Looking Glass*? Some historians will want to bypass such apparently unreliable accounts as Brendan's. However, historians of religion cannot afford to do so because they are interested in understanding the religious ideas and images of a people.

What does the legend tell us that is important to the shaping of American religious traditions, whose origins were European? It tells us that as early as the middle of the first millennium c.e.[3] the mind of Europe had already invested its imagination in the notion of a land westward across the waters, a promised land. Regardless of whether Brendan actually reached the shores of the western hemisphere, the idea that it was possible to reach a New World by sailing many days into the Atlantic was a prevalent one. Some historians, anthropologists, and history scholars have tried to reconstruct the possible path of Brendan's expedition from the evidence of manuscripts of his life and navigations. They have worked with a knowledge of geography to show the plausibility of the voyage. It would seem that some such event took place; very likely many such navigations were done. But what is significant for us is that the legend demonstrates what people in Ireland were thinking and believing.

European Attitudes toward America

The legend of St. Brendan is not the only evidence that indicates that people in Europe had America in mind before it was colonized beginning in the sixteenth century. Even before the idea of the earth as spherical (an old idea, actually) gained popularity during the Renaissance, the land across the waters was a mysterious place. The later assumption that the Atlantic could be a passage to India invested the lands encountered en route with the dreams of fabulous wealth and wisdom. Yet even before such notions as "going East by sailing West" were to become a motivation for voyages of exploration sponsored by monarchs and popes, there was already a Land Promised to the Saints across the terrible Atlantic.

The land across the waters was not like the world as it was perceived in Europe. In the minds of many people, it was an "other" world, a place of salvation, a refuge from the hells of Europe, the fulfillment promised to the faithful—a New World.

Europeans were accustomed to the idea of search and quest; they had been a very restless people. History informs us of the ages of what is called *Völkerwanderungen,* a German word that literally means "great wanderings of masses of people." Recall the so-called barbarian invasions during the last days of the Roman Empire. People in great numbers from the north, east, and west converged on the centers of Roman civilization to the south. After a time they settled in and became part of the medieval European civilization we call

Christendom, the society and culture ordered by the Holy Roman Empire. However, by the fourteenth century of our era there was already evidence of the erosion of lands and the erosion of culture. Forest resources had been depleted and the search for more arable regions was under way. The church was unable to keep in check the surge for power and wealth among some of its clergy, and the struggle between political and ecclesiastical administrations within Christendom weakened the forces of social and cultural cohesion. The emergence of new religious movements demonstrated the disorder within the church and its inability to address the needs of the people. Of course, it was also evidence of the regenerating and reforming potential already present in the Catholic faith.

The dark specter of disease and death accompanied the disorder, and people began to move about again. They were restless, in search of sustenance for their lives, and in hope of finding meaning and hope. So began massive movements of people, shifts of population within Europe and eventually across the waters in quest again of the Land Promised to the Saints. Would that land not also be a place like the Garden of Eden itself, where the needs of Adam and Eve were benevolently met? In a promised land the inhabitants themselves would be new Adams, new Eves, in a paradise of good. The eventual "discovery" and colonization of the western hemisphere must be understood as part of a great and continuing period of *Völkerwanderungen* that lasted for several centuries and has caused the intermingling of ethnic groups and religious traditions that is the mark of contemporary America. It is a measure of what is "coming on the world."

The peopling of America was accompanied by much greed and struggle for wealth. Europe was losing its wealth and was somewhat greedy to replenish it. The results were political manipulation, piracy on the seas, battles, and wars. And the church was concerned to carry its gospel to the children of lesser gods. Oftentimes the worst qualities of human nature sought to take control of history. As always, good and evil were a complex intermixture in human behavior. However, beneath all the noble motivation and the sanctification of greed, more subtle religious forces were at work. The ultimate order and meaning of existence that had served as the foundation of European thought and behavior for centuries was undergoing transformation. In quest of a new and firmer sense that life was still good and meaningful, Europeans fixed their sights upon the image of the Land Promised to the Saints. Whether in search of wealth, converts, refuge, or new opportunities, the people were on religious pilgrimage. They sought to replace an old world with a new one.

Living as we do not so much in a world as in a perception of the world, the perception is every bit as important as the place itself. The place does not exist without the perception. Images like the promised land that were borne in the myths and legends of Europe are inseparable from the land that was "discovered" and peopled by Europeans. And it is the Europeans who are responsible for the colonization that gave rise to the United States of America and contributed most to American self-understanding.

A Promised Land

For some, a promised land is a place of liberation from captivity. To think or speak of such a place is to impose that image upon a certain territory. The place is perceived as sacred, that is, other than ordinary. And once the place is perceived in that fashion, it will never again be an ordinary place unless total catastrophe eliminates human habitation and permits it to begin again. In the latter case, a new image of the land will reveal how it is perceived by those who possess it. If we experience a sense of bondage, the notion that we are hemmed in with little opportunity to control our own destiny, we will begin to construct images of escape, liberation, from that condition. The condition may be psychological or physical. If it is psychological, it may take the form of a belief in the lack of opportunity, or that life is weighted down by sin or severe limitations. In this case, our images of liberation may perceive a different state of being—a heaven, a nirvana—a state in which no such bondage exists. If, on the other hand, our captivity is physical, we begin to plot revolutions and escapes based upon images that perceive a different social order, a new physical world where our bondage is removed. Both conditions, both perceptions of the world, were part of the mind of Europeans who came to America.

A promised land is a place of new beginning, new birth. It is where we may start all over, even perhaps return to a state of innocence. There is a nostalgia for Eden, for recovery of the paradise we have lost. The voyages across the Atlantic were often in quest of regeneration for their world. Christopher Columbus asserted, "God made me the messenger of the new heaven and the new earth of which He spoke in the Apocalypse by Saint John, after having spoken of it by the mouth of Isaiah; and He showed me the spot where to find it." In his own mind, the great adventurer thought that he had discovered the rivers of the Garden of Eden, then reinterpreted his position in the light of Christian eschatology (doctrine of the end times).

Everyone has an eschatology because, presumably, we all have some notion of where history is going—what the goal and the terminus will be. Columbus's eschatology assumed that the discovery of the new continent was necessary before history could be completed. In his *Book of Prophecies,* he states that the end of the world would come after the conversion of the peoples of the newly discovered continent.

Columbus was understood in his time because he was not expressing ideas that had never been heard before. The people of Europe believed that the time had come to renew the Christian world. The literature of the times is filled with allusions to new beginnings and eschatological interpretations of the end of the old, the emergence of the new. To many Christians the great events spoken of in the Bible, beginning with Genesis, would be repeated before the goal of history could be achieved.

It becomes obvious that America bestowed a tremendous responsibility upon itself. From times long before its period of mass colonization began in the fifteenth century, America, in the mind of Europe, was a holy place, like a temple or a sacred garden. America has been the nation with the spirit of a shrine, our landscape like the grounds of a temple.

The Religious Meaning of America

The fact that America had religious meaning before it was colonized had its effect upon the religious traditions and movements that were to be part of our history. Individuals driven by the impulse to discover deeper truth, to renew their lives, or to find refuge from oppression were motivated by the image of a New World, a promised land. Groups of people hoping to find a new haven for the truths they had discerned often concluded that God had provided them with the place where God's expectations for them would be realized. The many denominations and representations from the world's religions would all be affected in some way by the religious meaning of America itself. Virtually every religious tradition that has come to our shores from outside or emerged full-blown from America itself (made-in-the-USA religions) has verified its own dreams by reference to the promised land. We shall discover that religions in America have been shaped by the religiousness at the heart of our land and its nationhood. Buddhism in America becomes American Buddhism. Certainly American Christianity has been distinctively different from that of its European forebears.

The difference will emerge in the telling of a story—a true story. Once upon a time, there was a young man who lived in the southern part of what became known as Germany. He was from a place called Heilbronn and he belonged to a group of people who were known as Mennonites, in the latter part of the seventeenth century. Now, Mennonites were the followers of Menno Simons, a parish priest in Holland who renounced his connection with the Catholic church in 1536 and joined a group somewhat loosely called Anabaptists ("re-baptizers," practicing believer's baptism). The young Mennonite heard of what William Penn intended to do in the "new world" across the ocean. Penn was about to conduct a "holy experiment," providing a haven in which people of many different religious views and practices could live together in political harmony. This was important to the young man because the area of Germany in which he lived had been devastated by wars and religious persecutions. Many people had said to each other, "There is another world, across the seas, where we may live out our salvation as we please, where we shall have food and shelter, where the lord shall bring in his promised Kingdom."

And so the young man left one world for another. He sailed on board a leaky old ship, setting out from Amsterdam, with some other Anabaptists from the Rhineland. They sang hymns and read psalms to remind themselves of a world that was so much better than the stench, sickness, and death that hovered about the holds, then crept along the salty planks to visit the unknown depths with each crash of a towering wave. The sailors cursed the pious Christians, abused them, and taunted them with heavy drinking, bawdy songs, and lewd jokes. Of course, the sailors had their religion, too, to help them face the precariousness of existence, but neither they nor the Mennonites understood what it was and how it was so.

At any rate, the young man and his friends finally found themselves in the Port of Philadelphia and settled in a place that came to be known as Germantown. He found some land and became a farmer, like his father and grandfather before him. Then one day he received a letter from his father. It read:

> America, according to your writing, must be a beautiful land. We rejoice greatly that your home is with such God-fearing people, and that the Indians in your community are a peace-loving people. Things are not so good here. They get worse instead of better. We have just been visited by a merchant who speaks of the hardships

and the suffering. He tells us there is another group of Rhinelanders who are preparing to leave for the New World. God help them; I wish we were with them. When I gave the good man your letter to read, he was greatly surprised, and said that you were in the land to which these emigrants are going. It is the good Providence of God that has shown these people so glorious a land. We, as also the Plattenbach family, are only waiting for a good opportunity when the dear Lord will bring us to you.

I do not know the young man's name. I only know that much of the story, and I know it only because I once discovered the scrap of the father's letter in some papers I found in a box. It was dated 1681. It is an American story, a story of American religion.

Isaac Mayer Wise was a Bohemian Jew who arrived in New York in 1846, after sixty-three tiring days on the ocean. He was to become one of the greatest rabbis in American history and a leader in the development of Reform Judaism. "We must become American Jews as speedily as possible," he said. Wise insisted that the divisions that had been forced upon the Jewish community by more than a millennium of isolation and oppression would be overcome in America. "Either I build up a Judaism suited to the age and breathing the atmosphere of American freedom, or I will be buried beneath the ruins of an old Judaism." He was the leader of a people who had arrived in a promised land, looking to the fulfillment of God's purposes after centuries of bondage.

Then there was Soyen Shaku, Lord Abbot of Engaku-ji and Kencho-ji, Zen Buddhist temples in Kamakura, Japan. He visited America from 1905 to 1906.

> Leaving Japan for America,
> Sea stretches out into sea, mountains into mountains.
> Where is the center of water?
> Where's the destination of clouds?
> I do not know!
> My heart tells me there is a happy field in the American land
> I presume myself to be a follower of Columbus.

And one of Soyen Shaku's disciples, Nyogen Senzaki, spent fifty-three years in America until his death in 1958, teaching the traditions of Zen. In 1944, he wrote,

What have I done in this strange land?
I have lived almost in vain,
The teaching having joined itself
To the revival of the American spirit.
Praise be to the wisdom of enlightenment.

These examples illustrate that America has its own religious meaning, a meaning that influences virtually every special tradition, teaching, and movement that comes to our shores. Of course, it is also true that religions like Christianity have had very profound effects upon America itself. This is especially true of Protestantism, that outpouring of Christian movements and ideas from the Reformation in sixteenth-century Europe. What we shall also expect to see is that this religious meaning of America will develop its own tradition, exist in some sense separately from and alongside the many denominations of American religion. However, before we begin to examine the many traditions of religion in America, it is necessary to turn to the Reformation and explore its meaning and significance.

chapter 3

Christendom and the Heritage
of Reformation

Christendom

What we have come to call *Christendom* was at least four hundred years in the making and has already lasted over fourteen centuries. Some scholars would say that we still live in the last days of its demise. The word *Christendom* refers to the unity of European society and culture that was established upon Christian ideas, beliefs, values, and practices. To speak of Christendom is to suggest that politics, economics, art, literature, and other forms of culture were shaped by Christian norms and ideas. Christendom does not simply refer to the inner life of the church and its doctrine. It is a social and cultural term demonstrating the sociological principle that religion provides the foundation of society. Religion is a culture's language for self-understanding.

Religion is always an establishment of some sort. That is, it is not truly religion unless it provides ultimate order and meaning of existence. It therefore establishes itself as a fundamental way of perceiving—at least, that has always been the case in human history. It is certainly true for the European history that has been shared by America. America has shared in the heritage of Christendom, which is the establishment of Christian ideas and practices in Western culture.

In order to understand how the notion of Christendom comes about, we must remember, first of all, that ancient people tended to assume that the social organism of which they were a part was "a single animal with one corporate life-blood." It would have been almost unthinkable that a tribe, nation, or kingdom would not share the same "life-blood." Therefore, a chief or a king was a sacred figure. He was the living symbol of their unity as an organism. The people believed, thought, worshiped as a single unit. The sacredness of living was shared in a common life of symbols, stories, and rituals that often had its focus in a single sacred person. To belong to a tribe, a nation, was to be a single sacred unit with established norms, symbols, and practices.

This observation relates to the sociological theory already discussed, that religion forms the foundation of the social reality and order. Christianity was at first a small Jewish religious movement. It emerged at a time when the Jewish people were refashioning their beliefs and practices after long experiences of exile from their homeland, enemy occupation, the destruction of the temple in Jerusalem, and their dispersion throughout the Roman Empire. The small Christian movement believed that the long-awaited Jewish Messiah had come in the person of Jesus of Nazareth. Jesus was to them the Messiah—the Christ (a Greek translation of *Messiah*). The Christ-group shared many of the Jewish notions of the sacredness and organic unity of the people of Israel. One of the early Christ-thinkers, Paul, spoke of the Christian movement as a new "single animal with one corporate life-blood." He called this social organism the New Israel and the Body of Christ.

At first, the new organism was small. It was one among several new Jewish movements, and it was one among many new sects and cults (as we tend to call them) that were part of the religious and cultural diversification of the time. Christianity was born in a time of great upheaval. The Roman Empire, which held much of the world together, was one grand festival of religious and political change. Old nations and ways were disintegrating and being reborn in new ways. It was a scene of great excitement and struggle.

The small organism of Christ-people found themselves dispersed like the rest of the Jews. However, they soon began to incorporate Gentiles (non-Jews) into their body and sought to understand themselves as a divine extension of Israel into a non-Jewish world. In this way they were forced to rethink what it means to be a religion whose sense of ultimate order and meaning applied only to their own body as Christ-people and not to the empire in which they lived. The empire itself had worked on the same problem in its own fashion. That is to say, the empire also inherited the assumption that a nation shares the same life, that it is a sacred, corporate organism with a common order. And so the empire solved the problem of unity in the midst of diversity by means of ritual. It required of all people within its realm the performance of certain ceremonial duties that recognized the sacredness of the empire in the person of the emperor. The empire developed a cultus, a ritual pattern or model followed by a particular group. The imperial cultus celebrated the life of a genuine Roman religious tradition and made the emperor a central figure in the religious order of imperial society. To refuse to participate in the cultus was to aid in the destruction of the social organism of the empire. The cultus was required maintenance for a religious world.

Christians and Jews were somewhat uncomfortable in this Roman perception of the world. How, for example, could Christians adjust to Roman requirements their perception of themselves as a new organism, the Body of Christ? This body, the church, the New Israel, shared with Israel of old the admonition to honor no gods other than the Creator God who had made a covenant with Israel centuries before. For a time there was conflict between the Roman and Christian perception of the world. Inasmuch as the Romans were the established political order that held together the diversity of the empire, they were in position to enforce their requirements upon all dissidents. Rome had to maintain law and order. It had to promote peace, and that could only be done if religious order prevailed. The result was the "persecution" of Christians. Many Christians became martyrs (Greek *martyros*, "witnessed"). They witnessed to their belonging to Christ's body, not the emperor's, and it often meant their deaths. The fate of the church, the Body of Christ, in the empire was a precarious one for several centuries.

Then something curious happened. In the year 312 C.E. the Emperor Constantine began to look with favor upon the Christ-people. He was convinced that he had won a battle with the help of a god known to him as the "unconquerable Sun." Certain Christian thinkers persuaded him that this deity was the Creator God who had become one with humanity in the person of Jesus Christ. The God who was present in all gods, including Sun gods, was the one God in Christ. Constantine granted toleration and imperial patronage to Christianity. The effect was the eventual establishment of Christianity as the religion of the empire. The social organism of the church, the Body of Christ, was to begin the process of becoming one with the entire empire and its people.

That process is what we mean by Christendom. Europe was to become Christian: In its social order, its culture, and its laws, it was to be an expression of Christian ideas, beliefs, and practices. To speak of Christendom is to refer to the unified social and cultural order of Europe. Christianity was no longer an isolated cult, a tiny organism in the pluralistic world of the empire. It was to be the dominant transfusion of life-blood into the "single animal" of European culture. Christianity, in sociological terms, was to become the social foundation upon which the European construction of reality and the world was based.

This unity of society and culture known as Christendom was not absolute, of course. The ancient ways of people in the various regions of Europe continued to have their place. Many of those ancient practices were "baptized"—embraced and initiated into the cultic system of Christianity. There was a kind of unity-in-diversity to Christendom. In the eastern part of Europe, Christianity began very early to show the influence of its proximity to the Orient. One of the teachings of Eastern Christianity was that "god became Man, that men might become God." Sharing of Christ's humanity meant that God was a presence to be appreciated and enjoyed. The goals of Christian life were present to all through certain spiritual disciplines, through the Divine Liturgy,[1] and through the veneration of icons.[2] By the eleventh century, the differences between Eastern and Western Christianity were accentuated by controversies both political and ecclesiastical, that is, having to do with matters of church order, authority, and organization.

The result of these controversies was the Great Schism, the division of Christendom into Eastern and Western churches, those in the East known as Orthodox Catholic, the Western church as Roman Catholic. Obviously, these titles are purely functional, inasmuch as both churches would want to be known as orthodox and as catholic.[3] From the time in 1054 C.E. that the patriarchs of Constantinople and Rome excommunicated each other, the division between Eastern and Western Christianity has persisted. In the West, particularly in America, we have tended to be quite ignorant of the Orthodox world. Most American Christians, familiar with the ideas and practices of evangelical Protestantism, would find it difficult to recognize their Christianity in the Orthodox culture of a Rumanian village.

The Reformation of the sixteenth century was a revolution in Western Christianity, in the half of Christendom that remained loyal to the patriarch of Rome as pope. It is sometimes also called Latin Christianity or Roman Christianity. Before we examine the Reformation and its significance for an understanding of religion in America, it is necessary to ask ourselves about the concept of Christendom itself. Why is it important for us to comprehend this concept in order to understand American religion? There are at least three reasons: (1) the concept of Christendom is inherited by the Reformation; (2) the concept of Christendom bestows on us certain assumptions about religion and politics; and (3) the concept of Christendom is related to the missionary impulse of our nation and its religious traditions.

We must remember that the Reformation takes place within Christendom. Loyalty to Jesus Christ and being part of a social organism known as the Body of Christ formed a total perception of the world for Europeans. To live in the world as a Christian was to live in a Christian world. When the rumblings of reformation began in Western Christianity, there was little thought but that Christian teaching and practice would be revitalized to provide a sounder Christian foundation for European society and culture. We shall learn that some of those who wished to reform Christianity in the sixteenth century dreamed of a Christian life untainted by the world. But most Reformers assumed that the world would be a Christendom, hospitable to the values of Christianity in politics, art, and economics. Even those who were more revolutionary than Martin Luther and John Calvin sought to establish a new world order that would be a more authentic Christendom than was the late medieval world of their birthright.

The United States has inherited the assumptions of Christendom. Our self-understanding as a nation and a people was born out of Christendom. There were those, such as the Native Americans, who did not share that self-understanding. However, in their encounter with Euro-Americans they shared their own understanding and practice of how to manage a common life of peace and harmony among people of diverse traditions. For example, the Iroquois comprised a people of five "nations" united by thirteen laws in a Great League of Peace and Power. Although this Native American experience was often in conflict with the assumptions of Christendom, we may observe here certain ideas of the inseparability of religion and political order that served as a bridge of influence upon the development of an American conception of nationhood.

Many of our American religious traditions and our political heritage are a development out of the heritage of Christendom. Hidden in that development is the notion that the political and social order must have a religious foundation. The unity and harmony of society and culture must be based on the sharing of certain images, ideas, values, and practices. As we shall see later on, although the new nation of America has lived "respecting no establishment of religion," it has never had total separation of religion from the social and political order. The heritage of Christendom assumes that religion and politics are logically inseparable even if there can be no establishment of a particular religious institution.

The concept of Christendom is also related to the missionary impulse of our nation and its religious traditions. There are many people who ask why it is that one religion should try to force itself upon others. That is, of course, a rather superficial question. "Force" has been a mode of conversion for Christians at some times in their history. Force has often been used by Marxists in the attempt to convert others to their quasi-religious perception of the world. Perhaps force is still attempted by some religions in those parts of the world where a militant religion exercises a dominant role. However, the issue is not so much a question of force as it is a question of whether a religious tradition that has a special message for which it claims universal significance has a right to try to persuade people of its truth. The answer has to be yes, so long as the persuasion does not interfere with personal freedom.

Some religions are what the sociologist Max Weber has called "emissary" traditions. They have a message to proclaim. Christianity, Islam, and to a certain extent Buddhism have been emissary traditions. It could very well be that the growing pluralism of the world will force a change upon the emissary character of these traditions. Meanwhile, they have a right to be true to themselves so long as they respect the freedom of their respondents. From its earliest days, Christianity has carried a strong emissary or missionary impulse. Christendom came into being partly because Christian spokespersons persuaded Emperor Constantine that his religious experience was the work of the Christ. Behind the religious insights of a pagan world was the pervasiveness of a Christ-nature, working to bring the world to enlightenment.

When the Europeans "discovered" the western hemisphere and began to settle, they understood that this New World was part of God's plan, to complete God's purposes for human history. The message that is called the gospel of Jesus Christ had to be carried from Europe so that Christendom would spread over all the earth. And when the religious movements that emerged out of the Reformation came to America, they believed they were establishing God's new order so that the kingdom of God would be fulfilled. History could end in the purpose of God. Even the early medieval notion of the Land Promised to the Saints implies that the land across the waters to the west is an outpost, a place of refuge, for Christendom to stage new beginnings.

The Development of the Reformation

And so we turn to the Reformation of the sixteenth century. First, it is necessary to understand that no great social, cultural, or religious revolution ever occurs instantaneously upon the scene. The Reformation was a revolution in thought, conviction, and practice that was a long time in the making. We should not assume that Western Christendom had been a tranquil world, carefully regulated in dictatorial fashion by the pope and his minions until Martin Luther got sufficiently aggravated and, out of utter frustration, nailed ninety-five complaints on the door of the castle church in Wittenberg, Germany. Some scholars would say that the Reformation owes a great deal to the rise of religious orders in the thirteenth century. These orders were comprised of communities of clergy and laity who devoted their lives to spiritual discipline, seeking to purify the church and serve human needs. The spirit of movements like the Dominicans and Franciscans certainly had its effect upon the mind and mood of the late medieval church. People were made aware of the fact that all was not well in the church and that its teachings and practices often seemed only remotely related to the gospel of Jesus Christ that had called the original Christian community into being.

The revival of learning known as the Renaissance also played a role in the development of the Reformation. At the heart of Renaissance activity was the notion that humanity must reclaim its ancient heritage. An educated person was one who knew the art, literature, and philosophy of the ancient world, before and during the early days of Christendom. A knowledge of ancient languages and classical texts was necessary. The Renaissance emphasized human wisdom and achievement. Renaissance scholars were known as humanists. Many of the early Reformers of the church were humanists involved in the examination of ancient texts in their original language. It is easy to see how a scholar knowledgeable in Greek and Hebrew would learn a great deal about the literature of the Christian Scriptures and might also discover much about the early church and its times—much that could lead the scholar to dissatisfaction with its fourteenth- and fifteenth-century descendant.

Renaissance scholars succeeded in challenging the authenticity of an eighth- or ninth-century document that had been used to strengthen the power of the bishop of Rome. Known as the Donation of Constantine, the document purported to confer on Pope Sylvester I (314–25) primacy over the other major centers of Christian strength. In it Constantine also allegedly gave the pope (bishop of Rome) dominion over all Italy, made him supreme judge of the clergy, and offered him the emperor's crown (which he declined). The discovering of this fabrication by humanists of the fifteenth century made them suspicious of many of the claims of the medieval church.

In England John Wycliffe began to challenge the accepted teachings of the church in the fourteenth century. He questioned the primacy of the pope, opposed monastic life, and denied any authority to the institutional church. His teachings on the meaning of the Eucharist were condemned by Oxford

University and by the Archbishop of Canterbury. Wycliffe's followers were known as Lollards, and his work must be understood as a movement leading to the erosion of ecclesiastical authority and therefore a major factor in Reformation history. When Wycliffe's writings made their way across the Channel onto the Continent, they were well received by figures such as John Hus. Hus was a Bohemian whose preaching was often violently directed toward reform of the church and society. He was excommunicated in 1411 and eventually executed in 1415.

Another movement that was to play a role in weakening the authority of the papacy and gaining momentum for the Reformation was conciliarism, which sought to reestablish the authority of General Councils. Conciliarism taught that decisions on doctrine and discipline were the responsibility of conventions or councils of bishops and other representatives of the worldwide church. The decisions were conciliar in nature—they were to be made *in council*. Such notions as this played a key role in laying the foundations for the great reforming activity of the sixteenth century.

It is certainly true that the work of persons such as Martin Luther, Ulrich Zwingli, Menno Simons, and John Calvin was directed against the corruptions of Rome and certain abuses of its authority. However, the Reformation may also be understood as a great historical movement in which radical change took place in the religious, social, and political history of Western Europe. Not least in the order of change was the intellectual and doctrinal factor. Ideas (matters of the intellect) were changing. The corruptions, abuses, and erosion of ecclesiastical authority may be understood as symptoms of a profound metamorphosis in religion and culture. The mind and spirit of Europe were being altered. Even in its political and economic phases, it was a religious affair, for the perception of the world was being transformed. The sense of ultimate order and meaning was undergoing a re-formation. Political and social factors were expressions of that fundamental religious transformation. People were thinking and acting differently than they had for centuries. Much of the struggle and warfare that accompanied the Reformation may be understood as symptomatic of the tension resulting from radical alteration in ultimate order and meaning.

This great revolution in the religious order was coming into its own at the very time that European nations were considering what they would do with the land they were claiming in the western hemisphere. The United States was itself part of the revolution. It was to become a symbol of the expectations of the many movements that arose in the midst of several centuries of

Reformation. Inasmuch as it is our purpose in this book to understand the shaping of American religious traditions, it will be necessary to examine some of the aspects of the Reformation that are directly related to the purpose.

Aspects of the Reformation

The Reformation may be divided into five basic formations: magisterial, separationist, spiritualist, humanist, and loyalist. The *magisterial* branch of the Reformation was an attempt to reform the whole of Christendom. It sought to reform the church by gaining the support of the political jurisdictions in which the Reformers were doing this work. The magisterial Reformers assumed that the reform of the church they were seeking would be reflected in social and cultural life. They were the heirs of Christendom. They knew that their reforms could not immediately affect the whole of Christendom, the Holy Roman Empire of the West. However, they sought to take advantage of the erosion of the political unity of Christendom by appealing to the rising authority of the rulers of the smaller states of Europe. The nations of Europe as we know them today were just beginning to affirm political independence. It was a time of rising national consciousness.

Small principalities and ethnic enclaves had begun to assert themselves in the move for political power and a measure of self-determination. Often the initiative for this new assertiveness came from members of the nobility who sought to cooperate with the rising merchant class for their own political reasons. Certain of the Reformers appealed to these new rulers for support, hoping the success of their ventures might eventually affect the whole of the Western church and Christendom. The word *magisterial* refers to political jurisdiction and authority; hence, it is assigned to that branch of the Reformation that sought the support of the *magistrates* (rulers). For the magisterial Reformers, true religion had to become the established order of the land. True religion always had its manifestations in the social and political realms.

Reformers such as Martin Luther, Ulrich Zwingli, and John Calvin are representative of the magisterial Reformation. In 1523–24, Zwingli used the support of the civil authorities in Zurich to carry out reforms that opposed the papacy, the power of the monastic orders, and the hierarchy of the church. Luther gained the support of the magistracy in Saxony, Brandenburg, Brunswick, and Hesse, as well as the rulers of Denmark and Sweden. John Calvin, a Frenchman (Jean Cauvin), established a reformed and miniature Christendom in the city-state of Geneva, Switzerland, afterward influencing the form of the Reformation in Holland, Scotland, and the German Rhineland.

For Martin Luther the Reformation began in his soul. We can almost take it for granted that many people were dissatisfied with much of the corruption that was present in the church of the times. It was nothing astonishingly new to protest against such abuses of doctrine as the sale of indulgences.[4] What was to be "new" was the recovery of the primacy of the gospel—the good news that God had acted to reconcile sinful humanity to himself and to each other. God had acted in and through the life of Jesus the Christ. Martin Luther discovered the simple and primary truth of that gospel announcement. Of course, in some sense he could not have discovered it without the church. It is the church that had preserved that teaching in its Scriptures and tradition down through the centuries. However, for Luther and others, the church had neglected the simple gospel in favor of practices that enhanced its own institutional power.

Luther was an Augustinian monk, a priest of the church of his day. He was an educated man, somewhat skilled in the humanistic traditions of textual analysis. He was a scriptural scholar and lecturer in the university. He was diligent in the pursuit of those disciplined practices that the church had taught were helpful to the process of salvation. But for Luther there was no peace of mind, only continuing anxiety. Then one day he was meditating on St. Paul's Epistle to the Romans (in the Christian New Testament). Suddenly he was convinced that nothing a person does can set him right with God. God accepts us in spite of our unacceptable lives. He had discovered the truth of "justification by grace through faith"; this truth was the gospel. It meant that God's unmerited love toward humanity and all creation (grace) elicits from us a trusting response (faith) when we discover the futility of our own thoughts and efforts. We are "set right" (justified) in our relation to God by grace through faith.

It was easy to find support for this truth in the writings of St. Augustine, a theologian and bishop of the fourth and fifth centuries. The discovery of this principle was electrifying. It was to become revolutionary, the basis for a change in the concept of authority for much of Christianity. Authority is an inescapable issue for all of us at all times. The question of authority is: What is the source, the foundation, for the convictions, ideas, and practices held by an individual or group? Authority is a matter of authorship—who or what is the author, the source, of your views and actions? Authority is important to everything we do, be it an affair of business, science, politics, or religious expression. The options are always interesting. One may conclude that authority rests with one's private and individual mind, experience, family, tradition, or academic discipline. The Christianity of Western Catholicism had come to the common conclusion that authority rests in the church—its hierarchy, its traditional teaching, and especially the bishop of Rome (the pope). Martin Luther was convinced that justification by grace through faith (the gospel) was made known in the life and work of Jesus the Christ. That revelation could only be encountered in the reading of Scriptures. For Luther the principle of authority was no longer the church; it became *scriptura sola*, Scripture alone.

The fiery German monk stood firmly on the ground of this principle of authority. On the basis of the principle he challenged many of the teachings and practices of the church in the hope that it might be reformed in conformity with the gospel. He was dissatisfied with all practices that implied that we could do anything about our own salvation other than admit our helplessness. He denied the primacy of the pope and abolished private masses, confessions, and fasts. The doctrine of transubstantiation, by means of which the medieval church had interpreted the Mass (Eucharist), was challenged, as was the denial to the laity of communion in both forms (wine as well as bread).

However, nothing in the authority of Scripture prevented Luther from inviting the German princes to take the reform of the church into their own hands, under his guidance. Luther's was a reformation that contained the assumption that the church that taught the Scriptures and proclaimed the gospel must be a church for all the people of the land. He was an heir of Christendom and of the ancient assumption that a nation is holy in its own special way, that a ruler is the sacred symbol of the holiness of the people.

Martin Luther was what Isaiah Berlin called a *fox*.[5] His intellect darted and jumped from one issue to another. He was an emotional person, one who probed the depths of his own psyche in the pursuit of peace. He was a son of German peasantry, his speech seasoned with images of the earth. He wrote and spoke without pulling punches and used language that could offend the sensitivities of "proper" society. His sermons and table talk are a joy to read. In contrast we turn to the other major figure of the magisterial Reformation: John Calvin, a brilliant, systematic thinker. Calvin was an example of Berlin's *hedgehog*—one who carefully organizes and sets a very logical model for whatever he thinks and does. Calvin's reformation was one of systematic thought and governance. Although he could have agreed with Martin Luther on many aspects of a program of reformation, Calvin was more convinced than Luther that the message of the gospel called for a transformation of society and the world as well as the church. He devoted a great deal of thought and energy to the question of what a political order would look like if it existed under the mandate of the gospel. Calvin's Geneva was an experiment in church and state living together in cooperative allegiance to God's hopes for a covenanted community that would be a blessing to the world.

Whereas Luther's concern was with the *experience* of salvation, the knowledge of justification, Calvin's concern seemed to focus on the *intellectual* principle of the sovereignty of God. For Calvin, the discovery of God's sovereignty was accompanied by an awareness of the fact that the individual was incapable of being master of his own spiritual destiny. Calvin's loyalty to the principle of God's sovereignty is rather like the Islamic notion of "*La Illa'ha Illa'lah*" ("There is no good but the God"). We can only know God through God's self-revelation, not through our natural inclinations. If this is so, said Calvin, the salvation of humanity is entirely in the hands of God. God knows who is likely to be concerned with salvation or justification; in fact, God *elects* those who are to be guided to salvation. Calvin's ideas eventually gave rise to a strict and systematic theological position known as Calvinism. We should not confuse Calvin's doctrine of predestination with popular notions of determinism. Determinism is concerned with the fated direction of events in our lives. Astrology is a form of determinism that understands events under the direct control of the planetary forces. Determinism decides that the "A" or "D" we may receive in a course on American literature was somehow planned, fated, and out of our control. It was determined. We have no "free will" in the matter. Predestination, on the other hand, is concerned with our destiny—our eternal relationship to God. Over such matters, says the doctrine of predestination, we have no free will. All we can do is hope. Even the signs that we may interpret as favorable to our salvation must be accepted without assurance. However, to treat the entire matter with indifference may be disastrous, inasmuch as it is a sign of damnation. Predestination is a complex doctrine. Long before Calvin, St. Augustine had struggled with its meaning in the fifth century. We shall return to other aspects of Calvin's thought in a later chapter.

For many of the people interested in the reform of the church in the sixteenth century, the magisterial Reformation of Luther, Zwingli, and Calvin was a continuing distortion of the truth of Christianity. These people became *separationists.* They were more radical than the magisterial Reformers in their interpretation of the gospel and its relationship to the world. The separationist impulse is a universal human response. It is expressed whenever a group decides that its discernment of the truth requires separation from those who do not agree. In the history of Christianity the doctrine of the fall has played an important role. The fall assumes that the world as it exists, the world as we know it naturally, is an estrangement or alienation from God's purposes. It is a fallen world—fallen from the state of paradise that is God's original and continuing intention. The doctrine of the fall leads some Christians to conclude that the Christian can have little or nothing to do with the fallen world. The separationists believe that because they have been restored to God's purpose by God's atoning presence in Jesus the Christ, they must live "separated" from the fallen world. The church must live by a set of values the world does not share.

The separationists were convinced that Luther and Calvin had permitted the church to exist in compromise with the fallen world. They believed that the church had existed for centuries, not as the true church, but as a worldly institution. They demanded a more radical reformation or separation from the world and the worldly church. Some of these separationists became known as Anabaptists, "re-baptizers." The first re-baptizers were simply a group of separationists who were convinced that, because Jesus was baptized as an adult, the only valid baptism was the baptism of adults, as opposed to the common practice of infant baptism. When these separationists began to baptize adults, they were referred to as "re-baptizers" by the followers of Luther and by the forces loyal to the bishop of Rome.

One of the basic practices of the Anabaptists was believer's baptism. In their minds, only discerning, believing people should be baptized. Only adults can be responsible believers; therefore, only adults should be baptized. The Anabaptists also held that the New Testament (the specifically Christian sacred writings of the first century, the apostolic century) was the authoritative source for learning how the church should live in separation from the fallen world. For them the New Testament became a textbook or manual to be consulted for answers to all questions of belief and practice. The New Testament writings contained the model for the life of the church.

This conviction of the Anabaptists concerning the church ultimately led to the conclusion that the church was basically a voluntary association of believers. The church existed only to the extent that people voluntarily gathered as an assembly of believers. This notion would eventually account for an emphasis upon the local institutional nature of Christianity. It would be a concept very congenial to an American setting, where no church could be established and the church could not readily exist without being an effective and successful organization. However, it would become increasingly difficult to understand some of the early Christian language about the church. The church as body of Christ, as existing in God's own realm, as bride of Christ, as the beloved family into which we are born, the body that exists before we exist—such conceptions would be difficult to comprehend in a society dominated by perceptions of the church as voluntary association.

However, Anabaptists seemed to be more concerned with the life of the church than with its thought. They preferred the Gospel accounts of the New Testament to the writings of Paul. To the Anabaptists, Paul was a theologian, a complex thinker; the Gospels gave simple evidence of the life and teachings of the Savior. Simplicity in worship and little distinction between clergy and laity were other marks of Anabaptist practice.

The followers of Menno Simons ("Menno-nites") were Anabaptists who were convinced that Christ's love required peaceful living. They became pacifists, separated from the values of the world by a devotion to nonviolence. They refused to take oaths and practiced foot washing as a ritual of love instituted by Jesus. There were many other groups of Anabaptists. Some were militant revolutionaries on behalf of a new age, a utopian society. Others emphasized communitarian living. The separationist impulse gave rise to numerous interpretations of Christianity and attempts to reform the church. Martin Luther called them *Schwärmerei*—enthusiasts, fanatics, anarchists— like a swarm of bees! Yet his principle of *scriptura sola* was somewhat in harmony with the motivation of the Anabaptists and other religious movements that sought a radical reform of the church by separation from the world.

A third type of Reformation was the *spiritualist* movement. *Spiritualism* is a term often used to refer to those beliefs and practices associated with the purpose of establishing communication with the spirits of the dead. That kind of religiosity might more readily be called *spiritism*, but spiritualism is a form of religion that insists upon spiritual meanings of beliefs and practices and tends to deny significant value to outward or formal expressions. Caspar von Schwenckfeld may be considered a spiritualist because he concluded that the real meaning of the Eucharist or Lord's Supper was "spiritual," that the external forms by which the ritual was performed and its elements received were of little consequence. Of course, if one is a consistent spiritualist, one is left without any religious need for practice except private meditation upon spiritual realities, a practice that, in the end, may be reduced to absurdity.

Nevertheless, there is probably a legitimate claim to the initial sentiment that gives rise to spiritualism. For some people it is more significant to reflect upon the meaning of something than it is to struggle with complex explanations or argue about proper administration. But, of course, it may be just as legitimate to say that the appropriate meaning is known by ritual participation without subjective reflection upon inner meaning.

It is quite understandable that the period of the Reformation should have spawned spiritualist notions. Schwenckfeld was not the only spiritualist. His convictions led him to separate from the followers of Luther, and eventually there emerged a movement that for a time experienced significant growth. Many Schwenckfelders came to Pennsylvania, where they contributed an important element to the formation of the culture. A few congregations still exist today.

There were also *humanist* Reformers who had discovered the essential divinity of human nature. They were convinced that Jesus was the paradigm—the model and example—for the discovery and nurture of the goodness that is in all of us. Humanists tended to deny any special divinity for Jesus and sought to form religious societies that had eliminated what they considered to be the superstitious elements of the church. The humanistic Reformers were not especially successful in their own time, for various reasons. However, they may be considered the forerunners who would influence the formation of later movements such as the Unitarians. Their ideas are shared by many inside and outside the more traditional Christian churches.

One of the most important of the reforming movements of the sixteenth century was that of the *loyalists*. They opposed the activities of magisterial, separationist, spiritualist, and humanist Reformers. Their loyalty was to the pope and the established order of the Catholic tradition that had developed through the centuries. Sometimes this movement is referred to as the Counter-Reformation. However, we must remember that the Reformation is not a single event. The Reformation is a term that refers to all the movements toward reform and renewal that took place within the Catholic Christianity of Western Europe in the sixteenth century. The loyalist forces were themselves concerned with reform. They were opposed to (counter) any reforming thought and activity that was not loyal to the papacy and that threatened the sacramental system of Catholic Christianity. Their reforming work sought to do three things: (1) they wished to reform the church of those corruptions and practices that had been arousing the protests of persons such as Luther and Zwingli; (2) they wished to prevent any further erosion of the fundamental teachings of Catholic Christianity by carefully defining doctrine and practice; (3) they tried to design an aggressive missionary program that would increase the teaching authority of the Church loyal to Rome. One of the reasons for this third concern of the loyalists was the opening of a new world to territorial expansion and colonization. "America" had again been "discovered" by Europe just prior to the Lutheran agitation. In the mind of Europe, it was a land waiting for the proclamation of the Christian gospel, waiting for occupation by the nations of Christendom.

The loyalist Reformation is also referred to as the Tridentine Reformation. That is because much loyalist activity was centered on the deliberations of the Council of Trent, which met in three sessions from 1545 to 1563 in Trent, Italy, and was first called by Pope Paul III in 1537. It is often said that Trent is the beginning of the Roman Catholicism with which the modern world was familiar until Vatican Council II (1962–65). Prior to Trent there seems to have been greater flexibility of interpretation and practice in loyalist Catholicism than afterward. Tridentine reforms were accompanied by careful definitions of doctrine, especially those that were challenged by the other reforming movements.

New religious orders, groups of people who set themselves apart in dedication and discipline for purposes either of contemplation and prayer or service to human need (or both), had already begun to emerge by 1520. They were followed by the formation of the Society of Jesus (Jesuits), founded by Ignatius of Loyola in 1534. The Jesuits were a major factor in the loyalist Reformation and have been known for their theological and educational work and their missionary program. The services of the order were to be at the loyal disposal of the pope in the fostering of reform and the saving of souls by way of loyalist faith and doctrine.

Those reforming forces that were not loyalist in sentiment were eventually referred to as Protestants. The word is a catchall term that came into use at the Diet of Speyer in 1529. This meeting was controlled by a loyalist majority and passed legislation to end toleration of the followers of Luther in loyalist districts in Germany. Some princes and municipal representatives launched a formal "protest." Henceforth the nonloyalists were known as "Protestants."

The Reformation in England

In some sense the term *Reformation* does not apply, therefore, to the movement in England. England's Reformation in its beginnings represents a simple declaration of independence from papal authority. Most of the existing traditions of Western Catholic Christianity remained intact. Catholicism in

England had always had its own distinct character. What had been the Catholic church *in* England became, during the sixteenth century, the Church *of* England. The short distance across the English Channel was sufficient to render British religion and culture different from those of the Continent. Ancient Celtic Christianity had left its mark, providing a curious blend of natural mysticism with a spirit of liberty. It had always been difficult to maintain Roman order in the church in England. It was as much a problem for the Roman hierarchy to control the Christian life of Britain as it was for the Roman Empire to exercise political sway over the destiny of the islands.

England has been a cradle of liberty. It was the tradition of English freedom that was to play so great a role in the development of the independent American nation in later times. The Reformation of the church in England owes much to this spirit of liberty. Late in the sixth century Pope Gregory I had sent a papal delegation to England, hoping to consolidate the church. Although the Council of Whitby in 664 C.E. managed to underwrite Gregory's plans, the monastic Christianity of St. Columbia had already established a more loosely organized and individualistic religious life in Britain.

When Henry VIII declared independence for the church in England in order for the archbishop of Canterbury to annul the king's marriage to Catherine of Aragon (Spain), he was expressing the English spirit. At first Henry wished to maintain the Catholic Christian tradition as it had existed in England for centuries. But it was a time of political and economic change as well as of religious change. Henry and his nobles began the suppression of convents and monasteries in order to lay hands upon the enormous wealth and property under the control of these institutions. In addition, there was unrest in England resulting from the influx of ideas and refugees from the continental Reformation. The Reformers of Europe had made ready use of the printing press. Sermons, Bibles, addresses, treatises, and theological works were published in great numbers as the religious revolution gained momentum. They made their way across the Channel and were read by clergy and laity. Refugees, exiles from oppression on the Continent, stirred the minds of the English people with their revolutionary ideas. Magisterial, separationist, spiritualist, and humanist ideas circulated, agitating further reform beyond the intentions of Henry VIII, whom Parliament had designated "the only Supreme Head in earth of the Church of England." Henry, of course, was not a cleric, not a priest or bishop. He could not ordain or celebrate the Eucharist (or mass), but he could serve as a force for unity in English Christendom. As Supreme Head, he symbolized the familiar and ancient prerogative of Christian monarchs in a world where church and state were but two aspects of a single undivided society.

The agitation for further reform within the Church of England gave rise to the Puritan movement. Puritanism sought to purify the Catholicism of the Church of England. Eventually this led to the pluralization of religion in England. Separationism resulted in the emergence of numerous denominational groups. Loyalism also had its devotees, and England became a land in which members of the established Church of England existed alongside Roman Catholics, Baptists, Congregationalists, and Presbyterians (the latter three born directly out of the conceptions of Puritanism).

The English Reformation produced no theological leaders of the caliber of Martin Luther or John Calvin. Instead, the intellectual efforts of English theologians were directed toward the design of liturgy and the justification of Catholic church order. No great systematic theologies such as Calvin's emerged; no theological treatises like Luther's received widespread acclaim. The genius of the Church of England was the Book of Common Prayer, which revised the prayers and practices of Catholic Christianity, making them available for clergy and laity alike. The Book of Common Prayer advocated a principle of unity. It was assumed that theological and experiential differences could exist side by side in a church that had a common liturgical practice. Diversity in the use of the prayer book was also permitted.

Richard Hooker's *Laws of Ecclesiastical Polity* was published during the reign of Queen Elizabeth I (1558–1603). It is a defense of apostolic succession[6] and the church order of the Church of England. Hooker also set forth a principle that continues to be important in the Anglican (Church of England) tradition. Arguing against the Puritan use of Scripture, he elaborated a theory of natural law as the expression of God's supreme reason, by means of which everything, including Scripture, is to be interpreted.

The English Reformation is discussed in greater detail than certain aspects of the continental Reformation because the first United States of America emerged out of a religious and cultural milieu that was fundamentally English. Puritanism is an unavoidable ingredient in American society and culture. We all continue to be Puritans, whether we are committed to its religious traditions or not. Many historians, such as Sydney E. Ahlstrom, have pointed out that the Puritan epoch ended in 1960 with the election of John Fitzgerald Kennedy as the first Roman Catholic president of the United States. As we shall observe in a later chapter, Puritanism was a dominant factor in the settlement of the English colonies. It was a tradition of nonconformity that was transformed into dissent. Americans have been dissenters. Puritans were rigorous in their morality, had a profound commitment to subjective experience, and were determined to make the state into a reformed Christendom. These qualities seeded the formation of American consciousness well into our own time and are still residual among secularists as well as among representatives of our religious traditions. All elements among the American people—whether Roman Catholic, Lutheran, Jewish, African, Indian, Asian—have had to relate to the Puritanism of America positively or negatively. Of course, as the American religious story unfolds, we shall see the entire heritage of the Reformation making its way to America, where it will be reshaped and bring its many influences to bear upon our way of thinking and perceiving the world.

To many Europeans the time of the Reformation coincided with their earlier hopes of a Land Promised to the Saints. The rediscovery of America in the late fifteenth century was closely linked to the momentum for Reformation that began little more than two decades later. Together they were thought to be a sign that the time had come for the renewal of the world. Something momentous was about to happen. A new history was beginning, a sacred history. An earthly paradise had been discovered across the western horizon, where the path of the sun beckoned colonists to follow. For numerous English thinkers, religion and culture always passed from East to West. America had been basically hidden to Europeans until the time of Reformation. Now it represented a home, a place of fulfillment, where the church would complete its reformation and its work of perfection.

Although we dare not minimize the importance of economic and political consideration in the peopling of America, we must remember that such motivations as those were most frequently understood as part of the design of Providence. That is to say, God as Creator is assumed to be a provider, one who makes provision for the people by leading them into a land of plenty. Paradise is a land of plenty, and God's plan to reform the church and bring divine hopes for humankind to fruition will find its setting in a Western land "flowing with milk and honey"—and gold! Much of the religious energy of the human race is spent on dreams of golden streets, visitors from other realms, and wealthy planets in space. It continues to be the religious illusion of the secular world.

Even the changing social order of Europe, reflected in the lives of the colonists of early America, can be understood religiously. Providence directs its compassion upon those people who had been previously neglected and oppressed. History will be fulfilled when the poor and the downtrodden have found their way to the earthly paradise where the new order of God's kingdom will be established. This was the thinking of thousands of Europeans, whether simple farmers, artisans, or more learned members of the society.

The ideas and institutions spawned at the time of Reformation were to find a ready home in the promised land of the West. It will be difficult to understand the shaping of American society, culture, and its religious traditions without remembering this important fact. America acquired the religious hopes of Europe. The oppression that always attends revolutionary times led many of its victims to come to America, where they believed God had led them. They came in order to pursue their own ways of thought, their own ritual life, their own welfare. Some came to experiment, to try new ways of living they assumed would be models of the new age toward which Providence was guiding them. Almost all of them knew that America was no ordinary place of refuge. To those of the magisterial, separationist, and spiritualist variety, it was the land for the flowering of Reformation. To them, loyalist Europe was a fallen world, a world of opposition-to-Christ (called Antichrist) from which it was necessary to escape. But to many loyalist Reformers, America was the place to which God had led them in order to bring all people into the Catholic faith before the advent of a "new heaven and a new earth."

chapter 4

The Native American Traditions

Long ago, before there was time like this one, there was a boy who hunted every day in the forest. One day in the late afternoon he sat down near a large rock to rest, repair his bow, and sharpen the points of his arrows.

Suddenly there was a voice, the sound of a man, that said, "I have a story to tell you."

The young hunter sat up quickly and looked around him. He was a little apprehensive. Who had spoken? He searched the area. It could only be the rock. The stone must have *orenda*, he thought. He had heard the grandfathers speak of the magic power. "What did you say?" he asked the stone.

"I spoke of stories. I will tell you about stories, traditions. But first you must give me a gift for telling you. You do not get such a story for nothing."

"I have a quail. Will it do?" asked the boy, laying one of the birds he had shot that day on the rock.

"You must come back tonight," said the stone, "and I will tell you about the world that was."

That night the hunter sat down near the stone and heard the voice tell him about the sky people, those of great magic who were the first people. There was an old grandmother who dreamed that the large tree that stood in the center of her village should be dug up by its roots. When she told the people about her dream, they immediately set to uprooting the tree. The hole was so great and awesome that the people nervously threw the old woman into it. She fell and fell until she hit the earth. It took a long time because the earth was completely under water then. So the animals had to prepare it to receive the fallen grandmother. They brought the earth up out of the water and put it onto the back of the turtle, where the beaver patted it with his tail and allowed it to harden and grow.

Some boys do not know how to listen, even to stories. By the time the tale was finished, the lad had dozed off. "It is important that you tell me when you become sleepy," said the voice. "Then we can rest. Otherwise, if you sleep while I speak, you will not hear. Come back tomorrow night and I will tell you more. And don't forget to bring me another present."

The young hunter returned the next evening with a string of birds he had hunted that day. This time he listened carefully and did not doze off. He did not miss a word and came back the next night and the one after that.

One day he was out hunting with a friend who became curious, "Where is it that you disappear every night?"

"I go to hear stories," replied the boy.

"What are stories?" asked the friend.

"It is difficult to explain, but if you will come with me tonight, you will hear for yourself."

That night the boy and his friend listened to the voice of the stone together. They heard the tales of Genonsgwa and the stone coats, the Flying Heads, and the Porcupine people, until they were so sleepy that the storytelling stone sent them home to their beds.

Before long the people of the village heard about the stone and its many stories. The young hunter introduced them to the stone. They began to bring fresh game and listen to the things called tales that came from the voice of the storytelling stone. The tribe learned many things they had not known before. They learned prayers for the harvest and songs of the corn. For four years they listened until they heard all of the tales. "Until the stone began to speak to the boy, we knew nothing!" said the wisest among the people.

"One day you will be an old man," said the stone to the young hunter, "and you may be unable to hunt. The tales will help you. Tell the stories to those who will listen, but always require a gift in return." So saying, the stone told the boy the final story one evening after the others had gone. And the voice of the storytelling stone became silent and never was heard again.

The boy became a man and then a grandfather. There were many who came to his lodge to listen to the stories he told. They came from near and far, and they brought fresh game, tobacco, and fur to hear the tales that were told to a boy long ago, stories that spoke of the beginnings of many different tribes. Crowds of people gathered in his lodge, catching the tales to take home with them to their own firesides.

That is the way that stories came to be and why there are so many stories in the world where once there were none. The stories tell us everything we need to know and without the stories we know nothing. Our tongues are tied, even today, if we do not know the stories of the people of powerful magic, the people of the world before us—the people made known by the storytelling stone.

The above is a tale from the Seneca, a Native American people whose name means "the stone folk." When we turn our minds from a consideration of Christendom and the heritage of the Reformation to the traditions of the peoples who inhabited the North American continent before the arrival of Europeans, we learn a great deal about ourselves as well. Perhaps it is not an exaggeration to say that these native people are aware of a truth of which Europeans were only dimly aware. It is a truth we tend to forget today: human beings live by story. Without stories we know nothing, and if we want to speak about anything that is important to us, we tell a story. The only trouble is, modern Americans do not tell very good stories nor very true ones, because they have forgotten the importance of story and because, sooner or later, the story must talk about the world before this one and the people who inhabited it. Time must sooner or later fade into the beginnings before time as we know it. It is the way to be human.

The storytelling stone of the Seneca was certainly a voice of wisdom to be able to make sense of the strangers who began to disturb the forests in the seventeenth century of the Common Era. The strangers were palefaced and did not dress like the people of the forest. They did not move easily among the bear, the deer, the wolves, and the badgers. The tales of the storytelling stone must include the stories of all of the tribes. From what part of that forest did the strangers come? Were they brothers and sisters to the otter, the panther, or the Great Fish Who Swims Like Islands in the Sea? Soon it became apparent that many of the strangers did not know the ways of the forest and its people. They acted as if the forest and its people were not there. They did as they wished with the trees and the animals. They ignored the stone people or pushed them away like unworthy dogs. Were the strangers pale devils sent from another world to punish? Or were they sent to help the stone people in their squabbles with the other people of the forests? The strangers were aliens, but they had curious power, a "medicine" unknown to the Seneca.

To reason is to try to remember the stories or to seek the wisdom of someone who knows tales you have not heard before. The ways of those called

Native Americans are traditional and are carried by storytelling. They are the ways of an orally dependent world. Communication is done by word of mouth, in singing and telling. Seeing and hearing are also important in such a world. There are signs to be seen and things to be known by careful listening.

We must remember, of course, that we always live in a perception of the world rather than in the rawness of the world itself. The Native Americans perceived the world by way of sounds and sights. Their perception was transmitted orally and by actions that told stories. The European strangers who appeared in their midst transmitted their perception of the world in reading and writing. It was literacy (the use of writing) that had fashioned their entire civilization through several millennia. Their mode of dress, housing, economics, and social order were determined by the written word. Native Americans were folk of the spoken word. They lived by the naming of things and the telling of tales.

Nonliteracy

We must not attempt to understand Native American traditions by judging them only from the perspective of our literate heritage. We must not think of them as illiterate. To do so would assume that a culture that depends upon literacy is superior to one that does not. They are a nonliterate (perhaps at some time a *pre*-literate) culture. In some sense, no culture, no people, is entirely one or the other. As individuals we are all nonliterate as well as literate.

Certainly our lives are greatly preoccupied with being able to read and write. Even a computer culture will depend for a time on the written word. However, much in our lives is dependent upon gestures and the spoken word. For example, if a man asks his wife where she has been, she will answer by telling him a story—giving an account, a narration, that satisfies his concern. Indeed, if she has spent a particularly bad day in a meeting where she did not fare so well, she may exaggerate or restructure the story so that her intelligence, righteousness, or courage stand out. "Good! I'm glad you did that!" replies the husband, happy to be related to so courageous a figure.

There are many occasions in which our lives are ritualized, hardly dependent upon written works. We do certain things, in certain ways, at certain times, not because they are rational or follow written instructions, but merely because "that is the way we do them!" We communicate by touch, by glance, by stories, and by ritual actions. We are nonliterate as well as residents of a world perceived through reading and writing.

There are two important things to remember about a nonliterate society. First, some oral communication is so important that few liberties may be taken in transmission. Second, oral communication generally permits great artistry in performance. Certain stories are generative; others are derivative. A generative account is one that displays many of the images, ideas, and values basic to a perception of the world. A derivative narration derives, plays with, or uses those images, ideas, and values generated by the basic story or stories.

An example of a generative account is the creation story. Scholars often call these narrations *cosmogonic myths*. Every society must have some sense of where it has come from, when and how its beginnings took place, and how it fits into the universe—the cosmos. Hence, the story it tells is cosmogonic; it has to do with the origins of the cosmos in which one lives. People do not create these accounts on demand; they are not fashioned by individual authors or by committees. They emerge out of the darkness beyond memory and gather meaning and power over generations of recall. Such stories are fundamental to the sense of well-being of a people. They are the source of attitudes, images, ideas, and beliefs. It is important that such generative stories be faithfully preserved and transmitted. Someone must memorize them and pass them on with a minimum of error. An oral and nonliterate society bases its very existence on the careful transmission of generative stories. Their telling becomes a sacred task performed in a proper manner by certain specialists.

What is transmitted is tradition. The ways and the wisdom of the people must be preserved and taught. Without tradition we do not know who we are, how to think, or what to do. To be human is to have a tradition. To the Native American, as well as to other tribal and nonliterate societies, tradition is especially important. However, its transmission is often a performance that is very joyful and entertaining. After all, good storytelling is an affair of pleasure and enchantment. There are some stories that are left to the artistry, skill, and voice of the storyteller. They transmit tradition that is derived from the generative accounts of the grandfathers and grandmothers. The storyteller serves an apprenticeship. Storytellers must learn the stories, but it is important that they know the frame, structure, and intention of them. They must also know when it is appropriate to tell them, and to whom. Stories are not to be told to people we cannot trust because stories are a gift. Many stories are harmonious with a certain season, a sacred time for which the story may serve as the conduit through which a timeless reality is made present.

Outsiders must be careful in their telling of the traditional stories of Native Americans. They must respect them and reverence them, trying not to tell them out of season. Sometimes scholars must remain silent about what they cannot understand and have no permission to possess. Stories are sacred. As their skills develop, storytellers may perform the stories in their own unique fashion, so long as they are faithful to the ways of their people. If they depart from the tradition, they lose credibility. The frame, the structure, and the intention of the story must be preserved.

The people we now call Native Americans have also been called Indians. The name was provided by European outsiders who sought to find a way of referring to those whom they encountered as "others." It is a practice similar to the use of the word *European*. In some sense there are no "Europeans." There are Italians, Germans, Greeks, Macedonians, Spaniards, Basques, French, Britons, Welsh, English, Scots, and so on. So perhaps there are no Indians, no Native Americans, only Navajo, Seneca, Hopi, Oglala Sioux, Seminole, Iroquois, Tlingit, Kiowa, to name a few. It is important to remember that there is great diversity among these people we call Native Americans. Among traditional, nonliterate peoples, diversity in tribal status and culture also means diversity in religion. To be of the Navajo people, for example, is to live the Navajo way, to know that one is Navajo. The religious tradition is therefore Navajo and is likely to be a different religion from that of the Zuni, the Apache, or the Ojibwa.

Their sojourn in the western hemisphere confronted Europeans with a dilemma that has never been completely resolved. Who were the swarthy inhabitants encountered on the shores and in the woodlands, and what was their place in the minds of the settlers and refugees of Christendom? Where had they come from? If the explorers had landed on the outskirts of Asia, perhaps these people were *los indios*—Indians. If they had "discovered" a "new world," then perhaps the natives were the descendants of the original residents of the Garden of Eden—innocent and noble in their nakedness before the institution of the "fig-leaf syndrome." Desiderius Erasmus, Dutch humanist, in his *In Praise of Folly* (published in 1509) described the American natives as "the simple people of the golden age . . . furnished with no school knowledge. Nature alone sufficed to guide them; instinct to prompt them how to live. . . . What would have been the advantage of jurisprudence to men among whom bad morals—the sole apology for good laws—had no existence?" This sentiment lay on the heart of the notion of the Native American as child of Eden or noble savage. Of course, the Indians also had to place these strangely attired "white" Europeans within their own perception of the world—were they saviors or white devils?

In our time, scientists have created their own myth of Indian origins. *Los indios* were probably Asiatics, immigrants who made their way across the land bridge where Alaska is now separated from Siberia by the Bering Sea and the Arctic ocean. Vine Deloria Jr., raised on the Pine Ridge Reservation of South Dakota and a professor at the University of Colorado, rejects the Bering Strait hypothesis as a form of conjecture with no evidence to support it. In *Red Earth, White Lies,* he points out that a Bering migration would have been scientifically impossible. Many Native Americans repudiate the doctrine because the memories and traditions of the ancestors provide no evidence of the Bering migration. "By making us immigrants to North America," writes Deloria, "they are able to deny the fact that we were the full, complete, and total owners of this continent."[1] Whether Deloria is correct in his conclusions or not, we are obligated to respect and think seriously about what Indian traditions themselves say about these matters.

This issue presents an opportunity to emphasize two principles central to religious studies: (1) What do we learn about ourselves, about being human, by studying a tradition? (2) It is necessary to *think with* the tradition in order to understand it—not to pre-judge it by the criteria of modern presuppositions or by what we ourselves believe or think. If scientists wish to be honest in their pursuit of knowledge, they will be prepared to *learn from* a tradition and its people—even about so-called scientific matters.

Common Characteristics

In this chapter we must confront the great diversity of Native American traditions and seek a common sense of them. Some scholars may tell us we cannot generalize in this way; however, generalization is a necessary and acceptable procedure in the academic world. We may generalize so long as we remember that we are doing so and realize that generalizations set limitations upon our understanding. We must risk generalization because this book is not a study of Native American traditions. We are being introduced to the shaping of American religious traditions and are forced to make many generalizations.

Accordingly, we shall ask, What are the common aspects of the traditions of *los indios*? What is the understanding of history shared by these people? And how are the native traditions shaped by the encounters of the common American experience?

What are the common characteristics of Native American traditions? First of all, the world is perceived as being alive, with a sense of continuity and relationship among all forms of aliveness. The world is filled with conscious vitality and unconscious vitality. It is very evident, says the Native American, that existence is experienced as widely distributed power—some of it conscious, willful, and personal and some of it impersonal, like the movement of a ray of the sun. It is like the *orenda*, first encountered by the boy in the Seneca legend of the storytelling stone. All things have *orenda*, the mysterious and magical power that flows through the world. Sticks and stones, the wing of an owl, the tail of the fox, the bough of the fir tree that hangs by the side of the stream—they all possess and share *orenda*, the vital energy. This kind of impersonal power must be understood, for it may be used to good advantage. Just as we harness something we call electricity (and do not know what it is), so it is necessary for the Native American to be alert to the *orenda* or the *wakan* (power) that is present in the things of this world. Not to be alert and respectful may be to court danger. One must be ready for good fortune and for bad. The *wakan* that is present in a rock or a fox's tail is not a conscious energy. It does not have knowledge. It cannot know, make decisions, or speak.

But sometimes there may be a stone through which unusual power moves. It may seem like all other stones, but there is a *conscious* force that makes itself known. It may become a *storytelling* stone. That is because some of the power that surrounds us in this world where everything is vital and related is personal. There is the personal energy of the dead. Ancestors continue in some form of life and power. Ancestors are present. For some Native American peoples, the living dead are dangerously present for a period of time right after dying. It is therefore necessary to be on watch and to perform certain ritual acts that ward off dangers that may be inflicted by contact with those who are unsettled and struggling in the transition from this existence to that of the living dead. Eventually, of course, the transitions are made, the dangers subside, and the living dead settle into normal relations with the other inhabitants of the universe.

There are other forms of personal energy. They are the beings that may reside in lakes, clouds, or certain mountains. If these spirits are extremely powerful and very purposive in their exercise of power, they assume the roles of deity, what we are accustomed to call gods. The Hopi live on the mesas of a reservation in the north-central part of Arizona. Their world is sacred, and they have lived near Old Oraibi and Hoteville for almost a millennium. They have been primarily farmers, scratching their corn, beans, and squash out of the harsh soil of the high deserts in their seasons. Almost everyone has seen a picture of the kachinas, the ceremonial dancers of Hopi society. From December through July, the male dancers in their elaborate masks and costumes enact the ceremonies that maintain the cycle of fertility upon which Hopi existence depends. During the course of their dancing, the performers are transformed into the spirits who visit the Hopi villages from their home in Arizona's San Francisco Peaks. The spirits possess the dancers as they bring fertility to the Hopi in preparation for the growing season. The costumes and the knowledge of the ceremonial dance are channels for the visitation of the spirits. The spirits are in fact the kachinas, who become one with the dancers. In a world where everything is alive, such transformations are an understandable reality. We would also assume that the San Francisco Peaks themselves are a sacred place for the Hopi. It is from such especially sacred places as the peaks that the people derive their sense of well-being, their understanding that the world is dependable.

If it is conscious being, if it is alive, it must be spirit. But the line between spirit and deity is a difficult line to traverse. It is quite likely that discussions about gods are not part of the original traditions of the Native Americans. With the coming of the Europeans—whose perception of the world was shaped by centuries of Christendom and its encounter with the gods of many peoples—language about gods, God, and the Great Spirit entered the Native American world. It is only when one comes into contact with others who perceive the world differently and who give different names to the powers that inhabit the cosmos, that one is forced to ask, Is the world greater than I have perceived? Is there a spirit who keeps all worlds together? Or are there simply many worlds, many spirits?

Originally, the Native Americans were probably satisfied with living in a world in which the traditions of the grandfathers and grandmothers taught how to get along with all the many personal and impersonal powers. Nevertheless, everyone's world changes. New creatures and spirits are discovered. Stones must change. New ones emerge. The tradition is always living; it is seldom a dead affair of past custom. The Native American discovers that some spirits are greater than others and may even conclude that a Great Spirit is the ultimate power to which everything relates. But does that American therefore speak about gods, about God? Ruth Underhill tells us: "Some Pacific Coast fisherman spoke of the One Sitting Above or the Lord of the Shining Heavens, but these beings are not mentioned in the origin myth and all do not appear in ceremonies. They and some other mentions of a sky god seem to belong to a level apart from the ancient myth."[2] This is probably so because it was related to the experience of white people's talk of the all-powerful being who creates, protects, and provides for both humankind and the realm of powers and spirits. Most often, scholars tell us, the traditions do not go beyond talk of the personalizing power of the sun or some other primary energy of the world. It is difficult to resolve the question of God or gods when trying to understand Native American peoples. In the absence of a canon of sacred writings, authority lives within the oral and ritual tradition. Words themselves are used differently at different times and by different people.

Among the Oglala Sioux of the north-central plains, *wakan* becomes so concentrated that it becomes *Wakonda,* and a speaker may give it a personal reference: "Wakonda is watching you." However, this does not settle the issue. The word shifts in meaning. Many times the Sioux may speak of *Wakan-Tanka* (Great *Wakan* or Sacred One). Even so it is the influence of Christian missionaries that defines the use of this name, so that it becomes equivalent to what Christians mean by God. Essentially the Native American has been satisfied with awareness of the great varieties and concentrations of power in the world. He or she may provide names for such experiences, but the use of the names is seldom really defined among a nonliterate people. It is probably safe to say that in our own times, God and the Great Spirit are important names in Native American societies, except in those cases where traditionalists react against the process of change and attempt to reverse it, hoping to return to the traditional world that existed before the encounter with Euro-Americans.

A second common characteristic, one that we observed earlier, is that transmission of knowledge and wisdom concerning the world relies heavily upon stories orally developed and performed. Of course, in nonliterate societies the auditors are as important as the storytellers. The performance that transmits sacred tradition includes the hearers. Storyteller and audience are performers together. There are ways of listening just as there are ways of telling. And the hearers all know the importance of the stories, when they must be told, where, and with what preparation.

A third characteristic, perhaps equivalent in importance to storytelling (sometimes accompanying it), is ritual. Nonliterate people depend very much upon ritual communication. In order to understand this we must set aside our prejudices about ritual. For many Euro-Americans, ritual bears the connotation of that which is superficial and unnecessary. Even if it is "nice" or acceptable to us, we think of it as either less than intelligent or perhaps nonspiritual. We often tend to assume that underlying ritual is something essential that is preferable to the ritual itself. Anyone who persists in this attitude will not understand people for whom ritual is basic communication. As a matter of fact, they will not likely understand themselves, inasmuch as all of us rely upon ritual performances of which we are often unaware. Human beings, regardless of education or intelligence, are ritualists.

Certain actions clearly demonstrate our attitude toward the world and other people. Ritual is enacted perception of the world. It need not be accompanied by words, although it often is. Much ritual is not done according to conscious thought. It is simply done. Ritual is learned from parents, school, culture. Some of it develops as we change our perception of the world through education or training. In any case ritual, like much of existence, is an affair of tradition. Scientists in laboratories are ritualists very much dependent upon tradition. Without ritual they would be lost and aimless creatures. We can tell something of how they perceive the world by observing their actions.

Ritual is patterned behavior, a set of actions that expresses our thoughts and feelings about existence in a cosmos we are unable to describe or define. Ritual is a dramatic demonstration of the principle we have been repeating— that we live in a perception of the world. Our perception of the world depends upon symbols communicated both verbally (in language) and by way of gesture and action. All human beings are ritualists to some extent, but nonliterate societies depend upon ritual perhaps to a greater extent than modern literate societies. We can certainly understand that Native Americans, who live in a world where everything is alive, imbued with personal and impersonal power, would celebrate much of their existence by way of ritual. One must learn how to act in the company of a diversity of powers. Rituals involve rubrics, special words, prescribed movements, and paraphernalia. *Rubrics* are the rules and instructions one learns either in a period of apprenticeship or simply as a result of living in a tradition in which people regularly participate in certain ceremonies, festivals, or habits of behavior. Special words refer to the songs or stories that accompany the rest of the action. These, too, are learned either by careful training (in the case of certain leaders or specialists) or by repeated participation. In addition to songs and stories there may be single words or phrases, formulae, which are important to the ritual events. The word *amen* is a single word of essential ritual power among Jews and Christians. Prescribed movements include dancing, processions, special signs, and gestures. Dancing is especially significant among most traditional or nonliterate societies like those of the Native Americans;

some of it is intricate and requires long apprenticeship. Most ritual action depends upon the use of special paraphernalia. Masks, rattles, fetishes (objects containing *orenda* or *wakan,* such as teeth, feathers, bones), costumes, fires, trumpets made from horns—these are all examples of the equipment that may be necessary for ritual to take place effectively.

Ritual is always an affair of tradition. It is a participatory event that must be learned and that will express the identity of those who perform it. A native of Rumania expresses his or her Eastern Orthodox Christianity in distinctive ways; there are ritual characteristics that are part of his or her tradition. It is unfair to conclude that ritual differences are incidental and unnecessary; such judgment is based upon our own biases, and it prejudices our ability to understand people as ritual beings.

Underhill tells us that the Navajo people participated in prayer and sweat rituals before going on a deer hunt. They traveled far from their ritual homes. When they camped, all actions—whether sleeping, cooking, eating, or placement of weapons—were subject to rubric. "The owner of the deer was sometimes thought to be Talking God."[3] The Wolf Way men would sing a hymn around the campfire:

> He [the deer] searches for me . . .
> I being the Talking God . . .
>
> On top of the dark mountain
> He searches for me
> Among the flowers
>
> He searches for me
> The finest of bucks
> He searches for me . . .
> With his death blood red in color he obeys me[4]

During the final stages of the kill, the group would apologize to the wounded deer before finishing it off with a club. Among some of the southwestern tribes the deer was brought home as an honored guest, decorated with beads, and sprinkled with pollen before it was killed. If the hide of a deer was to become part of the paraphernalia of a special ritual event, no arrow was used to mar the skin. Instead the animal was run down, captured, and usually smothered by filling the nostrils with ceremonial pollen.

A study of Native American ways reveals that ritual accompanied almost all human activity. Hunting, gathering, planting, and harvesting were of special significance because they were the activities of human subsistence. In the modern, nontraditional societies in which most of us live, subsistence depends upon the very artificial exchange of money. We are less likely to perceive the meaning of the activities that provide us with daily sustenance. Therefore, we tend not to express our sorrow and gratitude for the suffering and sacrifice that are central to everyday existence.

Of course, at special times of the year, at special passages in the course of life, on special occasions, ritual among Native Americans increased in dramatic crescendo. As Sam Gill has said, "It is through a tradition of formal ritual acts that Native Americans relate to the world, find significance of life, and uphold the responsibility for maintaining order as it was given to the world in the beginning. From the Native American view, their ritual acts are creative acts of the highest order, since the object of their creation is the world itself."[5] The Native American is no simple occupant of the world of nature, behaving instinctively like an animal or reflecting biological rhythms like a tree, but rather, a human being who transcends the biological world of which she or he is a part. Native American ritual acts are often complex responses to an environment that is very much alive with power. They are personal actions that reflect necessary behavior in the presence of an "other"—whoever, whatever, that "other" may be. As a child I must learn those gestures and responses that are required of me in relationship to other people. I know these people as mother, father, sister, brother, uncle, grandmother—on goes the list until it includes people who are strangers of different kinds. I must learn to do what is appropriate to survive among the people I meet. The Native American list of "people" includes many forces and powers that most of us do not include among people. Therefore, the Native American learns ways of response that have been established in the stories, songs, and prayers that are part of his or her tradition. Life without ritual is impossible in such a world, and the rituals are as significant an achievement as the published works of a great philosopher.

A great bonfire sends twisting tongues of red and indigo into the darkened sky. Flames thunder and roar like an angry Asian dragon, shedding sparks like spittle into the night. A safe distance away the crowd waits, huddled in groups around smaller warming fires. Incense from piñon, manzanita, and juniper lends friendly reassurance to the world of the raging monster. Suddenly, naked human dancers appear. They move about the great fire, carrying thick rolls of cedar bark. As the light trickles across their bodies, the shadows part to show painted stripes and daubs. The dancers crawl toward the flames, moving beneath the intense heat, to ignite the cedar ropes. They raise their torches and spray themselves and the crowd with sparks and bits of burning bark.

In this way the people know that the fire deities have come down from their mountain homes. They will drive out evil forces and bring healing power to the Navajo. The First Dance is a ritual that is part of the ancient ways of a people. It is not a luxury, a form of frivolous entertainment. It is life.

Gill tells us that Navajo sandpaintings are not framed as permanent works of art to be hung in the homes of tourists and art collectors. They are part of the ritual healing ways of the Navajo tradition. They are the work of a medicine man or singer, who must be carefully trained to remember the designs and their proper use. There are no books of patterns. Only human memory and the apprenticeship system preserve the hundreds of designs. The medicine man knows the sick person, and he is familiar with the illness and its symptoms. This knowledge determines the pattern to be selected from memory and constructed on the floor of a ceremonial house. The finished painting will depict in colors the mythic person who has some connection with the illness. The spiritual being becomes present through the form in which it is represented. Corn pollen[6] is sprinkled on the painting by both the medicine man and the sick person. The action serves as an invitation for the holy people to manifest themselves in the sandpainting.

The ailing person sits in the middle of the sandpainting in order to become one with the holy people. The medicine man takes sand from the legs, feet, head, and body of each of the mythic beings and presses them onto the corresponding parts of the body of the ailing person. Taking a feather-tipped wand, the medicine man completely destroys the defaced sandpainting and the sands are returned to nature in ritual fashion.

Native American ways of being religious are very profoundly shaped by storytelling, singing, and ritual. However, there is another element that is shared by many Native American people. It is what has been called the way of vision—the *vision quest*. Someone wishing to comprehend the way of vision may read Joseph Epes Brown's *The Sacred Pipe* or John G. Neihardt's *Black Elk Speaks*. These accounts are the records of those who have known and learned from the Sioux wise man, the shaman[7] Black Elk. Although secondhand, they are as faithful to the oral tradition as any account is likely to be.

The vision quest is the search for the spirit that will serve as the special support and guardian for one's life. The quest begins at an early age and usually takes place by means of the prescribed ritual ways of one's tribal tradition. In other words, the vision quest is not left to chance. There is a discipline that is part of tribal wisdom. The quest involves ascetic withdrawal from one's ordinary habitat and associates. The person leaves home and is to be alone; no male-female association is permitted. Various forms of austerity are required, fasting being the most common practice. One thirsts and starves in order that the body may lose its ordinary hold upon the mind and the imagination. The wonder that is fundamental to all humans and most evident in childhood is freed from its domination by daily need and desire. The individual may hallucinate (as a psychological explanation would have it) or go into a trance state. He or she has been prepared by the elders and has considered carefully the kind of power required. The spirit is called upon repeatedly until such time as the person enters the death world and receives the visit of that special spirit who will accompany him or her through life.

From the time of the first vision, life becomes a journey in companionship with the transnatural. Throughout a lifetime there will be periods of withdrawal and fasting that provide opportunity for the renewal and intensification of spirit power. Of course, the shaman and the medicine man are specialists in communication with the spirits. They become guides, helpers, in the vision quest. In some societies such visions are left to them alone; they share the results of their dreams with their people. The degree of female participation in the vision quest varies from one society to another. However, it is necessary to remember that woman has her own special power that begins its transnatural visitation with her first menstrual period and returns with each subsequent period.

It should be somewhat evident by now that Native American traditions have their religious specialists, just as other traditions do. Specialization of function and creativity is as natural to human societies as it is to the realm of plants and animals. We should not be misled by misguided individualism to assume that each of us is so independent and self-sufficient that he or she can do without specialists in the pursuit of religious meaning. One of the many lessons taught by the traditions of the world is that religious knowledge and practice are an interpersonal affair. It is the greatest of illusions to assume that these are private matters. Everyone needs a teacher, a guide. No one is human by himself; no one is religious by herself. To be human is to be social and interdependent. Our sociality is not really a voluntary issue. It is a fact of existence.

As traditions develop, preserving and teaching the wisdom of ultimate order and meaning, communicating means of transformation, they acquire specialists. Storytellers and singers must be carefully taught. Priests must be trained in the meaning and special details of ritual and ceremony, to preserve the ways of performing those actions that keep the world in meaningful order. Shamans undergo initiation into the guild of those who will learn how to go into trance, to die and visit the abode of the dead, then return to this level of being to share the experience with their people. And medicine people must be taught cosmology. They must comprehend the universe from its origins, and understand how various kinds of life and power relate to each other. Healing is a work that must restore to order what is in disorder, a task of setting things into proper relationship. Throughout history humans have been concerned with health. They have known that life is a movement from sickness to health and back again. Every individual and every family or group is aware of illness. We recognize that something is amiss—there are symptoms that intrude upon the flow of existence. We remember them and we remember the healing that restores life to greater wholeness.

Words like *health, healing, wholeness* are akin to salvation—the salving, healing, of lives that are somehow not what they ought to be; when we experience a brokenness, a disruption, a wrongness in our lives, we seek healing—salvation. Native Americans know traditionally that the well-being of the body is linked to the restoration of the mind, the health of the community, and their relationship to the landscape. The shaman and the medicine person visit the world of the living dead in order to restore health to individuals, clans, and tribes. Health and salvation are one and the same. In the novel *Ceremony,* Leslie Marmon Silko tells the story of Tayo, a young "halfbreed" whose life was disrupted by World War II. He was removed from his native people, their ways, and the landscape that was mother and aunt in the nurture of his childhood. Tayo becomes and stays ill, both physically and emotionally, until his visceral relationship to people and places is restored by the work of two medicine persons and a conjugal relationship with the landscape. In Native understanding, healing involves more than taking a pill, having surgery, or being psychoanalyzed.

Native traditions express their doctrine, their teaching and theory, in oral forms that rely heavily upon storytelling. They express the ultimate order and meaning of their world in the performance of colorful and carefully choreographed rituals. However, much of their perception of the world is expressed in their peoplehood. The people are a special people who have been given special gifts in a world where they occupy a special place. To be this people (this tribe, clan) is to be religious, for the sacredness of existence is expressed in a sacred history, sacred ways, and sacred space (plains, mesas, canyons, deserts).

Evolution of Traditions

Native American traditions have moved through several stages of encounter with others. This is, of course, a natural process: we all become aware of our ways of perceiving the world and expressing its holiness as a result of observing others, whose ways make us self-conscious. Children are born into a world of little distinction but gradually become aware of the fact that there are others—"out-there" realities of different types. They learn that some of these others exist as forces of living and conscious power, while others exist very impersonally. Nevertheless, the experience of otherness makes children increasingly aware of their separateness in relation to all these others. Life becomes a constant discovery of individuality-in-relationship.

So also do we become aware of our own traditions as a people. If there were only one tradition, we would not be aware of it. We would just do it, express it as we express hunger, thirst, the need to procreate, and the need to eliminate wastes. Every time we encounter a new tradition, a response is required of us. Our perception of the world must make a place for persons and practices it had not previously included. The others may be strangers with strange ways. Will the stranger and her ways remain strange, or will they find a place in our world? Of course, even as strangers they have a place in our world. Common sense informs us that others we encounter, and their traditions, may be good, bad, or indifferent. We may include some of their ways among our own. Whatever our response to others, some adjustment is necessary in our stories, our rituals, and our understanding of peoplehood and identity. The question "Who are we?" must now include the question "Who are they?"

It is obvious that Native Americans, as hunter-gatherers and even as agriculturalists, constantly found themselves encountering people very much like themselves. Through centuries of Native American encounter, roaming the plains, the mountains, and the wilderness, they adjusted their perceptions of the world. With each encounter, there were new forms of personal and impersonal power to be fought, domesticated, or avoided. However, no encounter was to have as great an influence upon the Native Americans and their traditions as the encounter with Europeans, who shared a variety of interpretations of what may be called a Christian perspective of the world. From the time of early European settlement and colonization beginning in the sixteenth century, the strangers had come as heirs of Christendom and the Reformation. Almost immediately it was apparent that the strangers had different kinds of power. They clothed their bodies differently. They came in large sailing vessels very different from the canoes and dugouts of the wilderness streams and ocean shores. They carried long sticks that poured out fire and destruction. To the natives the strangers seemed to know of spiritual power that was in many cases superior to their own. They brought these powerful new spirits into their own perception of the world, as they had frequently done in the past in their encounters with other native peoples.

In some cases the fair skin of the European was considered a sign of a visiting power. Who was the white man? Was he father? brother? devil? savior? Was he all of these, sometimes one, sometimes another, depending upon the channel through which the spirits moved? Certainly the strangers from across the waters had brought disorder, discord, to the carefully ordered world of the Indians. The stories and the songs, the visions and the dances of the native peoples had to change to make provision for understanding the strangers.

Many of the strangers spoke of the spirits and power of the cosmos in ways that denied the truth of existence to those beings who had long been part of the native perceptions of the world. The strangers did not seem interested in learning about the spirit world of the Native Americans; they had little respect for native stories and rituals and often interpreted their visions as satanic hallucinations. The strangers wanted to change the native perception of the world to include the white man's story of a great God who created all things and kept the world in order and who sent a Savior to help the people out of their distress and disobedience.

The powers of the strangers were so great that they forced the natives out of the forests where for centuries they had hunted, gathered fruits and nuts, and planted beans and squash in small, natural clearings. At times it seemed that the strangers intended to exterminate them. At other times the strangers seemed to want to Europeanize them or at least to force them onto lands that were inhospitable to their native traditions. With each move of the stranger, the world of the Native American altered radically.

Among some of the native peoples there emerged prophets who advocated a return to the life they had led before the coming of the strangers. By avoiding the food and other provisions that had come from the Europeans, they hoped to purge the Native American world of evil forces and effect the eventual disappearance of the strangers. A Pueblo man from San Juan by the name of Popé instigated the Pueblo revolt of 1680. A Delaware prophet emerged, and a Pontiac conspiracy occurred in 1672. These wars did not exterminate the Europeans. Nor did the new visions and dances that emerged among the Kickapoo in 1827, the Paiutes in 1870, or the Sokulks in 1889. A vision by the Paiute, Wowoka, led to the formation of the Ghost Dance religion, in which ritual was used to effect the magical disappearance of the Euro-Americans. Wowoka's gospel was misunderstood to be a conspiracy and resulted in the massacre of Wounded Knee.

Additional changes were made in tradition, which sought to adjust to or accommodate the world of the strangers. Handsome Lake of the Iroquois was influenced by Quaker missionaries and advocated peaceful coexistence with the Euro-Americans. He wanted a return to the old ways of his people, a purging of worldly ways, with no place for alcohol and modern dancing. "As celebrated today," writes Underhill, "in a house with a wooden floor and with sacred fire in an iron stove, [the old ceremonies] are still full of dignity. Farm people in calico and overalls go through some fifty dances, solemn, warlike, or picturesque in their imitation of animals. Corn is cooked and distributed. Tobacco incense is burned. This is a living religion."[8]

In 1881 John Slocum established Indian Shakerism in southern Puget Sound country. Christian elements were combined with native visionary experience. Perhaps the most widespread of the traditions shaped by American circumstances has been the Native American church, founded in 1918. This is a tradition combining old native practices, including hallucinogenic vision, and an ethical code designed to stabilize native life and provide it with integrity in a white person's world. The tradition finds its center in the use of peyote, a small orbed cactus with a long root containing mescaline. The Huichol of Mexico had long used peyote for elaborate ceremonies. Stories among southwestern tribes tell of a vision by a suffering individual who saw the peyote plant in human form and was given directions for a ceremony and provided with ethical teachings and a commission to share these ways with his people. Peyote is messiah to the members of the Native American church, as Jesus is Christ to the Euro-American. This tradition has emerged as a major form of religious adjustment to a complex world in which people provide order, identity, meaning, and the possibilities of transformation.

The native traditions have been shaped by encounter with the land that became known as America. When the landscape revealed the ways of other native people, traditions altered their stories and rituals. With the arrival of the Europeans, strangers with traditions unknown to native Americans, the ultimate order and meaning of the world changed to accommodate the new powers and accompanying spirits. To some Europeans the natives were "salvages,"[9] peoples "left over" from heathen days before the advance of Christian civilization. To others they were demons, denizens of the dark and foreboding wilderness that was Satan's playground. Of course, there were those who wanted to think of the natives as innocent inhabitants of Eden—darting about the garden like Adam and Eve, untrammeled in their naked beauty. From the time of Columbus, this particular European Christian perception of the world created an America that was a place of new beginnings, a return to paradise. Who else could the dark-skinned creatures be but the direct descendants of the first innocent residents of Eden? Savages, demons, innocents—none of these perceptions was accurate. The natives were human beings who lived with a very different religious perspective. Accordingly, as the Europeans gained control over the destiny of the American landscape, they learned that the Native Americans would not conform to the role assigned to them. They would not be converts, demons, or noble savages. They were creatures with all of the virtues and defects of human beings anywhere, anytime. With the Europeans came modernization and the age of expansion. The native traditions eventually had to contend not only with the tradition of Christianity but also with the effects of science, technology, and industrial development. Their perceptions of the world changed to make way for modernity. Native American traditions have been shaped into a blend of ancient ways, traditional Christian ways, and modern ways. In spite of it all, these changes still comprise their own ways. Their traditions, their ways of perceiving the world, have always been accommodating to the powers that are encountered on the hunt. To the Native American, change is a fact of existence, but even change is not what it seems to be. Change is the eternal return of the seasons, of life and death.

chapter 5

From Anglicans to Episcopalians

We turn now to a religious tradition that confronts us with a paradox for our understanding of religion in America. To discover a paradox is to learn that an apparent contradiction is a necessary relationship. On the one hand, the Episcopal church seems so much a stranger in the American religious scene. It is a tradition with a historic liturgical life, for the most part sedate and colorful. In the Episcopal service one walks in beauty. This kind of practical religious expression is quite in contrast to the American penchant for "no fuss, no fancy," only basic, "essential," and simple worship. This forms the one side of the paradox of Episcopalianism—it is so contrary to the American spirit. It is a tradition with a royal air inherited from its English parentage and theologically affirmed as participating in the kingly life of the Risen Lord.[1] The Episcopal church is not nearly so numerically successful in America as are the Baptist, Methodist, Lutheran, Roman Catholic, Pentecostal, and "Bible" churches.

The other side of the paradox has been the cultural and political influence of American Anglicanism. Throughout most of its history the Episcopal church has provided a disproportionate number of presidents, diplomats, congresspersons, and other political leaders. The worlds of business and education have been substantially affected by this tradition. It has set the tone for our thinking about America. Its beautiful cathedral in Washington, D.C., serves as a national cathedral. It is officially the Cathedral of Sts. Peter and Paul for the Episcopal Diocese of Washington, D.C., but it is also a national shrine and provides a place of meeting, prayer, and memorial services for people of many denominations and no denomination.

Popular historians Kit and Frederica Konolige have called their study of American Anglicanism the story of "America's power elite, the true establishment." There has been a certain aristocratic character to Episcopalianism; although America is a nation of levelers and democrats, it is also hospitable to the human need to aspire upward. Its emphasis upon the power of human reason, its dignity, and its affirmation of the importance of this world have made the Episcopal church a "semiofficial repository of national pride, national hope, and national unity." A distinguished and successful Southern Baptist preacher and writer in his mid-fifties left the Baptist family to study for the Episcopal priesthood. He was drawn to the church, he said, partly because Episcopalians he knew "were living more gracefully than I was. By that I mean they were enjoying life more; they weren't as intense and uptight as many of the people I knew. I was curious about where they got the freedom to be serious about important issues as well as to be playful and enjoy life. I learned the secret was in the Eucharist. I learned that going to the table really did nourish them with Christ's life." This man may be typical of the ministry of the Episcopal church, for it is reported that more than fifty percent of its priesthood have come from other denominations.

Sometime ago an entire congregation of Pentecostalists in Georgia were confirmed by an Episcopal bishop—the congregation became an Episcopal church. Recently, the novelist and essayist Frederick Buechner informed an interviewer that he had found his way into the Episcopal church. "Some ministers," he said, "are so professional and their performance so honed that there's no room for the Holy Spirit. My rector is very loose in the saddle. He preaches wonderfully but almost as if he's forging it out of himself as he goes along."

I cite these incidents in order to articulate an important factor in the paradox of American Anglicanism. In the twentieth century, this characteristic of Anglicanism to attract certain artists, scientists, and intellectuals led to the publication of *Modern Canterbury Pilgrims,* by James A. Pike. What accounts for this religious tradition? We remember that in its beginnings, the Episcopal church was the Church of England in America, that is, the Anglican church of the colonies. In the sixteenth century the Catholic church in England had become the Catholic Church *of* England, severing its ties and loyalties to Rome and becoming, in effect, a national church. King Henry VIII had intended the Catholicism of the Church of England to go on as before, with the exception that its monastic properties would be confiscated for their financial value and because otherwise they might serve as a continued base for Roman influence. However, it was not easy for the church of England to withstand the protestantizing forces that were unleashed by the Reformation on the Continent. And there were those thinkers who sought to reshape the liturgy and theology of Catholic Christianity in ways that would open the way to renewal. Anglican history became the story of a form of Christianity that attempted to maintain its Catholic order while accommodating the need for renewal and the changes in thinking brought on by the process of reformation and modernity.

Verbal Expression

Anglican theology has made much of the Christian doctrine of the incarnation. We might say that the verbal expression or theoretical foundation of Episcopalianism is incarnational. Of course, all of Christianity teaches that in the life and work of Jesus of Nazareth we can observe God's becoming what God is not—that is to say, God become "in-bodied," incarnate, in human existence. The selfhood of Jesus the Christ is both divine and human—another paradox, the fundamental Christian paradox. Although all of Christianity espouses some version of this doctrine, it becomes a matter of interpretation and of emphasis. Some Christian groups may emphasize the distastefulness of God's participation in humanity. They may focus upon the evil of human existence and the material world, teaching that God does this in order to satisfy the claims of Satan. They emphasize what are called atonement and sacrifice. Theology always faces the question of whether atonement is part of incarnation or incarnation part of atonement. *Atonement*, of course, means setting "at one" what has been torn asunder or fractured. Theology is the intellectual enterprise of the Christian religious tradition. It is the task of clarifying for our minds what we mean by certain teachings and practices. It is a matter of clarification and communication; for, unless we can communicate effectively with others, our personal clarification may be ineffective. Anglican theology emphasizes incarnation.

The Episcopal church, in harmony with Anglican tradition, tends to understand incarnation as inclusive of atonement. It affirms this world and this body, which is of great significance because it is the context of God's reconciling work as demonstrated in Jesus Christ. In other words, God cares enough for the material world to enter it and work at its transformation. When we are reconciled to each other and together find reconciliation with the mountains and rivers, the deer and the dove, it is the work of God as the Body of Christ in the world. Episcopal emphasis upon incarnation may account for what the aforementioned Baptist preacher discovered in this tradition as "living gracefully" and "enjoying life." Of course, no human tradition is perfect, and it is conceivable that emphasis upon the incarnation may lead some Episcopalians to affirm "unredeemed" wealth and the status quo. Bishop William Lawrence of Massachusetts in the late nineteenth century was known for his support of financier J. P. Morgan and for his aphorism, "Godliness is in league with riches."

Anglican theory also relies upon the interactive authority of reason, tradition, and Scripture. Richard Hooker, a sixteenth-century Church of England scholar, set forth the notion that God created reason, which may serve as channel for the revelation of truth even though we live in sin—in alienation from God's original creative intention. Reason, therefore, is an important aspect of authority. Presumably, authority is an inescapable problem for any human activity. This is certainly true in religion. The question always before us is, What or who is the author, the source, the foundation upon which judgments about truth and faith are made? What is the authority? Anglicanism says that reason is a valued authority, but it cannot stand by itself. It must be balanced by the teaching tradition of the church throughout its history and especially in the Apostles' and Nicene Creeds.[2] Authority is also balanced by the Scriptures and the sacred writings of the early Christian community, reflecting its tradition of teaching and practice. Reason, tradition, and Scripture serve as the vehicles for discerning God's will for the life of the church, which is God's people. God's truth is revealed in these three ways. Kept in balance, they help the church to continue to be loyal to Christ. Christ is God's truth for Christians, and Episcopalians maintain that Christ continues his presence in his body, the church. Of course, the church is also comprised of imperfect members. It is, as St. Paul described it, a "treasure in earthen vessels." Therefore, the truth constantly judges the church through the interactive authority of reason, tradition, and Scripture. This judgment calls the Body of Christ into conformity with its head.

Another distinctive feature of Anglican teaching is its emphasis upon the Catholic unity of common prayer and liturgical worship. The liturgical work of Archbishop Crammer in the sixteenth century set the tone of Anglicanism. Crammer and his associates sought to prepare a prayer book that could be used by all of the English people. Of course, the book was not a new creation. The Catholic understanding of the Christian faith, shared by Anglicans, is that the tradition of worship and doctrine going back to the apostles is the source of worship and doctrine today. Crammer sought to shape the English use of this tradition so that it would be available to clergy and laity and serve as a course of unity.

By the reign of Queen Elizabeth I at the end of the sixteenth century, the principle was established in such a way that it could become the basis of what is known as the Elizabethan Settlement. Two assumptions were made: (1) the unity of a people depends upon their sharing ultimate beliefs and values that shall be expressed through prayer held in common, so that liturgy becomes the foundation for religious and national unity; (2) a certain uniformity in common prayer permits flexibility in theological interpretation so long as the apostolic tradition serves as the source of theological reflection. The second of these two assumptions still serves an important theoretical function in Anglicanism. For Episcopalians, common prayer is the essential character of the Christian life. The Christian, in Anglican theory, is one who lives in common prayer with Christians of all ages in the Body of Christ. Loyalty to the creeds and apostolic tradition, along with common liturgical life, will permit freedom in belief and theological interpretation.

Practical Expression

In discussing this aspect of Anglican theory we have already slipped into a consideration of the practical expression of Anglicanism. In practice, Episcopalians have been a prayerbook people. It has been part of popular practice for members of the church to own personal copies of the Book of Common Prayer. Many Episcopalians carry their prayerbooks with them to services held on Sundays and often during the week. The Book of Common Prayer serves the private needs of the people as well as the common liturgical needs. From the time of the compilation of the earliest of the prayerbooks, the theologians sought to make available to all Christians as much of the rich prayer and liturgical heritage of Christianity as possible. Part of that heritage was the tradition of "offices," the name for those carefully designed, scheduled services by which from earliest times those clergy and laity who lived in monasteries regulated their days. Offices[3] formed the heart of monastic life and consisted of special prayers, psalms, chants, and Scripture readings. The liturgical scholars of the Church of England condensed and edited these offices in order to make them useful to the daily life of the people, rather than limited in use to monastic orders. Accordingly, the Book of Common Prayer has traditionally included forms for Morning and Evening Prayers. The 1979 prayerbook presents a greater variety of forms for daily prayer than previous books. These are not "new creations" but represent adaptations of ancient practice. The theology of prayerbook use is that one always prays in community with the church throughout the ages, even when one prays privately.

The Book of Common Prayer serves as a comprehensive guide to the Christian life. It is not "the Bible" for Episcopalians (American Anglicans) but provides a means for using and understanding the Scriptures and is a disciplined way for persons committed to the nurturing of their spiritual lives. The prayerbook includes prayers and forms for the private and public dimensions of Christian life. Whether one seeks a prayer for special and private needs or is concerned with the consecration of a bishop, one will find the proper guidance in the Book of Common Prayer.

In the introductory sections of the 1979 prayerbook, we find these words: "The Holy Eucharist, the principal act of Christian worship on the Lord's Day and other major Feasts, and Daily Morning and Evening Prayer, as set forth in this Book, are the regular services appointed for public worship in this Church." For Episcopalians, the heart of Christian practice is the Eucharist. This means that the Lord's Supper is understood to be the principal manner in which the presence of Christ is known in his Body, the church. Anglicanism is predominantly sacramental. Its practice is based upon the assumption that the Christian life is mediated by God through Christ. The Christian life is a lifelong affair of mediation, not an immediate experience of private salvation. One lives a lifetime in Christ's Body, receiving his body and blood—his life—in community with others.

Of course, there are many people who have been drawn to the Episcopal church for other reasons. They are attracted to the beauty of its buildings and its liturgy. Candles, vestments, priests, and beautiful language are pleasing to them. These motivations may tend to substitute an aesthetic mode of existence for a truly religious one. Nevertheless, it is still an acknowledgment of the transcendent aspect of our humanity. We stand above our biological existence and seek to make sense of it and/or find beauty in it. That is our religious nature at work, and it may often be satisfied with aesthetic living.

As we have observed, throughout the nineteenth and twentieth centuries many Americans were attracted by the refusal of Anglicanism to have the faith defined by any restrictive theological and confessional statements, and have been convinced of the power of liturgical life and the ability of its tradition to preserve the heart of Christian truth for living in today's world. Poets like T. S. Eliot and literary critics like Paul Elmer Moore made "pilgrimage to Canterbury"—meaning that their life's journey found meaning in the heritage of the Church of England, for whom Canterbury is a traditional symbol of the shared authority of the Catholic faith.

Social Expression

The social expression of Episcopalianism is one that it shares with other traditions representing the Catholic substance of Christianity. For the Episcopal church, Christianity is represented by a corporate reality, which may be called the "one, holy, catholic, and apostolic church" or the Body of Christ. The life and work of Jesus Christ has created a new people, a covenanted community in whose life Christ continues to live. The social expression of Christianity is the church, and it is more than an institution, more than a voluntary association of believers (as it is in the thinking of many Americans and of many American denominations). The church is more than the sum of its parts. The fact that the early creedal symbols of Christianity (such as the Apostles' Creed and the Nicene Creed) said, "We believe in the Holy Catholic Church" or "We believe in one holy, catholic, and apostolic church" is an indication that they spoke of more than an organization. This was something "believed in"—given credence to—in the same manner that there was a belief in "one God, the Father, the Almighty" and in "one Lord, Jesus Christ" and in the "Holy Spirit." The church was in some way a divine creation, an extension of Jesus Christ himself.

This is the theological basis for understanding the social expression of Christianity for Anglicans. Of course, sociologically the church is an organization. Its polity is "episcopal." American Anglicanism is named for its polity. All churches emphasizing the catholicity of Christianity tend to be episcopal in polity. This is because they seek to base their governance upon the practice of the early church, presumably in continuity with the practice of the apostles. Episcopal polity declares that the integrity of faith and practice is preserved by apostolic succession. Bishops (from the Greek *episkopos*) are the successors of the apostles. Their authority has been received by the laying on of hands of previous bishops going back to ancient apostolic practice.

The polity of the American Episcopal Church is extremely democratic, reflecting the intention of its shapers of the late eighteenth century. Although episcopal in polity, it invests no individuals or single administrative body with any ultimate authority. The bishop is the custodian of faith and practice, and the symbol of apostolic authority, but that authority does not confer absolute power. Decisions are made by the whole church, through its General Convention with its House of Bishops and House of Deputies, clergy and laity, respectively.

The General Convention chooses a Presiding Bishop who serves as head of the executive council that carries out decisions of the General Convention. Whereas the office of Presiding Bishop is a very respected one, the appointee is not administratively superior to other bishops. The Presiding Bishop heads sessions of the House of Bishops and sees to the consecration of new bishops.

A bishop guides the religious life of a diocese, which is a regional arrangement of local churches. This derives from the ancient practice in which the bishop was the pastor of all Christians in a given area. As these congregations grew too large and spread throughout the area, it became necessary to share that pastoral role with presbyters, who became known as priests. The priests served local congregations as representatives of the bishop as chief apostolic pastor or overseer.

In the Episcopal church the affairs of the local church are directed by a priest who is usually called a rector. If the parish is a mission, the bishop is officially rector and appoints a representative, known as a vicar. The rector or vicar directs the worship (according to the Book of Common Prayer), music, and educational program of the parish. Financial affairs and title to church property are left to an elected body called the vestry. The vestry presides over the selection of rectors, who are elected by the congregation with the approval of the bishop. Each rector or vicar *appoints* a senior warden from among the laity to assist in the direction of parish affairs. A junior warden is *elected* at the annual meeting of the congregation. The Episcopal Church in the United States is a member of the worldwide Anglican Communion. This means that the denomination recognizes its Church of England heritage and, like similar churches in Australia, New Zealand, Africa, and other parts of the world, acknowledges the symbolic and ceremonial authority of the Archbishop of Canterbury as a respected first among episcopal equals. There are regular and occasional meetings of representatives of the worldwide Anglican tradition, frequently at Lambeth Palace in England, the headquarters of the Archbishop of Canterbury.

History in the United States

After the War of Independence, which signaled the consummation of an American revolution that had been in formation from the beginnings of English colonization, the Church of England in America faced the necessity of adjusting to the life of a new and independent nation. It could no longer be the Church of England. The decision was made to organize a church in keeping with Anglican principles and the centrality of the Book of Common Prayer, which would also function somewhat democratically in the new republic. American Anglicanism titled itself the Protestant Episcopal Church at a general convention held in Philadelphia in 1784. For Americans it was not only necessary to eliminate the word England from the title, but also to reassure the people that it was a church in keeping with the predominantly Protestant character of America. In keeping with the continuing Puritan spirit of American Protestantism, things "catholic" were suspect and thought to be part of a papal conspiracy against freedom, the work of an antichrist. Accordingly, the church named itself for its polity and the doctrine of apostolic succession, but to prevent its being mistaken for Roman Catholicism, inserted the adjective Protestant.[4] Although a church of the English heritage of Catholic Christianity, the Episcopal church has been shaped from its beginnings by the religious and civil requirements of its American setting. It may be in communion with Anglicanism and the Archbishop of Canterbury, but it is an American tradition as well.

Anglicanism came to America in the midst of the Puritan revolution, which we shall discuss in the next chapter. The first permanent English settlers of the Eastern seaboard were loyal members of the Church of England. Those who established Jamestown, a Virginia colony, brought with them the Book of Common Prayer and sought to establish a church in keeping with Anglican order. They were members of the Church of England, establishing it as the social and cultural foundation of colonial America. However, these Anglicans were very much influenced by the Puritan movement at home. Although they supported the prayerbook and Episcopal church order, they tended toward simplicity in worship and shared many of the Puritan concerns for regenerate believers assembled as a visible church.

The Church of England carried to America the heritage of Christendom. Like the Puritans of Massachusetts Bay who sought to establish a holy commonwealth, the Anglicans assumed that true Christianity must serve as the unifying force of the social and political elements of a culture. Therefore, the church must be established as the conscience of the state—both are under a common Christian mandate. We must remember that when it comes to history, people think as children do—their thoughts take shape in particular time and place. We share many unexamined ideas and convictions that are out of the common storehouse of the early twenty-first century. The Europeans who came to comprise the American nation brought with them assumptions that were part of centuries of human experience. We always exercise our intelligence based upon certain assumptions. Eventually those assumptions may be challenged and disappear, but this is not likely to happen as a result of raw rationalism or even conscious decision. The assumptions behind establishment of religion, as we have seen, are among the oldest of human ideas. We are still not rid of them because they reflect very important considerations. The assumptions are: (1) that society depends upon a set of commonly shared religious beliefs, and (2) that the coercive power of the state must stand behind the institution that is responsible for preserving and disseminating those beliefs.

When the new nation emerged out of the Constitutional Period of American history in the late eighteenth century, the decision was made to eliminate the second assumption. Practically, there could be no effective establishment of religion; no institution or combination of institutions could receive the coercive support of the state. Theoretically, there were those like James Madison and Thomas Jefferson, who believed that coercion was ineffective in producing necessary religious beliefs. They believed that complete religious freedom would create an environment in which the art of persuasion would create the religious beliefs (which they reduced to a basic morality) essential to the existence and continued well-being of society. Notice the rejection of the second assumption does not imply the rejection of the first, and even in the minds of the most radical of America's political designers, there was an affirmation of the first assumption.

During the colonial period, however, most people held to some version of the necessity of both assumptions. They were, after all, children of Europe, where both assumptions had held court for centuries. The Church of England was a representative of both assumptions and sought to carry them out by establishing itself in the colonies. By the time the Episcopal Church emerged out of the ecclesiastical maneuvering of the Constitutional Period, it had become obvious that the second assumption was ineffective in the American setting. There had been nominal establishments in seven of the colonies. They had failed miserably in a land with so much space, very little established tradition, and great diversity in religion.

The Anglican tradition in America was reshaped by the requirements of its own doctrine in a frontier society. The Church of England took a long time deciding who was responsible for episcopal oversight of the church in the colonies. A church with episcopal polity that holds strong convictions about apostolic succession must have bishops on the scene to perform confirmations, ordain priests and deacons, and see to the consecration of other bishops. As chief pastor of the baptized Christians in a given area, a bishop must be available for general oversight of rectors and vicars (the pastor-priests of local congregations). Yet all during the colonial period there were no bishops in America. The best that could be arranged was a policy of appointment of representatives of the Bishop of London called commissaries. Some of these individuals played distinguished roles, founding libraries and schools and influencing young English priests to try their vocations in America. Thomas Bray, Commissary to Maryland, had been an Oxford professor who struggled on behalf of prison reform in England and founded two missionary organizations that are still in existence. His efforts on behalf of the consecration of an American bishop ended in failure.

It was not only the absence of bishops that affected the Church of England in the colonies. There was a dire shortage of priests to care for the Anglicans who came to America. In keeping with the thinking of establishment theory, colonies like Virginia had been divided into parishes, geographical areas in which all residents were assumed to be under the care of the church. Many of these parishes were so large that it was virtually impossible for a priest to provide effective ministry. Also, as was the case in many other American denominations, the church was ill-equipped to deal effectively with the vast amounts of space. Frontier America apparently hosted a religious style unimpeded by requirements of church order and education, which were more appropriate to the settled life of Europe and the British Isles. It seemed that the Anglican church was not made for America, even though it was the established church of the reigning government until the 1780s. Without a bishop, with an inadequate supply of priests, and with a dedication to establishment principles, the Anglicans were severely handicapped in competition with Puritan Congregationalists, Presbyterians, and Baptists, who grew in numbers and power as the colonial period progressed.

As early as 1660 the English colonies had adopted the principle of toleration. This policy meant that, although the Church of England might be established and favored, other groups were to be permitted. They were not considered illegal, and there was to be no suppression. Toleration represented a common approach to pluralism in America. Even the Congregational establishments in New England were forced to tolerate the existence of other denominations.

In the years preceding the Revolutionary War (1775–83), fear and suspicion of the Church of England reached almost frightening proportions. The agitation among colonial Anglicans for the consecration of a bishop to care for the needs of the Church was interpreted by many Americans of other persuasions as evidence of a conspiracy to bring the English crown into more evident control of the colonies. Many believed that miter was in tandem with scepter.[5] In the sixteenth century, when the English Catholic church declared its independence of the papacy and became the Church of England, Parliament proclaimed the King's Majesty to be "the only Supreme Head on earth of the Church of England." The sceptered ruler was given the right to "visit, reform, correct, and restrain all such errors, heresies, and abuses which by

spiritual authority or jurisdiction ought to be reformed and amended." This
was not a new or entirely English invention, but merely the application of a
fundamental assumption of the Christendom tradition—that the monarch
was responsible for the total welfare of the people. This was a prerogative
exercised by "the Kings of Israel . . . the Roman emperors . . . [and] the ancient
Kings of England," said Stephen Gardiner, Bishop of Winchester, who wondered why anyone should be offended by this assumption, "seeing that the
Church of England consisteth of the same sort of people at this day that are
comprised in this word Realm."

Although we may understand why many Americans feared that the introduction of bishops would consolidate the claims of the English crown, we
can also recognize that such a concern could become a ploy of revolutionary
agitators. The colonies were inhabited by English people who shared a heritage of liberty that emerged out of centuries of struggle and incitement.
These people were proud of their rights as English and they resented any
threat to that liberty. They were also dissenters by nature. They were rejecters,
rebels. Colonial America (perhaps all of American history to the present) has
been a hospitable land for those who will not be denied their freedom to follow their own convictions. As a result we have been a breeding ground of dissent. "Like the secretions of the pituitary," writes the historian Edwin S.
Gaustad, "the juices of dissent are essential to ongoing life even if we do not
always know precisely how, when, or where they perform their task." Such
"juices" aged in the American winery, fomented the revolutionary spirit, and
incited reaction against any specter of conspiracy. The Anglican church in
eighteenth-century America, in its efforts to have its own bishops, aroused
the dissenting suspicions of many of the colonial English, who were intent on
the pursuit of liberty. The Anglican Commissary of South Carolina informed
the Bishop of London that it would be as precarious for a bishop to be consecrated for America as it already was for a distributor of tax stamps. In
America the churches were becoming decreasingly representative of the religious life of the entire community and increasingly charged with the nurturing of inner piety. The Anglican understanding of the nature of the church
had to accommodate to this new religious environment.

Certainly it is true that Anglicanism in America suffered for its royal status. During the War for Independence many of the clergy were suspected of
being Tories—loyal to the Crown and Parliament. After the War and during
the National Period,[6] the new Protestant Episcopal Church worked against
almost insurmountable odds, adjusting to the new nation and finding the
strength and leadership for its role as an American denomination.

The first American bishop was Samuel Seabury of Connecticut, who was consecrated in Scotland in 1784 by three bishops of an independent Scottish Episcopal church. Seabury had failed to receive consecration by English bishops because the existing ecclesiastical laws prevented the consecration of anyone who could not take the oaths of allegiance to the king and to his supremacy as governor of the Church of England. Two years later the laws were changed to permit the consecration at Lambeth Palace Chapel of the Americans William White, Samuel Provoost, and James Madison in the English line of succession. Bishop White conferred holy orders on Absalom Jones, a domestic slave from a plantation in Delaware whose family had been taken to Philadelphia where White served as bishop. Jones went to night school, studied theology with White, and was granted his freedom at age thirty-seven. He founded St. Thomas Church for Americans of African descent and died on February 13, 1818.

The Book of Common Prayer was revised for American use. Prayers for the king were no longer appropriate and were reordered to become supplications for the President of the United States and others in civil authority. The American book was revised in 1928, 1952, and 1979. The direction of these revisions has been motivated by a desire for greater congregational participation in the liturgy, and for greater diversity and enrichment of services in keeping with ancient Christian practice and the uses of Eastern and Western Catholic Christianity.

The Anglican Communion has struggled to preserve and enhance the richness of Catholic Christian faith and practice in the face of Puritan influences. The nineteenth century witnessed the renewal of tradition and the formation of a distinctive prayerbook catholicity. In America this renewal began with the imaginative efforts of Bishops John Henry Hobart and Alexander Viets Griswold. Gradually the Episcopal church gained strength and confidence. During the late nineteenth century many of its clergy and churches were in the forefront of the liberal movement in theology. They sought to adjust Christian understanding to the new scientific world and the anxieties of living in urban and corporate society. Phillips Brooks became a celebrated preacher as rector of the famed Trinity Church on Copley Square in Boston. He is known to many as the author of the popular carol "O Little Town of Bethlehem."

In the twentieth century, the Episcopal church was a leading participant in the ecumenical[7] movement and the search for social justice in the name of the Christian gospel.[8] Charles Henry Brent was a bishop in the Philippines before becoming bishop of western New York in 1918. He was an ecumenical leader who served as president of the World Conference on Faith and Order, which met in Lausanne, Switzerland, in 1927. The Lausanne meeting was instrumental in the eventual formation of the World Council of Churches in 1948.

James Pike, an attorney who converted from Roman Catholicism, became the well-known Dean of the Cathedral of St. John the Divine in New York City, and later Bishop of California. Bishop Pike was a controversial figure, very much in the news as an advocate of ecumenicity, social change, and theological revision. He died under mysterious circumstances in Israel, where he had been searching for insights into the mind of Christ and the significance of the great ancient manuscript discovery of the twentieth century, the Dead Sea Scrolls.

In 1968 the Task Force on Women and Religion of the National Organization of Women (NOW) had passed a resolution urging the elimination of discrimination against women. For some time women had been dissatisfied with the patriarchal habits of church life and were seeking vocational opportunities beyond the long-standing work in women's fellowships and altar guilds. By the 1970s the Church had proceeded with the ordination of women priests.

The Episcopal church is somewhat of an anomaly in American society. In many ways a conservative church, seeking to preserve the rich liturgical and theological heritage of Catholic Christianity, it is also a liberal interpreter of doctrine. This is not to say, of course, that all Episcopalians are theological liberals. However, the tradition permits great freedom and latitude in theology, while emphasizing the nurture of common prayer. Perhaps this is its role in America—to demonstrate the importance of loyalty to the fullness of Christian tradition, while respecting the necessity of personal theological integrity. American Anglicanism is a tradition very much shaped by its American experience. It is at once un-American and profoundly American, a relatively small denomination of perhaps three million baptized members in a land full of Baptists, evangelicals, and other frontier religionists. Its role in our history and in the formation of American society and culture is a significant one. There are many unexplored aspects of Episcopal history, many interesting stories yet untold.

chapter 6

The Puritan Tradition:
Congregationalists, Baptists, and Quakers

Puritanism must be understood as a movement with its beginnings in the Church of England in the sixteenth century. Puritanism is a religious movement, not a denomination. It is a religious tradition with few distinctive institutional heirs. Indeed, there is no substantial Christian denomination that uses the name Puritan, although there are individual congregations with such titles as the Church of the Pilgrims. Puritanism is English Protestantism. It has been shaped by the English heritage of liberty, by association with ideas and leaders from the Reformation on the European continent, and by the religious significance of America as Land Promised to the Saints. The Puritans have generally suffered from bad press. It is easy to call someone a puritan and mean that she or he is a prude—rigid in opinions and moralistically religious or "pious." In common parlance a puritan is one who never has a good time and greets the world in dour-faced disapproval. Although some of these unpleasant attitudes may have their roots in Puritanism, the movement represents much more.

Origins of Puritanism

Once the church in England had declared its autonomy of the bishop of Rome and had become the Church of England, the English spirit of independence and fair play was released for all to express and to test. Over the centuries there had been many unpleasant conflicts between the English crown and the papacy. In the early thirteenth century, Pope Innocent III had appointed an archbishop of Canterbury whom King John refused to recognize. England was placed under papal interdict, which excluded the people from receiving the sacraments of the church. King John himself was excommunicated in 1209. Uncertain of the support of his barons and threatened with invasion by King Philip of France, John surrendered the realm of England to the hands of the Pope, receiving it back as a papal fiefdom. Only a half century before, Henry II had sought to regulate relations between the ecclesiastical and lay jurisdictions of England by means of a document known as the Constitutions of Clarendon. Thomas à Becket, Archbishop of Canterbury, refused to affix his seal, believing that the Constitutions interfered with the rights of the church and the authority of Rome. Thus began a feud that led to the assassination of the archbishop. The struggle between England (its sovereign, the people, and the church) and the claims of the papacy to universal Christian authority was itself a venerable tradition by the sixteenth century.

The plans of Henry VIII for the Church of England were misunderstood by some and disputed by others. The spirit of liberty linked itself to the spirit of reform, and there emerged movements for a more extensive reformation of English Christianity than what had been envisioned by the king and his advisors. Magisterial and separationist notions from Holland, Germany, and Switzerland had powerful influence on many of the clergy and laity. They sought radical reform of English Catholicism. They conceived of a veritable "purifying" of the church. Implicit in this idea of purification was the assumption that the lives of the people themselves would become pure.

The problem of the nature of the church is as old as Christianity itself. Christians had very early recognized that the reconciling love of God revealed to them in the death and resurrection of Jesus the Christ was a shared reality. Together they were the spiritual Body of Christ. Was the church in this life all that God intended? Theologians like Augustine of Hippo (in North Africa) in the fifth century wrote of the visible and invisible church. The invisible church was that body of true Christ-people known only to God. This was the pure church, which included those living, dead, or unborn, who were chosen through Christ. However, there was the visible church of all those who in some way professed to know God in Christ. The visible church contained those destined for salvation and those not so destined. The visible church was holy—it shared God's holiness in part—but not completely so.

To subscribe to this interpretation of what God accomplishes in Jesus Christ is to face at least two alternatives. On the one hand, inasmuch as the distinction between visible and invisible church is known only to God, perhaps we should go about our Christian devotion and responsibilities and leave the final judgment to God. On the other hand, if the invisible church presents a mandate to become as visible as possible, we may conclude that true Christians must become visible: they must be separate and unspotted from the world.

The Stages of Puritan Development

Many of the sixteenth- and seventeenth-century English Reformers struggled with this problem. Essentially, the Puritan forces were those inclined to give strong preference to the need for more visible evidence of the pure and invisible church. It seemed to the Puritans that the Church of England was too satisfied with considering all baptized English persons as part of the church. The Church of England seemed complacent, content in the assumption that it was all that it could be as an independent national continuation of the medieval Catholic tradition.

There were those puritanizers who began with an attack upon the externals of Catholic practice. They assumed that many of the visible practices of the church were merely external, superficial, and inessential to Christian life. Vestments, candles, altars, and crucifixes were thought to be not only unnecessary, but aberrations—demonic accretions to the simple faith of the gospel of Jesus Christ. Some Puritans understood these external trappings as evidence of magic and superstition. They advocated a church purified of these ritual embellishments and believed that simple preaching and unadorned sacraments would result in pure Christian living.

Although this Puritan position may be a correct one, it makes contestable assumptions. Modern Americans tend to be strongly influenced by this Puritan supposition that affects their ability to understand other people and other cultures. How can we understand the lives of the Bambuti pygmies of the Congo or the Hopi Indians of Arizona if we begin with the assumption that ritual practices are external and unnecessary to some core of simple teaching? How, for that matter, can we understand the everyday aspects of our own society and culture if we assume that ritual, ceremony, and adornment are inessential? It is much more helpful to human knowledge and understanding to recognize that ritual is itself a form of knowing and is basic to human expression. Our best thinking takes place in ritual contexts. Nevertheless, as students of the history of religions, we also acknowledge the fact that the Reformation of the sixteenth century was a period in which Puritan assumptions about the character of ritual gained considerable ascendancy. This Puritan attack upon "externals" quickly extended itself to the Catholic understanding of the necessity of bishops in apostolic succession. Puritans sought to rid themselves of bishops as readily as they exorcised altars and vestments.

There were some members of the Church of England who were sympathetic with much of the Puritan program, although objecting to the extremes of Puritan *iconoclasm*.[1] They were convinced of the Protestant teachings of Martin Luther and John Calvin, perhaps even Ulrich Zwingli. They wanted to have the church shorn of "excesses" and concentrate on the power of the Evangel—the message of God's saving work in Jesus Christ. They were the proponents of a simplified Catholicism. However, they stood behind the need for bishops as a visible guarantee of the continuing integrity of the apostolic message—the original evangel. These were the emergent evangelicals of the Church of England. Some scholars maintain that most of the Church of England was influenced by the Puritan movement in the late sixteenth and early seventeenth centuries. They would contend that the Virginia colony, which attempted to establish the Church of England in America, represented a strongly Puritan form of Anglicanism.[2]

Once the Puritan movement was under way, it was difficult to keep it from transcending mere iconoclasm. The psychology of the Puritan mind may demand more than the elimination of externals. If we try to find a way to purify the church of Jesus Christ so that it becomes more visible, we may say, "Well, just because we have gotten rid of bishops, altars, candles, and vestments doesn't mean that the pure and invisible church is now more visible. It still isn't a body of those who are visibly holy and pure witnesses to God's love for us in Jesus Christ. We have to go further in purifying the church."

Then we may ask ourselves, What further evidence of purity can we find? One answer is obvious: We can see purity in the kinds of lives people lead. *Morality* becomes a mark of purified sainthood, and it is a primarily private kind of morality. That is to say, purified lives are those that keep the commandments. Those who do not kill, commit adultery, or steal, who honor their parents, do not covet others' property, and avoid idolatry—they may be considered members of the true church. Their moral and honorable lives are a measure of their holiness, a sign of God's favor. This type of response to the Puritan quest is a reasonable and time-honored response, and it became a significant element in the Puritan movement. When we remember that Puritanism is an important factor in the formation of the American mind, it is easy to understand the strong moralistic character of American life.

Puritanism is not necessarily satisfied with the moral response to the problem of identifying the pure church. It becomes apparent to some that a genuine knowledge of the basic doctrine of Christianity is indispensable. Morality may quickly lead to self-righteousness, even cruelty, if the individual has no understanding of the Christian story. It is necessary to appreciate the cost of God's love for us. God's original intention in creation was thwarted by human self-centeredness and disobedience—sin. From the beginning, sin has distorted the relationship God intended. Humans deny God in favor of their own self-aggrandizement. What should God do? Is punishment the answer? Perhaps only to a point. God does not give up, goes the story. God decides to call together a special people with whom to covenant—they will live the life God expects of them and become models for all humankind. Up to this point, the story is shared by Jews and Christians. However, the Christian story asserts that the chosen people fail. God's covenant is broken. It is now necessary for God to demonstrate that the breaking of the covenant is destructive of the very purposes of creation. To break the covenant is to see God suffer. It is to see the God-that-is-with-us snuffed out, killed, crucified. This point is demonstrated by Jesus, the Jew of Nazareth. In this demonstration God is showing a new covenant—or at least a new way of understanding the covenant. However, God takes the process a step further and shows that, ultimately, divine intentions cannot be thwarted. Even when we kill the God-with-us, God, who is so much more than our petty self-centeredness, rises again. God's compassion is so great that there is resurrection. God's purposes are fulfilled by living in the light of resurrection. The old covenant is made through the commandments; the new is made in Jesus Christ.

This is a personal version of the basic Christian story, one that contains many spiritual and intellectual problems. It prompts questions about what this or that part of the story means. The questions and their answers are the history of Christian doctrine. They are theology, the intellectual interpretation and reinterpretation of the doctrine or teaching that is based on the Christian story. There are those who refer to this tradition of doctrinal interpretation as "the faith." Presumably it is fair to say that a Christian should have knowledge of and appreciation for the faith.

Many within the Puritan movement became knowledgeable about the faith. To become knowledgeable one had to know the Scriptures and perhaps be familiar with the teachings of the early Christian fathers, including Augustine of Hippo, and especially the writings of the great Reformer John Calvin. Puritanism became a very literate and intellectual movement. Many of the rank and file of the movement were highly literate theologically, as well as familiar with the classics of literature and the philosophical writings of their day. Knowledge and understanding of the faith were necessary for Puritanism because it became important for the individual Christian to make a *profession of faith,* thereby entering in covenant with others in the pure and visible church. To profess means to affirm, to make an open and public declaration of the faith. A profession connects one in mutual agreement with others.

Iconoclasm, morality, and *profession of faith*—these were three of the stages of development (to which we shall later add a fourth) in the Puritan attempt to reform the Church of England so that it would approximate the invisible church of St. Augustine. It is important to understand that most Puritans were concerned primarily with this purification—the substantial reform of the Anglican tradition, the Church of England. They were not proponents of any institutional or sectarian separation from Anglicanism. Nevertheless, we can see the cracks in their logic. We may ask, How far can the reform extend before it conceived of a church that is totally and extraordinarily different from the original? If we begin to demand reform that is fully consistent with a specific principle, teaching, or practice, we become rationalists—those who insist that a plan that is reasonable is the only reasonable plan. Presumably a church that is catholic must be concerned to hold together many reasonable positions, many differences of opinion and practice. The rationalist is almost always a sectarian who insists on the exclusive claims of "the reasonable plan."

Diversity of Puritanism

It was not long before the Puritan program of reform diversified to such an extent that it took the shape of many different groups and sectaries. Puritanism became a multiform movement. It included revolutionary bodies like the Diggers and Levellers, and eventually gave rise to Quakerism and in the English colonies to the Seekerism[3] and Antinomianism[4] of persons such as Roger Williams and Anne Hutchinson.

Broadly speaking, however, there were the separating and the nonseparating Puritans. The latter simply assumed that the established church could be reformed and purified from within. There was no need for separating from the Church of England; instead, the church could be transformed into the pure church. The former were those who came to the conclusion that the purity of the church required fresh beginnings. It was impossible, in their mind, to reform the Church of England; the pure and invisible church could only be an effective model for those who separated themselves from the indifference of an established church. For the separating Puritans the measure of the pure church was to be found in a body of intentional, believing Christians. Robert Browne of Norwich was imprisoned for establishing separating congregations and later emigrated to Holland. His tract *Reformation without tarrying for any* denies that Christians should wait for the government to reform the church. Browne was convinced that churches must exclude immoral people and all ceremonies and practices that are unscriptural. His name became associated with the cause of separation. Many separating Puritans moved to Amsterdam to escape persecution. Disputes among them led to the formation of several groups, one of which furnished the founders of the Plymouth colony in New England.

In England the Puritan movement often divided over issues of polity. An important question in the history of religions is: How shall a religious body govern itself in keeping with its basic teaching? What shall be its *polity*? Polity is more than a functional matter, more than a practical concern. For Christianity, it is a theological issue. Polity has to do with the nature of the church, and that, as we have shown, is an issue reaching into the heart of the story of how God's saving work in Jesus Christ is known. Like many of the magisterial and separationist Reformers on the European continent, the Puritans were generally convinced that Holy Scripture, not Catholic tradition, contained all necessary guidance and information. They consulted the Scriptures for direction concerning polity.

Some of the searchers discovered a pattern of polity that came to be called Presbyterianism. John Calvin and his reforming movement in Geneva, Switzerland, had already discerned this pattern. And Puritanism was strongly Reformed and Calvinist in its leaning. Scholars generally acknowledge the pervasive influence of Reformed Christianity upon the development of Puritanism. The Greek word *presbyteros,* found in the New Testament, may be translated "elder." Acts 14:23 mentions St. Paul's appointment of presbyters. Presbyterian polity assumes that government by elders was the original model of church government. Elders are in some way understood to be descendants of the apostles. The church is governed by elders at the local congregational level. However, in Presbyterian thought, the essence of the church is not exhausted by elders working at the local level alone. Instead, the church finds its self-understanding in ever-widening, representative bodies of elders, preserving the apostolic truth and administering the life of the church.

Some Puritans were *presbyterian* in polity, others *congregationalist* or independents. As might be expected, separating Puritans would of necessity be congregationalists. Only the local congregations of believers, professing their covenanted faith and living a moral life according to the Scriptures, worshiping in unadorned fashion, was the measure of the church to the congregationalists. Therefore the essential level of government was local and independent. A *congregationalist* is one for whom the essence of the church is to be found only in the local congregation and for whom church government admits no authority beyond the autonomous congregation. Many denominations on the American religious scene are congregational in polity, even if the term does not appear in their title. In fact, congregationalism is perhaps the most distinctively acknowledgeable form of Puritanism to become part of American society and culture. For the moment, however, we are concerned with understanding the nature of congregational polity as an element in the development of Puritanism. Controversy about polity eventually led to a hardening of positions. It became possible to identify "camps" of those who were presbyterian, those who were congregationalist. However, it would take many years before the camps would become denominations.

We have examined the diversity of Puritanism as the distinctive character of the Reformation in England. Parties of Puritans were already forming before Puritanism came to America. There were presbyterians and congregationalists, separatists and nonseparatists, seekers, antinomians, revolutionaries, and baptists. And there were those people of Puritan sentiment who still clung to the importance of bishops and apostolic succession and preferred to remain loyal to the established Church of England. They became the evangelical wing of Anglicanism and were the dominant force of the founding of Jamestown and Virginia colony with its Church of England establishment.

With this background, we are ready to be introduced to three important religious traditions shaped by the English Puritan heritage and the religious power of America, the Land Promised to the Saints.

Congregationalists

The Puritan tradition has played an important institutional role in the United States. Those scholars who characterize America as a Puritan nation would almost certainly be forced to rely on the role of Congregationalism to enhance their case. Congregationalism emerged in direct lineage out of the Puritan movement. Congregationalist pastors and theologians have been prominent figures in our history; through the nineteenth century they were at the forefront of our religious and cultural life—this in spite of their decreasing numerical strength in the American religious landscape. Prestigious educational institutions such as Harvard and Yale are the heritage of Congregationalism, and throughout much of their history they were led by clergy. Even from the times of our independence from Britain as a new nation, the story of Congregationalist influence continues. Famous New England families have shared Congregationalist ideas and values with the rest of America. Names like Parker, Phillips, Beecher, Bushnell, Abbott, and James are inescapable in the attempt to understand the formation of the American mind and its habits. Documents like the Mayflower Compact and John Winthrop's "Model of Christian Charity" set forth principles that became typically American and have played a significant role in our self-understanding. The Puritan experience is at work in the Declaration of Independence, the Constitution, and the pronouncements of presidents from Washington and Jefferson through Lincoln, Franklin Delano Roosevelt, and John F. Kennedy. Congregationalism has been an important denominational vehicle for the dissemination of the Puritan assumptions that make America what it is.

Congregationalism has its roots in the congregationalist party of the earlier Puritan revolution in England. In America it takes shapes as a distinctive denomination as a result of Puritan efforts to adjust their ways to North America. Puritan settlements in Plymouth, Massachusetts Bay, New Haven, and Connecticut held a variety of interpretations of the experiment they wished to conduct in the New World. However, they were all basically of the conviction that God had led them to this American wilderness where they were to be tried and tested and where they would have a supreme opportunity to do what European Christians had never been able to accomplish. The church had for centuries sought to be a body of mutual concern and love, helping the world to become a political and social order of righteous living. The Puritans now had a special commission to achieve that end. America was the place for the "city upon a hill" to be built, where it would serve as a model for all the world to see. Note that the Puritans did not come to America to seek freedom of worship—either for selfish ends or as a principle for all future Americans to uphold. Freedom of worship was a secondary, pragmatic issue. Foremost among concerns was the mandate, the divine commission to be a New Israel—a nation of people whose social and political lives were under God's direction and shared God's promise.

The Puritans in America soon discovered that their shared motivations made the old Puritan portals of England somewhat obsolete. The distinctions between separating and nonseparating groups seemed to break down. It might be possible to say that one was not separating from the Church of England, only reforming and purifying it. However, in the American wilderness there was not much evidence of any established Christianity other than their own attempts to promote the ideal church and society. Separatists and nonseparatists were faced with the same problems, the same opportunities.

However, the conflicts between congregationalists and presbyterians took on new meaning as the Christian congregations in New England struggled to implement the Puritan way. The congregationalists, or independents, concluded that the attempt to create the pure church as a body of "visible saints" (representative of the invisible church) required maximum *local* control of Christian life. Any deference to the wider, representative nature of the church would weaken the procedures by which the membership of the church could be monitored.

This growing congregationalism was expedited by a growing tendency among the Massachusetts Bay Puritans to carry the puritanizing process we discussed earlier to a *fourth stage* of development. They added *the test of saving faith* to the more external evidence of purity—iconoclasm, morality, and profession of faith. In so doing, the character of the church was internalized and individualized. Puritan leaders in old England and Holland, as well as in New England, had dabbled with the idea of requiring evidence of saving faith as a criterion for true membership. The *profession* of faith was the external acknowledgment that a person understood the fundamental doctrines of Christianity and was willing to go on record as subscribing to that doctrine. However, there were those who reasoned that there may be some internal, private evidence that God really considered an individual to be among the elect—to be among those destined to benefit fully from the salvation made known in Jesus Christ. There had to be a way to discern saving faith as opposed to mere external affirmation of Christian faith.

Can the individual be diagnosed for evidence that God is at work, directing the world to salvation? If so, then the pure church would be comprised of those who could provide that evidence. Certain of the leaders in Massachusetts began to take this issue seriously. They scoured the writings of Puritan theologians like William Perkins for help. The result was the development of a process in which steps to saving faith could be discerned. The individual might require assistance in probing for this evidence. However, it was essentially a private affair, which then became a narrative to be recited before the church, where cross-examination could determine its authenticity.

With this development in Puritanism, the importance of private experience became a strong and significant characteristic of American religion and of American thinking in general. This Puritan heritage made common cause with the growing penchant for the workable, the practical. The frontier spirit of the nineteenth century was guided by the spirit of individual democratic experience. We can see in William James's championing of "those religious experiences which are most one-sided, exaggerated, and intense" a certain growth from Puritan roots. Congregationalism became the early custodian of this experientialism. The Congregational way was the institutionalization of the test of saving faith within the life of an independent, local society of believers. Congregationalism was a form of American Puritanism that held court in New England and asserted its influence upon the American mind with a power quite beyond that of the denomination that came into existence.

"The New England churches," writes Edmund S. Morgan, "were fully equipped with powers of discipline and exercised them to expel members who lapsed from good behavior. But the new demand for signs of grace gave the New England churches a different character from the old Separatist churches. . . . In New England, membership required an experience that was beyond the power of a man to attain by his own efforts."[5] However, a person could *own up* to the signs of grace and in so doing "own the covenant" that God sought to make with God's elect. To own the covenant was not to possess it, but to be possessed by it and to make one a member of the community of the covenant—the new Israel of God. In the Congregationalist conception, the private "owning" of the covenant made one a member of the covenanted community, the church, which in turn served as the foundation of civil society. The New Israel was to be a holy commonwealth, its politics, economics, and social life measures of its holiness. The Congregational way was that of an ideal society, held together by common commitments, values, and experiences. It was a form of democracy, assuming that church and civil order were both under holy order—both were forms of covenant, both required the full participation of an intensely committed, moral, and holy people. It is, of course, possible to see the heritage of Christendom at work in this covenanting experiment. It is still assumed that righteousness and salvation are more than a private affair—they are expressed in civil society and culture.

In the idealism of the Congregational way is a disregard for a key insight of Christian history. Martin Luther had emphasized the understanding that the saved person is simultaneously saint and sinner. In some sense he was echoing the insights of the early Christian thinker St. Paul, who wrote, "I do not know my own actions. For I do not do what I want, but I do the very thing I hate. Now if I do what I do not want, I agree that the law is good. So then it is no longer I that do it, but sin which dwells in me" (Romans 7:15-17). This principle is easy to ignore, but it represents a chiding of idealism. It is a reminder that becoming a saint by owning the covenant does not mean that one can fully escape one's inclination to self-interest; nor does it mean that the groups to which one belongs (visible church and civil society) can become the sum total of holiness. Christian theology maintains that all human society is simultaneously saint and sinner. Idealism is doomed to failure, except as an impossible possibility—as a norm that both calls us to continuing commitment and effort and judges our performance. The original idealism of the Congregational way was short-lived. Major adjustments in theory and practice became necessary. Out of the fifteen thousand inhabitants of Massachusetts in the 1640s, less than half had passed the test of saving faith and were part of the inner covenant of the true church, and thus propertied "freemen"—franchised members of the civil covenant.

Nevertheless, Congregationalism became the dominant form of Christianity in New England. Congregational churches enjoyed an established status. They were supported by taxation, and numerous laws required attendance at worship services. Attendance at Congregational services was much greater than the small sum of those who were able to "own the covenant." We must remember, of course, that large numbers of people were believers who read the Scriptures and were able to make a profession of faith. Many were well-informed theologically—they just could give no evidence of *saving* faith.

By the end of the seventeenth century, Congregationalism had been shaped into a denomination of the American way. This Land Promised to the Saints demanded that religious convictions and movements adjust their conceptions of sainthood to the increasingly obvious fact that there were always "others" whose vision of sainthood was at variance with their own. The Puritan dream of Congregationalism was forced to live in its own house. It had to accept the fact that its notion of a covenanted people living in a holy commonwealth was not shared by others who came to America. The vision had to be denominationalized. The rest of America had separate and differing visions that were also forced into a denominational pattern. Visions and dreams meant for "all the world" to share are seldom accepted in the way they are presented.

However, although Congregationalism became merely a single American denomination, its polity was attractive to much of the American spirit. It would seem that congregational polity has left its mark on American religion. Even those traditions that subscribe to other forms of polity are strongly influenced in practice by the inherent independence of local congregations. Roman Catholicism, with its hierarchical, episcopal polity, finds itself adjusting to the demands of people on the local level. Congregationalism also succeeded in disseminating its vision of a New Israel of God, a holy commonwealth, into the American way of thinking and acting. America itself became the "nation with the soul of a church," a nation with a chosen, divine mission.

If we were to visit a town in New England even today, we would see evidence of the Puritan perception of the world. We would gain an understanding of the verbal, practical, and social expressions of Puritanism as a religious movement. In the midst of every town is the square, where originally the meetinghouse occupied the center. Puritans thought of their places of assembly and worship not as churches but as meetinghouses. The resulting Congregational church (herein used interchangeably with meetinghouse, inasmuch as it has become the acceptable American usage) was a spare, pure building. There were no images, no altars, no stained glass. Set at stage center was the pulpit, sometimes massive, high, with a canopy above that served as a sounding board for acoustical purposes. In front of it on a lower level was a table that was used for commemoration of the Lord's Supper.

The building was often white—because the Congregationalists perceived holiness as simple and devoid of decoration and so that worshipers would not be tempted to lapse into fascination with images or fall into idolatrous adoration of anything other than God, who says, "Thou shalt have no other gods before me . . . thou shalt not make unto thee any graven image." The pulpit is central because the Scriptures and the sermon are the central act of Puritan worship. Scriptures contain the Word of God—words that represent the will of God—and the sermon is meant to be the "breaking open" of that Word. Congregational worship was primarily a ministry of the Word. The most practical (that is, practiced) expression of Congregational religiousness was the assembly of people to hear and heed the intelligent and sound reading and preaching of the Word of God. The table, which served as the focal point for the Lord's Supper, emphasized the point that no sacrifice was being reenacted before an altar by a priest. This was no Mass, no Divine Liturgy, no great eucharistic offering. There was no assumption that the bread and wine were in any way transformed into the presence of Christ. It was a commemoration of the last supper of Jesus with his apostles, a supper that for Christians becomes the Lord's Supper—the meal that symbolizes Jesus' victory over death and the grave.

The Congregationalist perceived the world as God's rational creation, a world fallen from God's intention, but restored by God in Christ. Christ himself was God's Word, which made the Word not only the center of the meetinghouse (church building) but the center of life itself. Therefore the meetinghouse was placed in the center of the town. As the symbol of the center of the universe, it could be used for education or civic activity—all of existence was under the judgment and guidance of the Word. The houses and fields of the New Englanders were laid out with the symbol of the Word at the center. And when the Congregationalist world finally settled on school and court as distinctive arms of Christian civilization, the town square possessed three sacred public buildings, all under the authority of God's covenanting Word.

During the colonial period of American history, Congregationalism was the largest and most prominent denomination. By the beginning of the nineteenth century it had exerted an influence on the formation of American consciousness that was to be virtually unmatched by any other single tradition. The effect was irrevocable. However, as a denomination, Congregationalism began to lose ground in the nineteenth century. It was to a certain extent the victim of the revivalistic evangelicalism that was its own offspring. The frontier spirit of the new nation began to have little time for educated clergy, for theology, and for the more churchly elements of Congregational life. Harvard, Yale, Dartmouth, Williams, Amherst, Smith, Wellesley, Mount Holyoke, Carleton, Oberlin, Grinnell, and Pomona colleges all emerged from the Congregational heritage. Prominent pulpits and congregations played prestigious roles in American religion and culture well into the twentieth century.

In 1931, the Congregationalists united with a small denomination called the Christian Church and formed the Congregational Christian Churches. And in 1957 most of Congregationalism merged with the Evangelical and Reformed Church to form what is the United Church of Christ (not to be confused with denominations that use the title Church of Christ or Churches of Christ).

It is interesting to reflect upon the fact that Congregationalism became more and more liberal as the decades wore on. Not only did it spawn much of the Unitarian and Universalist movements in America, but it also generated its own liberal theology[6] and became active in programs of social and political justice.

Baptists

Baptists in America are the result of several different influences. The ideas and practices of the Anabaptist movement discussed in an earlier chapter are important elements. Anabaptists believed that the church is a community of believers. Belief is an activity for adult, responsible human beings whose lives are regenerated and ready for commitment. Therefore baptism is a seal of the regeneration that takes place in a believing adult; it is not for an infant. Anabaptists were also convinced that the life of Christian holiness is lived in separation from this sinful world. The church is an order of living quite distinct from the order of life in the world. They were committed to the idea that the simple faith and practice of the New Testament church were recoverable. The New Testament became their handbook.

Anabaptist notions made their way into England through the writings of Menno Simons and the presence of Anabaptist refugees from Holland and Germany. They also came to America late in the seventeenth century when William Penn opened his colony to people from Frankfurt and other parts of Germany where people had been victimized by oppression.

Another factor in the development of Baptist denominations in America has been the adaptability of their principles to the frontier spirit of practical, down-to-earth, and democratic sensibilities. Americans were quick to dismiss the traditions of Europe. They wished to get on with the business of living without deference to older, established ways. In religion, this meant that educational requirements for clergy and hierarchical notions of truth (as learned under the guidance of those who preserved it) were not only suspect but considered impediments to God's direct work in people. Baptists are congregational in polity. They assume that the local autonomous congregation is the fullness of the church. Any gathering of adult believers can constitute itself as a Baptist congregation. There are no frills, and there are many Baptist denominations. The word *Baptist* by itself on a believer's lips or on a church's letterhead does not tell you whether the congregation belongs to the Southern Baptist Convention, American Baptist Churches, the predominantly black National Baptist Convention, or any of a number of other associations of Baptist congregations. Sometimes a single Baptist congregation is its own denomination.

The third and very important element in the shaping of Baptist tradition is the Puritan heritage. Much of Baptist tradition in America emerged out of Puritanism. If we recall the earlier discussion of Separatist Puritanism, we can understand the logic whereby certain Separatist Puritans became "Baptists." For those Puritans who concluded that the true church is an association of believers, visibly distinct from others by virtue of simple worship, moral probity, and profession of faith, it was a short step to conclude that only responsible human beings could make such a claim. Responsible choice and mature experience are associated with adulthood, or with a certain adolescent stage in which the individual assumes direction for his or her life. It is, therefore, possible to conclude that baptism should occur when a person is initiated into the true church as a responsible adult. Infant baptism becomes invalid to this way of thinking. Baptism becomes a ritual action that separates the believer from the world under the dominion of sin. It is a believer's action; infants are incapable of being believers. The result of that, for Baptists, is that baptism no longer is a sacrament but becomes an ordinance—a necessary ritual process and seal of an experience and commitment that has preceded it. Adult baptism, usually by immersion, is the way Baptist life is initiated and ordered. It certifies a regeneration that has already taken place. A sacrament, on the other hand, it itself the channel of God's gracious love. The sacrament affirms the fact that God's covenant is for all people, that it does not depend upon the individual's belief or experience.

The Baptists remained a small movement in America until after the War for Independence and the National Period of our history. On the frontier, however, the tradition was lifted to its present predominant status. There are those who would say that whatever else Americans are, they are Baptists by nature. Although the tradition gained its fullness of power in the nineteenth century, it was released by the fervor and intensity of the Great Awakening of the eighteenth century (to be discussed later). In this latter movement, New England Puritanism experienced both renewal within and a breakdown of its structures that changed the shape of American religion and led to greater diversity (denominational and otherwise).

Roger Williams is often claimed by Baptists as the "father" of their tradition in America. Williams was a Puritan clergyman, ordained originally as a priest of the Church of England. As a citizen of Salem and the Massachusetts Bay Colony, he quickly became a figure of controversy and was finally exiled, becoming the founder of Providence and the colony of Rhode Island.

Williams was probably "rebaptized" and active in a group of Baptist Puritans for a short time. However, he was convinced that only God can know the membership of the true church and that no visible church can ever demonstrate that it is in true succession to the faith of original Christianity. Perhaps Williams was not so much a Baptist as a Seeker who trod the earth as a lonely pilgrim, committed only to the dictates of his private search for grace.

Nevertheless, Williams's convictions provided support for the growing assumption that the civil order must be radically dissociated from the ecclesiastical order. Puritan thought had clung to the Christendom ideals expressed in Calvinism. It sought to have civil and ecclesiastical orders as partners in the fashioning of a holy commonwealth under the mandate of Scripture. However, if Williams was correct in his belief that no visible church can claim to represent God's truth, then it was easy to conclude that no government had any right to meddle in religious affairs. Roger Williams is often considered to be the progenitor of the American ideal of "separation of church and state."

The Baptist movement gained its first institutional success with the founding of the Philadelphia Association of Baptist Churches in 1707. The association included churches from New York to Virginia and served as the foundation upon which denominational growth developed. One of the most important figures in eighteenth-century Baptist tradition was Isaac Backus. Backus was one of those Congregationalist Puritans who concluded that the experience of saving faith called for separation from those who considered themselves part of the church but were obviously not "visible saints." His dissatisfaction eventually led to "rebaptism" by immersion. He was the founder of the First Baptist Church of Middleborough, Massachusetts, in 1756 and spent the rest of his life trying to win freedom from the effects of different forms of established religion in New England. It must be understood that principles of toleration and local option could often have oppressive results. By the eighteenth century, Congregationalism in New England had lost its singular hold upon the religious life. It was no longer necessarily the one established church in any specific town. Diversity had taken its toll upon such establishments. After all, there were Baptists and Anglicans in New England by this time. The laws frequently permitted local elections to decide which religious body should receive the tax monies mandated for support of religion. Minorities such as the Baptists frequently suffered under this kind of establishment, even though their existence was tolerated.

Quakers

Quakerism was a mid-seventeenth-century development out of the Puritan revolution in England. It has never been a large denominational family. Although there are several denominations that make up the family, much of the movement has departed from the evangelical moorings that motivated George Fox (its founder) and his early followers. Like many names given to religious movements, "Quaker" began as a nickname with a derisive, negative connotation. During a magistrate's trial in Derby, England, George Fox told the magistrate that he should tremble at the Word of God. His followers became known as tremblers or quakers. Early members of the movement referred to themselves as Children of Light, Children of Truth, or Friends of Truth. The Gospel of St. John (in the Christian New Testament) records a passage in which Jesus addresses his followers, "Greater love has no man than this, that a man lay down his life for his *friends.* You are my *friends* if you do what I command you. No longer do I call you servants, for the servant does not know what his master is doing; but I have called you *friends,* for all that I have heard from my father I have made known to you" (John 15:13-15).

Quakers have reserved for themselves this conception of being friends—of imparting love, compassionate action, and truth. Friends of Jesus! Friends of God! They are appropriately known as the Religious Society of Friends.

Certainly Quakerism emerged with unique and precious insights out of the experience of Fox and his followers in northern England. Yet it must be understood that the Puritan movement unleashed a wide-ranging set of spiritual emphases. Latent within Puritanism's struggle to effect the pure life in community with others are the seeds of Quaker teachings. George Fox wrote of his dissatisfaction and alienation from the religious life of the times. "At the command of God" he left the company of those who were supposed to be important to him. Like Joseph Smith[7] almost two hundred years later, he despaired of his own life and the truth of those "religions" with whom he had associated. "I continued in that condition for some years," wrote Fox, "and . . . went to many a priest to look for comfort, but found no comfort from them. [Then I] . . . looked more after the Dissenting people.[8] . . . But as I had forsaken the priests, so I left the Separate preachers also. . . . And when all my hopes in them and in all men were gone, so that I had nothing outwardly to help me, nor could I tell what to do; then, oh! Then I heard a voice which said, 'There is one, even Christ Jesus, that can speak to thy condition'; and when I heard it, my heart did leap for joy."

This pattern of experience is familiar to the evangelical tradition and is at the heart of Puritanism itself. First, one has a customary religious upbringing. Then, in the course of adolescence or the continuing maturation process, one experiences alienation. Life seems aimless, and it becomes difficult to figure out why it does not submit to one's desire to control it. It is not easy to find comfort in the midst of this anxiety. The individual often finds his or her religious heritage inadequate. In complete despair, he or she discovers that all accepted ways are false and that a simple and direct experience avoids the complexities of decision. Private and individualistic experience is the answer. It is immediate and overcomes the impatience one may have with the fact that religion may be a lifelong nurturing process. It is also a helpful resolution of our inability to understand why churches and their members continue to be sinful and imperfect.

The teaching of Fox and his followers had much in common with the Puritan movement. The Quaker emphasis on equality and the assumption that God approaches each of us directly through the inner light that is the Christ within are shared by other Puritans. It was the Quakers, however, who drew heavily upon these convictions and made them the essence of their tradition. Friends believe that God's will is available to us through the inner light, by means of which we can gain direction for all human affairs and receive the power to live the abundant life. The most impressive development of the doctrine of the inner light was provided by a Scottish Quaker theologian named Robert Barclay. His *Apology,* published in English in 1678, makes the case for the inner light against any external authority, including the Bible. Barclay became governor of East New Jersey in 1683 after helping another Quaker, William Penn, with the founding of the "holy experiment" of religious pluralism and toleration in Pennsylvania. There is in Quakerism a certain continuation of the principle of Christendom and the Puritan desire for the holy commonwealth. Even Penn's experiment assumed that toleration and pluralism would permit God's will to effect itself in an ideal society. It is assumed that God's will for human affairs is to be discerned and put into effect by the art of friendly persuasion. The inner light within each of us will respond to God's will, and we can all be instruments for the perfection of human society.

Education is not an absolute qualification for ministry. Consecrated buildings are not necessary for worship, and services are under the guidance of the Holy Spirit, which is God's way of making contact with the Christ-within-us, through the inner light that awaits the awakening of the Spirit.

Friends share the Puritan preference for unadorned places of worship. The
ritual aspect of their religious life is one of silence and simplicity. The ritual
is a meeting and takes place in a meetinghouse. The meeting is a "meeting"
with the Spirit and with other people of friendly persuasion; it is shared by a
community that exists by virtue of the equalizing presence of the inner light.
For the Quakers the true church is thus a spiritual community. Although
there is a certain "invisibility" to this community, it is easy to see that the
Friends share the Puritan separatist concern for visible saints who will transform human society into the kingdom of God.

In its beginnings Quakerism was strongly evangelical and concerned for
its orthodoxy. However, it has suffered schism throughout its history. Resident within its teachings is a liberalizing tendency that wishes to deny all
external forms (doctrine, worship) in favor of inner and essential[9] truth.
Such assumptions as this often run counter to concern for orthodoxy. The
notion of the inner light also opens Quaker teaching to the mystical inclinations of human beings, and there has been a rich intellectual vein of mysticism in Friends' history. Besides Fox himself, who may be considered
mystical, there is John Woolman. Born in 1720 in America, Woolman "began
to be acquainted with the operations of Divine Love" by age seven. He lived
with a sense of being in the presence of the "pure spirit of truth" and became
one of the earliest opponents of slavery, which he believed was totally "incon-
sistent with the Christian religion."

One of the greatest American students of mysticism in the twentieth century was Rufus Jones, a Quaker professor of philosophy at Haverford College
in Pennsylvania. "The mystic," he wrote, ". . . is . . . a person who has culti-
vated, with more strenuous care and discipline than others have done, the
native homing passion of the soul for the Beyond. . . . The result is that he has
occasions when the larger life with which he feels himself kin seems to surround him and answer back to his soul's quest."[10]

Quakerism is a pacifist tradition that eschews oaths and the bearing of
arms or the commission of intentional violence. Although this may be a
noble and desirable religious and moral posture, it made for difficulty in the
governance of Pennsylvania in the eighteenth century. Quakers were among
the economic and political elite of the power structures of the colony. During
the skirmishes of colonists with the Native Americans, they were often negli-
gent in the defense of life and property. German and Scotch-Irish colonists
were shouldered with most of that responsibility, to the detriment of human
relations.

The polity of the Religious Society of Friends is entirely pragmatic. It has little theological concern and is based upon the necessity of transacting the common business and program of any human association. The polity is therefore associational and connectional. The association of Friends at local levels is weekly and monthly. Beyond the monthly meeting, there may develop quarterly meetings and yearly meetings in which Friends from a region are associated. Friends, therefore, have connectional relations to others in various areas of jurisdiction. They may have further denominational connections with the Five Year Meeting or the Friends General Conference. As you can see, the term *meeting* bears an almost sacred connotation for this American tradition.

The Quakers have always been in the forefront of activity on behalf of social conscience. The American Friends Service Committee has fed the hungry, promoted peace, and worked effectively for human rights and social justice. Even though the Friends are a small denominational family, they have made profound contributions to American society and culture. Their emphasis upon the privacy and immediacy of religious experience is in harmony with much of the American spirit. However, their tendency to reject all external authority runs counter to the American practice of associating private judgment with the external authority of Scripture. Friends have become more intellectually private and independent than much of America, and their advocacy of pacifism and championing of liberal social issues tends to make them an elite. The American public does not turn to such groups in large numbers. Like most religious traditions in our nation, Quakerism has been shaped by America itself. It is one of the many traditions that express the diversity in the American perception of the world. Shaped by its minority status and the political and economic power of a nation it helped to found, it lives as a conscience far removed from its evangelical heritage. It is as American as it is Christian.

Postscript

When we examine religious ideas and practices from within the broad context of history since the sixteenth century, we may well conclude that America has been the stage on which the drama of equality and freedom has been working itself out. From the beginning of the American experiment there have been people and ideas that have contributed to the emancipation of African American slaves and the struggle for women's full participation in the religious and social life of the emerging new republic. Anne Hutchinson (1591–1643) was a woman whose Puritanism led her to the conclusion that human beings have direct access to the voice of God without mediation from any external authority—neither sacred scripture nor tradition are essential to communication with the divine. Her close friend, Mary Dyer, eventually became a Quaker and, like Hutchinson, ran afoul of the Massachusetts Puritan clergy as she witnessed to her spiritual experience.

Hutchinson and Dyer serve as examples of women whose thinking represents the beginnings of the erosion of patriarchal dominance in American religious history. By 1853 Puritan Congregationalism gave way to the ordination of Antoinette Brown as a pioneer in the feminine struggle for full participation in the structured religious life of America. By this time, of course, women had been recognized as the custodians and nurturers of piety and morality in a society where males were increasingly removed from familial influence by the competitive activities of the industrial and commercial age. This "feminization" (as it has been called) of American society and culture imposes a role for women that is still not of their own choosing and has failed to provide access to the equality that is essential to a free exercise of power and decision making.

It should be emphasized in this regard that Congregational women were active in the voluntary societies that in the nineteenth century were to open the doors to the emancipation of slaves and women. Societies such as the Antislavery Society, the American Education Society, the American Peace Society, and the Women's Christian Temperance Union were aligned with the churches by interlocking membership and served as workshops for the development of radical ideas and political experience.

chapter 7

The Reformed Tradition: The Scotch-Irish and English, the Dutch, and the Germans

Members of the Reformed tradition in America may use the word *Reformed* or the word *Presbyterian* to designate their denominations or to identify their forms of Christian persuasion. The Reformed traditions are an alliance of churches owing a great loyalty to the theological work of continental Reformers like John Calvin and Ulrich Zwingli and governing themselves by a presbyterial polity. Whether they call themselves Presbyterian or Reformed is to a great extent an accident of history. Perhaps it is true to say that the Anglo-Saxon world prefers pragmatic issues and is therefore prone to concentrate on matters of organization and polity. Its religious traditions are often termed Congregational, Methodist, or Presbyterian. The continent of Europe, particularly in the Swiss and Germanic realms, has sustained an interest in theoretical and philosophical concerns. Its religious traditions are often termed Reformed or Lutheran—designating a concern for ecclesiology[1] or for reformation based upon theological principles.

Generally speaking, we may apply a rule that says that the Reformed tradition on the Continent is expressed in the lives of Reformed churches. In the British Isles, the Reformed tradition calls itself Presbyterian. The Reformed heritage of Europe, England, Scotland, and Northern Ireland migrated to America, where it continues to reflect the diversity of its Old World origins.

In our examination of the Reformed tradition in America we shall confine ourselves to the Dutch and German Reformed churches and to the Presbyterians. Of course, it is not easy to maintain simple boundaries of the mind when thinking of the Reformed tradition. Some scholars would remind us that Puritanism is itself the English manifestation of the Reformed heritage. It must certainly be remembered that the ideas and practices of John Calvin were extremely important to the development of Puritanism. The Church of

England itself sought the assistance of Swiss Reformed scholars like John Henry Bullinger in its polemics with the papacy.

However, Puritanism has its distinct heritage (see chap. 6). And in America, the Presbyterian and Reformed churches have developed a history of their own. Even though Presbyterianism especially has close ties with Puritan origins, its custodianship of an orthodox Reformed Christianity distinguishes it from Puritanism. In the final analysis, I must confess to a certain convenience in separating Puritanism from the Reformed tradition. Let us hope that the separation is justifiable. The renowned nineteenth-century historian Philip Schaff, himself a representative of German Reformed Christianity, wrote in 1854 an evaluation of religion in America for a German audience:

> The religious character of North America . . . is predominantly of the Reformed of Calvinistic stamp, which modifies there even the Lutheran Church, to its gain, indeed, in some respects, but to its loss in others. To obtain a clear view of the enormous influence which Calvin's personality, moral earnestness, and legislative genius, have exerted on history, you must go to Scotland and to the United States. The Reformed Church, where it develops itself freely from its own inward spirit and life, lays special stress on thorough moral reform, individual, personal Christianity, freedom and independence of congregational life, and strict church discipline.[2]

By the time of Schaff's writing, much of the Calvinistic bent of the American character was being softened by the independent perfectionism of the frontier spirit. The colonial mind of America was decidedly Calvinistic and Reformed; the emergent nineteenth-century mind was distinctively Wesleyan or Methodist. The full meaning of this observation will be discussed in a later chapter. However, it is important to note that Americans are still very Methodist in spirit and have a difficult time understanding many of the ideas of Calvin and the Reformed tradition. This fact represents a significant reorientation for the American mind, a change from Reformed and Puritan origins.

Verbal Expression

The verbal or theoretical expression of the Reformed tradition bears three discernible manifestations. First, there is the unmistakable emphasis upon the sovereignty of God, which is the mark of Calvinism. As we have seen in a previous chapter, John Calvin was inspired by the awe and majesty of God. Those Christian thinkers who followed in his footsteps made this emphasis a first principle for the doing of theology. The more we focus upon the sovereign God, the more we sense a great separation or discontinuity between God and ourselves. God becomes the "Other" whom we cannot really fathom. God as sovereign is not like anything else but is "Other" than all else, Creator and not created. Inasmuch as we are members of the created order we can only comprehend what is created, not what is uncreated—the Creator. The gap between ourselves and God is constantly widened, deepened. Who are we, we ask ourselves, to approach so awesome a being as God? We are nothing—except what has been created. But God is Other, sovereign. We are in God's hands.

This is an important lesson in theology, in *all* thinking for that matter. We should note how a first principle in thinking will determine the shape and outcome of the rest of our thought. If, for example, the first principle of theology focuses upon the experience of God's love, God's compassion, then the issue of God's Otherness, or sovereignty, will be a much modified consideration. After all, we shall have known God in terms of God's identification with our finite human condition. We might say that we know only of the love, not the almightiness, or the sovereignty, of God. The remainder of our thinking about God and human history, about the universe, will be influenced by the first principle.

The Reformed tradition makes much of the chasm between God and humanity, of what must be overcome in order for God to relate to the creation. That is because a second aspect of Reformed and Calvinistic theology is consideration of the continuing sinful condition of humanity. It is not only that God is Other because God is Creator and we are created, it is also that we who are created do not accept the finiteness of our condition. The created bears the image, the stamp, of its Creator—just enough to help it assume that it is itself creator, that it can be self-sufficient. This tendency is what is meant by sin. Sin is the condition of living in deliberate alienation from our created status, of assuming the ultimate control of our own lives and of the realms of nature. Sin aggravates the separation between the sovereign God and God's creation. As a matter of fact, there would be no great chasm but for our sinfulness. The things we leave undone and the actions we take that harm others are symptoms of our sin. In other words, sin begets sins; sins verify our sinful condition.

The Reformed tradition is keenly aware of this constant condition. No true member of this tradition would make the mistake of assuming that humans are to be finally trusted. Neither a conversion experience nor a commitment to Christ and his teachings means that the individual will depart from the state of sinfulness. Only God's redeeming love, known in Christ's crucifixion and resurrection, can reconcile us to our deity, even though we remain sinners in this life. There is no illusion here about human nature, no naïve utopian idealism. John Calvin was convinced that the kingdom of God is precisely that—God's and not the property of any government (civil or ecclesiastical) or the vision of any thinker. When the kingdom of God comes, it comes as a surprise to the individual, to the orders of human history. It is not something available to the schemes of natural, sinful humanity.

Out of this emphasis upon the sovereignty of God and the continuing sinful condition of humanity emerged an attitude that influenced the framing of the American Constitution. The Reformed tradition believes that human sinfulness must be restrained. No person or human agency must ever be given unlimited powers; not even the best intentioned person must be left unrestrained. Some form of power must balance a person's claim to power. No matter the sincerity of the ideals an individual or group represents, they can be expected to permit inordinate self-interest to involve them in acts of injustice. A balance of power must be provided to see to the restraint of self-interest. No person is God, no matter that person's intelligence or commitments. All are sinners, under the best intentions and circumstances.

A third distinguishing feature of the Reformed tradition is its emphasis upon cultural transformation. The sinful world is, after all, still God's world; therefore, not only must evil be restrained, but the world must be transformed. God's redeeming work, represented in Jesus the Christ, extends itself into economics, politics, and education. All of culture is under mandate to show forth the kingdom of God. Both church and state live under the same constitution—the kingdom of God proclaimed in Scripture and in creation. Reformed theology has always led to an activism on behalf of social justice. The tradition has never been satisfied with any kind of withdrawal from the natural and social orders. It has not been content with private religiosity. Life must be restored to harmony with God's kingdom, even though our vision and understanding of that kingdom is always partial, given our alienation and continuing sinfulness. The kingdom may never be known in fullness, in historical existence as we know it. But it can be approximated because redemption has been revealed to us in Jesus Christ.

Reformed theology has often been strongly confessional. That is, it has affirmed the importance of doctrinal statements that serve to identify true Christian teaching. Confessionalism maintains that Christians can be identified by their willingness to subscribe to—to confess or profess—a statement of orthodox principles. Throughout much of American religious history the Reformed traditions have been preservers of confessional orthodoxy in the face of threats from modernity and secularization. The Presbyterian-based theological seminary at Princeton has been a citadel of orthodox Reformed theology. Charles Hodge, Archibald Alexander Hodge, and Benjamin Warfield were prominent in nineteenth- and early twentieth-century theology. Liberal currents in theology finally eroded the confessional authority of Princeton and, indeed, of Presbyterianism itself. A schism in the Princeton Seminary led to the formation of a new theological school and a new Presbyterian denomination under the influence of the fundamentalist evangelical theologian J. Gresham Machen. However, a significant portion of the Dutch Reformed heritage, both in the Reformed Church of America and the Christian Reformed Church,[3] continues to be custodian of confessional orthodoxy. Colleges like Calvin and Hope, Western Theological Seminary, and New Brunswick (New Jersey) Theological Seminary serve the Dutch Reformed tradition and are dedicated to the preservation of classical Reformed doctrine.

The representative of the Reformed tradition that has been most socially active and in conformity with the mandate to bring about the transformation of society has been Presbyterianism. In the twentieth century it has also been the most flexible denominational family with regard to its confessionalism.

Practical Expression

What practices are in some sense distinguishing features of Reformed Christianity? Calvin had been more sparing in his liturgical practices than had Martin Luther and his followers. The Reformed tradition, therefore, tended to assume that practices not specifically sanctioned by Scripture were at least suspect. At first the liturgies used in Reformed churches were heavily didactic, that is, they used language in order to teach rather than to evoke congregational response to God. Calvinists and Zwinglians were so concerned to separate their worship practices from the habits of the Roman church that their language of prayer often seemed like courses in doctrine. Inasmuch as they rejected the meaning of the Roman Mass and the theology of works implicit in much Roman liturgical observance, they sought to spell out their theological refinements in new liturgies. They wanted to be sure that the people understood at all times how and why they were worshiping. They believed that prayer and theology go hand in hand.

The Reformed tradition affirmed two of the seven sacraments that were at the heart of the inherited Catholic Christianity of the Middle Ages. Only two sacraments were distinctly biblical; only two were directly instituted by Christ—Baptism and the Lord's Supper. The theological principles behind any sacraments insist upon dominical[4] institution and assume that the sacrament itself confers or channels God's grace. A sacrament uses nature's resources for divine communication. This means that a sacrament is not a mere sign or seal of something already present. If this is the interpretation given a ritual action, it is no longer a sacrament because the question of its necessity may be raised. We may ask whether baptism plays an essential role in the reception of God's saving grace. Is baptism necessary to salvation in the Reformed tradition? The Reformers were faced with these questions because of their emphasis upon justification by faith. Calvin and the Reformed tradition held that infants should be baptized as a sign and seal of the covenant that God would bless divinely chosen children just as God had blessed the children of Abraham and instituted circumcision as a sign of the covenant. They did not wish to go to the extremes represented by Zwingli in Zurich, or those taught by the Anabaptists. Baptism was to be more than a sign or seal but perhaps not necessary to salvation.

The Reformed practice of the Lord's Supper takes its interpretation between the position of Medieval Catholicism and Martin Luther, on the one hand, and Zwingli on the other. For Zwingli the supper was really no longer sacramental. It was more like the ordinance of the Anabaptists, a simple remembrance of the last supper of the disciples with Jesus. The view held by medieval Catholicism and the loyalist Reformation was that the mass reenacts the sacrifice of Jesus Christ and that the bread and wine are changed in inner substance into the body and blood of Christ. Martin Luther rejected the view of Mass as reenactment of Christ's sacrifice but maintained that the body and blood of Christ were indeed present in, with, and under the bread and wine. The latter were not changed in substance but were the occasion for the presence of the body and blood. Calvin and his followers held that Christ was present to the church in the receiving of bread and wine, but that the substances of bread and wine were in no way changed or altered.

The line between Luther's and Calvin's interpretation is a fine one. The Reformed tradition, however, has tended to neglect Calvin's notion of spiritual, real presence. In the middle of the nineteenth century in America, a professor in the German Reformed Theological Seminary in Mercersburg, Pennsylvania, tried to remedy that neglect. John Williamson Nevin, a former Presbyterian, published a book titled *The Mystical Presence.* In it he deplored the manner in which Reformed practice had softened the understanding of the Sacrament of the Lord's Supper. For Nevin, the presence of Christ in the bread and wine was real. It was neither a subjective dream nor a simple memorial. The presence of Christ was an objective reality; the truth of Christianity must rise or fall on that fact. Christ's presence was not a natural presence—not like a human's. It was the presence of the risen Christ, a transnatural presence, a mystical presence. However, by the time of Nevin's writing in 1846, the strength of American theology had already been weakened by revivalism and the new subjectivism of American culture.

Most Reformed denominations today would advocate an interpretation of the Lord's Supper that is more substantial than the memorial view. However, the celebration or use of the Supper tends to be quarterly in the church year, with perhaps additional observance on special occasions. There are exceptions among those congregations that have sought to restore the liturgical and theological traditions of the Catholic Christianity from which all Western churches have emerged historically. One of the assumptions of the sixteenth-century magisterial and separationist Reformation was that the church had trivialized the Supper by a too frequent and magical use of the Mass. Reformed Protestantism, therefore, celebrated the Supper less frequently (hence, the eventual quarterly practice) and stressed the importance of serious preparation for those occasions. Christians were expected to examine their lives carefully and reconcile any differences with other Christians before communing with Christ in his Supper and sharing that communion with other members of Christ's body, the church.

Social Expression

The social expression of the Reformed tradition is based upon Calvin's theology of the church as that community where the Word is rightly preached and the sacrament faithfully administered. The churches of the magisterial Reformation were quick to develop preaching into a skill and practice that were new to the history of Christianity. The Reformed tradition has contributed greatly to the rise of a new type of religious leadership that eventually reached the zenith of its development in America. Americans tend to speak of a clergyperson as a "preacher." Often Roman Catholic, Orthodox, and Episcopal priests are called "preachers" in America. This means that sociologically the function of preaching came to be so dominant in Protestant Christianity that the clergy or other religious leaders were identified by way of this single function. In the perspective of priesthood, preaching is only one aspect of liturgical and pastoral responsibility. A priest may be a preacher, but not necessarily so.

In Reformed tradition preachers must be skilled in the interpretation of Scripture. When they use the Scriptures faithfully, preaching and the written word of Scripture become the Word of God, the occasion in which the Spirit speaks to the minds and hearts of people. The Word must be preached regularly to the community of faith; it must also be preached to confront the fallen world with God's judgment in the hope that individuals might repent and seek to be included among the chosen of God. When the Sacraments of Baptism or the Lord's Supper are to be administered, the Word has to be preached. Preaching makes faith possible, and faith is necessary to the receiving of the sacraments.

This emphasis upon the preached Word and prepared celebration of sacraments in the Reformed doctrine of the church affected the architecture of church buildings. Increasingly, they featured a central pulpit, high and often ponderous; the remaining areas were often barren and austere. After all, what was central was the Word of God who was sovereign, unlike anything in nature or the human scene. One had to have a clear head to worship such a God. There could be no distraction. All that took place was directed toward confrontation with God's law (focused in the Decalogue, or Ten Commandments). Only such an encounter could produce repentance and thanksgiving for God's sacrificial love in Christ. The church was God's chosen family. Only God knows who is chosen, and it is a knowledge best left to God. However, repentance and a transformed life may be signs of chosenness. Some within the tradition came to believe that success in life might be evidence of divine favor. Nevertheless, the best of Reformed theology would always caution us against too naïve an assumption of chosenness, regardless of the apparent evidence.

The church is God's chosen family, hidden in the life of the churches and the world. Accordingly, the Reformed Christian is a person very faithful to the Word and its preaching, zealous in adherence to the doctrines of the confessions, in awe before the majesty of God, and impressed with no lesser authority. Of course, the state must guarantee and protect true religion; it is to be obeyed as long as it keeps God's law and violates no religious obligation. The world is judged by the sovereign God, who seeks to transform it by his redeeming love in Christ. The Word of God, contained in Scripture, judges state and church—both of them orders of creation, under the sign of the kingdom of God.

A discussion of the social expression of a Christian religious tradition leads inevitably to the issue of polity. Reformed polity is presbyterial. Followers of Calvin in Europe and Great Britain thought that the earliest Christian model of ordered community life was government by presbyters—elders. Consequently, the tradition developed a pattern of representative order in which lay persons play a prominent role. There are teaching elders, who are ordained pastors, and ruling elders, elected from the ranks of the congregations. In each local church of Presbyterians, for example, the ruling elders form a court known as the Session, which is moderated by the clergy. Deacons are also elected in each congregation, where they form a board for distributing charity and performing other special responsibilities.

A presbytery is a regional assembly of teaching and ruling elders, representing the congregations of a given area. The synod, in turn, is composed of representative elders from congregations within a large district, comprised of several presbyteries. The General Assembly is the representative court of the whole denomination and is made up of delegate elders from all presbyteries. Variations in this presbyterial system are found among the many denominations of the Reformed tradition.

The largest denominational family of the Reformed tradition in America is the Presbyterian. A recent merger of Presbyterian denominations has produced the Presbyterian Church (U.S.A.), bringing together the two largest Presbyterian bodies. This represents a union of the United Presbyterian Church of the U.S.A. (a previous merger) and the Presbyterian Church in the United States, which was the Southern denomination that had resulted from schism over different attitudes toward slavery prior to the Civil War.

History in the United States

For the most part, American Presbyterianism is the formation of the unique circumstances of American history. It is a heritage of Scotch-Irish and English parentage. English Puritanism had fostered many internal debates over polity. As we saw earlier, there were the independents and the Presbyterians, among others, who made up the factions of Puritanism. These differences of opinion were exported to America, where it soon became apparent that the Presbyterians had much in common with the Reformed immigrants from Scotland and Northern Ireland. The latter churches had already forged a strong tradition that emphasized the theological significance of presbyterial polity. They were indeed Presbyterians, fashioned by the temperament of the Scotch and Irish realms, and based upon a loyalty to the model of Christianity developed by John Calvin in Geneva, Switzerland. The Scotch-Irish arrived in America in the early eighteenth century, locating in Pennsylvania, western New Jersey, and western Maryland. Some of them wandered southward into Virginia and the Carolinas.

The great expanse of wilderness and undeveloped frontier had its effects upon Presbyterianism. The Scotch-Irish were an independent and hardworking people who took their Calvinism seriously. Many of them were farmers, who sought the rich soils that were not too encumbered by the limestone formations of the eastern seaboard. They tended to leave those rocky lands for the Germans, who were more accustomed to that kind of agriculture. The Scotch-Irish scattered into the hinterlands, pioneering and stretching the boundaries of the colonies. Their Calvinism was often refashioned into a folk culture, still rich and unexplored by historians of American religion. The organization of Presbyterian congregations was difficult, and many of the people lost contact with these institutional elements of their tradition.

The College of New Jersey, which became known as Princeton, was an early educational enterprise of colonial Presbyterianism. It was there, for example, that the Scotsman, John Witherspoon, became president and influenced the thinking of many of those who were to become leaders in the forming of the Constitution and the development of the new and independent United States of America. Credit for formation of the first American presbytery in 1705 goes to Francis Makemie. Before long this Philadelphia Presbytery was divided to form three, and a synod was formed. Presbyterianism was establishing itself as one of the continuing traditions of American pluralism.

The Puritan Congregationalists of New England continued to have much in common with the Presbyterians of the Middle Colonies. They shared an allegiance to Calvinism and many of the pragmatic notions of British Christianity. The Congregationalists, although advocating the primacy of the independent local congregation, frequently found themselves functioning as consociations or associations of representatives from local churches. Congregationalists in theory, they discovered the expedient necessity of regulation beyond the local congregation. Perhaps they were Congregationalist in theory, Presbyterian in practice.

As the American frontier moved rapidly westward during the National Period, Presbyterians and Congregationalists agreed to a so-called Plan of Union. This agreement was meant to avoid unnecessary competition between two traditions that held much in common. When a new congregation was formed in the western territories, the leaders were to be free to call upon clergy from either one of the two denominational groups. The Plan of Union benefited Presbyterianism more than Congregationalism. Continuing immigration from Scotland and Northern Ireland swelled the ranks of Presbyterian churches. Their missionary activity was more effective than was the case with Congregationalism, and more congregations called Presbyterian pastors than Congregational clergy. The result was the increased strength of Presbyterianism in the nineteenth century. Of course, although no denomination could match the frontier efforts of Methodists and Baptists, Presbyterianism maintained its loyalty to the sovereignty of God and divine election of the saved at a time when Americans were more and more convinced of their own potential and responsibility for salvation.

As a representative of Reformed confessionalism, Presbyterianism looks to the Westminster Confession, a statement of faith drawn up by the Westminster Assembly that was appointed by Parliament in 1643 to reform English Christianity in keeping with Puritan expectations. Parliament approved the Confession in 1648. During the previous year the document had been ratified by the Church of Scotland, thus making it the definitive Reformed confession for the English-speaking world. American Presbyterians revised the Confession in 1967 in order to produce a doctrinal statement more likely to be understood by contemporary humankind. Many of the Calvinistic doctrinal positions have been softened, especially the traditional Reformed emphasis upon the sovereignty of God and the doctrine of election to salvation. It should be understood, of course, that Presbyterianism in America had been undergoing a liberalization of its theology throughout the twentieth century. The doctrine of election and its concomitant notions of predestination have long been an identifying characteristic of Presbyterianism in the public mind. These doctrines are exceedingly complex and have been an embarrassment in those situations where the public lives with its own understanding of what the teachings mean, without sufficient theological education. The gradual liberalization of Presbyterian doctrine has produced its expected reactions. From schisms have emerged new denominations, which in sectarian fashion consider themselves to be restorers of the true church. There have also been defections of clergy and laity; often certain congregations, such as the First Presbyterian Church of Hollywood, have adopted the style of a more evangelical and revivalistic American Christianity.

Presbyterianism has been very important in American history. Its clergy and laity have been profound contributors to our cultural and political life. President Woodrow Wilson and Secretary of State John Foster Dulles were knowledgeable and dedicated Presbyterians whose Reformed faith was instrumental in their understanding and conduct of their public responsibilities.

Holland had found its way to America early in the seventeenth century. The Dutch Reformed church came with Dutch immigrants to what became known as New Amsterdam. Peter Minuit, the first director of the New Netherlands, had been a ruling elder of the French Reformed church and saw to the pastoral care of the early settlement. Jonas Michaelius was the first dominie[5] to arrive and organize a congregation. When Peter Stuyvesant became director of the colony in 1647, he sought to impose a policy of religious uniformity according to the practice of the Reformed church. However, his attempted restriction of Lutherans, Quakers, and Jews was detrimental to the economic well-being of the colony, and Stuyvesant was ordered to follow a policy of toleration. Michaelius had discovered the necessity of ministering to the French-speaking Walloons as well as the Dutch. Both were Calvinist in tradition. Early on the colony was an asylum for dissenters and reformers seeking freedom from the religious restraints of Europe. Although the dominies frequently spoke in French as well as Dutch, and the French Reformed congregants often understood the Dutch tongue, many congregations developed according to lines of nationality. When the New Netherlands became an English colony in 1664, there were eleven Dutch Reformed churches. By the end of the century, there were several French Reformed churches as well, even though many of these Huguenots had become members of the Dutch congregations.

New York continues to be a stronghold of the continuing Dutch Reformed tradition. Early English governors had to recognize the presence of the Dutch churches and the role they had established in the colony. Religious toleration continued, with a certain deference and public financial support for the Dutch clergy. Gradually, however, this special status was lost, and the Dutch tradition was left to exert its influence upon the culture of the state.

New Jersey was also a Dutch Reformed outpost. It was in the Raritan River Valley that Theodore J. Frelinghuysen, pastor of four Dutch Reformed congregations, sparked a revitalization of religious commitment that became part of the movement known as the Great Awakening (see chap. 11). Frelinghuysen was a German ordained in the ministry of the Dutch Reformed church. When he came to America in 1719, he was displeased by what he considered to be complacency among his Dutch parishioners. They seemed content with churchgoing and being members of the church as an expression of social identity. Perhaps being Dutch Reformed was for many of them a means of ethnic security in a frontier society peopled by many different faiths but dominated by the English language and political order. To Frelinghuysen this was unacceptable Christianity, and he sought to renew and deepen the experience of the people. He did not understand that churchgoing as ritual event and religion as social identity are also important aspects of human religiousness. From a theological standpoint, they may not be at all incompatible with the Christian gospel. However, Frelinghuysen was under the influence of the Pietist and Puritan spirits of his age. He was convinced that evidence of saving faith, and experiential piety, were the essence of religion.

Frelinghuysen's preaching was directed toward confronting the people with the shallow character of their commitments. He enforced the Reformed discipline of penitential preparation for participation in the Lord's Supper and instituted the pastoral practice of family and small-group conferences. The latter practice was in keeping with the program of European Pietism and English Methodism, in which conventicles and classes were directed toward personal renewal through prayer, Bible study, and spiritual examination. By 1726, a period of conversion and renewal had overtaken the Dutch communities of northern New Jersey and New York.

Queen's College (later Rutgers University) was chartered by the Dutch revivalists to serve the increased concern for proper Christian education and the growing number of recruits for the professional ministry. During the War for Independence, the Dutch, like many other groups of non-British origins, supported the revolutionary cause. Perhaps the revivalist effect upon the Dutch church accounts for a gradual weakening of the confessional orthodoxy that is so characteristic of the Reformed traditions. By the early twentieth century a reaction set in against this revivalist softening of doctrine in favor of experience. Some Dutch Reformed clergy found doctrinal deviations among supporters of an emerging American religion that was to emphasize the Puritan notion of "evidence of saving faith" over against concerns for theological integrity. The American religion in the making, a religion that was to affect the many religious traditions of the nation, was losing the Calvinism of its earlier days. It was becoming increasingly anti-intellectual, unconcerned with the history or consistency of ideas.

Reaction against deviation from Reformed confessionalism eventually led in 1857 to the founding of the Christian Reformed Church among Dutch immigrants in Michigan. This firmly confessional denomination has emerged as a body equal in strength to its parent. Together the Reformed Church in America and the Christian Reformed Church represent the ongoing heritage of the Dutch tradition in America. The parent church has established a number of community churches, which are devoted to a conservative evangelical Christianity that attempts to avoid denominational characterization. The Garden Grove Community Church in Pasadena, California, serves as the parish of television celebrity Robert Schuller, whose message is considerably remote from Reformed confessionalism and belongs to the "positive thinking" school of American religion (see chap. 18).

In the nineteenth century Mercersburg, Pennsylvania, was the site of a small theological seminary responsible for educating young men for the ministry of the German Reformed church. It had a small faculty and a small student body. Two of the faculty were to set in motion a way of understanding Christian theology that was somewhat contrary to the mainstream of American religion. John Williamson Nevin was a former Presbyterian who came to Mercersburg in 1840 after having taught at Princeton and the Western Seminary in Pittsburgh. Nevin was influenced by his reading of German philosophy, theology, and church history and assumed he would find congenial surroundings in the German Reformed church in this country. Nevin was joined in 1844 by the young Swiss-German scholar Philip Schaff, who was to become America's foremost church historian. Together, Nevin and Schaff fashioned a mode of thinking that sought to put the German Reformed church in touch with its Reformation heritage in such a way that it would also appreciate the truth of its Catholic parentage. These thinkers thought that American religion was too much influenced by Puritanism and the evangelical revivalism that was fast becoming the style of Protestantism. Their assumption that Protestantism was a positive outgrowth of Catholic Christianity was too much for the anti-Catholic sentiments of American society.

Nevertheless, Nevin and Schaff are two very important figures in any understanding of the shaping of American religious traditions. They represent an intellectual movement that has still not been adequately assessed in relation to the whole of American religious history. However, in the present context we see the Mercersburg theology as a development in the German quarter of the Reformed tradition in America. The movement provides evidence for understanding the manner in which European religious traditions were "Americanized." Nevin and Schaff were reacting against what was happening to the Reformed tradition in America. Pluralism and denominational proliferation (what Nevin called the "Sect System") were combining with the voluntary principle of religious participation to make America a place of competition and hasty decision. This was a land with much space and very little time. Emphasis was upon experience rather than knowledge, commitment, and understanding. Religion was possessed of a democratic spirit in which personal experience and immediate results were the rule, tending to ignore the priestly and nurturing character of the Christian church.

The homeland of the German Reformed church was the Pfalz, the German Rhineland or Palatinate. Its first immigration came as the result of William Penn's "holy experiment" in bringing the victims of religious oppression to the haven of Penn's Woods. Quakers, Mennonites, and representatives of other European minorities were among the first arrivals. However, many of those sympathetic to the cause of these Pietist and separationist Christians were also members of Lutheran and Reformed churches on the Continent. Accordingly, members of the German Reformed Church were early on the scene in Pennsylvania.

The German Reformed Church was distinguished by its loyalty to the Heidelberg Catechism, a sixteenth-century teaching document that sought to mediate between the seemingly rigid polarities of Lutheran confessionalism and Calvinistic orthodoxy. German Reformed teaching has been moderate and conciliatory, its theology attempting to prevent divisions. In America the center of its strength was Pennsylvania, where it shared the German culture and language with Lutherans and Anabaptists such as the Mennonites, Amish, and Church of the Brethren.

For a while the people were without pastors and adequate economic resources. John Philip Boehm (1683–1749) was the son of a Reformed pastor in Germany, where he had been a schoolmaster. He settled in Pennsylvania as a farmer in 1720. Persuaded by his neighbors to conduct services for them, he eventually assumed pastoral responsibilities and was ordained by the Dutch Reformed church in New York in 1729. During the next two decades Georg Michael Weiss and several other German Reformed clergy came to America to serve their compatriots. However, the farmers and craftsmen scattered throughout eastern Pennsylvania and eventually through the Cumberland

Valley into western Maryland and the Shenandoah Valley of Virginia. They were frequently without the pastors and established congregations necessary to keep their faith alive and disciplined. They learned to improvise, reading the Bible, German-language devotional classics, and the works of mystical writers such as Jacob Boehme, Johann Arndt, and Gottfried Arnold. By the time the denomination achieved any degree of stable organization in Penn's colony, the German Americans had already developed a religious lifestyle that was independent and lay-oriented. They sought to adhere to the Heidelberg Catechism and Reformed liturgical practice, but they were accustomed to improvising without clergy, seeing to the education of their children, and meeting in homes and schoolhouses for services of worship and scriptural study. The pattern of their religious life was shaped by the expediencies of a frontier existence without benefit of clergy.

The Reformed synods of Holland first came to the assistance of the Germans, sending a native of Switzerland to visit existing congregations and organize them according to Reformed polity. By the time Michael Schlatter returned to Europe in 1757 he had organized a "coetus."[6] The following year he brought six young clergy to America, representing a considerable improvement in the pastoral conditions of Pennsylvania, where fifteen thousand German Reformed inhabitants had had to depend upon four ordained pastors. The people, who were poor and self-reliant, found it somewhat difficult to assume responsibility for the support of pastors and church buildings in a colony where no establishment of religion provided for public support. However, the German Reformed church was taking its place in the denominational system of American religion.

By the middle of the nineteenth century, it was evident that the new American nation was to be an English-speaking country, its culture being shaped by a kind of deference to Anglo-Saxon and Germanic elements. The German Reformed church officially became known as the Reformed Church in the United States. Still somewhat regional in its constituency, it reached into Ohio and certain parts of the old Northwest where Pennsylvanians had resettled and new German immigrants had swelled the ranks. In 1934, in the midst of concern for Christian unity, the Reformed Church in the United States merged with a sister denomination of German parentage, the Evangelical[7] Synod of North America, to form the Evangelical and Reformed Church. The Evangelical synod was partly the result of early nineteenth-century immigrations from sections of Germany affected by the Prussian Union of 1817, which had brought Lutherans and Reformed together in a single institution. The Evangelical Synod of North America was the nurturing tradition of some of the most important American theologians of the twentieth century. Reinhold Niebuhr, his brother, H. Richard, and his sister, Hulda, were the children of a Missouri Evangelical pastor. Reinhold was to become a leading public theologian who influenced many of the nation's politicians, political philosophers, and social ethicists. Richard, on the other hand, was a philosophical theologian who taught at Yale Divinity School. Hulda became a professor at the McCormick Theological Seminary in Chicago. Together they represented a great theological renaissance in America in the mid-twentieth century.

In 1957, the Evangelical and Reformed Church merged with the Congregational Christian Churches to form the United Church of Christ. This was an American union of denominations with divergent ethnic and theological traditions. Of course, they share some common heritage out of Reformed origins. Nevertheless, the Puritan and Anglo-Saxon character of the Congregational Christians has been difficult to harmonize with the Germanic Christianity of the Evangelical and Reformed Church. More than forty years after the merger, there is evidence of efforts to preserve the distinctive theological habits of the original participants. The heirs of the German Reformed church who are now members of the United Church of Christ often find themselves searching their history for the liturgical and theological insights that they deem necessary for meaningful existence in a secular world.

Like most of the Europeans who had made their way to North America, the leadership of the Reformed traditions sought to conduct missions among the Native Americans. They had difficulty adjusting their worldview and their sense of European Christian civilization to the religious life of the Indians and assumed for a long time that the faith and rituals of the latter were irreconcilable with Christian understanding. Although they often resisted the concept of removal to reservations, they nevertheless worked to reform Indian life in harmony with the ideals of European Christian civilization. The student of religion will want to ask whether European Christianity is the norm by means of which the insights of the Christian gospel are to be interpreted. Certainly the Christianity found in India or Egypt contrasts sharply with the Christianities of Europe and America. Another important question for the historian of religion is whether the experience of the gospel may become part of the traditions of Native American peoples.

Throughout the nineteenth century, women began to argue that their prominent roles in the lives of the churches was justification for their access to ordination and the right to preach. The Reverend Isaac M. See of Newark, New Jersey, was brought before the Presbytery of Newark in 1876, charged with encouraging a woman to preach and teach in his congregation. See maintained that, inasmuch as women spoke and taught in smaller meetings of the church, there was no scriptural basis for distinguishing between larger and smaller meetings. His argument was rejected by the Synod of New Jersey. Nevertheless, by the middle of the twentieth century, and before the advent of the feminist liberation movement, there were ordained women in several of the Reformed denominations, although they were frequently assigned the role of professional Christian educator in charge of church schools and other educational programs.

The Reformed traditions have helped to make the United States what it is. There is a nostalgia in us that seeks the assurances once held by our forebears. The academic and the professional, who have lost the explicit faith of the mothers and fathers, still assume that their thoughts and actions lie under a special mandate to transform the world, even if they do not understand the image of the kingdom of God. And, stubbornly, they like religion to remain recognizable; they want to know that it is "there," even if only to ignore or scoff at. Perhaps, just perhaps, they even know that there is no God but God—that their own postures and pretensions stand upon feet of clay. If these playthings of the theological mind still move upon the winds of our time, it may be because the Reformed tradition has made an ineradicable contribution to the American soul.

"The 'Calvinist' side of this new man," writes historian Martin E. Marty, "this American who has neither fear of hell nor hope of heaven, is nostalgic. This man looks back, as his father before him looked back, to a society and a religious context in which spirituality grew out of an agreed-upon frame of reference. He expects religious institutions today to propagate something of that earlier context's assumptions. He feels cheated when religious leaders want to lead him away from those assumptions."[8]

chapter 8

The Lutheran Tradition

> It is also taught among us that we cannot obtain forgiveness of sin and righteousness before God by our own merits, works, or satisfactions, but that we receive forgiveness of sin and become righteous before God by grace, for Christ's sake, through faith, when we believe that Christ suffered for us and that for his sake our sin is forgiven and righteousness and eternal life are given to us. For God will regard and reckon this faith as righteousness, as Paul says in Romans.

Those are the words of Article 4 of the Augsburg Confession, prepared by Philip Melanchthon for presentation to Charles V at the Diet of Augsburg in 1530. Melanchthon was the brilliant young follower of Martin Luther who helped to systematize the latter's teaching.

Verbal Expression

The Augsburg Confession expressed the heart of the Lutheran tradition of Christianity. We must remember that Luther and his followers thought of their work as a reforming activity within the Catholic Christian church of the West. The Lutherans, like all other reformers, had recovered what they considered to be the essence of Christian teaching and wished to refashion the church in accord with their discovery. When it became evident that the loyalist Reformation could not reconcile its deference to the papacy and the teaching tradition of the Church of Rome with the claims of Luther and Melanchthon, Lutherans were faced with the necessity of organizing themselves into reforming churches separate from Roman allegiance.

By the end of the sixteenth century Lutheran Christianity was well established throughout the German states and Scandinavia. In places like Sweden, Denmark, Norway, and Finland, the Lutheran Reformation tended to be successful according to its original intention. That is, the Catholic church in those countries was reformed according to the Augsburg Confession and other Lutheran principles. The Lutheran church became the established national church in those states and maintained loyalty to the Catholic order and the practice of apostolic episcopal succession.

The first Lutherans to arrive in America were Swedes and Germans. Eventually immigrants from all the Lutheran nations of Europe contributed to the diversity of American denominationalism. The Lutheran family consisted of many denominations, most of them constituted by ethnic and nationalistic ties with their European origins. Some Lutheran denominations emerged as a result of conservative reaction to the influence of modernization upon the larger Lutheran constituencies. In May 1987, three Lutheran bodies merged to form the Evangelical Lutheran Church in America, making it, with almost five and one-half million members, one of the nation's largest denominations. Only the Lutheran Church—Missouri Synod and the Wisconsin Evangelical Lutheran Synod, among major Lutheran bodies, remain outside this new Lutheran denomination.

Lutheranism is a distinctive tradition, maintaining a certain distance from the mainstream of American evangelical Protestantism, while at the same time reflecting a Pietistic aura shaped by its confessional mentality and its subjective concern for the warm assurances of justification by grace. Lutheranism has a patina all its own that awaits the careful polish of historians of religion. It is like so much of the United States in its concern for the religion of the heart, yet it is stubborn in its emphasis upon doctrine. It has a European flavor and carries the weight of centuries of experience with the consequences of human sinfulness. There is present in Lutheran faith and practice a sense of the continuing tragedy of human life, resulting from our constant disobedience to the Creator. Lutheranism focuses upon the suffering that God assumes in sharing our tragic existence. For Martin Luther there was no ladder from earth to heaven; aspiration to immediate unbroken communion with God is an illusion of the human condition. Religious speculation and thirst for knowledge gets us nowhere in our relationship with God. Ethics and right living are equally ineffective. The "theology of the cross" stood at the center of Luther's thought, and it lingers in the most Americanized versions of Lutheranism.

"To Luther," writes Lennart Pinomaa, "the cross of Christ is more than a historical event, for it demonstrates the fundamental nature of the relationship between God and man. Like a flash of lightning it illumines the life which we live. . . . But no one can appropriate this reality of the cross simply by trying to understand it. There is no room here for mere spectators. The cross of Christ decided the fate of the spectator. If he wants to enter into this life, he must . . . sink into it with his whole being."[1] There are similarities here to Mahayana Buddhism, where it becomes necessary for the individual to face the suffering at the heart of existence by transcending it through meditation or participation. When the disciple, the *bhikku,* sees through the illusions that make existence a tragedy, it is "like a flash of lightning" that "illumines the life which we live."

We have been exploring the essence of Lutheran teaching, a theoretical note that plays at the heart of all that Luther taught and wrote, and cries out from every Bach chorale. However, the intensity of Lutheran concern for the experience of salvation by faith, its emphasis upon the theology of the cross, also made the tradition open to the movement known as Pietism. And in America, Pietism easily became a work designed to gain results.

Pietism began in Europe with a mind to put some heart into the dry-as-dust Protestant orthodoxy that had taken shape by the latter seventeenth century. Almost two hundred years of doctrinal debate and polish in Protestant history had produced a stifling concern for right theology and spare-and-proper worship. This is the Pietist claim. Accordingly, the movement sought to renew the existing Lutheran and Reformed churches. It began as a movement within and was successful in affecting much of Lutheranism. There were those Lutherans who opposed it, but it left its mark upon the tradition. The earliest of German Lutherans to come to Pennsylvania were Pietist Lutherans.

Although the intentions of Pietism may be noble, it promotes an assumption that may run contrary to Luther's theology of the cross. Pietism seeks to renew. It judges the spiritual life of the church and finds it wanting, leading to an attempt to work for the evidence of justification, rather than to receive it by grace. Pietism may also become anti-intellectual and therefore theologically indifferent. It may develop a sentimental attitude about matters of faith, thereby leading to stereotypical behavior.

Historian Martin E. Marty, in an essay on "The New Face of Southern Evangelicalism," notes the Lutheran divergence from mainstream evangelical Protestantism: "Even on a statistical basis, Evangelicalism is small compared to the Roman-Orthodox-Anglican-Lutheran complex."[2] For Marty, the United States is comprised of numerous religious subcultures; there is no "*the* culture," no consensual dominance, yet he can speak of that greater "other"—that out-there Evangelicalism—against which Lutheranism stands in contrast.

We have already examined one of the themes that makes Lutheranism distinctive as an American tradition. Its confessionalism and its theology of the cross keep it from being submerged in the great wash of American subjectivism and pragmatism. No doubt the ethnic character of American Lutheran history is also a contributing factor to Lutheran distinctiveness. The tradition exists today as a major element in the understanding of American religion and culture.

Before more can be said about the verbal or theoretical expression of Lutheran religion, we must be certain we understand the nature of justification by grace through faith. It is not easily understood, and the questions raised are timeless. As a student once asked, "If it doesn't matter what you do or don't do—if you're always forgiven in the end—then what does it matter how you live?" But we must be honest learners and attempt to understand the teaching even if we do not ultimately advocate the doctrine. We are not primarily concerned with the truth or falsehood of the concept, or whether it is one we might choose to live by. We must recognize that many intelligent and honorable people live by the truth of this doctrine.

In Lutheran thought, God is holy and sovereign. In a sense, that goes without saying; after all, no Jew, Christian, or Muslim would ever agree to a notion that would deny that God is God and there is no other. However, Lutheranism approaches the doctrine of God with a heart that is intent upon finding peace of soul. Like St. Augustine, Luther was driven to find the source of his restlessness. God is the seeker, working away to draw all of us in. The holy and sovereign God is partly hidden from us and known primarily through love for us. This means that we are aware of God's presence in the judgment that stirs us up, disquiets our lives, in order that we might learn of our true natures and find peace.

Therefore, in Lutheranism, the central doctrine of justification points to the fact that God is that reality that works within us to change our wills. People who think that they may fulfill all personal wishes because it is always possible to obtain God's forgiveness are ignoring the signs in their lives that are judgments upon sinfulness and evidence of God's loving concern that they should be more than they are. Justification means that God is working to set our wills on the right track, a task we cannot accomplish by ourselves but only as we discover our helplessness. "Man's acknowledgment that God is right in judging him is the beginning of faith and justification." This acknowledgment is already faith. From this we see that faith is not belief—at least not in the sense of willing assertion or assent to doctrine. Faith is a new way of knowing. Faith is the discovery that we are more than we think we are, more than we know ordinarily. Faith is the human consciousness of God's justifying grace at work in us.

Most of our lives are spent trying to justify our own existence—to ourselves and to others, sometimes to something we call God. According to Luther, our outward lives are constantly seeking to pretend to holiness by our talents, our intelligence, and our actions. Whereas some Christian teaching assumes that the more we turn from our own self-seeking to seek the will of God, the more we are freed from sin, Luther maintained that this idea is self-deceptive. To Luther we remain sinners even when faith turns our inward lives to God. Our life's work is a constant warfare, a constant discovery of our sinfulness, a constant repentance, even though we feel that our lives have already been transformed, that is, turned in the direction of God's justification.

This teaching of Luther is a profound heritage. In these few paragraphs we have touched the surface of its complexity. Decisions about its efficacy should not be made purely on the basis of this introduction, but should be grounded in the many careful studies of Luther's theology or in the works of the great Reformer himself. Luther was a learned and penetrating thinker. His insight into the meaning of justification by grace through faith is a unique contribution to human thought, quite apart from our personal religious inclinations, and is a part of the special heritage of Lutheranism. Of course, there are many American Lutherans whose lives are informed less by the profundity of this doctrine than by the influence of American evangelical revivalism and by Pietism. The author begs leave of his status as observer in order to say: more is the pity.

Apart from the theology of the cross and the doctrine of justification, there is one other distinctive feature of Lutheranism that deserves our attention: the doctrine of the two kingdoms. "We must firmly establish secular law and the sword," wrote Luther, "that no one may doubt that it is in the world by God's will and ordinance." The state and secular authority are one of the sacred orders in this world. They are one of the orders of creation. The state functions according to its own basic nature, to keep order in a sinful world. The state is the secular authority meant to regulate the ordinary world. It operates according to its own special God-given rule: "Whoso sheddeth man's blood, by man shall his blood be shed." To Luther it was "clear and certain that it is God's will that the sword and secular law be used for the punishment of the wicked and the protection of the upright."

One of God's two kingdoms was the kingdom of this (the ordinary) world. However, there is another realm, the kingdom of God. "Those belonging to the kingdom of God are all true believers in Christ and are subject to Christ. For Christ is the King and Lord in the kingdom of God." If all people belonged to the kingdom of God, secular authority would be unnecessary. Inasmuch as we all continue to be sinners even when justified by grace, we are citizens of the ordinary world and its kingdom as well as of the kingdom of God. Luther wants us to understand that the world cannot be ruled by the gospel of the kingdom of God, nor can we expect the kingdom of this world to be transformed into the kingdom of God. We must live in two kingdoms by two different authorities under God. To the extent that we are justified Christians, we will live by the spirit of the kingdom of God; we will not go to the secular authority.

"Since, however," writes Luther, "a true Christian lives and labors on earth not for himself but for his neighbors . . . he submits most willingly to the rule of the sword, pays tax, honors those in authority, serves, helps, and does all he can to further the government. . . . Although he needs none of these things for himself and it is not necessary for him to do them, yet he considers what is for the good and profit of others." The state is that government necessary for the righteousness of our neighbors in the world under God. Spiritual government is the Christian's own, although it represents a righteousness that God expects of the world, a righteousness that judges the ordinary world and keeps its politicians and philosophers busy trying to comprehend. "Where there is only secular rule or law, there, of necessity, is sheer hypocrisy." The gospel is not directly applicable to the ordinary world, nor should the earthly government try to act as if it is the representative of God's perfect righteousness.

Again we are faced with a very complex set of theological issues. No doubt Luther failed to work out many of the implications of his thought. He was, after all, primarily a reformer of the church, a preacher, a spokesperson for the gospel and the righteousness of faith. The Lutheran tradition has maintained a steadfast loyalty to this theology of the two realms—two *regiments* of governments. This means that in contrast to the Reformed tradition, Lutherans work at the reform of society because of the needs of their neighbors, who are citizens of this world. They work with a sense of tension between the two kingdoms. Christ and culture are in paradox; the kingdom of this world is not to be transformed as it is in Calvinism.

Practical Expression

When we turn to an examination of the practical expression of the Lutheran tradition, we are faced with some curious anomalies. "It is taught among us," says the Augsburg Confession, "that the true body and blood of Christ are really present in the Supper of our Lord under the form of bread and wine." Here the objective character of the sacrament is set forth as against any memorializing tendencies such as those of Ulrich Zwingli, the Swiss Reformer. Although Luther repudiated the Roman doctrine of transubstantiation, he wished to affirm the real presence of Christ through the elements of bread and wine. Hidden in, with, and under the substances of bread and wine was the active presence of the body and blood of Christ. Yet, for Luther, grace is always present through faith. Faith, of course, is the awareness of God's judgment and reconciling love. However, the emphasis upon faith may lead people to assume that the Mass or Supper is a more outward sign of something that could take place without it. A sign bears no power. A sacrament is a bearer of power, of grace. The symbols bread and wine participate in the realities that they communicate. Article 13 of the Augsburg Confession says that the sacraments "require faith, and that they are rightly used when they are received in faith and for the purpose of strengthening faith." Without the guidance of a Luther on such matters, the people may understand the Lord's Supper not as a sacrament, but as a sign of the presence of a faith that precedes the reception of bread and wine. This way of thinking leads part of Lutheranism in the direction of a kind of Pietism that makes faith into a work, rather than evidence of grace.

This observation is made not to disparage the Lutheran tradition but to try to account for the diversity in Lutheran thought and practice. There is little doubt that many congregations and pastors practice a Christian piety that does not celebrate the sacramental objectivity of God's justifying grace but instead focuses upon the subjective faith of the individual. Initially, Martin Luther was concerned primarily with the reform of the church's theology with regard to salvation, to the justifying relationship between God and humankind. He thought that the church's use of the Mass was magical and misleading. "The sacrament was replaced by the Word," says one Lutheran historian, "and the sacrifice of the Mass was replaced by faith. . . . Luther's doctrine of the sacraments places the Word above the sacrament. . . . The life of the church is the cultivation of the Word and sacraments, but the preaching of the Word is absolutely the more important of the two."

Yet Luther wished to preserve and protect the centrality of the Mass as true worship. He defended its importance against the spiritualizers who championed the spiritual meaning of the Supper and cared nothing about the outward celebration. Against the loyalist Roman contingencies, he argued that humans do not sacrifice to God; the Mass is not a sacrifice that elicits God's favor. Nothing we can merit God's favor. Only God can confer favor upon us, favor that has been effected through Christ, once and for all. We learn this fact, receive it in our inward being when the Word of God speaks to us in Scripture and the preaching of the church. The Supper is the visible sign of this Word spoken in Christ. To receive the supper faithfully is to receive God's gift of reconciliation.

"We are unjustly accused of having abolished the Mass," says the Augsburg Confession. "Without boasting, it is manifest that the Mass is observed among us with greater devotion and more earnestness than among our opponents. Moreover, the people are instructed often and with great diligence concerning the holy sacrament . . . in order that the people may be drawn to the Communion and Mass . . . no conspicuous changes have been made . . . except that in certain places German hymns are sung in addition to the Latin responses." The Lutheran tradition shares the conviction of the magisterial Reformation that the life of the church is defined by the faithful preaching of the Word and the proper administration of the sacraments. A distinctive practical expression of Lutheranism is its preaching. The tradition arrived on the American scene in the heat of debates with the loyalist Reformation. Much of the early tradition was formed, therefore, in negative response to Roman Catholic practice. Pietism and Anti-Romanism shaped early American Lutheranism into a religion in outward appearance not unlike the Reformed. Church buildings tended to be pulpit-centered, reflecting the high esteem given to the Word of God as revealed in Scripture and preaching. The Lord's Supper may have held a more sacramental interpretation than it did for the Dutch and German Reformed churches, but it was no longer a mass and its importance was emphasized by its infrequency of celebration. Certainly theological and sociological differences separated colonial Lutheran and Reformed practice, but the differences were often too delicate in nuance for the masses of people. Their loyalties were frequently familial, regional, and ethnic—and certainly anti-Roman, antipapal.

Today, in many American churches of sixteenth- and seventeenth-century heritage, whether Lutheran, Reformed, or Puritan, there is marked similarity in liturgical practice. At one time, earlier in the century, only some Lutheran pastors and clergy of the Mercersburg tradition of German Reformed ancestry would have been seen in the traditional vestments of the Catholic heritage. The magisterial Reformation had separated itself visually from Catholicism by adopting the black gowns of Geneva. Today cassocks, surplices, white albs, and eucharistic vestments are worn by clergy of many denominations. A visitor to a Lutheran church will observe a building appointed with an altar-table at the center rather than a pulpit. In many instances the mass has returned as the central act of Christian worship, although today it is frequently called the Eucharist rather than the Mass. Historical scholarship has uncovered the liturgical practice of the early church and discovered that the Lord's Supper was celebrated whenever the Christian community assembled. It was celebrated as a great thanksgiving (a eucharist) to God, for God's justifying work in Christ. This discovery has led Lutheran and Reformed churches away from their anti-Catholic posture and practice and has returned them to the common liturgical habits of the early and the medieval church.

Lutheranism is distinguished by its theology; the verbal expression of its tradition is rich in interesting and often complex ideas. There is little doubt that Luther's emphasis upon justification by grace tended to make all other considerations of lesser consequence. Hence, there is little that is distinctive when we turn to Lutheran practice. The practical expression of Lutheranism bears no great distinguishing characteristics, unless diversity of practice is itself significant. This is not to say that the ethnic divisions of Lutheranism exhibit no unique features. We would certainly sense the differences in Finnish, Norwegian, and German Lutheran practices. We would know that Luther and the Augsburg Confession have settled into distinctive ethnic and cultural worlds where matters of dress and piety have left their measure. However, the ethnic features are not characteristically Lutheran. Governor Johan Printz instructed the Swedish Lutherans on the Delaware to give proper attention to their responsibilities of worship: ". . . and to that end all proper care shall be taken that divine service be zealously performed according to the unaltered Augsburg Confession, the Council of Uppsala, and the ceremonies of the Swedish Church." The governor saw to the decoration of the first Lutheran church building in American in 1646 "according to Swedish customs" and reported to the regent in Sweden that "the service with its ceremonies are conducted as in old Sweden" and in the "good old Swedish language."

From a practical (or practicing) standpoint, what distinguishes Lutheranism is its emphasis upon the primacy of Word and Sacrament. Sacrament without the Word becomes magic or works-righteousness; Word without sacrament risks an unhealthy emphasis upon spiritual realities that have no relationship to the world of matter in which we exist. However, as we have seen, there was an emphasis upon the Word that seemed to give it priority over sacrament.

Social Expression

The social expression of Lutheranism is a further demonstration of the diversity of a tradition with a strong confessional and theological heart. It is true that justification by grace makes all other issues pale in contrast so far as liturgical and other ritual practice is concerned. It is even more the case when we examine such matters as polity and the social forms of Lutheranism. Although Luther and his contemporaries tended to abide by the threefold ministry of Catholic order, episcopal polity and the doctrine of apostolic succession soon became issues of lesser consideration than the apostolic authority of the Scriptures and the preached Word. Many of the national Lutheran churches lost appreciation for the importance of tradition and the value of the historic ministry. Doctrine and piety became more important than church order, implying that church order could not of itself be a communicator of God's justifying grace. For a while some of the national churches deliberately maintained the ancient episcopal succession, just as Luther and his followers had done. But it was soon apparent that such matters were not of primary importance.

The United States was a natural field for diversity of polity to emerge. It was likewise conducive to the Lutheran attitude that episcopal succession was not an affair of the gospel, but incidental. America was not hospitable to the inherited tradition of Catholic Christendom. There was too much space and very little time to reach the people with the demands and promises of the gospel. Furthermore, it was often cumbersome to rely upon the efforts of bishops in a wide-ranging frontier society in which bishops were not readily available. Until recent decades, most of American Lutheranism functioned by way of a presbyterial polity. Its synods were administered by executives who were presidents—presiding officers. However, the historical and theological scholarship of the twentieth century has recovered the reality of an early Christianity that saw gospel value in the historic ministry, the sacraments, and liturgical worship. American Lutheranism has gradually turned an appreciative ear in this direction and recovered an episcopal polity, in which bishops are chief pastors and not merely administrators. Whether there is genuine understanding of the power of apostolic symbolism remains to be seen.

Luther himself had been primarily concerned that bishops remember that their office did not belong to the kingdom of this world, to the *regiments* (government) of the state. "What, then, are priests and bishops?" he asked. "I answer, their government is not one of authority or power, but a service and an office; for they are neither higher nor better than other Christians . . . their rule consists in nothing else than in dealing with God's Word, leading Christians by it and overcoming heresy by its means." And the Augsburg Confession affirmed this practice: "According to divine right . . . it is the office of the bishop to preach the Gospel, and exclude from the Christian community the ungodly. . . . All this is to be done not by human power but by God's Word alone." A bishop has no authority in the secular realm, should not assume it or be given it.

How and why is it that these priests and bishops are "neither higher nor better than other Christians?" Behind this expression of equality is the concept of the church itself in Lutheran tradition. For Luther the church is a religious reality. It is the whole company of those who have ever known God's justifying grace in Christ. The whole company is a priesthood of those who are called by Christ, who have received the gospel—the good news of God's justifying and reconciling grace. The priesthood is therefore Christ's priesthood shared by the company of believers throughout all time. This is what is meant by the phrase "priesthood of all believers." It does not mean, as popularly interpreted, that "each person is his own priest"; it is not an individualistic and subjective concept. Priesthood is shared; it exists as a divine reality or community.

The social expression of Lutheran tradition focuses upon this reality of church as priesthood of all believers, the community or fellowship of the Word. "Their community," write John Dillenberger and Claude Welch, "is anchored in a common faith in a common Lord; they meet together to hear God's Word preached and considered; they participate in the sacraments as particular and significant acts instituted in the time of the New Testament."[3] However, this Lutheran understanding goes beyond what those words may imply to the average reader. They mean that the truest form of reality is social. In the ordinary understanding of the world, reality is what is observed by the individual observer. The gospel, on the other hand, provides for a transcendence of this reality. For the gospel, reality is the reconciling work of God, known in Christ's priesthood and encountered by us as gospel in the priesthood of all believers.

In this priesthood there are no "highers" or "betters." In whatever calling we find ourselves, as believers we are called to responsible fulfillment of our tasks. The difference between the farmer and the bishop is one of function. Even though bishops, as teachers of the gospel, may be better versed in doctrine and Scripture, they are not necessarily closer to the justifying faith of the gospel than the farmer. Each of us has a vocation, a calling to fulfill a certain task in life as a member of the priesthood of believers and a citizen of the kingdom of this world.

History in the United States

"The story of the Lutheran Church in America," writes Lutheran historian Abdel Ross Wentz, "is best told as a part of the great fabric of American history, for the religious life of a people is enmeshed in political and social life. . . . Thus there are significant parallels between the nation's political history and the story of the Lutheran Church in America."[4] The latter story begins in the New Netherlands, where Lutherans shared the commercial development of the colony with their Reformed compatriots beginning in 1623 and 1625. Forced to attend the services of the established Dutch Reformed church, these Lutherans adopted many of the practices of the Reformed tradition. Wentz tells us they resembled their neighbors in polity and liturgical order. "The only distinctive Lutheran element in the order of service was the requirement that the sermon be based on the Gospel appointed for the day."

The Swedish Lutherans along the Delaware had the benefit of direct support from their homeland. Their devotional literature, hymnals, and catechisms were supplied. A pastor served the colony and saw to the careful observance of Swedish Lutheran practice. In the outlying areas, laypersons were appointed to lead simplified services of prayer and Bible reading, along with the use of collections of sermons especially prepared.

With the opening of Penn's colony, Lutheran and Reformed colonists from the German Rhineland began settling the territory. They came from an area where religious oppression and strife had virtually decimated their lands. They came as simple farmers and artisans and were often determined to live together in harmony. These Germans had come to a new and promised land in which they hoped to avoid the dissensions of the Palatinate. The Lutherans wished to remain loyal to the Augsburg Confession and their own practices while avoiding conflict with their fellow Germans of the Reformed tradition. There were two loyalties to preserve in a culture that was increasingly English: it was important to be Lutheran and to respect the German language and culture. Often this led to the sharing of a church building with a Reformed congregation. In rural and small-town Pennsylvania, it is still possible to see the evidence of this practice. Union churches, as they were called, still exist as buildings shared by Lutheran and Reformed congregations. In the affluence of the twentieth century, many union church congregations have managed to grow and to acquire the means to construct separate buildings. The result has been the buying-out of the share of a common building and frequently, the construction of a new edifice across the street from the former union church building. In the villages and countryside of Pennsylvania, we may see Lutheran and Reformed congregations with their own buildings, one of them usually occupying the original union edifice. By 1771 there were eighty-one Lutheran congregations in Pennsylvania and neighboring colonies, along with thirty more in other sections of the American settlements.

The Lutheran and the German Reformed managed to live in relative harmony. They were not so hospitable to the Mennonites, Amish, and Church of the Brethren people—the Anabaptists who also shared the German language. Luther himself had called these folk "crude spirits" because they misunderstood his emphasis upon faith and made faith a prerequisite for baptism. "Baptism," he said, "is water with the Word of God, not water and my faith. My faith does not make the baptism but rather receives the baptism, no matter whether the person being baptized believes or not; for baptism is not dependent upon my faith but upon God's Word." Anabaptists could not keep the two *regiments* apart; they tried to impose the righteousness of faith as norms by which the world should be governed. They left the "Kingdom of this world," which was also of God's ordering, to madmen and evildoers, because they insisted on separating themselves from the world in favor of living a righteous life—rather than living by the righteousness of God's Word.

When their fellow German Lutheran, Count Nicholas von Zinzendorf, came to America in 1741 as a member of the Unitas Fratrum (or Moravians), he sought to bring together all Christian groups into a single communion. He was especially zealous in this kind of ecumenical or interdenominational activity among his fellow Lutherans and the German Reformed. The Moravians had settled in Georgia in 1735, working among the slaves and Native Americans. They moved to Pennsylvania in 1740 and established the towns of Nazareth and Bethlehem. Pennsylvania at this time was a colony of diverse religious groups, many of them German in background. They had little organization and almost no educated leadership. These circumstances provided an excellent opportunity for Zinzendorf to attempt to bring these people together in "the Church of God in the Spirit." He held several consultations toward that end.

Zinzendorf did not understand that religion does many things. It is not only an affair of the spirit dealing with the salvation of souls. Even if this is the major intention of a religious tradition, it rather quickly takes on other religious features. One of these is the need for social identity. Whatever else religions do, they help us know what kind of world we live in and who we are in relation to that world. Inasmuch as reality is social, identity is a social and cosmological affair. It is important to be able to identify ourselves not merely by private name (which is itself a social practice), but also by being a Buddhist, a Christian, a Lutheran from Frankfurt. The people with whom Zinzendorf consulted were not certain of what he was trying to do; they were not sure they wished to give up being Lutheran in order to belong to "the Church of God in the Spirit." And religious leaders began to wonder whether Zinzendorf was not trying to capitalize on the shepherdless conditions of German-American religious life. Was he hoping to create a large "Moravian" church under his own control and direction?

The situation was serious enough to motivate decision among Lutheran authorities in Germany. They had either to provide adequate pastoral leadership for their people in Pennsylvania or to give up their tradition to the designs of an idealistic zealot who had been consecrated a bishop by the Unitas Fratrum. They responded by dispatching from Halle the man who was to become the "patriarch" of American Lutheranism, Henry Melchior Mühlenberg. He arrived in 1742, in the midst of the movement known as the Great Awakening (see chap. 11). For the present, it is sufficient to know that this movement marked the beginning of American revivalism, a distinctive tradition in American religion and culture. The movement brought about renewed interest in the church and Christianity, but sometimes its excesses led to chaotic results. Mühlenberg came among a people who had been influenced by Zinzendorf and were frequently the easy victims of religious enthusiasts who sought a following among those who despaired of life on the frontier.

The German immigrants came as individuals and families, not as communities like the Plymouth and Massachusetts Bay Puritans. Many were too poor to manage their own fare for the ocean voyage. They came as "redemptioners" who agreed to specified years of service as indentured servants in payment for their trip's passage. Most were ill-prepared to support a clergy and, by the time Mühlenberg arrived, had been accustomed to laxity in ecclesiastical matters. He began service as pastor to Lutherans in Philadelphia but quickly extended his care to include other congregations in eastern Pennsylvania. There was no bishop in the American church, but Mühlenberg played an "Episcopal" role as overseer of many of America's Lutherans. He was frequently called upon to solve problems in places quite distant from Philadelphia. His diaries provide significant insight into the religious and social life of America in the mid-eighteenth century. Mühlenberg was the right man for the times. The ministerium of Pennsylvania was organized in 1748, setting the stage for further development of colonial Lutheranism.

With the birth of the new nation, the burgeoning of the frontier, and the sweeping influence of nineteenth-century revivalism, came an Americanizing influence that awakened the slumbering confessional soul of the Lutheran tradition. Americanization was, of course, a natural and understandable process in a pluralistic frontier society concerned with the fashioning of a new nation, a new people. To many, the times called for a diminution of ethnic distinctions in favor of the English language and the development of a common national culture. Inasmuch as evangelical Protestantism appeared to be the dominant religious orientation of Americans, it made sense to many that certain denominational distinctions should be sacrificed in favor of a common heritage. Samuel S. Schmucker (1779–1873), president of the Lutheran seminary at Gettysburg, was himself a graduate of Princeton, a Presbyterian institution, and became an advocate of Americanization. His *Fraternal Appeal,* issued in 1838, called for the formation of an Apostolic Protestant church. A certain reaction against this de-Lutheranizing summons was intensified by the increased numbers of German immigrants who swelled the ranks of the tradition by mid-century. Like all first-generation immigrants, the new Lutherans wished to preserve their identity in an alien land. They sought the special security of their faith and practice. The result was a renewal of confessionalism in the face of revivalism and Americanization. Charles Philip Krauth and his son Charles Porterfield Krauth emerged as leaders in the movement to affirm faithfulness to Lutheran orthodoxy and to reclaim the liturgical and sacramental heritage of Catholic Christianity.

The eastern Lutherans were aided in their renewed confessionalism by the arrival in Missouri of those who were to form the Evangelical Lutheran Synod of Missouri in 1847. These people had come from Saxony where they had despaired of preserving the integrity of the Augsburg Confession because of the efforts in that homeland to bring Lutheran and Reformed traditions together. The Missouri Synod Lutherans have remained a conservative force for strict doctrinal interpretation of Christianity. Although they participate in the discussions of the national Lutheran Council and in certain ecumenical organizations that do not compromise their confessionalism, the

Missouri Synod Lutherans frequently consider other Lutherans to be compromisers with modernity.

During much of its life in America, the Lutheran tradition has been fragmented by its ethnic pluralism. Lutheran immigration tended to seek lands where the people could live their lives in relative isolation from other populations. Their communities were ethnic islands where their Lutheranism was a major force in their social order. In the Upper Midwest they managed to keep their perception of the world in a self-contained manner, affecting the social and cultural history of Missouri, Minnesota, Wisconsin, and parts of Illinois. Pennsylvania, of course, bears the unmistakable stamp of the Lutheran influence of earlier German immigrations. Lutheranism, as a whole, had grown to the point where its unorganized diversity accounted for a major proportion of non-Roman Christianity. Lutherans stood behind Methodists and Baptists in numerical strength by the beginning of the twentieth century. By 1960 the number of Lutheran denominations was reduced by the gradual merger and union of German and Norwegian groups to form the American Lutheran Church, and of the United Lutheran Church in America with Swedish, Finnish, and Spanish bodies to form the Lutheran Church in America.

The Lutheran Church—Missouri Synod, writes Edwin S. Gaustad, "stepped away from broader cooperation, even within the Lutheran family itself. All this occurred in the context of what one religious journalist called 'the Great Lutheran Civil War'" of the mid-1970s. The "war" was fought over the "authority of the Bible," an important Lutheran issue. Some Missouri Synod leaders were concerned that the faculty of Concordia Seminary in St. Louis were compromising that authority as a result of the influence of critical and historical biblical scholarship. Liberal interpretations were viewed as a threat to biblical authority. Perhaps the scholars were too susceptible to the temptations of modernity and ecumenical cooperation at any price. An attempt was made to stem the tide of "liberalism" within the seminary. The president of Concordia was fired, along with many of the faculty. Two hundred or more congregations withdrew from the Missouri Synod and eventually formed the Association of Evangelical Lutheran Churches. These ecumenically minded schismatics joined with the American Lutheran Church and the Lutheran Church in America to form the most recent of Lutheran mergers, mentioned at the beginning of this chapter.

During the early centuries of Lutheran history in America, the church was often hindered by its ethnicity, its lack of coordinated national authority, and its inherited interpretation of the doctrine of the "two kingdoms," which we have discussed. As Sydney E. Ahlstrom points out: "Lutheran synods . . . tended to be organized on a territorial basis, so that the extreme views did not meet at [the level of national coherence on the slavery controversy]. . . . For Lutherans . . . a truly 'national' echelon was virtually nonexistent, since the General Synod, which often took a strong antislavery stand, had little more than advisory or coordinating functions."[5]

Moreover, the doctrine of the two kingdoms was interpreted to mean that issues like slavery were not in the domain of the church as representatives of the Kingdom of God, but of the political order, the state. Relations with Native Americans during the colonial period were shaped by missionary attempts to provide Bibles and Luther's Catechism in the Indian languages. Lutherans from the Austrian province of Salzburg, who settled in General Oglethorp's Moravian colony of Georgia, deprecated slavery and worked at the Christianization of Indians. Slaves who converted pledged not to use their Christian status to break the bonds of obedience to their masters, and Indians were expected to conform to Euro-American church life, rejecting their traditional religious life and culture upon conversion. A Lutheran layman, Conrad Weiser, father-in-law of Mühlenberg, became well-acquainted with the Indians. His influence among Eastern tribes is thought to account for the fact that the Iroquois remained neutral during the French and Indian War (1754–63). Yet an Iroquois leader expressed his confusion on these matters by saying: "We don't know what you Christians, English and French together, intend; we are so hemmed in by both, that we have hardly a hunting place left. . . . We are so perplexed . . . that we hardly know what to say or think."

As the Indians retreated farther into the wilderness, their hostility increased and contacts with the Euro-Americans were diminished. Nevertheless, Lutheran clergy supported the advance of the whites and continued to assume that conversion to the ideals of European Christian behavior was the surest way to deal with the effects of encounter between the two peoples.

Until well into the twentieth century, Lutheran attitudes toward women tended to be conservative, confining their roles to the leadership they provided for missionary societies and other women's organizations. Here again, the continuing ethnic character of Lutheranism and its lack of effective ecclesiastical unity combined with its doctrine of the two kingdoms to make radical change in women's roles in theology and practice unlikely until very recently.

It would be interesting to explore in detail the manner in which the Lutheran tradition has been shaped by the particularities of the American religious experience. Certainly it is a unique feature of our religious landscape. It has emerged in the twentieth century as a very churchly and liturgical tradition, concerned with renewing the relationship with the church of Rome, especially since Vatican Council II. Lutheranism in America has reclaimed its appreciation for episcopal succession and often understands itself as non-Protestant, as does Anglicanism. Certainly its confessionalism and devotion to careful theology make it a tradition set apart from much of American religion. Yet it has been shaped also by American brands of Pietism and by the strongly private and salvationist character of revivalism. Both in its confessional reaction to mainstream evangelical Christianity and in its subtle adaptation to individualism, Lutheranism shows its American religiosity.

Without Lutheranism, our history and culture would be much the poorer. Lutheranism provided influential leadership and, along with the German Reformed church, gave a distinctive character to colonial Pennsylvania, a character that is still evident in our own time. In the great ethnic enclaves of the Midwest and the old Northwest, the Lutheran tradition offered its teaching, its pastoral care, and its church buildings to sustain the lives of a pioneer people who fashioned the soul of America.

chapter 9

The Roman Catholic Tradition

As an introduction to this chapter we may consider the true story of a semi-retired Episcopal priest who had converted to Anglicanism from Roman Catholicism many years ago. A native of Spain, he had been born and raised a Roman Catholic and had come to the United States as a priest of the Roman church. He had changed his priesthood in the 1950s, before the days of Vatican Council II and before the disaffections of those Roman priests who sought marriage and family life in the 1960s and beyond. Father Perez (not his real name) was assigned to a small Mexican-American mission in the Southwest. Although most Mexican-Americans are Roman Catholic in culture and tradition, this little mission of San Miguel was an Episcopal mission. Many of the people in that section of the city were no longer active participants in the life of any church. Father Perez visited them when they were sick. He helped them when they were hungry or in trouble. He saw them in their homes, in the hospital—sometimes in prison. To Father Perez the mission of the church was one of sharing the grace of God, not getting members. Some of the people began to come to Eucharist, or mass, at little San Miguel. They were confused at what took place.

"Father Perez," they asked him, "Why does this church seem so much like the Catholic church?"

"This *is* the Catholic church!" replied Father Perez. "It is the Catholic church without the pope!"

It is our purpose here to gain some understanding of Roman Catholicism, the Catholic church *with* the Pope.

Richard P. McBrien of the University of Notre Dame wrote in 1975:

> What finally differentiates Roman Catholics from all other Christians is in the realm of ecclesiastical order. Roman Catholics alone are committed to the papacy as a necessary and indispensable office within the Church. The Pope, by the will of Christ, exercises the Petrine ministry

of supervision for the whole Church. . . . Roman Catholics are committed to the view that the Church cannot fully be the Church without the Pope. . . . The ecumenical question which still divides Roman Catholics from all other Christians is the question of ecclesiastical office. Authority, infallibility, apostolic succession, and the like, are but component parts of that issue.[1]

It may not be the case any longer that the question of ecclesiastical office and the papacy is what "divides Roman Catholics from all other Christians." Certainly, many traditions that share a loyalty to Catholic order—such as Anglicanism, Orthodoxy, and Lutheranism in an increasing manner—no longer see the papacy as a necessary obstacle to reunion. They are at least able to accept the symbolic value of the papal office. They may accept its value as a symbol of unity and a means of significant encounter with a secular world that is no longer familiar with the claims of the Christian gospel and the teachings of Christianity. It could be said that the papacy is more essential than ever before. It could represent a perception of the world that has important implications for the future of humankind. There may still be differences of interpretations of the papacy among churches of Catholic persuasion. However, the importance of the papal office is no longer an insurmountable obstacle to greater Christian unity.

Nevertheless, it remains true that the Roman Catholic tradition of Christianity is the only tradition bearing the long history of the unique office of the papacy. The loyalist Reformation (see chap. 3) held to the necessity of faithfulness and obedience to the authority of the bishop of Rome. Therefore, any understanding of Roman Catholicism must begin with a discussion of that authority. Who is the pope? What is the origin of the papacy?

The Verbal Expression: Papal Authority

The pope is the bishop of Rome, who is heir to the authority of the first bishop of Rome, which tradition claims was Simon Peter. Accordingly, the theoretical basis for papal authority is what has been called Petrine doctrine. The early and apostolic Christian community very soon developed a tradition that claimed a special order among the apostles—disciples who are sent forth as messengers. Apostles have a special authority inasmuch as they are the bearers of an original message or mandate. The tradition of an apostolic order is already present in the writings (Scriptures) that became the New Testament.

At the head of the order were Peter and Paul, the latter a later addition to the original apostolic community. However, it was Peter who shared a special relationship to Jesus the Christ. Peter was apparently a rather impetuous person who would jump to his master's defense unthinkingly, sometimes even to the point of cutting off the ear of the assistant of a high priest (cf. Matthew 26:51; John 18:10). Peter did not always comprehend the sayings and actions of his master/teacher, but he was faithful. A very human and conscience-smitten person, he had even denied his loyalty at the time of Jesus' crucifixion in order to avoid detention himself. But he repented; he always came back. Somehow he was a typical follower—an ordinary human being—filled with courage at one moment, frightened the next.

Tradition tells us that this man eventually went to Rome to establish the apostolic community there. He was a faithful apostle and bishop (*episkopos,* overseer) who was finally crucified himself—upside down at his own request, in order not to assume that his crucifixion was on a par with that of his master. The scriptural basis for the primacy of Peter in the apostolic order is found in Matthew's Gospel:

> "But who do you say that I am?" Simon Peter replied, "You are the Christ, the Son of the living God." And Jesus answered him, "Blessed are you, Simon Bar-Jona! For flesh and blood has not revealed this to you, but my Father who is in heaven. And I tell you, you are Peter, and on this rock I will build my church, and the powers of death shall not prevail against it. I will give you the keys of the kingdom of heaven, and whatever you bind on earth shall be bound in heaven, and whatever you loose on earth shall be loosed in heaven. [16:15-19; note that the man's name was Simon, Son of ("Bar") Jona.]

Simon made a confession, or a profession, that Jesus was not merely a teacher. He gave witness to the fact that in Jesus the Messiah (the Christ) had come. Simon said, "You are the Christ. . . ." The scriptural tradition informs us that Simon also believed that God was present in Jesus—God in the fullness of humanity. For Simon, the role of the Messiah was not merely that of a political leader come to restore the Davidic kingdom of Israel. The Messiah (the Christ) was the incarnation—the embodiment—of God. "You are the Christ," professed Simon, "the Son of the living God." On the basis of this confession, Jesus observed that Simon had been granted the power of a transformed perception. He no longer perceived with an ordinary mind—the secret at the heart of the world's great religions. Jesus recognized this in Simon's confession, which is why he said, "Blessed are you, Simon, son of Jona! For flesh and blood [that is, ordinary knowledge] has not revealed this to you, but my Father who is in heaven." This is like saying, "Only God can know God. What you have just professed cannot be known by ordinary mind (flesh and blood). God has revealed it; God has transformed your mind in order for you to perceive this truth." Because Jesus recognized this divine action in the life of the simple fisherman Simon, he told him, "You are Peter [Greek: *petros,* rock], and on this rock I will build my church, and the powers of death shall not prevail against it."

This statement of Jesus, recorded in Matthew, is the basis of Petrine theory, the substance of which is that the foundation of the church is Simon and his confession. That Simon was able to make this confession was itself a sign of his chosenness. Simon becomes Peter, the rock (foundation) of the divine institution, the church. This Petrine theory is what distinguishes Roman Catholicism from the rest of Christianity. The selection of Peter as the foundation of the church gives rise to the teaching that his office as bishop (first apostle) of Rome has been bestowed with a primary authority in the life of the church. His successors in that office share the distinction. The authority of Peter and the office established by his confession is further clarified by the last sentence of the above scriptural quotation: "I will give you the keys of the kingdom of heaven, and whatever you bind on earth shall be bound in heaven, and whatever you loose on earth shall be loosed in heaven." This is why it is always St. Peter who sits at the gates of heaven in legends and jokes about the afterlife. He holds the "keys."

Petrine theory, in other words, insists that the authority of Peter and his successors is the basic authority for judgment about God's promises on earth. Peter has understood the promises of God made known in Jesus the Christ. That insight now serves as the authority by means of which all of humanity may share those promises. Just what "heaven" means is a source of theological debate. In the folk understanding of Christianity, heaven means primarily an afterlife state of being. However, there is little doubt that it means more than that. It implies a new social order, a new way of apprehending what is real. Heaven is a new set of relationships that is shared by those who apprehend "eternal life" in the here and now. In Buddhism we would find a similar problem with the meaning of "nirvana" or of the "Pure Land to the West." These terms connote a present reality, but they are filled with future and afterlife implications—especially on the folk level. So, when

Peter is given the keys of the kingdom of heaven; he is given something that is the basis for a lifetime of meditation. To Roman Catholicism, Peter's authority is shared by his successors. It is an authority over the forgiveness of sins and the key to "eternal life." The reader should not be hasty in drawing conclusions about the meaning of the "kingdom of heaven" or assume that she or he knows what that means. Instead, the reader should accept the fact that its meaning is something to be learned, and to the extent that she or he begins to understand it, it may be because "flesh and blood" has not revealed it. It is possible that its meaning is only comprehensible to one who does not think with an ordinary mind.

In trying to understand the history of the emergence of papal priority, we are faced with a chicken-or-egg situation. Many historians of early Christianity will acknowledge the fact that a Christian tradition existed prior to the development of Scripture (writings). That is, there was a body of Christian teaching and practice—a tradition—which is later reflected in the writings (scriptures) of those who produced the Gospels and Epistles of the first-century church. A reading of Scripture leads us to the conclusion that a proclamation about Jesus the Christ and a way of celebrating his significance was in existence shortly after the time of Jesus' death and resurrection. The Scriptures reflect a developing Christian tradition. In the Scriptures we may read of the prominence of Peter and later Paul among the apostolic followers of Jesus. Peter is already a leading figure in "scriptural times"—some scholars would say that his leadership was foremost only among those Christians who wished to remain Jews.

Early church history also indicates a certain deference given to the bishop of Rome, for whatever reason. After all, Rome was the seat of the Roman Empire. Until the fourth century it dominated the cities of the empire, and the church of the capital city became strong and politically significant. When Emperor Constantine tried to establish his new capital in Constantinople, the power of Rome was threatened. It may have been at that time that the church in the western part of the empire sought to preserve the power of the West by emphasizing the spiritual supremacy of the church of Rome and its bishop. By that time (the fourth century) the empire had begun to look favorably upon Christianity as the spiritual foundation of the empire, its society and culture.

Petrine theory alone could not account for the rise of papal authority. Peter's authority had already been established in Christian tradition. The Church of Rome had emerged as a leading and powerful representative of

Christianity. And the Christianization of the empire, along with the rise of Constantinople, called for a leader who could bring the barbarian chieftains and their peoples into the Christian church so that the religious, political, and cultural unity of the Western Empire would be guaranteed. A combination of theory and political reality were refined in the fires of history to create one of the most unique forms of religious leadership in the entire history of religions. Although there may be parallels to the role of the papacy, such as the Dalai Lama of Tibetan Buddhism, none is as universal in its extension throughout history and the earth. The faithful Roman Catholic might well say that the continuing existence and authority of the papacy is a vindication of the Gospel of Matthew's claim that the church is built upon this rock "and the powers of death shall not prevail against it."

An examination of the papacy as a distinguishing feature of Roman Catholic tradition should include a discussion of the doctrine of papal infallibility. This is a teaching that easily lends itself to misunderstanding, and the outsider does not often find guidance to understanding from Roman Catholic friends and acquaintances. Many Roman Catholics speak of the strictness of their tradition. They remember the priest or the nun who told them they should not question the church's teaching, but they did not realize that it was the defensive inability of the particular priest or nun to answer the questions that made him or her hide behind some false notion of authority. The Roman Catholic church has always questioned its teachings. Without questions there would be no theology. Some of the world's leading artists, scientists, and intellectuals have been converts to Roman Catholicism, even in the twentieth century, as a result of questioning that has found answers in the Roman Catholic tradition. Walker Percy, a psychiatrist turned novelist, who also converted to Catholicism toward the end of the past century, put it this way: "The salient truth of life is not the teaching of a great philosopher or the enlightenment of a great sage. It was, rather, the belief that something had happened, an actual Event in historic time." The conditions of life, said Percy, are such that what we need is a "message in a bottle." For Catholicism, the bottle is very important.

Stereotypical views of the teaching authority of the church and of papal infallibility must be cast aside if we are to understand this religious tradition. First of all, papal infallibility does not mean the pope can do no wrong, that he is not a sinner. Only Jesus Christ is without sin. Sinlessness is present in the church and its bishops only to the extent that Christ's sinlessness is present in his Body, the church. The members of the church are "earthen vessels" (as St. Paul called them)—the treasure of Christ is present in less-than-perfect containers, including that of the pope. Only the Body in its wholeness is perfect, and that perfection is not visible in life as we know it.

Papal infallibility does not mean that everything the pope says or does is infallible—to be accepted and obeyed without question. Obviously, there is a significant and important authority to the papacy. A faithful Roman Catholic will take the statements, the circular letters, the teachings of the papacy with great seriousness and seek to understand and learn from those statements because they derive from the office that bears the authority delegated by Jesus to Simon bar-Jona. The faithful Roman Catholic will not confront a papal encyclical[2] with an attitude of defiance, but with recognition that the teaching seeks to represent the wisdom of the church on the matter discussed. It is not likely to be the pope's personal opinion but the result of his prayerful deliberation with other bishops and theologians and a careful study of the past teaching of the church. Nonetheless, this important teaching authority of the papal office, distributed by encyclicals, is also not infallible.

In a sense, a papal pronouncement is infallible only when it is said to be so. Only when the pope speaks *ex cathedra* (from the throne of St. Peter) on matters of faith and morals proclaimed as infallible teaching is the teaching in fact infallible. The throne of Peter obviously plays an important symbolic role. The pope is not likely to proclaim a doctrine from that throne unless it is a matter of utmost importance to the faith of the church. That is to say, infallibility is related only to those matters considered necessary to eternal salvation. An infallible teaching would be part of the deposit of divine revelation. An infallible pronouncement would contain nothing new or novel; rather, it would be a clarifying of something that had been implicit in the revelation since earliest times, or part of the faith and practice of the church that had never before been carefully defined.

The dogma of papal infallibility was formulated in 1870 during the sessions of Vatican Council I. One of the reasons for its formulation was the increased strength of the Roman Catholic Church in this country. As the United States reshaped the traditions of Europe to fit its own religious needs, in the case of Roman Catholicism a hierarchical and monarchistic polity had to adjust to the democratic ways of the youthful nation. It took the Vatican and European Catholicism a long time to understand the independent ideas and practices of America. The polity and the theology of the church in this country were gradually adapting to the promised land of freedom, equality, and opportunity. The Vatican and the papacy were for a time disturbed at these American developments; one of their early responses was the dogma (teaching) of papal infallibility, a reminder to Roman Catholics everywhere (perhaps especially in the United States) that matters of fundamental doctrine were not to be tampered with but were under the protection of the papacy. Only once since the formulation of 1870 has an infallible pronouncement occurred. In 1950 Pope Pius XII defined the dogma of the Assumption of the Blessed Virgin Mary, teaching that Mary, "having completed her earthly life, was in body and soul assumed into heavenly glory." According to the church's theologians, the dogma was meant to confer doctrinal authority upon a practice (practical expression) that is at least as old as the seventh century. Many faithful members of the Christian community had believed that the purity of Mary as the vessel of incarnation was not stained by death, that Mary was assumed into the celestial realm in a manner similar to the ascension of Christ, and they celebrated this belief in many ways. In 1950 it was given proper clarification and proclaimed a dogma necessary to salvation.

Although papal authority is a distinguishing feature of the Roman Catholic tradition, it is not the only one. At least until Vatican Council II,[3] the tradition had been a highly elaborate and sophisticated system of faith and practice. Roman Catholic theology is too extensive a subject to comprehend within the pages of an introductory chapter. The thought is intricate and intellectual on the one hand and highly influenced by folk beliefs and practices on the other.

Other Features of Verbal Expression

Roman Catholic theory is characterized by a high doctrine of revelation. The theology of this tradition has been notably affected by the system of the medieval theologian Thomas Aquinas, but something about the nature of Roman Catholic thought from its inception inclined in the direction of what came to be Thomas's system. Thomas wished to resolve the problem of the relationship between faith and reason. He wanted to construct a system of Christian thought that would be as magnificent an edifice as a Gothic cathedral or as Dante's literary masterpieces. This system presumes that reason is a God-given human attribute, provided in order that we may "read" the universe of things and beings, and gain a glimpse of the Creator. However, reason no longer sees as it should; the fall has had a traumatic effect upon our vision. We can still see, of course; reason still functions. It can tell us *that* God

is or *that there is* God. But from that point on, reason is lost, except as it is res-
cued by faith. Faith provides the necessary vision to see *who* God is, what
God is like, what God requires of us. Faith can only accomplish this task by
way of revelation. Revelation is the means of knowing God (not of knowing
the fact that God is, which reason can accomplish); the knowing itself is different from the knowing done by reason. The knowing made possible by revelation is faith; it is a message in a bottle, floating in to stranded people.

The record of revelation is found in Scripture (the writings of the Hebrew
Bible and New Testament) and in the ongoing tradition of the church. "This
tradition which comes from the apostles," says the Constitution on Divine
Revelation of Vatican Council II, "develops in the Church with the help of the
Holy Spirit. For there is a growth in the understanding of the realities and the
words which have been handed down. . . . Sacred tradition and sacred Scripture form one sacred deposit of the word of God, which is committed to the
Church. . . . The task of authentically interpreting the word of God, whether
written or handed on, has been entrusted exclusively to the living teaching
office of the Church, whose authority is exercised in the name of Jesus
Christ." Most Protestant traditions grant no authority to anything other than
Scriptures and private judgment. They ascribe no teaching authority to the
church and acknowledge no authority for anything known as "sacred tradition." (It might be said in passing that this set of distinctions between Protestantism and Roman Catholicism may be breaking down. Critical and
historical scholarship of Scripture and early Christianity has had the effect of
demonstrating the importance of a tradition in existence before the writing
of the New Testament documents, and it is more and more recognized that
interpretation of Scripture should not be done privately but in the context of
a community and, acknowledging the interpretations of theologians and
others, recorded in commentaries throughout Christian history.)

Roman Catholic emphasis upon the comprehensive and hierarchical
character of divine revelation (the Word of God) has been in keeping with its
understanding of the gospel as a truth entrusted to Peter, a truth that is
"handed on," passed down from apostolic authority to those who would
receive it. Richard P. McBrien writes of a "configuration of characteristics
within Catholicism that is not duplicated anywhere else in the community of
Christian Churches." This configuration is comprised of the principles of
sacramentality, mediation, and communion.[4] Some scholars might say that
these three principles are characteristic of all catholicism—Roman, Anglican, or Orthodox. However, it may help our understanding of the Roman
tradition to examine McBrien's meaning.

Sacramentality, according to McBrien, is the perspective that sees God in and through all things. He states that the Catholic (that is, Roman), "unlike Luther, espouses no doctrine of the Two Kingdoms." All authentic human progress and achievement of peace and justice are part of a "movement of and toward the Kingdom of God." Sacramentality, says McBrien, insists that all things are potential carriers of divine presence. We may agree with McBrien that sacramentality is a feature of Catholicism that distinguishes it from other forms of Christianity. However, it is not because God is every-where an immanent and abiding presence; rather, it is because God has demonstrated in the incarnation the potentiality of nature as the vehicle of grace. The Protestant tends to understand faith or experience as a precondi-tion, signed, in effect, with an action called sacrament. The Catholic (Roman, Anglican, or Orthodox) is aware of the fact that God makes a sacrament out of nature by taking a natural action and making it the occasion for the grace that is known in Jesus the Christ. The grace elicits faith because it is the church—the body of Christ—that celebrates the sacramental occasion.

"Catholicism holds," writes McBrien, "that the encounter with God is a *mediated* experience, rooted in the historical, and affirmed as real by the crit-ical judgment that God is truly present here or there, in this event or that, in this person or that, in this object or that." Again, the definition of Catholic mediation holds until McBrien has God truly "present, here or there, in this event or that" (and so on). The latter ideas suspiciously resemble so much theophany,[5] God present everywhere God chooses. The *mediational* principle of Catholicism really points to the fact that God is only observable by those who have eyes to see. By nature we have lost the ability to see clearly, but the necessary perception is mediated by the presence of Christ in his body, enabling us to see God. We cannot do it by means of private judgment and Scripture, only by living in the mediating life of the Body of Christ, the church.

The sacramental and mediated way is also a *communal* way, says McBrien. "Even when the divine-human encounter is most personal and individual, it is still communal, in that the encounter is made possible by the mediation of a *community* of faith." All three of these principles are characteristics of Christian catholicity. They may at one time have been most carefully pre-served by Roman Catholicism, Orthodoxy, and Anglicanism. However, catholicity is no longer the unique heritage of these great Catholic traditions; rather, it has asserted itself into the thinking and practice of a wider segment of the Christian world. Only when these three principles are related to Petrine theory and a high doctrine of revelation do they point to a distinctive religious tradition. The "outsider" who observes Roman Catholics at worship and reads Roman Catholic theology is usually confronted with a form of Christianity that he or she must be at pains to understand. Perhaps this is less the case than was so before Vatican Council II. Now, frequently, the observer is aware of a certain "protestantizing" of worship and a modification of Roman dogma to conform to the mythology of the modern world. McBrien's three principles have become isolated from their association with revelation and apostolicity. The mystery of the church is lost by folksy identification with the unexamined "needs" of modernity.

We must remember, of course, that much of what we have known as Roman Catholicism in modern history has been the result of the loyalist Reformation (explored in chap. 3). The Council of Trent gave concise defin-ition to much of what had remained loosely contained within the Catholic church prior to the sixteenth century. Medieval Western Christianity had permitted more diversity in practice and thought than is generally imagined. Much of the supposed "rigidity" of Roman faith and practice is the result of a defensive posture in relation to a reformation that threatened the authority of the church and fractured its unity. Roman Catholicism was faced with an increasingly hostile Protestantism. In northern Europe, the British Isles, and most of North America, anti-Romanism was to hold sway for generations, causing a greater rigidity in Roman faith and practice than might ordinarily have been the case.

Practical Expression

In considering the practical expression of the Roman tradition, we come face-to-face with one of the most unique of religious practices, the Mass. This is the central act of worship and an illustration of all three of McBrien's principles. The Mass is a sacramental, mediating, and communing practice. Its meaning has been developed through centuries of observance. As a ritual process, the Mass reveals a structure that has influenced all forms of Christ-ian worship. However, it has been a more objective event than most Protes-tant worship. For much of Roman theology, the Mass does not depend upon the intentions of a congregation of worshipers. The Mass, in effect, is some-thing God does. It is as objective an occurrence as the consummation of a marriage, the flight of a condor, or an anniversary dinner. It takes place. Its meaning is not subjective, but objective. Or better, regardless of the degree of subjective meaning derived from it, it is there for us. For a time it was so objective an event that the priest could celebrate it alone, apparently disregarding its communal dimension.

The Mass begins as a ritual reenactment of the last supper of Jesus with his disciples. This reenactment takes place, says the tradition recorded in Scripture, because Jesus *instituted* it. The supper became the Lord's Supper, the solemn yet joyous occasion of communion with the one who had become Lord by his victory over death. In earliest practice, the apostolic community reenacted the Lord's Supper regularly. For them it was a thankful moment in which they communed with their risen Lord. The scriptural tradition even spoke of the postresurrection appearances of Christ as occasions in which recognition depended upon a shared supper.

Even the earliest of supper traditions suggests a certain objective character to the event; Roman Catholic teaching assumes that the church is custodian of an ever-developing understanding of the apostolic faith. Accordingly, the meaning of the supper and the necessary ritual reenactment may have been issues that awaited postscriptural development and definition by the teaching authority of the church. In this interpretation the Mass became a representation of the sacrifice of the crucifixion. It perpetuates that sacrifice by offering it anew and receiving the transformed life of Christ through the elements of bread and wine. Although the Mass remembers and memorializes Christ's last supper, it is now a new and continuing Lord's Supper. The word *mass* itself is derived from the *missa* or *mittere*, meaning to send or dismiss, and came into use as a way of ending the communion with the Lord in his Supper.

The structure and much of the content of the Mass are traceable to early Christian practice. The *first part* of this ritual event is interpreted as an encounter with the Word of God. In other words, as the Christ-community assembles, it is taken into the presence of the God first revealed to Israel, who then took personal action in the life of Jesus of Nazareth. Through the reading of Scriptures, the singing of psalms or scriptural songs, and the interpreting words of priests, deacons, or other faithful members of the body, the Word of God addresses the people. God's Word is God's presence made real through words and actions. This early action is sometimes called the Liturgy of the Word. A liturgy is always a special and regularized work—something done as a service. Accordingly, the Christian community in assembly first engages in the Liturgy of the Word, thereby encountering the God who was in Christ reconciling the world to the divine. After the Liturgy of the Word, it was apparently the practice of the early church to dismiss "catechumens," those being instructed in the meaning of the Gospel but not yet initiated into the church by baptism or the laying on of hands.

Only the baptized and confirmed "faithful" were to continue their participation in the *second part* of the ritual event, called variously the Liturgy of the Mass, the Liturgy of the Faithful, or the Eucharistic Liturgy. This action began with the bringing of offerings, most particularly the bread and wine, which were to represent the offering of the people and the offering of Christ himself through the elements of his last supper. There followed a prayer of thanksgiving, the form and substance of which were established very early. This eucharistic prayer set the death and resurrection of Christ within the context of the whole story of the creation, the exodus, and the faithfulness of God in trying to draw all humanity and creation into relation to his purposes. Certain responses and songs were attached to this great prayer. The *narrative of institution* was the recital of those words that tell of the last supper of Jesus with his disciples, the words that institute the sacrament. All of this led to a ritual sharing of the bread and wine, which had become the presence of Christ, reconciling all to God and to each other.

The question of how, in what manner, the bread and wine constitute the body and blood of Christ has been a complex issue that has exercised the thought and imagination of countless theologians throughout Christian history. Until Vatican Council II, the standard interpretation was the doctrine of transubstantiation, which, briefly stated, taught that bread and wine were the "accidents," the external forms within which a certain substance existed. Through Christ's own action and the subsequent action of the priest's consecration of the elements, the substances were no longer bread and wine even though the "accidents" were not changed. This entire event is viewed as a banquet with the risen Christ, who is not known by ordinary means. It is a "banquet in which Christ is consumed, the mind is filled with grace, and a pledge of future glory is given to us."

In Roman Catholic teaching there are seven sacraments, seven ritual occasions in which the church shares the grace that lives in it as the abode of the risen Christ. The seven are called Baptism, Confirmation, Eucharist, Penance, Extreme Unction, Holy Orders, and Matrimony. Right matter and proper form or words, used with right intention, are necessary to the validity of any sacrament, which is independent of the worthiness or unworthiness of the ministering priest or bishop. The significance of all sacraments depends upon Baptism, which initiates the person into the sacramental family. All sacraments are at one and the same time a reflection upon one's baptism and a sharing of its meaning. A sacrament is meaningless unless one is part of the

Body of Christ, which is the occasion for the encounter with grace in this sin-ful existence. Baptism brings one into the Body; Confirmation confirms Baptism for our entrance into responsible adulthood. The Eucharist is the everyday nurture of the Body of Christ, a thankful participation in the life that has been offered in Baptism. Penance (repentance for sin) and Confession are possible only on the condition of Baptism. That is, forgiveness of sins is not an abstract principle of natural existence; it is based upon the compassion of Christ. Without Baptism we do not know the cost of forgiveness. The anointing of the sick is a sharing of the healing power of grace and a benediction at the time of death. Holy Orders are the means whereby one shares the ministerial priesthood of Christ. Matrimony is the sacramental union of man and woman, reflecting the same grace that unites Christ and the church.

Some of the sacraments are once-in-a-lifetime occurrences, others are nurturing sacraments, often functioning like rites of passage through the various stages of human existence.

> The Church has always believed that the apostles and Christ's martyrs who had given the supreme witness of faith and charity by the shedding of their blood, are quite closely joined with us in Christ. She has always venerated them with special devotion, together with the Blessed Virgin Mary and the holy angels. The Church too has devoutly implored the aid of their intercession. To those were soon added those who had imitated Christ's virginity and poverty more exactly, and finally others whom the outstanding practice of the Christian virtues and the divine Charisms recommended to the pious devotion and imitation of the faithful.

These words are recorded in the Constitution on the Church, a document of Vatican Council II. They underscore a perception of the world that many Protestants and contemporary secularists would have a great difficulty understanding. The fact is that the Roman Catholic Church has always been hospitable to the religious needs of the masses. In some sense, there is much greater tolerance of those needs than among those of Puritan and modernist sensibilities. The tradition permits and nourishes a diversity of religious practices that others often find unacceptable. Only Eastern Orthodoxy shares a similar openness to the devotional needs of people.

Many of us know that we are "compassed about by a great cloud of witnesses." We believe that we live in the presence of those who have lived in the past, that the lives of some who have died are of special value to us in this life.

Christ's resurrection is a mode of existence of which we have a foretaste in the sacrament of the church. However, the church is not limited to life as we know it. The church is a communion of the living and the dead. The living and the dead exist in Christ's resurrected body. Therefore, those who have "gone before us" are present with us in the church. The apostles, the martyrs, and those whose lives served as inspiration and models for others—all these were among the saints. Inasmuch as they were present in the "Church Triumphant," the living could appeal in prayer for their special aid.

The Roman tradition also recognizes the fact that not all of reality, not all being, is present in the same way. We know from our understanding of science that things are not what they seem to be. That which seems solid and impregnable (like a table or a wall) is in reality in a state of fluidity or wave length. The arrangement of atoms, molecules, electrons, neutrons, and all the other images created by the language of science is varied and diverse. Roman piety makes room for the age-old notion that there are many levels to the scale of being. On the "higher" levels of the scale is conscious, willful, and intelligent being. "The holy angels" are a form of intelligent being between God and humanity. However, they are "spiritual" beings, meaning in this case that they do not have bodily form like humans. There are those theologians who suggest that angels are not necessarily superior to humankind, inasmuch as their freedom is curtailed (they do not become sinners) and they have no bodily existence. Nevertheless, these beings in God's celestial realm are worthy of devotion and intercession, along with the saints and the mother of Jesus.

The veneration of the Blessed Virgin is one of the oldest practices in Christianity, although it came into prominence in the late Middle Ages. Some scholars tell us that increased devotion to the Virgin was a folk reaction to the austerity attributed to God, whose almightiness made him unapproachable. At the same time, the elevation of Christ in trinitarian thought made the Son equally inaccessible. The result was an appeal to the feminine, to the warm and receptive mother, through whose loins the Son had come into the world. Marian devotion finds popular expression in the "Hail, Mary" prayer, based on the greetings of the archangel Gabriel and Elizabeth, mother of John the Baptist, recorded in St. Luke's Gospel (1:28, 42). The prayer is part of the Rosary, a form of devotion to the Fifteen Mysteries associated with the life of Christ. Marian piety appears to represent an important religious need—the appeal of feminine receptivity and compassion in relation to divinity. It has been suggested that the practice developed out of the ancient cults of the

Mother Goddess, or is evidence of some universal presence of the divine feminine. In Mary's case it was important for the faithful to emphasize the purity associated with her role as *theotokos*—bearer of God. The result was an accent upon virginity and sinlessness that led to such dogmas as the Immaculate Conception and the Assumption. The former teaching was defined by Pope Pius IX in 1854, stating that "from the first moment of her conception the Blessed Virgin Mary was . . . kept free from all stain of original sin." Again, it may be observed that the dogma was probably defined as a result of Americanist threats to the authority of Vatican teaching. The doctrine had always been a matter of dispute even though it had been an important element in Roman Catholic practice from the sixteenth century onward.

Social Expression

The distinctiveness of the social expression of Roman Catholicism is to be found in its high doctrine of the church and the strength of its hierarchical understanding of priesthood and practice of episcopal polity. The word *hierarchy* literally means the rule of the sacred. The Roman church had built upon the Roman legal system partly in order to prevent the erosion of civilization in the western part of the empire. The Roman tradition, therefore, has tended to express itself in terms of administration, organization, and legal modes of thought and action. It is a tradition of canon law, of carefully wrought regulations in governance and ethics. There is a parallel between the great Jewish tradition of Talmudic interpretation and commentary and the Roman Catholic development of canon law. Like all law, it depends heavily upon precedent and *casuistry,* the art of bringing general principles to bear upon specific cases.

For Roman Catholicism the church is a highly visible institution. It is Christ's own institution, based upon Petrine theory. It is the Body of Christ on Earth. "Christ, the one mediator," reads the Constitution on the Church, "established and ceaselessly sustains here on earth His holy Church, the community of faith, hope, and charity, *as a visible structure* [my italics]. Through her He communicates truth and grace to all. But the society furnished with hierarchical agencies and the Mystical Body of Christ are not to be considered as two realities, nor are the visible assembly and the spiritual community, nor the earthly Church and the Church enriched with heavenly things. Rather, they form one interlocked reality which is comprised of a divine and a human element." Hierarchy in the Roman system means the rule of the ministerial priesthood within the priesthood of the laity. Apostolic succession, with primacy for the successors of Peter, stands at the head of the hierarchy and represents a magisterial authority that applies gospel teaching to matters of saving faith, ethical responsibility (private and public), and ecclesiastical governance. No other form of Christianity, except perhaps the "new" religion of the Latter-Day Saints, has so complex and powerful a system of authority.

Bishops are of the order of apostles; there is no higher authority than apostolic authority. The pope signs himself as bishop. However, the bishop of Rome is heir of Peter, who was given special distinction by Jesus. He becomes "vicar of Christ" because Christ gave Peter what he himself possessed—the "keys of the Kingdom." So the pope is bishop, but more than bishop. And, in effect, the tradition has fostered de facto differences in authority for other bishops as well. Some are archbishops—chief bishops because of the size or special significance of their see (seat of authority). For example, the bishop of New York is an archbishop because of the size and importance of his diocese. In addition, some bishops become cardinals, representing the pope and assisting him in the special administration of his universal responsibilities. They have been frequently called the "princes of the church."

The Roman concept of authority is based on the notion that the revelation of truth that was present in Christ has been preserved by the church through Scripture and tradition. The teaching authority of the church, given supreme recognition in the pope's special commission, is divinely guided by the Holy Spirit. This concept means that the church is custodian and interpreter of revelation. It has a teaching authority that cannot be reduced to the typical American conviction concerning religious authority (that it is an affair of Bible and private judgment).

Roman Catholicism has maintained a monastic tradition that goes back in history to at least the third century. Monasticism is a form of religious life designed to further the possibilities of ascesis—one's effective withdrawal from the world in order to enhance one's understanding of the world and to achieve a degree of spiritual maturity not possible under ordinary circumstances. Monks are of two kinds: eremitic or cenobitic. The eremite lives in great solitude. He lives alone, although his solitude is sometimes shared with others who live in surrounding cells, caves, or hermitages. The cenobite lives his vows in direct relation to a community in which manual labor, study, and prayer are carefully regulated. Different models of monastic practice developed in East and West. Since the sixth century the Rule of St. Benedict has become the basic model upon which all Western monastic orders have relied.

These orders are often comprised of both laity and clergy. Some of them are primarily contemplative, devoted to prayer, meditation, study, and the life of enlightenment. Their contemplation is always for the church and for the world. Other orders are active in the service of education, health and medicine, or the poor.

Monasticism is a religious phenomenon found in the Roman, Orthodox, and Anglican traditions of Christianity. However, Buddhism and Hinduism have rich monastic heritages (especially the former), and the Sufi tradition of Islam has some of the elements of the monastic life. There is a certain romance to monasticism. It may be the ultimate romance, an expression of intense longing for the Other not satisfied by the many "others" one knows. Needless to say, monasticism has been a great civilizing influence in the history of Christianity. It has produced some of the noblest lives and greatest literary expressions of Christian history. Monasticism has been the custodian and preserver of the Christian tradition through time of warfare, oppression, disease, and spiritual deterioration. Monastic history is at the heart of any attempt to understand Roman Catholicism in any depth.

History in the United States

When the Protestant and Anglican traditions arrived in America in the seventeenth century, they came out of the great religious and cultural upheaval of the sixteenth-century Reformation. They were ready for America, the promised land. They understood themselves to be liberated from the bondage and captivity of an Old World that was tired, oppressive, and diseased. They left much behind them in Europe. The vast expanse of a new land offered the opportunity to complete the Reformation that had begun in Europe. These Protestants and Anglicans were generally anti-Roman, antipapacy. To them the Pope was the Antichrist and the Roman church was the whore of Babylon (an image derived from the New Testament book, The Revelation to John). Although the Roman church had made its way into the Spanish Southwest, the South, and Florida almost a century before the coming of the Protestants, Roman Catholics represented a distinct minority in the original thirteen colonies that were to become the first United States of America. Roman Catholics from England and Germany were among these first colonists.

In England the Romans had been barely tolerated, sometimes oppressed, because the Church of England thought of itself as the Catholic church in England. However, the English Roman Catholics were the heirs of liberty, along with all other English persons. It was relatively easy for many of these English Romanists to adjust to the style of life found in the colonies. After all, they were English, too, and English governance, however torpid and ugly at times, was plagued by the spirit of liberty. The second Baron Baltimore, Cecil Calvert, sought the support of Protestants to make the proprietary colony of Maryland into a place where people of different religious faiths could live in peace and good will. Baron Baltimore was a Roman Catholic, a realist who sought refuge for his fellow religionists but knew that the financial success of the colony depended upon avoiding religious conflict. He also understood that there could be no Catholic establishment and that he was a proprietary representative of a nation that had established a form of Christianity not loyal to the bishop of Rome. As proprietor he was to erect churches "to be dedicated to and consecrated according to the Ecclesiastical laws of our Kingdom of England." Accordingly, he arrived at a policy of toleration long before the famous Maryland Act of Tolerance of April 1649. Among the first arrivals in the colony in 1634 were two English Jesuits who offered their first American mass on St. Clement's Island in Chesapeake Bay. English Roman Catholicism thus played an interesting role in the early formation of the United States.

From its earliest contact with the original thirteen colonies, the Roman tradition was shaped by the uniqueness of American circumstances. It was an early sign that pragmatic adjustment to the plurality of religion and the vast American spaces was to have a sustained effect upon all of the European imports. An American version of the Roman tradition was in the making. As more immigrants saw the North American continent as a refuge from persecution, a place for beginnings, they attached themselves to images of a New World and a promised land. Even Roman Catholics began to comprehend the guiding light of Divine Providence bringing them to a place of hope and fulfillment. Like many of their Protestant and Jewish counterparts, they were the legatees of an exodus, the residents of a world of promise.

In eighteenth-century Maryland the Carroll family rose to prominence as Charles Carroll and his cousin became active in the cause of liberty and independence. John Carroll was a Maryland native educated at the Jesuit College of St. Omer (France). When the Jesuit order was suppressed by the Vatican in 1773, Carroll returned to the colonies. In 1776 he accompanied his cousin

Charles, Benjamin Franklin, and Samuel Chase on a mission to Quebec, with the purpose of winning Roman Catholic support for the colonial cause. Charles Carroll was the leading Catholic layman of his times, a member of the Continental Congress and a signatory of the Declaration of Independence. John, on the other hand, was named superior of the American Missions in 1784, a step that made the Roman church in America independent of its English jurisdiction.

For a time the Roman priests in America opposed the appointment of an American bishop. The spirit of the colonies was generally anti-Roman and all prelates[6] were hated figures. The appointment of bishops was therefore a sensitive issue. (We have seen the same concern expressed with regard to Anglican bishops during the same period.) By 1789 national independence was an established fact and the mood of America somewhat modified. Carroll himself was convinced of the necessity of bishops but advised the Holy See that the first appointee should be the nominee of the American clergy rather than an arbitrary appointment of the Vatican. The Roman authorities reluctantly agreed, and John Carroll was named bishop of Baltimore. In 1808 the diocese was divided into four sees, and Carroll became archbishop. In this incident we may again observe the manner in which the tradition was being shaped by the American context. Another stage of the shaping of an American Roman Catholicism is evident. The Vatican was forced to adjust its European mode of operation to the circumstances of the New World. The Carrolls were champions of the cause of independence in the face of an ecclesiastical history long supportive of monarchical institutions. And even the selection of the first American prelate was made in deference to the republican spirit. A new form of Catholicism was in the making.

As bishop, Carroll faced a shortage of priests. At the time of his consecration, there were thirty to serve a constituency of about twenty-five thousand in Maryland, Pennsylvania, New York, and Virginia. By the time of the archbishop's death in 1815, there were one hundred parishes in the nation, served by as many priests.

For some time, Protestants in the United States had assumed the right of laypersons to control ecclesiastical property and finances and to select their own pastors. In fact, the nation was fast becoming congregationalist. Regardless of presbyterial or episcopal polities, many churches assumed the rights and decision-making power of the local, independent congregation. This often occurred because judicatory authorities beyond the local church were not available or because of controversies arising from the peculiar pastoral needs of a frontier society. Religious needs are universal and people sought ways to meet them unhindered by the demands of a tradition shaped by the established culture of Europe. The United States was shaping its own religious tradition. In polity it began to appear amazingly congregational, ecclesial theory to the contrary notwithstanding.

The congregational and democratic spirit of American religion played a role in the "trusteeism" controversies among Roman Catholics in the United States. Here and there the laity incorporated themselves legally as a church and proceeded to assume responsibility for the selection of pastors. Typically the property of a church was under the administrative direction and legal ownership of the bishop. Presumably there was nothing in canon law[7] that would prevent the development of a system of lay trustees, and the church often found it convenient to rely upon the laity for financial management. The business of selection of pastors was another matter; appointment and dismissal of clergy was an episcopal prerogative.

Often these trusteeism controversies were aggravated by the ethnic diversity of the American circumstance. In Philadelphia in 1787 a group of German-born Catholics separated themselves from St. Mary's Church and constituted a parish for themselves. They had been ill at ease in a parish in which both the ministry and constituency were predominantly English-speaking. Frequently the Irish chafed under the ministrations of French clergy and sought to exercise control over their own ecclesiastical destiny. When the hierarchy sought to stabilize their control over the churches and their property, it was often interpreted as one more instance of un-American authoritarianism. As such it fed the so-called "nativist" (not to be confused with Native Americans—Indians) sentiment that was gathering momentum in the 1840s and 1850s.

Nativism was directed mostly at Roman Catholicism. It was partly a response to the changing religio-cultural climate of America. As the numbers of immigrants from Ireland, France, and Germany increased, the "native" (i.e., basically Protestant) Americans experienced a threat to their culture and to the set of largely British and Puritan religious assumptions that had been predominant in the United States for more than two hundred years. The "natives" were white, Anglo-Saxon, and Protestant. They wished to preserve their way of life. Nativist agitation mounted as the immigrants threatened the solemnity of the Puritan Sabbath-Sunday and altered the American landscape with crosses and convents. There were riots in Germantown, Pennsylvania, and a convent was burned in Charlestown, Massachusetts. A political party, the Know-Nothings (the American Party), sought to maintain Protestant hegemony, sometimes through devious means, of which they claimed to "know nothing." The nativists produced books and pamphlets, all of them exposés, attempts to demonstrate that Roman Catholicism was a conspiracy of Satan himself. Romanism, said the nativist literature, sought to undermine democracy and permit the pope and his minions to rule the United States. Some of the literature was quite sensational, not least in importance of which was the *Awful Disclosures* of Maria Monk, a lurid account of life inside a Montreal convent supposedly written by a former nun. The book remained in print long after its content was proven to be flagrant untruth.

The pervasiveness and the intensity of nativism required a response on the part of the Roman church. Some apologists, such as Orestes Brownson, Isaac Hecker, and later the well-known James Cardinal Gibbons, sought to demonstrate that Catholicism belonged in America, that America was to be the place where the real genius of Catholicism would be fulfilled. Here we may observe a theoretical effect upon the tradition. If the democratic spirit of America forced adjustment upon the administrative policies of Catholicism (as in the case of the trusteeism controversies), nativism required a rethinking of the theology in relation to the self-understanding of the new republic. "No constitution," wrote Cardinal Gibbons, "is more in harmony with Catholic principles than is the American. And no religion can be in such accord with that constitution as the Catholic. . . . Both [church and state] derive their life from the same interior principle of truth."

In 1884 the Third Plenary Council of the American Church, meeting in Baltimore, decreed that "near each church, where it does not exist, a parochial school is to be erected within two years." The development of these schools had begun years before in response to the fact that the American common and public schools reflected the historic hegemony of Protestantism. To many Roman Catholic leaders the public schools were in effect Protestant schools, teaching the values of a Protestant society and even using the King James Version[8] of the Bible in both curricular and devotional fashion. Thus, one of the largest nonpublic school systems in the world came into being, shaped by reaction to the dominant religiosity of American life.

By the end of the nineteenth century, adjustments in Roman Catholic theology and practice had accelerated to such an extent that the European hierarchy and the Vatican were concerned about reported deviation from authentic teaching. Rumors of an "Americanization" of the church in this country were circulating. Isaac Hecker had founded the Missionary Society of St. Paul the Apostle (the Paulist Fathers) as an organization with special sensitivity to the missionary needs of America. Hecker tended to recognize a measure of truth in Protestantism, and he later accepted that truth in his attempt to demonstrate to a potential convert that Catholic faith and practice fulfilled and completed what was partially present in the Protestant system. To foreign observers a new scenario seemed to be emerging in the American church. Perhaps it was not yet heresy, but it could well become so. "Americanist" teachings supposedly threatened the orthodoxy and uniformity of Roman Catholic teaching. In 1899 a papal encyclical circulated by Leo XIII dealt seriously with "Americanism," rejecting the idea that "the Church ought to adapt herself somewhat to our advanced civilization, and relaxing her ancient vigor, show some indulgence to modern popular theories and methods." Of course, the American adaptations were already in process; although the church in America experienced almost sixty years of reaction and isolationism, as a result of the Americanist and modernist condemnations, the adaptations were never completely undone. American religion and culture make demands of every tradition that lives within their sacred grounds. Roman Catholicism is no exception. The student may explore numerous incidents of theory and practice in which this great tradition has been shaped into a distinctively American tradition.

Vatican Council II (1962–65) represented an opening of the doors of the Roman temple. The Roman church has not been the same since. Its liturgy, its theology, and its popular piety have been given new shape. Perhaps the changes required by the American context—changes more than a century in the making—had finally come of age. Today the Roman Catholic Church in the United States looks very much like its sister denominations of catholic and liturgical heritage. Lutherans, Anglicans, and Roman Catholics tend to have a common demeanor. An outside observer of the freestyle adaptability of a post-Vatican Council II mass frequently comes away shaking his or her head, wondering why these people want to recapitulate several hundred years of Protestant, free-church, and Pentecostal history.

Roman Catholic women have been in the forefront of the feminist and women's liberation movements that have emerged in the wake of Vatican Council II and the civil rights and liberationist struggles since the 1960s. The theologian and teacher Rosemary Radford Ruether has reminded her readers that feminism, racism, anti-Semitism, and environmental destruction exist together at the heart of contemporary social alienation and oppression. Ruether advocates a women's church in exodus: "As Women-Church we claim the authentic mission of Christ, the true mission of the church, the real agenda of our Mother-Father God who comes to restore and not destroy our humanity. . . . God's Shekinah, Holy Wisdom, the Mother-face of God has fled from the high thrones of patriarchy and has gone into exodus with us." Not all Roman Catholics have acknowledged this exodus. Many women continue to work at a reform of Catholicism that will be expressed in women's ordination and a married priesthood.

Roman Catholicism in America is today one of the few traditions of long-historical standing and European origins that have grown significantly in membership. Immigration from Europe and Latin America continues to be a relevant factor in this growth. However, only a small percentage of this increase is African American, in spite of the fact that the Roman Catholic Church is virtually alone among the major white denominations experiencing any growth in black membership. This emergent black middle class is the primary source of this increase.

For many years the tradition in America was affected by its classical theory of slavery. In keeping with its origins in the early centuries of the Christian era, the Church maintained that slavery in itself was not a necessary evil. It was a fact of human history. The Christian ethic required that slaves be treated with justice, respect, and goodwill and that they be given religious instruction. Whether slave or free, wrote St. Paul to the Galatians, a new "law" is at work. He wrote: "There is neither Jew nor Greek, there is neither slave nor free . . . for you are all one in Christ Jesus" (Galatians 3:28). This was interpreted to mean that in the Body of Christ the slave was heir to all that a free person was heir to. However, instead of eliminating slavery itself, the Church assumed that it was one of the orders of creation; that a slave should be a good slave, doing what was expected of him or her as laborer or servant. In America, the Church recommended manumission of slaves if they were improperly treated and not provided with the nurture and instruction due to a member of the Body of Christ.

Archbishop John Carroll directed that his "black servant Charles" be freed after the archbishop's death. The Church condemned the slave trade more than once in the nineteenth century, and many plantation owners manumitted their slaves in response to the Church's teaching. However, social order and the unity of the Church were always primary concerns for Roman Catholicism. Therefore, the condition of African American slave life was often determined by the local or regional point of view. One prominent Georgian of Irish ancestry, Michael M. Healy, owned seventeen slaves by

1831 and married a mulatto woman who became the mother of his ten children. Healy was the father of a future bishop and president of Georgetown University. Bishop John England, along with other Church leaders, sought to provide schools for free blacks.

Nevertheless, it was not until the presidency of John F. Kennedy and the civil rights movement of the 1960s and 1970s that the social order of the nation and the spirit of the Vatican Council afforded an opportunity for forthright Catholic participation in black liberation.

chapter 10

The Methodist Tradition

He was the fifteenth child of the Reverend Samuel Wesley, an Anglican priest and sometime rector of Epworth in Lincolnshire, England. From 1727 to 1729 he served as his father's curate, then later traveled with his brother Charles on a missionary journey to the new colony of Georgia. But John Wesley was a man tormented by the struggle for assurance of salvation. Like Martin Luther he sought peace where there was none and a sense of joyful liberation from deep self-disdain.

One night in 1738 at a meeting in London he experienced a profound rebirth:

> In the evening I went very unwillingly to a society in Aldersgate Street, where one was reading Luther's preface to the *Epistle to the Romans*. About a quarter before nine, while he was describing the change which God works in the heart through faith in Christ, I felt my heart strangely warmed. I felt I did trust in Christ, Christ alone for my salvation; and an assurance was given me that He had taken away my sins, even mine, and saved me from the law of sin and death.

From that moment on, John Wesley was determined to share his discovery with the plain people of England. He became an evangelist, one who understands his vocation to be that of appealing to the individual to surrender his life to the claims of Christ and his gospel (evangel). Because of the direct personal appeal of Wesley's preaching he incurred the displeasure of the hierarchy of the Church of England. This was a time of great concern for sanity in religious behavior; *enthusiasm* was a term of opprobrium. It denoted unseemly emotional behavior. Through the history of Christianity there had been apprehension regarding these matters. *Enthusiasm* meant literally *en theoi*, possession by the gods. Theologians were wary of such possession because to them it represented the pagan forces out of which many Christians had been delivered. The Church had come to support a policy of decency and order. Enthusiasm might mean not only possession but also disorder and chaos, the breeding ground for satanic connivance. To encourage the enthusiasm of common folk was to promote chaos and foster un-Christian practices. In addition, there were those who disapproved of the concern for one's "salvation" that characterized the personal evangelistic appeal of preachers like Wesley. Presumably the salvationist perspective of much American evangelical Christianity is not the way in which the gospel has been understood and practiced through the earlier course of history.

John Wesley was to have a tremendous impact upon the formation of American religion and culture. If the colonial period of our history was the age of Calvin, the nineteenth century was the Wesleyan era. Something about the spirit of the United States resonated with the tenor of Methodism. Although he was no great orator, Wesley took the gospel out of the churches and into the fields, the parks, and the streets where people lived. "I love the poor," he said. "In many of them I find pure genuine grace unmixed with paint, folly and affectations." In taking the evangel to the people, he was to break the molds in which Christianity had been cast for centuries. The parish system, with its assumption that the nation could be divided into geographical jurisdictions within which a church and its clergy were responsible for total pastoral care of all people, was shattered by Wesley's evangelistic practices. The cause of itinerancy was advanced. He performed a clerical role, developing a form of religious leadership that was not dependent upon either the call of a congregation or the appointment of a bishop. Wesley's style was to find a natural setting in the unsettled life of the United States, where parish structures meant little and where the religious needs of the people seemed to cry out for the peripatetic preacher. The moving frontier, the migratory life of the American continent, were congenial to the itinerant evangelist. The United States is the home of the "preacher," the evangelist whose only mandate is his or her message, who may know of such things as holy orders and apostolic succession but thinks they are evil impediments to the free delivery of the evangel to those who should hear it. Ordination and the pastoral responsibility for an established congregation were presumably not for everyone. Certainly not in America. Wesley and his English colleague, George Whitefield, brought itinerancy to America in the early eighteenth century. It has been a distinguishing feature of American religion since that time and has played an important role in taming the frontier and refashioning the American mind.

Wesley had been a "methodist" even before his Aldersgate experience. While a student at Oxford University he had belonged to a group of young men who met regularly for Bible study and prayer. This practice was no doubt the English version of the Pietist conventicles that were prominent on the Continent toward the end of the seventeenth and into the early eighteenth centuries. Conventicles were small groups or classes, similar perhaps to Communist cells. They were part of the Pietist program of renewing the church from within. Accordingly, methodism is English Pietism. Wesley's "methodists" agreed to discipline their lives by a strict rule of prayer, Bible study, and service to the poor and imprisoned. Their methodical spirituality was directed against what they considered to be moral laxity and churchly formalism.

The intensity of the methodist circle aroused the ridicule of fellow students who dubbed them the Holy Club, Bible Moths, Methodist—all in a disparaging manner. In this we may observe a frequent phenomenon in the history of religions: the manner of the naming of a tradition. It is often the outsider who provides the name, at first pejorative and rejected by the movement itself. Eventually the term becomes acceptable even to adherents of the movement.

Wesley was concerned with what he believed was the necessary renewal of the Church of England. Like Martin Luther more than two hundred years earlier, he did not intend to be the founder of a new tradition. He apparently never left the Church of England, remaining to the end of his days a firm believer in the importance of the sacraments and the necessity of catholic order. Even when he was forced to commission leaders for the evangelistic work in America, because the Church of England would not provide suitable bishops and clergy, he assumed that his societies and their new organization would form a special religious order within the establishment. However, his wishes were not to be fulfilled. Much of the Anglican Church continued in opposition to the evangelistic fervor, the zealous methodist societies, and their supposed threat to the order and rationality of the church. And the methodists themselves gradually perceived their work as a valid representation of the church of Jesus Christ. They could justify their separation from the Church of England because of their own commitments to the righteousness of their cause and the perversity of the establishment. Thus methodists became Methodists. A new denominational family took its place in the history of Christianity and in the American pantheon of religions. The Methodist Episcopal Church was organized at Baltimore on Christmas Eve,

1784. Note that its name distinguishes it from the rest of American Anglican-ism, from which it emerged.

To a great extent Methodism is Wesleyanism, yet it is a family of denominations. It has undergone many changes in the course of its history, especially in the United States, but has remained a religious movement "mystically joined" to the genius of the United States and dedicated to the spiritual potential of every individual. By 1850 Methodists numbered well over one million adherents. Methodism had a message congenial to the soul of the new nation.

Verbal Expression

Methodism, writes William Warren Sweet, preached a doctrine of "free will and free grace, as opposed to the doctrines of limited grace and predestination preached by the Calvinistic Presbyterians, or even the milder Calvinistic Baptists. The frontier Methodist preachers brought home to the pioneers the fact that they were masters of their own destiny, an emphasis which fitted in exactly with the new democracy rising in the West, for both emphasized the actual equality among all men."[1] Sweet's emphasis on the development of frontier Methodism as a key to understanding the consensus of evangelical Protestantism has to be qualified today. It was a thesis constructed out of perspectives gained in the Methodist environment of Baldwin City, Kansas, in the late nineteenth century. Sweet's eye was not trained for perceiving American diversity, the role of Roman Catholics, Jews, and those who resisted the revivalistic Americanization of religion.

Nevertheless, Sweet's generalization about Methodism stands firm on its moorings. Catherine Albanese of the University of California, Santa Barbara, points out that the nineteenth century "has been called the Methodist era because it was the time in which Methodism became the predominant form of American Protestantism. But Methodism also gave its name to the period because it was a generic name for the religious style that swept Protestantism."[2] Actually the style characterized by Sweet swept more than Protestantism; it swept the United States. Every major tradition, including Roman Catholicism, was affected.

Theoretically, Wesleyanism is shaped by its reaction to what Sweet called "the doctrines of limited grace and predestination" of Calvinism. John Wesley's Aldersgate experience was in many respects little different from the experience of Martin Luther, the Rhineland mystics, and the great mystics of medieval Western Christianity. What distinguished Wesley's religiousness are the conclusions he reached on the basis of his experience. He concluded that such an experience as his was just the beginning of the Christian pilgrimage rather than the result of the discipline and nurture of the church. Secondly, he directed his efforts toward the transformation of the individual soul. Although Wesleyanism was to have tremendous social effects, preparing English society for significant reforms, its salvationist emphasis was ultimately individualistic. Wesley himself never ceased being a loyal member of the Church of England, stressing the significance of the sacraments. However, the movement seemed to remember only his emphasis upon personal religious vitality. Wesley was impatient with the human condition and seemed convinced that a "saved" person could escape the circumstances of his sinfulness. He was a Christian idealist and expected perfection of all Christians. He wondered how it was possible for a Christian to do evil, to be involved in any injustice. He could not accept our constant and paradoxical involvement in a sinful world. He expected people to love their neighbors and walk as Jesus walked. "I am sick of opinions," he said, "am weary to bear them; my soul loathes this frothy food. Give me solid and substantial religion; give me a humble, gentle lover of God and man; a man full of mercy and good faith, without partiality and without hypocrisy."

It is this drive toward the perfection of humankind that distinguishes Methodism. Wesley believed that the individual who is justified by grace through faith is set on a course of sanctification. Sanctification means holiness, perfection. To Wesley this sanctification is positive and readily discernible. To thinkers like Martin Luther sanctification is constantly shattered by our continued sinfulness, therefore not so easily discerned. One must leave sanctification to God's own good time and grace, and not dwell too much upon it, according to Luther. Concern for sanctification can lead to self-righteousness and temptation.

Not so to Wesley. He readily divided Christians from Christians. There was no such thing as a drunken, cursing, lying, cheating Christian. The "bulk of parishioners," he said, [are a] "mere rope of sand. . . . We [Methodists] introduce Christian fellowship where it was utterly destroyed. And the fruits of it have been peace, love, joy, and zeal for every good work and word." The reader may understand from this emphasis upon the capacity to judge the Christian life that Wesleyanism would ultimately find itself in schismatic relationship to the Anglicanism that Wesley himself claimed to appreciate. We may also expect emphasis upon perfection to become moralistic in the spiritual life of many people. Perhaps it also leads to a fastidiousness about duties and responsibilities akin to a belief in works-righteousness—justification by doing one's duty.

"A Methodist," said John Wesley, "is one who has the love of God shed abroad in his heart by the Holy Ghost given unto him." This statement places his thought within the context of catholic orthodoxy, for it attributes the love of God to the work of the Holy Spirit and not to human intention. However, Wesley follows this theological affirmation with a characterization of a Methodist as one who is always "happy in God," is constantly thankful to God for his glory, prays without ceasing, is pure in heart, and keeps the commandments. Although this is certainly a hortatory statement, one might want to ask, "Are there then any Methodists, Mr. Wesley, yourself included?" As the gift of the Holy Spirit, these characteristics are qualities not discernible by ordinary knowledge, perception, or judgment. They are theological realities. They may have been so for Wesley, but his characterization is one that leads to assumptions about the possibilities of human perfection in the ordinary course of natural existence.

Sweet wrote that Methodism preached a gospel of free will and free grace, meaning, essentially, that the unmerited love (grace) of God was freely available to all and that each individual was free to respond to free grace. The will is free to do what it must do. Wesley himself was subtle in his understanding of this matter. He was aware of the problems involved in a doctrine too humanistically inclined. His writings reveal a theological sophistication about justification by grace, sanctification, good works, and predestination. But Methodism came to the United States and shaped Wesley's passionate concern for personal salvation into a tradition suitable to the optimism of the new nation.

Wesley's own thought was in part a reaction to Calvinism, which was a well-constructed theological system. Wesleyanism is accused of being Arminian. Arminianism is a softening of the Calvinism of the sixteenth century. Already in 1591 James Harmens (in Latin, Jacobus Arminius), a Reformed minister in Amsterdam and later Professor of Divinity at Leyden, had sought to reinterpret some of Calvin's ideas. Arminius's teachings were condemned at the Synod of Dort in the early 1600s, a full century before Wesley's Aldersgate experience. We have seen, in a previous chapter, the importance of the sovereignty of God in the theology of John Calvin. This emphasis took Calvin in the direction of a doctrine of unconditional predestination. Essentially this means that inasmuch as God is sovereign, wholly other, we cannot know

God's ways. Our destiny is unconditionally in divine hands. We, of our own accord, cannot know or determine our ultimate destiny. Furthermore, our wills are not free; they are captive to a selfhood that assumes it can control its own destiny. When we observe our lives carefully, it is apparent that it is not a matter of talent, will, intelligence, or knowledge that determines our concern for justification. It is a matter of God's initiative. This led Calvin, like St. Augustine before him, to posit a doctrine of predestination, which meant that our ultimate destiny, our salvation, is a matter of God's election.

It was the rigidity of Calvin's predestination that Arminius challenged. He held that through God's sovereignty a condition for salvation is provided. God has decreed that those who believe that Christ died for all shall be saved; those who do not believe shall be condemned. Predestination was therefore conditional for Arminius. John Wesley was sympathetic with the softened predestination of Arminius. It coincided with his own experience. But he was an irenic person; he did not condemn Calvin or Calvinists. "John Calvin was a pious, learned, sensible man," he wrote, "and so was James Harmens. Many Calvinists are pious, learned, sensible men; and so are many Arminians. Only the former hold absolute predestination; the latter, conditional."

Wesley's concern was for the individual soul and its movement toward sanctification and perfection by the grace of God. Therefore, to be "pious, learned, and sensible" is more important than precision of doctrine. Wesley's was an idealistic and harmonious theology, directed toward the experience and perfection of the common person. Faith, he said, was a divine evidence and conviction that God is able to perfect us right now. Although sanctification may be gradually wrought in some, "it is infinitely desirable, were it the will of God that it should be done instantaneously; that the Lord should destroy sin 'by the breath of his mouth,' in a moment, in the twinkling of an eye. And so he generally does; a plain fact, of which there is evidence enough to satisfy any unprejudiced person." Although there were those for whom this instantaneous destruction of sin was not at all "a plain fact," there were many who heard the liberating force of the message and became Methodists, inflamed by Wesley's affirmation of their perfectibility. It was a message that the American, Crevecoeur's "new man," was waiting for. This new man had little time; he was always in a hurry. What mattered was potential! One must assume that a person is essentially good, not sinful; and one must be more concerned with experience and a pious life than with any complicated theological notions. That was the mind of the new man, and Methodism was the affirmation of that mind.

Practical Expression

The advance of Methodism in the shaping of America required more than the doctrine of sanctification and its emphasis upon free will and free grace. It required a strategy and a set of tactical maneuvers commensurate to its mission. Perhaps the true genius of Methodism is to be found in its practical expression. Certainly this was true in the age of Methodism, the nineteenth century. Although the tradition inherited many of the working assumptions of its parent tradition of Anglicanism, it was shaped by the demands of a frontier society. Early on, the liturgical patterns of the Book of Common Prayer continued to inform the drama of Methodist worship. But this was to be a liturgy for the poorly educated and those with little time or equipment appropriate to the ritual process of catholic practice. Vestments, altars, and sacramental proprieties were not of great significance. Two forms of the practical expression of religion stand out as distinctive of the Methodist tradition. They are the camp meeting and Methodistic discipline.

To understand the significance of the camp meeting we have to try to imagine life on the frontier. People lived great distances from each other under the constant anxiety of life "at the edge of existence." Every moment of every day was an occasion filled with the threat of extinction, nonbeing (as the existentialists would put it). Accident, disease, starvation, the menace of wild animals, and hostile encounters with the resistant Native Americans were an unremitting presence. Loneliness, despair, and fear reduced human existence to its lowest denominator.

At first the camp meeting was a spontaneous response to the need for affirming one's humanity in the face of the dehumanizing and merciless aspects of frontier life. The meeting occurred as a response to the call of a traveling evangelist, or to the news that circulated by trader and pioneer. There was to be a gathering at some place, perhaps along a river or fordable stream. Some traveled a hundred miles and more. Trees were felled and a clearing made for an open-air auditorium. On the edge of this center was a circle of fires, lanterns, and torches. Beyond this a row of tents and improvised quarters sheltered the families for the several days of the meeting. The outer rim of the camp consisted of wagons, with the horses tethered behind them.

A camp meeting was a place to find order and meaning in the chaos of frontier existence. The meeting grounds themselves were temples in the wilderness, models of the frontier universe. They were like a sacred center in an otherwise hostile environment. It was a fragile world into which the preached Word of the Christian gospel was brought, organizing existence around the worth of the individual soul in the eyes of God. Here was worthiness in the midst of conditions very threatening to human worth. Sometimes the preaching, the praying, and the singing led to rather extraordinary behavior. People shouted and screamed in pain and in ecstasy. Some danced and others experienced violent spasms and jerking movements. They crawled, they rolled, and they lost consciousness. They experienced the liberating action of the Holy Spirit. Emotions and passions that had been pent up in the anxiety of on-the-edge existence were released, and the people knew that God was good, that God restored their lives to new meaning. These were humans like us, no less intelligent or gullible. They were mortals in dire circumstances, discerning whatever ultimate order and meaning were available to them. No doubt, many or most of us would have been among the ecstatic creatures of the camp meeting.

Reports of the camp meetings spread eastward and caught the attention of Methodist leaders like Francis Asbury. Asbury had been consecrated as the first bishop of the Methodist Episcopal Church. He saw his first wilderness revival in 1800 and was impressed. The camp meetings appealed to Methodist sensibilities because they were not afraid of passion and emotion. If such enthusiasm led to disorder, it had to be forestalled by proper organization and supervision. There had to be rules. From the beginning Methodism operated by rules and regulations. It was not a tradition without demands. But the camp meeting was suited to the Methodist goal of confronting as many individuals as possible with the fire of the gospel, with the blessing of receiving the love of God instantaneously. Asbury had only to hear the reports of the results of the sylvan revivals to sustain the impression he had gained by participating in the outdoor meeting in Drake's Creek, Tennessee. From Pennsylvania, Maryland, Delaware, New York, and Vermont, as well as Tennessee and Kentucky, came word of human harvest. "God has given us hundreds in 1800," said Asbury, "why not thousands in 1801, yea, why not a million if we had faith? Lord, increase our faith."

Asbury began to refashion the wilderness revivals of the frontier into a design appropriate to his intentions. They had to be carefully organized and promoted, to guard against disorder and immorality, and to assure the harvest he was seeking. Presiding elders of the districts and local preachers were instructed to use the camp meetings regularly. They were standardized in form and duration for the best possible results. The camp meeting was transformed into a methodistic strategy, a carefully regulated ritual process that assured Methodist success on the ever-moving frontier and altered the religious life of the more settled eastern United States. The mass meeting, designed to encourage individual revival and conversion, became a feature of American religion. Even the evangelistic campground became a prominent part of the settled life of congregations and denominations. Like their frontier paradigm, they were settings for evangelistic meetings and social gatherings where stories were told, horses were traded, boys met girls, and women exchanged recipes and found friendship.

The Methodist tradition in the United States was thus shaped in its practical expression by the frontier character of the nation as well as by its modified version of John Wesley's concern for sanctification. However, as we have just observed in our discussion of camp meetings and mass evangelism, Methodists have been methodistic. This concern for structure and discipline is another distinguishing characteristic of the practical expression of the tradition. Although John Wesley sought to maintain loyalty to the Church of England and its sacramental theology, he had embarked upon a course that would lead to a distinctive and separate practice of Christianity. So convinced was he that holiness was to become the full measure of Christian faith, that his enthusiasm led to the development of methods for separating "sheep from goats." First, he welcomed those who were "justified by faith" to gather together in societies where they would "taste of the heaven to which [they] were going," where they would be "holy and happy," treading down sin and fear, sitting "in heavenly places with Jesus Christ." These societies were a comfort against the world that rose up against them.

To Wesley, this world that rose up against them was comprised of many who called themselves Christians. How can they be Christians? asked Wesley. "What! drunken Christians! cursing and swearing Christians! lying Christians! cheating Christians! If they are Christians at all, they are devil Christians." Creating Wesleyan societies does not divide the church, the Christian world, said Wesley; it merely separates true Christians from the world. He was not willing to leave this kind of judgment in the hands of God, was not prepared to understand that justification and sanctification may be difficult to perceive in a world that is alienated from its Creator's intent. There was a moralistic and Puritan character to Wesley's Christianity that would find hospitality in the United States. Wesley's Methodists were to be the purified church. Proper discipline and method could assure holiness and morality.

Wesley soon discovered that it was difficult for members of a society to be successful in watching over each other. "I do not know that any hypocrites were crept in; for, indeed, there was no temptation; but several grew cold, and gave way to the sins which had long easily beset them." Something had to be done. Discipline had to be tightened. "I called together all the leaders of the classes [societies], and desired that each would make a particular inquiry into the behavior of those whom he saw weekly." Soon Wesley was able to assert, "A Methodist is one who has the love of God shed abroad in his heart by the Holy Ghost given unto him, one who loves the Lord his God with all his heart, and with all his soul, and with all his mind, and with all his strength." We can observe the growing propensity for being able to discern and develop true Christians. The emphasis is on the possibilities for discernible holiness in this world.

Eventually there emerged a book called *The Discipline of the Methodist Episcopal Church,* which detailed the governance and spiritual practice of the tradition. The Methodists in the United States devised an ingenious strategy for the evangelistic conquest of the frontier. At the heart of the system were the circuit riders, charged with the responsibility of preaching for conversion, covering a vast territory. The riders were each assigned specific stretches of wilderness, making contact with all major points of settlement, visiting families, and assembling people to hear the gospel of Jesus Christ. They made circuit on a regular basis. Certainly this strategy accounts for the tremendous success of Methodism on the nineteenth-century frontier. They were rough-hewn lay preachers, common folk with common speech, but powerful personalities bringing the message of justification and holiness to the starved spirits of the new nation. Like the crusader knights of Europe's Middle Ages, they were courageous members of Wesley and Asbury's "Army of the Lord." In the history of religions, they may be compared to the Society of Jesus (Jesuits), those militant representatives of the loyalist Reformation who carried Roman Catholicism into many corners of the earth.

When the circuit rider discovered a few people who experienced justification, he gathered them into classes, according to the prescription of the Methodist *Discipline.* They were ready for their venture into sanctification. A leader was appointed and the group was put under strict regulation. The class met weekly and members were expected to account for the progress of their faith and personal conduct. A white ticket was issued to each class member by the circuit rider. It served as admission to class meetings, was validated by the local leader, and would not be reissued if attendance was irregular. The itinerant on his rounds would make special effort to meet with as many classes as he could. This helped to stabilize the work of local leaders and provide a valuable assessment of the spiritual development of the Methodist tradition.

The practice of Methodism has always been characterized by its careful organization and its strict devotion to rules and regulations for the spiritual and moral life. The largest denomination of American Methodism today is the United Methodist Church. To a great extent this denomination has yielded to liberalizing and modernizing tendencies that no longer adhere to the methodistical discipline. *The Book of Discipline* today is largely a general guide and symbol, without much direct impact upon the lives of Methodists. Still, the denomination shared that spirit of perfection and moral potential that coincided so deftly with the formation of the American consciousness. Much of United Methodist perfectionism and holiness today are directed toward the achievement of social justice rather than to disciplined personal morality. However, throughout the history of our nation, the Wesleyan sensibility has emerged again and again, judging the spirituality of denominations and often inspiring schism and the formation of new groups.

Social Expression

The social expression of the Wesleyan tradition has also been shaped by a combination of American context and the evangelistic priorities of Methodist origins. As we have seen, those priorities were also tied to a functional disposition—a methodistic program for separating true Christians from the chaff of the world. Denominations within the Methodist tradition vary in polity. It is safe to say that the original Methodist Episcopal Church (the predominant element in the contemporary United Methodist Church) maintained a form of polity reminiscent of its Anglican heritage. However, the functional and evangelistic priorities of early Methodism tended to refashion episcopal polity into what is termed connectionalism. The church is governed by a carefully monitored connection of administrative levels and clerical functions. The Methodist bishop is not of an apostolical order or ministerial priesthood. There are only two orders of ministry: elders (presbyters) and deacons. The elders have not become priests (presters, from "presbyters") but are preachers of the evangel with a diversity of administrative responsibilities. The bishop is merely a presbyter, selected to sustain the connectional order of the church in a given geographical jurisdiction. The bishop, therefore, is not in apostolic succession, preserving the teaching of the apostles. His office does not impart divine grace; it is not a sacramental or symbolic authority. The authority of the Methodist bishop is functional and administrative. In effect, he wields more power than his namesake in the

Episcopal church, where apostolic succession is affirmed. The bishops of Methodism appoint the clergy of local congregations.

Methodism is not congregationalist, although the effects of the independent spirit of American congregations are evident. Today especially, large and influential congregations have their way with the bishop and his powers of appointment. In the days of Francis Asbury and Thomas Coke, the emphasis upon methodist organization and discipline gave the bishop an iron hand in the direction of the life and work of the church. Gradually the presiding elders (today, District Superintendents) and the local preachers and laity began to exercise a greater share of representative authority in the connectional system.

At the head of the connection is the Council of Bishops, elected by jurisdictional conferences of clergy and laity. Each bishop is president of an annual conference, made up of district conferences, guided by district superintendents. Laity participate in all levels of the denomination's governance. General Conference is a legislative body that meets every four years. It is obvious that the United Methodist Church has been influenced by the representative character of American republicanism. However, Methodism exercises a very supervisory form of polity; its connectionalism is designed to work from the top down, regulating the spiritual life of the church.

From this discussion of Methodist polity, it is possible to draw some observations about the social expression of Christianity. For the Wesleyan tradition, the church is a community or society of those who subscribe to a Christian idealism. The church is expected to be a society of holiness—what John Wesley described as a class of those who love God, are happy in God, are pure in heart, and do everything to the glory of God. Holiness and perfection are possible and expected. This is the spirit of Christian idealism that affects the thinking of Americans with regard to their understanding of religion. Americans cannot understand why people who call themselves Christian are not exemplars of certain ideals readily visible to the rank and file. The American intellectual satisfies the spiritual queasiness in his or her soul by speaking of the inability of church people to be realized idealists. He or she does not consider the fact that idealism of the Wesleyan order is only one way of understanding the nature of Christianity. For some Christians the church is a body of nurturing and mediating grace that helps people live with the realization that they constantly do what they know should not be done and leave undone what should be done. There are those who would argue that the ideals of the kingdom of God are not ordinary ideals; we cannot attain them by ordinary means. They are gifts of grace when they are realized, always beyond our willful reach. Methodist piety has coincided with the spirit of America on such matters. Methodism has implanted its spirituality in the soul of the secular and ecclesial United States.

Methodist Diversity

There are several denominations that owe their origins to the Wesleyan tradition. Many of them do not share the parent church's concern for a strong connectional polity. They have been more fundamentally influenced by the American passion for independence and private judgment. Several Methodist denominations are almost exclusively African American and owe their origins to the late eighteenth and early nineteenth centuries. The African Methodist Episcopal Church came into being as a result of the work of freemen Richard Allen and Daniel Coker, both of whom had been ordained by Asbury. An African Methodist church in New York City (named Zion) was the nucleus of another denomination, the African Methodist Episcopal Zion Church. Both these denominations were founded by ex-slaves and were designed for blacks who encountered discrimination in the predominantly white congregations. These denominations followed the Methodist Episcopal Church in polity and doctrine.

James O'Kelly was a Methodist preacher in good standing with the church who began to question the power of Bishop Asbury to move preachers around and otherwise rule the new Methodist church with a heavy hand. As early as 1790 O'Kelly objected to the episcopal authority of Asbury. A Virginian who had been raised on the republican principles of the post-revolutionary era, O'Kelly began a subtle agitation for reform. When it proved unsuccessful, he left the Methodist Episcopal Church to form the Republican Methodist Church. Eventually, in the Wesleyan spirit, he changed the name of the denomination to the Christian Church.

The efforts at reform continued within the parent church in spite of O'Kelly's schism. By 1830 a group of reformers had formed another separate body, the Methodist Protestant Church. The new denomination rejected bishops and presiding elders, and it permitted the election of class leaders by the membership of classes. Again the schismatic group was Wesleyan in spirit but republican and democratic in its polity and understanding of the nature of the church. The American sympathy for private judgment and the experience of justification and aspiration to perfection were giving expression to a diversity of Methodist formations.

In the Wesleyan understanding, the lowly and poor were of infinite worth in the sight of God. "All God's children had a soul, and the only problem was to find it and save it." Souls were neither black nor white, and early Methodists spoke out against slavery. The Christmas Conference of 1784 had declared that all Methodists were to free their slaves within a year. The discipline of the church was to be used to execute the order, and no slaveholder was to be admitted into membership. However, on the local level it was not expedient to free slaves, and preachers began to develop a theological position that concerned itself only with the saving of souls and left social ethics to the government. Gradually the Methodist perspective on slavery was modified. By the 1830s abolitionism had become a crucial issue in America.

In 1836, a presiding elder named Orange Scott headed the New England delegation to the General Conference meeting in Cincinnati. An abolitionist, Scott sought to get the conference to take action against slavery. When he was unsuccessful, he withdrew from the Methodist Episcopal Church. However, he was still a Methodist in polity and doctrine; accordingly, he helped to organize a new Methodist denomination that would set its standards against slavery. In 1843 the Wesleyan Methodist Connection of America was established at a convention held in Utica, New York. The Christian Methodist Episcopal Church, until 1954 known as the Colored Methodist Episcopal Church, was born in the post-slavery South. These African Americans had been members of the Methodist Episcopal Church, South, a tradition that resulted when national Methodism split over the issue of slavery in 1844. In establishing the Colored Methodist Episcopal Church, these blacks were exercising their need for a religious community of their own people, independent of the denominations in which they had been second-class members. According to Hunter D. Farish, the Methodist Episcopal Church, South, had declared that it was "unprepared to revise radically its conception of the proper place of blacks in the Connection. Though the Negro was invited to remain in the church, it was expected he would continue in an inferior and subordinate relation."

By the middle of the nineteenth century much of Methodism had begun to lose its Wesleyan fervor and to grow careless in the use of methodistic discipline. Holiness had been tamed, and Methodists lived as children of the world. A wave of reaction and reformation against the institutionalization of Methodism began. The cry went out for a return to the "old-time religion," to evidence of holiness and for attention to the Wesleyan experience. The result was the birth of the Free Methodist Church and the Holiness-Pentecostal movement (see chap. 18). Denominations such as the Church of the Nazarene, the Church of God (Anderson, Indiana), and the Christian and Missionary Alliance are Wesleyan movements; however, their development relates to the revolution in ideas and society that took place in the latter half of the nineteenth century. Although the Holiness-Pentecostal movement has Wesleyan roots and sympathies, it is a peculiarly American phenomenon, very much a product of the modernization of Western culture.

Several Methodist denominations were partly the result of the ethnic diversity of the United States. Something about Wesleyanism was in harmony with the spirit of Pietism which had emerged in Germany shortly before Wesley's Aldersgate experience. The romanticism and intuitional power of the German people sought the curious warming of the heart so cherished by John Wesley. Some of the Germans who came to the United States in the eighteenth century had already been awakened to the possibilities of the renewal of personal spirituality. Philip Otterbein was a German Reformed pastor who underwent a Methodist type of conversion and found himself in sympathy with Wesleyanism. After Bishop Asbury concluded that English should be the standard language of the Methodist Episcopal church, Otterbein began special evangelistic work among the Germans. By 1800 the United Brethren in Christ had become a separate German-speaking Wesleyan denomination.

In similar fashion Jacob Albright, a Lutheran layman, became a Methodist after experiencing justification and sought to establish a German-speaking branch of Methodism. Asbury remained firm in his decision that the Methodist church should be English-speaking. Accordingly, Albright began to organize classes independently of the Methodists. In 1803 a conference of his followers formed an independent ecclesiastical organization called the Evangelical Association. In 1946 the United Brethren and the Evangelical Church united to form the Evangelical United Brethren Church. It is interesting that this latter denomination joined with the Methodist church in 1968 to form the United Methodist Church. Divisions that had been occasioned by differences in language and ethnicity were resolved in the course of a history that rendered such divisions obsolete.

The General Conference of the Methodist Episcopal Church in 1844 had adopted a strong antislavery measure, resulting in the formation the following year of the Methodist Episcopal Church, South. The two churches reunited in 1939 in company with the Methodist Protestant Church, making the Methodist Church almost comprehensive of the Wesleyan tradition bearing the name Methodist.

History in the United States

Having examined the nature and shape of the Methodist tradition, at least in its original development into the nineteenth century, and having noted several ways in which it was a tradition congenial to an emergent United States, it remains for us to make some general observations about Methodism in the scope of American history.

The Wesleyan tradition was coming into its own on the eve of the War for Independence. It can be suggested that Wesleyanism shares with the Great Awakening[3] in the creation of a national spirit of the common folk of America. Both phenomena, although led initially by educated clergy, were expressions of the emerging spirit of democracy and independence that eventually transformed the American republic into a democracy. Both movements fostered that spirit and became universal enough to create Americans out of a diverse group of colonies and colonists.

Although Wesley himself was opposed to American independence, he had unleashed a set of assumptions that made independence and democracy inevitable. Although many of the Wesleyan lay preachers returned to England at the outset of hostilities, they had already made their bequest of equality and holiness to a host of native preachers. Under Asbury's supervision these American itinerants served the cause of freedom and increased the membership of the Methodist classes in spite of the war. The connectionalism and emphasis upon the leadership of laity gave exceptional advantage to the Methodists during the time when other traditions suffered from lack of trained clergy.

By 1784 the Methodists were ready for their own American church. Wesley provided them with ordained clergy, circumventing the requirements of episcopal polity and dispatching Thomas Vasey and Richard Whatcoat as presbyters to guarantee the future of the American church. The newly emergent Methodist Episcopal Church would have its ordained ministers as well as its lay preachers. "In 1784 at the time of the Christmas Conference," writes Winthrop S. Hudson, "Methodists had numbered almost 15,000. Six years later, in 1790, there were 57,631 members. By 1820 they had overtaken the Baptists and had become the largest American denomination."[4]

Revivalism is in many ways an American religious phenomenon;[5] it is both an expression of the American spirit and a powerful contributor to the formation of an American way of thinking. Certainly it represents a dominant characteristic of American religion, affecting all religious traditions. There is little doubt that Wesleyanism has been one of the primary exponents of the revivalistic spirit. Methodist growth, especially on the nineteenth-century frontier, coincided with its advocacy and support of those measures necessary to the saving of souls. Methodism, under the leadership of talented and charismatic figures like Francis Asbury and Peter Cartwright, was strong in strategy and tactics. It succeeded where others failed as the representative of a carefully disciplined revivalism that subdued the frontier and prepared America for its role in the world. To be initiated into a Methodist class as a result of conversion was to be born into the body of a chaste and purposive United States.

When the age of mass immigration brought millions of foreign-born peoples to the strange but promised land of America, Methodists rose to the challenge of initiating the newcomers into the world of the Christian United States. They provided relief programs, sought to make the Bible and worship services available in the languages of the immigrants, and helped them adjust to the customs of the United States. Millions of people had to be integrated. Their former religious identity was not important. The society and culture of the United States had been shaped by Protestant Christianity, and the American religious spirit was Wesleyan and revivalistic. The only real hope for integration and for avoiding barbarism was to transform the newcomers into true Americans by offering them the possibility of that powerful warming of the heart that creates new and holy people.

Frances E. Willard (1839–98) was a devout Methodist whose personal religious life had been strongly affected by revivalistic evangelicalism and the holiness tendencies of her tradition. It should be emphasized that nineteenth-century evangelicalism was fervently involved in social reform, which was considered a necessary continuation of the conversion experience. Willard, as president of the WCTU (Women's Christian Temperance Union) urged the movement against the abuse of alcohol in the direction of support for labor unions and women's suffrage. Inasmuch as the romanticization of women had led men to say that women's virtue was superior to male virtue, Willard cunningly agreed and suggested that it was up to women to reform society.

Some Methodist women, such as Jarena Lee (1783–1850?) became prominent preachers in the Methodist tradition. Often they were licensed to preach without granting ordination, but it was not until the 1950s that women were granted full clergy rights.

The twentieth century was to be the Christian century in the minds of many Americans. A Methodist layman named John R. Mott spoke of the "Evangelization of the World in this Generation" and worked with students to create the World's Student Christian Federation in 1895. Mott's amazing skills were directed toward overcoming denominational differences (a Methodist goal from the beginning of the movement) and bringing the simplicity of the gospel message to the people of the world. The assumption was that this was a message for all people, one that would transform them into citizens of the kingdom of God.

Mott's efforts were interrupted by the terrors of World War I, an indication of the fact that Christianization had not taken place and that the optimism focused on the new century had been misplaced. Methodists renewed their evangelistic efforts in support of the Interchurch World Movement of 1919 and 1920. According to the idealism that lay at the heart of Wesleyanism, the war had to be interpreted as an aberration, an intrusion into the process of world conversion and Christian civilization. The Interchurch movement sought to raise millions of dollars to complete the task. The Methodist Centenary Movement set a goal of $40 million and received pledges of $100 million. But the mood of America and the world had altered. Unpaid pledges and dwindling enthusiasm led to the failure of the Interchurch movement.

World War I ended "the Methodist era" of American history. Although many of the ideas and assumptions of Wesleyanism still reside within the American psyche, its people have laid aside much of their optimism. Many are no longer concerned with the saving of souls and have embarked on a pilgrimage of spiritual satisfaction through consumerism and the sanctification of personal desire. Even those who concern themselves with the salvation of their souls do so in an almost narcissistic fashion, as if salvation were a possession and a guarantee of success in this life and the expectation of a golden paradise beyond. Although some commentators may wish to say that this narcissism was already present in the Methodist concern for personal salvation, it is far from the spirit of John Wesley.

Modernization has had its effect on Methodism. Perhaps it was so congenial to the American spirit that it has become secularized—universalized and incorporated into the worldly assumptions of America by the beginning of the twenty-first century. Methodism today is concerned with Christian unity and social justice. In many ways it was a pioneer in the former and a great practitioner of the latter. In the twentieth century the Methodist Bishops Francis J. O'Connell and G. Bromley Oxnam stood in the forefront of leadership in matters of ecumenicity and social ethics. But certainly the United Methodist Church has become a prominent member of that phalanx of

American Christianity known as the mainline. It is against this seeming lack of conviction that a whole new religious phenomenon has emerged out of the fires of modernity. William McLoughlin has called it the "third force" of Christianity, that body of churches and preachers, too numerous to mention, that came to maturity in the twentieth century—whose number may be equivalent to the remainder of mainline Protestantism.

In the middle of the last century J. Paul Williams called attention to the prominence of Methodism. He quoted Theodore Roosevelt, who once said:

> I would rather address a Methodist audience than any other audience in America. . . . The Methodists represent the great middle class and in consequence are the most representative church in America.

Williams also referred to a comment in *Life* magazine:

> In many ways it is our most characteristic church. It is short on theology, long on good works, brilliantly organized, primarily middle class, frequently bigoted, incurably optimistic, zealously missionary and touchingly confident of the essential goodness of the man next door.[6]

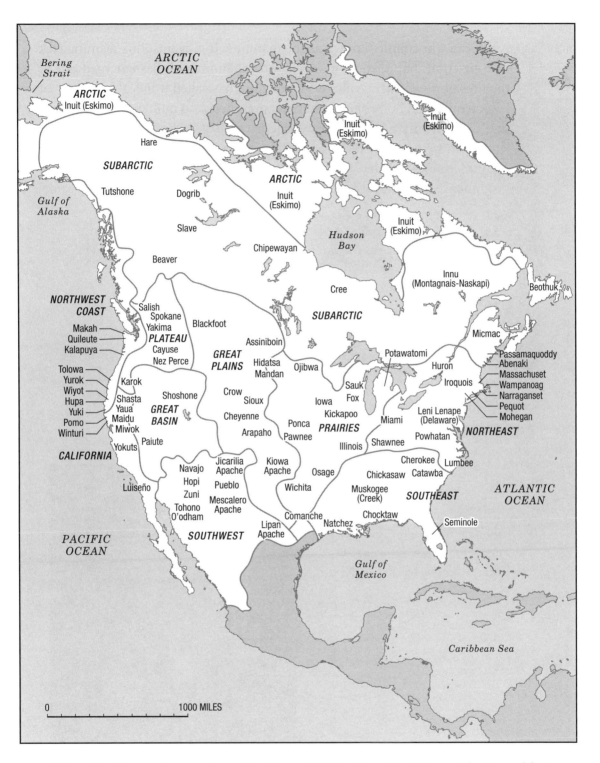

Cultural regions and approximate locations of Native American tribes at the time of first contact with Europeans.

Left: **John Winthrop**, colonial statesman, in an etching and engraving by Amos Doolittle published in Benjamin Trumbull's *A Complete History of Connecticut* (1797).

Right: Portrait of **Joseph Smith**, founder of the Church of Jesus Christ of Latter-day Saints, by Adrian Lamb (1971).

Right: **Frances Willard** (1839–1898), the American temperance campaigner. Circa 1870–1880.

Left: **Isaac Mayer Wise** (1819–1900), a rabbi who became a leading organizer of Reform Judaism. Date unknown.

Left: **Mary Baker Eddy** (1821–1910), American founder of the Church of Christ, Scientist. Date unknown.

Below: Making sweet grass medicine—Blackfoot ceremony. Painting by Joseph Henry Sharp (1920).

Right: **Harry Emerson Fosdick**, on August 29, 1925, aboard the S.S. Duillio sailing from New York to Europe, where he delivered a sermon before the League of Nations at Geneva.

Below: **Clarence Darrow** and **William Jennings Bryan** have a friendly chat in a courtroom during the Scopes trial in Dayton, Tennessee (1925).

Left: **Reinhold Niebuhr**, theologian, social ethicist, and scholar. 1958.

Right: On February 26, 1964, in Chicago, a man distributes the newspaper *Muhammad Speaks* outside the Nation of Islam's convention. The photo on the front page is of **Elijah Muhammad**, the leader of the Nation of Islam.

Right: On July 18, 1972, Senator George McGovern, Democratic presidential candidate, met with **Ben Black Elk**, seventy-three-year-old Oglala Chief, during a visit to Mt. Rushmore National Memorial in South Dakota. In the background are the sculpted heads of Presidents George Washington, Thomas Jefferson, Theodore Roosevelt, and Abraham Lincoln. McGovern was vacationing in his home state.

Below: **Billy Graham** preached on July 13, 1973, at the Upper Midwest Crusade. He likened each person's judgment day to the Watergate hearing: "Have you noticed how the TV cameras zoom in when the witness is asked difficult questions?" There is a judgment day, he told his audience of 21,000, that no one can escape.

Left: Two men pray in a mosque in the Chicago suburbs (1993).

Right: A Passover Seder plate.

Left: Roadside graves.

Part 2

Restructuring, New Beginnings, and Preservations

Thus far we have been examining American religious traditions whose origins were European or British and settled primarily on the eastern seaboard during what is called the Colonial Era (prior to 1783) of the history of the United States. The exception to this generalization are those Native American traditions whose subsequent history was profoundly affected by the presence and behavior of the European Christians. The effects of the European heritage on American Indian religious life are still under investigation, with many chapters of the story yet to be compiled. The reverse is also true: There is little doubt that the story of American Christianity has been influenced by Native American ideas and practices, both on the popular and institutional levels. For example, among the Pennsylvania Germans, the Christmas visitor Belsnickel was a figure costumed in buckskin, wearing moccasins, and carrying a quiver of arrows on his back. The history of missions among Native Americans also represents an extended period in which Christians had to rethink the significance of the Christian gospel in relation to people and cultures that did not share the heritage of European Christendom.

In part 2 we shall be discussing religious traditions that either had their origins during the early decades of the new American Republic (after 1789) or grew in stature and significance as a result of mass immigration during the nineteenth and twentieth centuries—both of which centuries belong to the story of the coming of age of the new nation. This is an age in which many traditions were being restructured to adjust their ideas and practices in harmony with the hopes of the people of a new nation or the assumptions of modern knowledge. It is also an age of new beginnings, in keeping with the American tendency to seek escape from the past or to recover a past presumed lost over many centuries. However, religious traditions often attempt to preserve the past, maintaining that past knowledge, faith, and understanding are not necessarily displaced or canceled out by modern scientific or philosophical discoveries.

These are the issues to be examined in the development of American religious traditions after the Colonial Period of our history.

chapter 11

The Revivalist Evangelical Tradition

Religious movements akin to American revivalism occur among many people and cultures, from the traditional peoples of Australia and Africa to certain Hindu and Islamic societies of Asia and the Middle East. We call the movements under discussion in this chapter revivalistic *evangelicalism* because it is a Christian phenomenon in which the gospel/evangel is directed by scriptural mandate toward the experience of individual transformation. We shall use the terms *revivalism* and *revivalistic evangelicalism* interchangeably. The revivalist heritage has affected all of American religion, at least until very recent times. What we are discussing is not a tradition that has assumed any one denominational form but one that has influenced almost every denomination, yet exists in a somewhat differentiated form alongside all denominations.

That is, revivalistic evangelicalism has its own religious form and character. Some might say that it is an American religious institution even though it has no one denominational standard-bearer. To a great extent, it is an American creation, a tradition shaped by the currents of history that came to confluence in the American experience. It is not entirely the product of our own history, but the United States has provided the time and place for the development of this religious tradition, which has been very individualistic and pragmatic, as we shall see in further discussion.

Revivalism is a religious tradition that emphasizes the centrality of the individual's experience of saving faith. It is not to be identified with Puritanism but bears the unmistakable stamp of the Massachusetts Puritan heritage. Revivalism demonstrates the manner in which a single important emphasis in religious history (in this case Massachusetts Puritanism) becomes a primary criterion for the formation of a new "way." In an earlier chapter, we examined the Puritan experiment—its attempt to define a pure church composed of pure and visible saints. Iconoclasm gave way to moral definition and to profession of a doctrinal statement of faith. Eventually, however, these were considered insufficient evidence of true sainthood, and the prospective saint had to provide a testimony—a narrative that gave evidence that faith had indeed transformed her or his life. It is this evidence of saving faith (often with its corresponding testimonial narrative) that becomes a prominent feature of American religion. Revivalism is the tradition most responsible for the promotion of that distinction.

Basics of Revivalistic Evangelicalism

Although revivalism focuses upon the individual's evidence of saving faith, the heritage began out of concern for the loss of moral and religious vitality in society and culture. The earliest practitioners, the forerunners of modern revivalism in eighteenth-century America, spoke of revivals of religion, of the need for such revivals. Essentially, they were not referring to the revival of an individual's spiritual life but to a general "stirring up" of the public. To point to a revival of religion was to call attention to the fact that people in general were renewing their commitments to the essence and practice of their religion. The incidence of one or two people experiencing transformation (giving evidence of saving faith) would not have been cause for speaking of a revival. Only if such incidents as these were quite numerous, and if the effects upon the society were observable, would there be evidence of a revival.

A revival implies the stirring up of the comatose, the awakening of the slumbering. A revival is an indication of the overcoming of spiritual lethargy and indifference. Eighteenth-century observers of the American scene began to report what they called *awakenings* occurring all along the eastern seaboard from Massachusetts to the Carolinas and Georgia. The events appeared to be spontaneous, unplanned, suggesting that a major alteration in the American mind was under way. Reports of the "awakenings" came from the rural valleys of Pennsylvania and western Maryland, from the Connecticut River Valley in Massachusetts, from New Haven, Connecticut, and from the Raritan River Valley of New Jersey. When we remember that the first half of the eighteenth century was hardly a time of rapid transportation and communication, the reports of these "awakenings" are all the more remarkable. It would have been difficult to "program" a network of awakenings in those days. The incidence was spontaneous and wide-ranging, so much so that historians have dubbed the circumstances the Great Awakening. Accordingly, we may define the Great Awakening as a concurrence of spontaneous awakenings (or "revivals") that took place in colonial America during the first half of the eighteenth century.

Theologians like the renowned and brilliant Jonathan Edwards, himself involved in the awakenings, began to address some fundamental questions raised by these religious phenomena. He wondered how it would be possible to determine whether such goings-on provided evidence for a genuine revival. He applied the insights of philosophy and science in order to make a theological analysis of conversion experience. Edwards was a man of his time. A child of Puritan upbringing, precocious, educated at Yale, he had served as a tutor there before joining his grandfather, Solomon Stoddard, in the pastorate of the Congregational Church in Northampton, Massachusetts. Edwards had read John Locke and Isaac Newton as an adolescent; he understood the new philosophy, new psychology, and new physics. But he was a Puritan with a highly moralistic interpretation of the Christian life. The strength of Calvin's understanding of God undergirded his moralism. He deplored what he considered to be the moral laxity of the youth of Northampton, addicted as they were to "night walking, and frequenting the tavern, and lewd practices. . . . It was their manner very frequently to get together in conventions of both sexes for mirth and jollity, which they called frolics." (Today we might call it "partying.") The people were not very serious about their destiny, according to Edwards. They were consoling themselves with the idea that they were no better, no worse, than others—that they were relatively "good" folk and God would judge them accordingly.

To Edwards this was a flagrant denial of the truth of Christian salvation. The complacency of the people needed jarring. They needed to hear the truth of the gospel as St. Augustine, Luther, and Calvin had presented it. They had to learn that they were justified by God's grace alone, that their destiny hung in the fragile balance of God's election of them. There is a certain terror in that realization, an anxiety that reduces one to a helplessness that enables the truth of God's gracious election to be experienced. Edwards began preaching the Reformation doctrines, using his knowledge of modern human psychology and his skills of language and rhetoric. The results were extraordinary. People were transformed, sometimes dramatically overwhelmed by their sinfulness and the subsequent liberation of their souls by Christ's saving power. There was weeping, emotional collapse, trance, and renewed attention to the disciplines of the spiritual life. Northampton was aglow with an awakening.

However, the news began to trickle in that awakenings were occurring throughout the valley, or that the towns and congregations were eagerly awaiting the same experiences. Sometime before Edwards's "narrative of the surprising word of God in Northampton," there had been reports of awakenings among the Dutch Reformed in New Jersey. They were partly the result of the persistent efforts of Theodore J. Frelinghuysen, who confronted the people under his care with the seriousness of their spiritual responsibilities. Frelinghuysen's methods were partly an outgrowth of the Pietistic movement in Europe. He utilized personal meetings in the homes of people and directed his preaching to matters of renewal and commitment. In addition, he sought to enforce the Reformed discipline of requiring intense examination and preparation before celebrations of the Lord's Supper. His approach was often direct and personal, embarrassing to some. However, the results were phenomenal. A revival was in motion.

Meanwhile among the Presbyterians in Pennsylvania and New Jersey there were similar awakenings as the result of the preaching of William Tennent and his sons, John, Gilbert, and William Jr. From the rural outposts of central Pennsylvania and the Shenandoah Valley of Virginia came the reports of what was later to be known as the Great Awakening. From this widespread revival of the eighteenth century came the methods and the ideas that were to become fundamental to the heritage of American revivalist evangelicalism.

Revivals generally occur at a time when the accepted modes of order and meaning in society appear to be incapable of sustaining life. Of course, there are always forms of vice, immorality, and the experience of anxiety or despair. However, in normal times we may expect that persons engaging in immoral behavior acknowledge their misconduct, admit error, and perhaps express penitence—even though they continue to be immoral. Somehow these persons still feel like a part of a meaningful and ordered universe. Although they may digress from the norms or experience meaninglessness, they continue to trust and care for what ought to be.

However, there seem to be times when people are self-satisfied with whatever way they may be living. They are not much interested in issues of right and wrong; perhaps they care very little whether the universe is meaningful. They will claim whatever life has to offer at any moment. Of course this expression of disorder and amoral circumstance derives from our perspective in the late twentieth century. We have been living through times of great social and religious disruption—times in which morality, order, and meaning are subservient to the subjective standards of individuals. It may be unfair to speak of the past with the words of our own anxiety. Twentieth-century words and ideas may be inappropriate to the description of previous centuries. Nevertheless, the findings of historians and anthropologists provide us with a certain license for observing patterns in our history.

The early eighteenth century was a period in which the inherited traditions of Europe were under great stress. Two hundred years and more had passed since Martin Luther and John Calvin had forced the Catholic Christianity of Western Europe into a new stage of development. There had been times of religious oppression and warfare. The relative stability of Catholicism had been shaken to its foundations and from the rubble had emerged a great proliferation of religious movements, all seeking the loyalty of people, all staking some claim to represent the essential truth and form of the gospel of Jesus Christ. This great diversity of claims was exported to America. We must remember that until the early decades of the nineteenth century, almost all American religions were imports from Europe. Even the most radical of them perpetuated many of the assumptions of European religion and society. For example, they retained some measure of the Christendom model, assuming that the commitments and transformations of people were to be shared in such a way that they become the basis of civic and political life. Many of the European traditions also functioned with some version of the inherited parish system. This system was based upon the notion that all people in a given geopolitical area were in some state of loyalty to the same religious institution. The area could be divided into parishes, which were religious jurisdictions under the care of the proper ecclesiastical appointees.

It is easy to understand that such assumptions would not find great hospitality in the American setting. It is difficult to maintain a parish system in a place of open settlement where people may move about freely and where it is difficult to limit the constituency to folks of a single religious persuasion. We have seen how the Massachusetts Puritan experiment in establishing a holy commonwealth (essentially a model of purified mini-Christendom) was doomed to failure because it was difficult to maintain control over the spiritual well-being of constituents. The attempt to exile deviants and exclude the uncommitted and unorthodox was ineffective in the long run. As Sidney E. Mead expressed it:

> From the beginning, the subtle magic of space began to work upon the tight little islands of the transplanted authoritarians themselves, eroding their most ingeniously contrived and zealously guarded barriers of creed and logic and doctrine, until, by the time of Crevecoeur, it was no more than the repetition of a platitude to say that "zeal in Europe is confined; here it evaporated in the great distance it has to travel; there it is a grain of powder enclosed, here it burns away in the open air, and consumes without effect."[1]

Of course, "both transplanted and indigenous zeal continued to burn, even in the open air, and *not* without effect." But the point is well made that by the early eighteenth century, the inherited structures of European religion were greatly modified in America. The parish system in its European form was ineffective and the attempt to regulate the spiritual life by external control was victimized by space. There were always visitors from somewhere else who held another vision or little vision at all. And there was always more space to invite the visionary and dissenting members of one's own "parish" to go elsewhere, to start anew, to "do their own thing."

The Great Awakening

The Great Awakening occurred because of the breakdown of the old order. It contributed greatly to the creation of a new order. This revival of the eighteenth century was an occasion of great social and cultural significance. When we remember that religion always has to do with the manner in which the ultimate order and meaning of the world is perceived, we should expect that these pervasive religious awakenings were to be of profound consequence. It has been said by scholars that the revival was a sign of revolution. The democratic spirit was asserting itself in the voice of people. It was a sign that the inherited hierarchical and traditional assumptions of Europe were no longer applicable—at least not in this New World. The inhabitants of America had been returned to primordial time and place, to sacred space and time, the time of beginnings. Here the old ways no longer applied. Each person was Adam and Eve at home in the garden with the voice of God as companion. Priests and hierarchies were of the old order created by old boundaries and distinctions. Even education was a boundary without meaning. The Presbyterian Gilbert Tennent preached and published a sermon that serves as the watchword of the new order. Titled "The Danger of an Unconverted Ministry," and delivered in Nottingham, Pennsylvania, on March 8, 1740, it levels the qualifications of ministry to the evidence of saving faith. In effect, it informs the people that their own experience of justification (conversion) makes them the equal of anyone, be he prelate or Oxford don. Tennent also challenged the parish system head-on. What was most important, he said, was preaching that comes from the soul of a converted speaker. The people must go wherever such preaching may be found; they need not be bound to the congregation or parish to which nature had assigned them and where they might be in danger of receiving unconverted nonsense. By the same token, the converted preacher was free to move about and preach wherever he was led by the call of God and the needs of the people. Thus was born a new form of religious function—the itinerant preacher. This was a preacher who was not pastor to a congregation in an assigned parish location. This was a person, like the wandering prophets of ancient Israel or the mendicant friars of the late Middle Ages, who carried the gospel into fields, street corners, and warehouses.

In England, as we have seen, John Wesley broke from the restrictions of the parish system at the same time that Tennent and others took to the highways of the New World. The most prominent of the itinerants in America was an Englishman named George Whitefield, who was the forerunner of the American evangelist, that long string of itinerant revivalists that includes such names as Lorenzo Dow, Charles Grandison Finney, Dwight L. Moody, Billy Sunday, and Billy Graham. Whitefield had come under Wesley's influence at a time when both had had opportunity to read Jonathan Edwards's *A Faithful Narrative of the Surprising Work of God in the Conversion of Many Hundred Souls in Northampton and Neighboring Towns* (London, 1737). Both were influenced by Edwards's *Narrative* and by what was reported of the awakenings in America. Whitefield's work attracted the attention of Benjamin Franklin, who thought that the preaching of the former could be an important factor in fostering morality and social control among the colonial masses. Franklin, for all his republican maneuvering, was an intellectual elitist. In his own mind, the masses of people needed the preaching of churches and itinerant evangelists like Whitefield. He, of course, being an enlightened *philosophe,*[2] did not. Franklin was impressed with Whitefield as an agent of moral order and supported his work, even assisting in the sponsorship of a tabernacle capable of housing the crowds who came to hear the young evangelist in Philadelphia.

If there was any integration or coordination to the awakenings of the eighteenth century, it was provided by the work of such itinerants as George Whitefield. He traveled throughout the colonies and, along with other traveling preaches like Gilbert Tennent, helped bring a new and democratic order into being. The experience of the individual was being raised to prominence so that everyone could say, I speak with the authority of what I have personally known and felt. My voice has the right to be heard. It is a voice that is equal to the voice of any other person. It is the voice of the people.

There is little doubt that the Great Awakening was symptomatic of democracy in the making and that it was a grand facilitator of that democracy. The world had waited for the appropriate time and the fallow open fields of America for this child to be born. Here, in America, said Jonathan Edwards, will occur the fulfillment of the ages, the redemption that God has planned. H. Richard Niebuhr, in his classic work *The Kingdom of God in America,* sums up this important insight into the significance of the Great Awakening:

> Such in briefest outline seems to be the story of the great renewal of Christ's kingdom which, not in America alone, but in America not least, came upon the land like the sun and rain of spring, refreshing life and promising abundant harvests. . . . For America . . . it cannot eradicate if it would the marks left upon its social memory, upon its institutions and habits, by an awakening to God that was simultaneous with its awakening to national self-consciousness. It was no wholly new beginning, for the Christianity expressed in it was a more venerable thing than the American nation. Yet for America, it was a new beginning; *it was our national conversion.* [italics mine][3]

It may not be true that the Christianity expressed in the Awakening was an old and venerable tradition. Perhaps it was a new form of Christianity, being fashioned in the American Eden out of the experiential overexertions of Puritanism. New or old, it was a source and symptom of "our national conversion."

There were other consequences of the eighteenth-century revival. On the theoretical level, there were those who opposed the revival, calling attention to the reasonableness of Christianity, for dedication to its Calvinist temperament of decency and order. Viewed from the perspective of the history of religions, these awakenings were at least partly an example of enthusiastic religion. (*Enthusiasm* is a word derived from the Greek *en theoi*—"in the gods," or possessed by the gods.) Human beings everywhere in the world, from tribal traditions to the centers of the world's literate traditions, have always provided evidence for possession. Trances, ecstatic dancing, visions, convulsions, voices, and immunity to pain and injury have all been understood to be the result of possession by a divine being or beings—enthusiasm. Christian and Jewish history have their own chapters on ecstasy.[4] There has also been a tradition of suspicion of ecstatic, enthusiastic religion. In the history of theology there is a wariness, a concern that what seems to be God-possession may in fact be demonic, satanic possession, or a temptation to delight in such experiences. Enthusiasm may be a form of illusion or idolatry, detracting us from the truth of God's merciful love.

Many clergy and people in New England and the Middle Colonies were concerned about the potential chaos and disorder that would be unleashed by the awakenings. There were some examples of excesses that seemed to support these suspicions. Charles Chauncy cautioned the members of First Congregational Church in Boston and extended his opposition in a book, *Seasonable Thoughts on the State of Religion in New England.* The reasonableness of these seasonable thoughts got out of hand as Chauncy castigated the revivalists and accused them of lawlessness. It did not take long for sides to be chosen. In Congregationalism, those who opposed the revivals and stood by right doctrine, reasonableness, and order in worship were called the Old Lights. Followers of Edwards and the awakenings were known as New Lights. Presbyterianism settled for Old Sides and New Sides. The seeds were sown for theological controversy, and, although it may well be true that New Light-New Side Christianity has become the American way, the controversy lingers.

Of course, Jonathan Edwards was more than an apologist for revivals. He was a creative and constructive thinker; some would say he was one of America's greatest theologians and philosophers. Edwards was a Calvinist, but he was also an intellectual whose ideas had been shaped by the philosophy and physics of his day. As a student of John Locke, he demonstrated the manner in which traditional Reformed theology was perfectly consistent with the new way of understanding the human mind as a function of the total sensate person. Edwards's thought led to the establishment of a new direction in theology, orthodox in its intentions, but set over against the old Calvinism of many of his contemporaries. Revivalism and John Locke had fashioned a new form of religious thought—Edwardsean in tone, a New England theology that would carry the weight of creative thinking for several generations.

The institutional consequences of the Great Awakening were of almost equal significance to those of a social, cultural, and intellectual character. Membership increased in the many existent churches and religious societies. To understand the importance of this, we must realize that statistical measures do not provide an adequate insight into the religious situation. Statistics were somewhat loosely regarded in those days; they were not the measure of things they have become for us in later times. Statistics became important when institutions were thrown into competitive circumstances wherein their success was determined by voluntary membership and financial support. The early eighteenth century was a world characterized by biblical ideas, images, and concepts of morality. The perception of the world was biblical, predominantly Christian. Religiously speaking, the ultimate order and meaning of existence for virtually every American colonist were shaped by Christianity and the Bible. Most people were Christian in some sense; many were Christian in conviction and intention, whether their names were entered upon the roles of congregational societies or not. The Great Awakening increased active and committed participation in the Christian life and added to the roll call of the congregations.

In addition, there were new congregations and new denominations. It is understandable that the rising tide of the revival should have inundated the countryside with numbers of people who had no home in the established congregations. And, of course, in some instances the numbers were so great that the churches were too small to contain them. Rural outposts and small villages acquired new congregations to meet the needs. Then too, the newly awakened often found themselves in congregations of old Calvinist or Old Light persuasion, where the enthusiasm of revivals was suspect and opposed. Many of these people formed their own societies.

Once the practice of itinerancy and the voice of the laity had broken the inherited social and cultural order, religious democracy had its way in America. It was a small step from the experience of conversion in a New England meeting house or an open field to the conclusion that a true congregation of God would be comprised of those with an adult evidence of saving faith. Baptism of infants would be suspect under those conditions, and the baptism of "saved" adults by immersion would become a matter of spiritual logic for many. The Great Awakening gave encouragement to the Baptist spirit. This new denomination gathered momentum and eventually became the largest of non-Roman Catholic traditions in America.

The evangelical mind is convinced that the evangel of God's justifying grace in Jesus Christ must be carried quickly and effectively to all the peoples of the earth. The evangelical mind is convinced that God intends to confront each individual with the claims of Jesus Christ, that an immediate response will produce immediate and lasting transformation of life. Revivalism gave full play to the evangelical mind. Missions to the Native Americans were organized or given renewed effort, and the cities and countryside were soon filled with organizations directed at evangelical goals. When we remember that the Great Awakening was in some sense the revolutionary American counterpart of European Pietism and English Methodism, it is easy to understand why certain charitable projects emerged as institutional effects of the revival. Schools and hospitals were founded, and orphanages were built. Most such institutions had long been the result of religious efforts. They were Christian institutions, supported by the church. The eighteenth century still retained the assumptions that learning and service to human need were essential expressions of the religious life and in some way mandated by the church. The ravages of disease, the precariousness of frontier existence, and skirmishes with alienated Indians left many orphaned children who required the care of benevolent Christians. There were many opportunities for awakened laity to express their newly discovered thanksgiving for the grace and mercy of God.

Many of America's premier institutions of higher education owe their origin to the Great Awakening. The College of New Jersey (Princeton), the College of Rhode Island (Brown University), Queen's (Rutgers of New Jersey), Dartmouth, Hampton-Sydney, Washington and Jefferson, Dickinson, and what later became Washington and Lee are among them. They began in response to the need for more facilities for the education of clergy. There was an insufficient number of older, established colleges like Harvard, Yale, and William and Mary. These older institutions were also inaccessible to the people of an expanding frontier, who were demanding an affordable education for their newly enlightened existence. Also, the Awakening convinced many that the millennium, God's new age, was about to dawn on American shores. It was necessary to prepare for this grand moment of history by extending the boundaries of Christian civilization.

The Great Awakening was the beginning of a distinctively American brand of religion. Although it is true that Pietism and revivals had their counterparts in Europe and Great Britain as well as in America, nowhere else did the unique circumstances of history and geography create an environment that nurtured revivalist elements in so profound a manner. There was a transition from the spontaneous and revolutionary awakenings of the first half of the eighteenth century to the revivalism that took shape in the nineteenth century. By the beginning of the new century, Americans knew that they were a different breed of humanity. They were to be people of success, of competition. They had been offered a measure of divinity and were to be responsible for mastering a continent. The United States was not like other nations, which were hindered by the past and stuffy with deference to established ways of protocol and social and educational standing.

A New American Spirit

"American" was becoming Daniel Boone and Davy Crockett, demonstrating that formal education lacked common sense and courage. A Crockett or

Mike Fink could make a fool out of a fancy, educated easterner any day of the week. The American Revolution (not the War, but the Revolution) and the American landscape had created a new kind of person. The American Enlightenment, with its emphasis upon reason's ability to discover all it needs to know about God, nature, or humanity, was an expression of this revolutionary being. Benjamin Franklin, with his pragmatic wisdom (as evidenced in *Poor Richard's Almanack*) and air of self-made pride, was an incarnation of this new humanity, and George Washington was its heroic and divine icon.

But the people had their own way of discovering the Franklin and Washington in their own lives. That way was the way of awakenings, and God had found a way to bring out the best in a person, having waited until America was settled to try it out. As the new nation came to terms with itself and its vast frontier, its people were in a hurry, with little time for the refinements of the intellect and aristocratic culture. Theological nuances and distinctions seemed of little consequence. Barbarism could be averted and Christian civilization advanced by the application of principles learned at the time of the Great Awakening.

The eighteenth-century revival had taken place in the context of a reasonably established congregational life. Awakenings first occurred in the parishes of Congregational, Dutch Reformed, Presbyterian, and even Episcopal churches along the eastern seaboard. However, in the 1790s and early 1800s it was often the unsettled areas west of the Alleghenies, western New York, Vermont, and New Hampshire, that beckoned for the message of a saving faith that could still the savage passions and bring order and meaning to the capricious life of the wilderness. Nineteenth-century revivalism was to be different from the revivalism of the Great Awakening. Memories of the eighteenth-century awakenings were kept alive by sermons, books, and aging fellow travelers. Nostalgia for the enthusiasm and the revitalized spirits of people led some clergy to try to *stage* revivals. Remembering the kinds of gatherings, the styles of preaching, the character of revival messages, and narrative testimonies of saving faith, they sought to re-create the miraculous moments. Nineteenth-century revivalism became much more contrived and intentional than its parent tradition, with its spontaneity and integrity. And the heritage of modern revivalism owes much more to the nineteenth century than it does to the Great Awakening.

Of course, the earlier movement gave way to the later one. In spite of the parish orientation in its beginnings and the stabilizing influence of Jonathan Edwards, the Great Awakening yielded to the democratizing tendencies of

George Whitefield's itinerancy and Gilbert Tennent's emphasis upon saving faith as the basic criterion of church and ministry. Nevertheless, it is the individualistic evangelicalism of later revivalism that removes the evidence of saving faith from the context of the covenant community. The revivalistic message is one that requires only a messenger and an auditor or an audience. The messenger's qualifications are personal experience, personal declaration that he or she is called to speak on behalf of saving faith, and persuasive skills. We must remember that, in the Puritan tradition in which evidence of saving faith became an important qualification for "visible saints," that evidence took place in the context of a covenanted community for whom other qualities such as knowledge of Scripture and doctrine were also important. And throughout much of the history of Christianity, the doctrine of the one, holy, catholic, and apostolic church served as the medium in which the truth of salvation was heard, interpreted, and mediated. Some theologians would say that a doctrine of the church avoids subjectivity of experience. The church is the embodiment of salvation. It exists prior to the message, in the message, and is the continuing community in which the individual exists who has given evidence of saving faith.

Focuses of Later Revivalism

It is purely a historical observation that American revivalism removes the evidence of saving faith from the context of the covenant community (Puritanism) or from the life of the church that nourished it. Revivalistic evangelicalism is the new religion fostered by the new nation. By evangelicalism, we mean that the focus of Christianity is directed toward the evangel (gospel)— a proclamation that Jesus Christ atones for the sinfulness of individuals, who must in turn confess their sinfulness and accept Jesus Christ as Lord and Savior. Of course, some aspect and interpretation of that proclamation belong to all of Christianity. However, the American experience provides a unique formation for this religious phenomenon.

In the United States this proclamation is addressed primarily by one individual to another individual—even if the latter individual is part of a gathered assembly. As we have said, the proclamation requires no covenanted community and no theological understanding, and it depends upon the skills of a speaker and the expectations of the assembly. There is no assumption that salvation may apply as much to the reform of the social order as to the individual. Instead, it is assumed that society is the sum of its parts and that society will be transformed when its constituents are individually converted to give evidence of saving faith.

This evangelicalism is revivalistic in the sense that it is directed toward the individual for the purpose of reviving the person. The true individual is revived—restored to God's intentions; hopefully, sufficient numbers will be revived so that the world stands ready for the second coming of Christ.

Accordingly, revivalistic evangelicalism is individualistic in keeping with the spirit of America. The message of salvation is directed toward the benefit of the individual. The twentieth-century Russian philosopher Nicholas Berdyayev called this form of religion "transcendental egoism." By this, he meant that it is sanctified self-interest. In other words, it is our religiousness directed toward self-satisfaction, self-realization. It is consumer religion, concerned with gaining for the self whatever will meet the needs of the individual narrowly considered. The assumption is that the individual is in a position to know what her or his needs are. Be all this as it may, the idea of private judgment and experience is certainly characteristic of American religion and culture, a characteristic celebrated by revivalism.

Revivalism, as mentioned above, also focuses upon subjective experience. It is less concerned with social experience, that is, with the experience of having a history, of belonging to a people, of having lived through a certain time or crisis, or having learned to do a certain task. Experience tends to be psychologically oriented in revivalism. This form of evangelical Christianity is pleased with emotional jarrings that animate the person in a new direction. For Jonathan Edwards, the "holy affections" that were awakened in the revivals were "dispositions" like love and fear. That is, "an affection is a determinative disposition towards the whole of reality"—as M. Darrol Bryant puts it.[5] "There are," wrote Edwards, "no other principles which human nature is under the influence of that will ever make man conscientious, but one of these two, fear or love." Accordingly, awakenings were good because the whole of one's being was redirected in a responsible manner. Presumably, it is only with the "whole of one's being" that a human lives and moves. Edwards was sympathetic to revivals because they could alter the dispositions of people by their effects. By the nineteenth century, Edwards's sophistication concerning "religious affections" was transformed into an emphasis upon an experience that the individual could *have*. Although such "experiences" frequently converted the lives of people, they tended to become things that individuals could get, then talk about in a narrative witness to evidence of saving faith.

Revivalism transformed the Bible into a repository of texts that served the requirements of private judgment. Traditionally, the Scriptures of Christianity had been part of the church's teaching; they were an early written testimony to the tradition of the apostles. As such, they were especially sacred and served as an important authority for Christian teaching. Through them, the spirit of God worked to activate and encourage the response of people to the evangel. However, they were to be interpreted in and by the church as the custodial community, the embodiment in this life of Christ's own life. As reflection of the earliest Christian witness, the Scriptures were the church's writings. The Bible was the church's book.

Even when Martin Luther, John Calvin, and other Reformers of the sixteenth century restored the gospel (evangel) to prominence and maintained that the Scriptures alone *(scriptura sola)* were the means to knowledge of the gospel, they understood that scriptural interpretation would take place in the context of the church as community of faith—the priesthood of *all* believers. This is quite removed in concept from the understanding of the nature of the Bible that is most common in America. The heritage of revivalism has transformed the Bible into a textbook of religion. It becomes a reference book whereby the private individual can obtain satisfaction for her or his own needs. Both the needs and the satisfaction are assumed to be an affair between the individual and God. The church as catholic priesthood of all believers through time and space is no longer essential. Instead, the individual seeks personal salvation by reference to the Bible. Religion becomes a private, literal deference to the words of a text. Religion becomes biblicist.

Revivalistic evangelicalism is, therefore, privatist and biblicist in its emphasis. It concentrates on the immediate rather than the mediacy: what is necessary to the salvation of the individual is immediately available to him or her; it is not mediated by a community through a lifetime of nurture. There were those preachers of nineteenth-century evangelicalism who maintained that without the immediate experience of salvation—the subjective evidence of saving faith—there was no redemption, even if one lived a devout lifetime in the bosom of the church. And certainly that is also the message of many representatives of this religious tradition in recent times. Many Americans who are not remotely concerned with participation in religious traditions share these values with revivalistic evangelicals. Americans, in general, tend to value the private and individualistic; they have little regard for mediation and the creative power of tradition.

Revivalism is very pragmatic. It is concerned with results, immediate results that can demonstrate benefits. Converted ("born again") evangelical Christians are aglow with a knowledge of their salvation, having sought happiness and found it. Frequently, material success and prosperity become marks of their conversion. Although previously unhappy and unsuccessful, now they are able to narrate a story in which evidence of saving faith has been followed by victory, in which the individual has found something that works. Out of revivalistic evangelicalism emerges the power of positive (or possibility) thinking, one of the most pragmatic forms of American religion, which is not concerned with orthodoxy or sinfulness and salvation, but with spiritual and material success. Bolstered by a doctrine of humanity that is optimistic and convinced of the divinity of human potential, this form of religion has led to the formation of several denominations and twentieth-century preacher celebrities like Norman Vincent Peale and Robert Schuller.

History of Modern Revivalism

Having discussed the nature and development of revivalism, we turn now to the history of nineteenth- and twentieth-century revivalism. We begin with attention to the role of the frontier camp meeting in this history and its democratizing influence (see above, chap. 10). Camp meetings were at first wilderness assemblies of people who had few other forms of socialization. They were people with deep emotional needs and in search of some validation of existence. Theirs was a religious dilemma—how was one to discern ultimate order and meaning in a chaotic wilderness? There was little time for the subtleties of theology or the refinements of a fully developed religious tradition. What was necessary was a short time away from work and danger—a time to visit, to release tensions, and to hear a message that could turn misery into a blessed assurance that God loved the repentant sinner. Good news was welcome. The style and mandates of revivalism were tailored to the situation, and the awakenings of the past had already begun the process of fashioning a new type of religious leader just made for the camp meeting. The "preacher" was in the making—the common person, the itinerant, with an experience to proclaim, with the gift of persuasion, directing the truth of Bible texts to the broken lives of peers.

Camp meetings were soon part of the trappings of revivalistic evangelicalism. If extended meetings away from the ordinary circumstances of existence could work in the frontier wilderness, they could also be used outside the cities, in the countryside of the more settled eastern United States. By removing people from the scene of their anxieties and providing them with an intense message and an intense experience for a few days, the churches sought to create vitality and newly directed lives. The camp meeting became a means of *ascesis,* withdrawal from the ordinary in order to encounter the superordinary, thereby transforming the ordinariness of existence.

The revivalists discovered other measures as well. In the person of Charles Grandison Finney (1792–1875), evangelical theology found its spokesperson. He was a man of the people, somewhat representative of the Jacksonian age of the common person. A lawyer in the days when one became professional by reading and examination, Finney found the evidence of saving faith in his own life at age twenty-nine. With short notice, he embarked on a career as an itinerant. He was still a lawyer and his preaching had the style and effect of a prosecuting attorney, driving intensely and logically toward the conviction of his auditors. His language was simple, but his effect upon people was spellbinding. He seemed to force his message into each private life, breaking down all the defenses of the "sinners."

Finney had studied theology after his conversion. His skills and demeanor as a lawyer helped him to master the system of theological study and translate the doctrines into language that people could comprehend. He was the new American speaking to new Americans. Finney was also convinced that God had provided humanity with a free will to obey divine commandments. His Calvinist background was converted to make way for the values of decision and personal resolve. Break down the barriers and a person will change his life, thought Finney: God has established this perfectly logical and simple principle. And so Finney began the development of techniques that could be used to bring about conversions. They were called "new measures," although in some sense none was really new. These new measures, however, mark the beginnings of modern revivalism with its careful organization and use of tried methods that could be counted on to produce the desired results. God will not make a revival, said Finney, we have to do it; God gave us the will and the way. This understanding is a far cry from the thought of Jonathan Edwards, who understood revivals to be the surprising work of God.

Finney's new measures included the use of direct, plain speech. He did not discuss theological issues but spoke to the people (sometimes naming individuals) about their particular sinful lives. Another new measure was the anxious bench, a front seat to which a person was led and where, in the presence of the assembly, he or she could be appealed to or cajoled—a practice similar to the lawyer's use of the witness stand. Finney organized home visitations and "anxious meetings"—small group prayer and examination sessions in which the intensity of personal appeal could be sustained. Still another such technique was the "protracted meeting," an adaptation of the camp meeting to the setting of town and city. Protracted meetings lasted a week or more and had the effect of sustained and intense appeal. These measures drew people out of the ordinariness of their lives, where they could exist for several moments or several days on the boundary of existence. It is often in such situations that transformative experiences occur, affecting the individual's perception of the world. This, in effect, is what all religion seeks to do. Subjective conversion experience seeks to do it quickly, immediately, assuming continuing results.

Revivalism provided opportunity for initiation into the new nation, the new American world and civilization. It was not only a ritual designed to bring about immediate, individual conversion (whether by camp meetings or Finney's "new measures"), but also a means whereby lives were prepared to express those values and behavior patterns that were thought to be the characteristic of this new human, the American, and to be necessary for the continuation of a Christian civilization. "Consider," wrote the evangelical patriarch Lyman Beecher in 1835, "that the mighty resources of the West are worse than useless, without the supervening influence of the government of God. To balance the temptation of such unrivaled abundance, the capacity of the West for self-destruction, without religious and moral culture, will be as terrific as her capacity for self-preservation, with it, will be glorious." Revivals provided the means for initiating people into "the supervening influence of the government of God." An individual could enter a revival service, an anxious meeting, a protracted meeting, or a camp meeting as a representative of an old world of self-destruction and sin and could emerge a new person, prepared for the glorious capacity for responsible existence in the "unrivaled abundance" of this new world of the United States.

Revivalism has been a dominant force in the shaping of American religious traditions. It may well be that it has shaped the American mind and its culture more than any other single influence, save perhaps its Puritan progenitor. But revivalism is itself a uniquely shaped American tradition. A mood, a movement, an attitude of life, it has taken form in many of our denominations as well as in our ways of thinking and writing.

Revivalism has its own long and complex history, which in its entirety is beyond the scope of this book. Yet, like all human ways, revivalism has changed. We have seen its development from the Great Awakening to the so-called Second Awakening of the early nineteenth century. Here lies the birthplace of the more contrived and willful pattern of present-day revivalism. After the Civil War, increased urbanization and industrialization altered revivalism so that the tired, poor, working classes might hear the message of an evangel that could change their lives, making their lives livable in a promised land of plenty. Whether the tired and poor ever heard that message is not easy to determine. However, the efforts of Chicago's shoe-salesman evangelist Dwight L. Moody were dedicated to the conversion of masses. And a number of new denominations and religious movements like the Young Men's Christian Association (YMCA) and the Salvation Army were exponents of the principles and techniques of revivalistic evangelicalism.

In its early nineteenth-century formations, revivalism remained linked to the idea that the converted person would voluntarily and without concern for personal righteousness associate with others who would direct their efforts in organizations concerned with the welfare and reform of society. America's penchant for voluntary philanthropic activity has its roots in revivalistic evangelicalism's vast network of reform societies. Education, peace, temperance, missionary enterprise, woman's suffrage, and abolition of slavery provided objectives for these associations. However, there was a strong tendency to seek the reform of society by addressing the private sins of individuals. Gradually, the concern for ethics became moralistic—directed toward the perfection and purity of the individual human body as "God's temple." Alcohol became an absolute evil, and dancing was so associated with lust and sexual license that even the ritual movements of Shakers[6] were suspect. American evangelicalism began to lose its true social vision, failing to understand that the ills of society must be addressed by reforms that seek to change collective and institutional structure as well as private lives.

By the time of Moody and the end of the century, the transformation of revivalism was almost complete. Mass campaigns of preaching aimed at the salvation of souls became the order of the day. Throughout Christian history conversion had always been manifest in two ways: (1) in the conversion that takes place when the individual experiences saving faith; (2) in the conversion of social realities—groups, families, nations, and institutions. Much of evangelical Christianity was confining itself to the conversion of individuals. Christianity was becoming an affair of the private person, concerned with the transformation of the world as a result of the collective transformation of the individuals in it.

In the course of this evolution, American evangelicalism divided. The mass evangelism, in the tradition of Whitefield, Finney, and Moody, continued its own development. The evangelists became more and more skilled in addressing masses of people in such a way that individuals experienced overwhelming compulsions to alter their lives. The speaking style of these "preachers" adjusted to the purpose and the setting of what were to be called campaigns. Billy Sunday, Billy Graham, and many of the stars of the "electronic church"—the television celebrities—stand in this tradition of revivalistic evangelicalism.

However, there was another strain in the evolution. Some evangelicals, still convinced of the importance of preaching for personal conversion, began to be concerned for the disunity of the Christian world and the deplorable conditions in which the people of other nations lived. They became involved in missions that ministered to the need for the ability to improve one's life: how to earn a livelihood, how to remain healthy, and how to read and write. These evangelicals also became active on behalf of the unity of Christianity—what is called the ecumenical movement. As a result of these efforts on behalf of personal welfare and church unity, theology and preaching were modified in this strand of evangelical development. There was increased attention to knowledge and education. Ideas became important, and theology as an intellectual enterprise rather than a recital of scriptural texts experienced a rebirth. Perhaps some lost sight of the evangel and were more interested in modern knowledge, social reform, and church union than their evangelistic brothers and sisters on the campaign trails. Or perhaps they understood the evangel as something other than a message designed to collect individual converts. History will offer us a clearer perspective on this issue. Meanwhile, we have observed the interesting story of a unique development in Christian history. The United States has indeed been the setting for the shaping of the distinctive tradition of revivalistic evangelicalism.

chapter 12

The Public Religious Tradition

It is hard for those who have never known persecution,
And who have never known a Christian,
To believe these tales of Christian persecution.
It is hard for those who live near a Bank
To doubt the security of their money.
It is hard for those who live near a Police Station
To believe in the triumph of violence.[1]
        —T. S. Eliot, "Choruses from 'The Rock'"

It is not difficult to understand that a republic "conceived in liberty and dedicated to the proposition that all men are created equal, that they are endowed by their Creator with certain inalienable rights," should be a "nation with the soul of a Church." Yet, somehow it seems puzzling that historians of American religion should want to point out that there has been a cumulative tradition of religion associated with the nation itself; that, as Robert N. Bellah points out, "there actually exists alongside of and rather clearly differentiated from the churches an elaborate and well-institutionalized civil religion in America."[2] It is difficult for Americans to acknowledge this public religious tradition.

With apologies to Eliot, perhaps it is very hard for those who live near the flag and the Declaration of Independence to observe the religiousness of their behavior. And, of course, Americans are so accustomed to associate religion with churches, synagogues, Bible, and Jesus, that it is hard for them to take seriously religiousness in any other package. Frequently, the response to such matters seems to be, Yes, that's cute—to talk about all these matters *as if* they were religion. But we all know that this is not *really* religion.

This chapter will demonstrate that there has been a public religious tradition in our American experience that must be taken very seriously. After all, it is certainly true that some of our fellow citizens find all the religion they need in the activities of service clubs, the American Legion, or the Veterans of Foreign Wars, where many of the beliefs and practices of our public tradition are constantly exhibited. And, even outside such organizations, there are those who are secure in the knowledge that they belong to a country where belief in a Supreme Being who wills our success as individuals and as a nation is worthy of celebration and prayer—if not all the time, at least on certain "holy" days like Thanksgiving, the Fourth of July, and Memorial Day. In that statement, we can observe all three expressions of religiousness at work in such a way that they may be said to constitute a religious tradition.

This tradition has been given various names by historians and sociologists of religion. It has been called (with Bellah) civil religion, the American Way, the Religion of the American Republic, civic piety, and public religion. Since we do not wish to enter into the scholarly controversies that arise over the proper terminology, the term *public religious tradition* will suffice. In this decision, we recognize the fact that the lives of all of us are at one and the same time public as well as private. The study of history, wrote Benjamin Franklin, would "afford frequent opportunities of showing the necessity of a Public Religion." Public religion is an acknowledgment of the fact that any given individual who expresses himself or herself religiously in a variety of ways is also a member of various publics—groups—from which to draw identity and in which to anchor private life. "The public," writes Parker J. Palmer, "is the human world of which [we are] a part on which [we are] dependent, a world which brings color and texture . . . life, energizes and educates [us], enlarges and enlivens [our] human experience. The word 'public' as I understand it contains a vision of our oneness, our unity, our interdependence upon one another. . . . We occupy a common space, share common resources, have common opportunities."[3] The public realm is the household in which our private character and individuality come to maturity.

Obviously, every religious tradition has a public character, inasmuch as there are public implications to being an Anglican, a Reform Jew, or a Jodo Shinshu Buddhist. Belonging to a religious tradition is never a merely private matter. To belong is to identify with others. In addition, almost every form of enlightenment or salvation has to do with our relationship to others in a meaningful cosmos. However, in this chapter, we are not discussing the public character of every religion; rather, the public referred to is the American public. And the public religious tradition of the United States is of a kind with the "Public Religion" of which Benjamin Franklin wrote, a tradition attached to the nation and its society so that we become what the British journalist G. K. Chesterton called "the nation with the soul of a Church." There is surely an *American religion,* just as there are churches, denominations, Islamic societies, and Buddhist centers.

Verbal Expression

How has the verbal expression of this tradition come into being? What is the theoretical basis for American public religion? What is the teaching? One contributing factor is that we believe that our role in history is unique, that a certain "chosenness" has brought us into being. America was constituted a special people on a special mission to a special land, like the ancient Israel reflected in the patriarchal stories of Genesis:

> Now the Lord said to Abram, "Go from your country and your kindred and your father's house *to the land that I will show you.* And I will make you a great nation, and I will bless you, and make your name great, *so that you will be a blessing.* I will bless those who bless you, and him who curses you I will curse; and *by you all families of the earth shall bless themselves."* (Genesis 12:1-3)

This use of Israel as a paradigm for understanding the settlement of North America was at the heart of the Puritan enterprise of Massachusetts Bay. However, the Puritans did not invent it. Christianity had long understood itself as a New Israel, a people of God who inherited through Jesus Christ God's promises to the Israel of old. The magisterial Reformation and the Puritan Revolution in England drew heavily from this convention as it formulated its theology and went about the task of reforming Catholic Christianity. Here were images that helped to form their way of thinking and their perception of the world.

The Puritans, especially, did not come to this continent primarily to promote religious freedom or to have the adventure of new investments. They came because, in their understanding, God had called them to do what Christians for centuries had hoped to do without success—be a beloved community in which all the burdens of life were shared, while awaiting God's close of the historical page. They came to be a blessing to all the families of the earth. They were a "city upon a hill" with the "eyes of all people" upon them so that people would say of future attempts at civilized governments, "the Lord make it like that of New England," *where ecclesiastical and civil or political orders* were both under the mandate of the beloved community and the kingdom of God. Not only Puritans but Calvinists in general were concerned that the kingdom of God should furnish the norm for a just society as well as for the true church. Covenant was the key to their measure of all relationships and responsibilities "on earth as it is in heaven."

Covenant means that all of existence depends upon God's "call" (such as the call to Abraham and Israel) and God's promises and that the harmony of existence depends upon human response to those promises. Relationship with God, with nature, and among humans is a covenant business. God has *intention* for existence; its success depends partly upon keeping the covenant. In these images of Israel, covenant, and the blessing of all creation, we find the metaphors in which Americans live, move, and have their being—*as Americans*. At the heart of the theoretical expression of our public religion is the Puritan and Calvinist understanding of existence. This set of ideas and convictions has been bequeathed to the broad public base of American self-understanding. Although the images may have undergone a secularization that in our own day robs them of the fullness of their original symbolic power, they still undergird the American sense of a unique national character and destiny. We Americans tend to believe we are judged by high standards, that our nation is expected to do more than merely function. We are a model for the world; our mission places tremendous responsibility upon us.

Of course, this sense of mission was part of Europe's religious investment in the New World long before the settlements of the sixteenth and seventeenth centuries. Europe long knew, with St. Brendan and his confreres, that there was a Land Promised to the Saints across the waters—a land that would be fully revealed and available at the right time in history (see chap. 2). America became a place of liberation from the bondage of an old world. It was a place and a moment of new birth, so that the voyages of explorers and colonists were like rituals of initiation into a new life. The oceans were the waters of baptism, sometimes dangerous, but from which people would emerge triumphant—either in the American Israel or the kingdom beyond death itself. The history of the religious importance of the images of new birth and salvation that were associated with America from pre-colonial times has not yet been written, but it is a history that all Americans share in some way, even today. It is a profound contributor to the theoretical substance of the United States' public religious tradition. For humans live by images and metaphors, by narrative or story; their thoughts and actions take place in a matrix of images. Without images there would be little action, hardly any thinking.

Behind the idea of the unique destiny of the United States was the public religious belief in the existence of a Supreme Being, who had created the world and provided for its continued governance. The symbol of Providence refers to this providing governance of the Creator. The presence of this belief in the public mind meant that Americans did not completely accept all of the precepts of the Enlightenment. The latter movement tended more strongly to the idea of a hands-off creator, one who had completed the work and left it solely in the hands of human beings. The American public tradition affirms a doctrine of Providence, whereby the presence of God continues to make history, to bring order out of the chaos of human foibles. This sense of the providential ordering of history began to diminish after World War I. Perhaps this is why a certain public reaction to the decline forced the inclusion of the phrase "under God" into the pledge of allegiance to the American flag.

American society was "constituted" by shared experience and common beliefs among the colonists. Without this "constitution," there would have been no free and independent nation, indeed no Constitution. Prior to the 1950s the "constitution" that undergirded the social and political order of the United States was still religiously intact—it was assumed that the nation was under God. Once this "constitution" weakened, Providence was no longer as powerful a factor in the thinking of many Americans. Accordingly, by the 1950s there were those who felt it necessary to assert that the nation was "under God." What had been previously assumed now had to be asserted. Nevertheless, even in these times when belief in a Providential Creator (what James Madison called the "Governor of the Universe") seems remote to our common experience, most Americans retain some notion of a special destiny for America. Where there is a sense of destiny, Providence is implicit and remains a significant element in the verbal expression of our public tradition.

Related to this belief in the Creator has been the public religious assumption that no person, no system, no earthly and natural authority is absolute. If God is God, reasoned our mothers and fathers, then there is none similar. The American sense of independence emerges out of the conviction that all human authority is relative before the "Universal Sovereign." No creature can have absolute knowledge; we should permit no one to claim it. "The opinions of men," wrote James Madison in his "Memorial and Remonstrance," "depending only on the evidence contemplated by their own minds, cannot follow the dictates of other men." If we ask how this is so, Madison provides us with the logic involved:

> It is the duty of every man to render to the Creator such homage . . . as he believes to be acceptable to him. This duty is precedent *both in order of time and degree of obligation,* to the claims of Civil Society. Before any man can be considered as a member of Civil Society, he must be considered as a Subject of the Governor of the Universe: and if a member of Civil Society, who enters into any subordinate Association, must always do it with reservation of his duty to the general authority; much more must every man who becomes a member of any particular Civil Society, do it *with a saving of his allegiance to the Universal Sovereign.* [emphasis mine]

Human authority and power must always be limited. This conviction was part of the constitutional character of America as it took shape in the new nation. It was expressed in the Constitution, a document that sought to provide checks and balances for all duly constituted authority. It led to a Bill of Rights that sought to keep the order of duties, of which Madison had written, under constant check and in proper perspective. Inasmuch as duty to the Creator is of the first order of human responsibility, serving as the foundation for civil society, there can be no coercion. Each individual must be free to discover a proper mode of response to the Creator.

Of course, there could be no establishment of one religion in a nation with the religious diversity of America. No single religious institution or combination thereof could be permitted to make a claim that must be saved for "allegiance to the Universal Sovereign." It was obvious that no institution could really make that claim anyway—witness the multiplicity of denominations. At least in the realms of nature, what John Locke had said was correct: "no man is *by nature* bound to any church." Perhaps, in the private domain in which individuals take seriously the hope of salvation, it is possible to discover that we are "bound to [the] church" in profound and subtle ways. However, that is not the immediate concern of a government that exists both in and by nature to regulate the affairs of humans whose knowledge and power are limited.

Another aspect of the verbal expression of the American public religious tradition is the principle of equality. Although no individual or groups in the natural order of things have any supreme knowledge or abilities, it is certainly true that there are inequities. Some persons are more intelligent than others. Some have skills and talents that far outshine the rest. And by virtue of birth, environment, dedication (or a combination thereof), there are those who have special advantage or power. Wealth and position, as well as talent and intelligence, lead to inequities. Sometimes just being in the right place at the right time is an occasion for inequality. The obverse, of course, is also true. In a very real sense we are not equal by the ordinary nature of things.

If we permitted nature to take its course, these inequalities would lead to horrible results. Suppression of ideas, oppression of the less fortunate, manipulation of the intellectually weak would be the order of our existence. One has only to read a fictional work like Aldous Huxley's *Brave New World* to imagine the character of a world where natural inequalities run their course. However, the public religious tradition of our nation has taught that inequality is relative in the sight of the Universal Sovereign to whom we owe our primary allegiance. A civil society cannot exist without responsible people who "render homage" to their Creator. Among ourselves, by ourselves in the natural order, we have unequal advantages. However, we are "endowed by our Creator" (not by the government, the state, or natural design) with "certain inalienable rights." We are created equal in terms of the *rights* we have only in relationship to the Creator and to one another. In other words, because only God is sovereign, we cannot take our unequal advantages with ultimate seriousness. We must live politically as equals even though inequality exists. We do not live a completely natural existence as Americans. We live with what Thomas Jefferson in his original draft of the Declaration of Independence called "sacred and undeniable" truths. We live as a civil society that gives due homage to the Creator.

Some scholars tell us that the United States' public religious tradition has always honored what Benjamin Franklin called "the essentials of every religion" that were "found in all the religions we had in our country," although in each religion these essentials were "mix'd with other articles" unique to that particular denomination. "I never was without some religious principles," wrote Franklin in his *Autobiography.* "I never doubted . . . the existence of the Deity; that he made the world, and govern'd it by his Providence; that the most acceptable service of God was the doing of good to man; that our souls are immortal; and that all crime will be punished and virtues rewarded, either here or hereafter." No doubt these principles of Franklin's, derived in some measure from the Enlightenment and its deism, have been an ever-present element in the public mind. Probably many Americans, like Franklin himself, listened to the special doctrines of churches and their preachers, all the while transposing those particularistic teachings into the idiom of the "common essentials." It is very likely true that, even in our own times, many Americans "believe" the common essentials whether or not they adhere to the system of a particular religious tradition.

All of this means that the very idea of common essentials is itself an important aspect of American religion. We believe that religions have something in common. Today, historians of religion tend to be irritated with the notion that there are common essentials to the religions of the world. They tell us that each world tradition has its own special history, a history that must be honored for its own uniqueness. They remind us that it is somewhat fraudulent to speak of such things as the "transcendent unity" of religions. They ask us whether it is possible to translate the meaning of a foreign experience described in a foreign language into the language and meaning-system of another culture. Is it proper to use the English word *love,* for example, to speak of what lies at the heart of another tradition? After all, to say that Buddhism and Christianity are both concerned with love and compassion is not to say very much. The question remains whether love and compassion have the same meaning. Nevertheless, Americans believe there are common essentials to all religions. That belief has been an integrating factor in the public faith that undergirds our diversity as a pluralistic nation.

Of course, there are differences of interpretation to the "common essentials" and to the public tradition as a whole. Thomas Jefferson retained certain subtle biblical and Christian precepts and images that mingled with his Enlightenment religion. He proposed a picture of Moses leading Israel across the Red Sea for the Great Seal of the United States, and spoke of the guiding hand of Providence in American history. Abraham Lincoln, whom Sidney Mead has called "the most profound and representative theologian of the religion of the Republic," was deeply influenced by the ideas and metaphors of the Bible. His interpretations of American destiny and the crucial issues of the Civil War are derived from a biblical theology unparalleled among the presidents of our country. There have been those among our leaders and our citizenry who have made the nation itself into a supreme or ultimate reality. They have said, "My country, right or wrong" and have asked us to have "faith in ourselves and in America" rather than in the Divine Being who calls us into responsible life as a people with a special task.

It must be emphasized that the idea of America's special destiny rests on the notion of a chosenness by God and responsibility to God. What St. Brendan contemplated as a Land Promised to the Saints became very real for the New England Puritans, the framers of our Constitution, and the people of the new and independent nation. It was a nation biblically conceived—an Israel, that is, a New Israel, a people of God. Such images and metaphors are seldom lost completely. They may lose their particularity in the secular mind of our own times, but they exist invisibly, in subtle ways in altered metaphors that continue to communicate their power. Perhaps this is dangerous. Perhaps metaphors that function invisibly and unrecognized have a way of becoming demonic—forces of evil.

For example, the notion of Manifest Destiny may be understood as a secularization in which the Christian symbols of mission and millennial kingdom become invisible and distorted into jingoism and nationalism.

Practical Expression

Our consideration of the practical expression of the public religious tradition begins with the long-standing practice of special episodes of fasting, prayer, and thanksgiving. New England again serves as the cradle of this interesting practice. During much of the colonial period, there were occasions when sermons were preached before legislative assemblies, reminding the lawmakers of their responsibility to be faithful to the Word of God in Scripture. They were told that God had made a covenant with them; they were to be a people who bear one another's burdens and keep the commandments of God. Although there were two forms of government—one ecclesiastical, the other civil—both were under the rule of God's Word, judged by God's law.

Whenever the towns and colonies of New England faced a crisis, whether natural calamity or social disorder, the people were reminded that something was spiritually awry. Some form of disobedience, a breaking of the covenant, was at the root of the crisis. A pattern of preaching known as the *jeremiad* came into practice. One who is familiar with the Hebrew Bible (Christian Old Testament) will recognize in that term the name of the prophet Jeremiah. The structure of the jeremiad consisted of a description of the crisis, a reminder of the covenant, a judgment upon the covenant-keeping of the people, a call to repentance, a renewal of obedience, and a prediction of what was to come should there be insufficient renewal of the covenant. The student of the Hebrew Bible will recognize this structure as the frequent technique of the prophet, for whom Jeremiah serves as a paradigm.

Of course, the pattern of the jeremiad could be used in the regular preaching of the churches. But we must remember that clergy and people were aware of the civic and public implications of their piety. The churches belonged to the ecclesiastical order, but their responsibility for the interpretation of the Word of God was related to the civil order. They were the teachers of a tradition that regulated the political realm in which they lived. The jeremiad has been a practical expression of the public religious tradition since the colonial era. William Warren Sweet tells us that "as early as 1633 in Massachusetts and 1674 in Connecticut the practice of preaching election sermons . . . before the governor and assembly year by year" was established. These sermons "were printed at government expense and distributed among the towns." This is an example of a ritual action in which the public character of religion was at work in the domain of civil government itself. Governors frequently called for times of fasting in moments of crisis. They proclaimed days of thanksgiving for the harvest, for survival and sustenance. Here we have public religious practices that are continued by governors, mayors, and presidents in our own day. In taking such actions, these political leaders play a priestly role for the nation, or for its other levels of governance.

From the earliest days of its nationality, the United States has had its "holy days." Independence Day, Memorial Day, and Thanksgiving are high holy days in the American "sacred" calendar. They are days of celebration, traditionally of thanksgiving and remembrance. We thank God for the harvest, we call the people to remember those lives given that we might live. In the tradition of the jeremiad, we pray that our unfaithfulness to our special destiny may not bring upon us a crisis too great for our survival. To this day, in small towns of the East and Midwest, Memorial Day is a festival of the dead. Families gather to visit the cemeteries where generations have been buried. There are parades and services of worship held in the cemeteries. This ritual combines elements from the worship of the churches with public practices such as the use of the national anthem, the Pledge of Allegiance, and such songs as "America," "America the Beautiful," and "God Bless America." The leadership of these public rituals is usually shared by clergy, elected officials, and representatives of the military. Prayer, preaching, and singing are important ingredients. It is to be emphasized that these ritual events are not under the call and direction of the churches but of our public leaders. They are sacred moments in the national and public calendar, not the ecclesiastical calendar.

And, of course, our public tradition has its own "saints," its own saints' days. Secularization has affected the public religion as much as the ecclesial traditions. Our secular calendar is increasingly functional or directed toward the self-gratification of American consumers. We have, therefore, created a Presidents' Day in place of our commemorations of the birthdays of George Washington and Abraham Lincoln. Presidents' Day is much less a public religious occasion. It is a day added to the weekend that enables many Americans to continue indulging themselves in shopping malls, lakes, and ski resorts. However, our first president and the president who saw us through one of our greatest crises have been saints in our national memory. Washington was given the aura of an Olympian figure who could do no wrong and tell no lies. In portraits and sculpture he was not like other men but became the "father of our country," worthy of our reverence. Lincoln, on the other hand, was the common man whom the nation came to honor. He was a savior, raised up from the common life of a log cabin with little formal education, only the Bible to guide his thoughts, his speech, and his life. There was no room for him in the inns of the powerful. Rough, homespun, sad and humorous, he came to us in our time of need. Like Christ, he was cut down by the force he sought to save.

At one time, the birthdays of Washington and Lincoln were truly religious occasions. Schools held special assemblies, often with clergy present to pray or to speak. Children ate candy cherries in honor of Washington, made pictures of hatchets, and cut out of construction paper the bewigged silhouette of the father of our country. Every child knew stories of the two presidents, whose days were sacred to the memory of a special nation whom God had favored with such saintly and courageous persons.

There were lesser saints, of course. For Euro-Americans, Columbus was the man who had finally opened up the continent. The Land Promised to the Saints had waited for the pious Genoese navigator to carry the flag of Spain into its hallowed waters. It was in "1492 that Columbus sailed the ocean blue"—a creedal phrase that once rose spontaneously from the lips of Americans. Without his faith, skills, and perseverance, the "fullness of time" for the United States might not have arrived. Providence had raised him as the man of the times, to make possible the rebirth of European humanity in the promised land. He was an Abraham. Columbus Day has become a parade day for Italian-Americans and a time for America's furniture warehouses to offer their special sales; however, Columbus remains a minor saint, even though the historians and archaeologists write ever more confidently of the earlier voyages of Norse, Welsh, and Irish explorers. In an increasingly pluralistic America, where the power of the ideas and symbols of Christendom have waned, Columbus no longer retains his saintly Euro-American halo. He has come to represent the abuse of the public religious tradition, wherein notions of Christian and European superiority and manifest destiny combined to justify the suppression of Native American peoples and traditions. There have been efforts to raise American Indian protagonists to the status of American sainthood, placing them on the reredos of Mount Rushmore. Of course, the image of a solitary individual on the face of the sacred mountain is quite contrary to the Native understanding of individuals as part of the community. It remains to be seen whether Black Elk, Sitting Bull, Geronimo, or Red Cloud will find their way into the sainthood of America's public religious tradition.

During the 1960s the United States experienced several tragic deaths—assassinations of public figures, struck down while still young and vigorous in their leadership. The first was that of President John F. Kennedy, who was killed by an assassin's bullet in November 1963, as he visited Dallas, Texas. The Kennedy era had been the age of Camelot, a time that the President himself had dubbed the New Frontier. Kennedy was a well-to-do Harvard man, sophisticated and ambitious. He caught the imagination of the youth and the intellectuals of the United States. Although a member of a brash new breed of Americans, he had deferred to the public religious tradition in many of his public statements. In his inaugural address in January 1961, he said,

> We observe today not a victory of party, but a celebration of freedom—symbolizing an end as well as a beginning—signifying renewal as well as change. For I have sworn before you and Almighty God the same solemn oath our forebears prescribed nearly a century and three-quarters ago.
>
> The world is very different now. For man holds in his mortal hands the power to abolish all forms of human poverty and to abolish all forms of human life. And yet the same revolutionary beliefs for which our forebears fought are still at issue around the globe—the belief that the rights of man come not from the generosity of the state but from the hand of God.

President Kennedy had instilled a new spirit of hope and dedication. Even if his brief administration was merely the rapture at the end of an epoch, it was an occasion of renewed dreams and courage. For Kennedy had advised:

Whether you are citizens of America or of the world, ask of us the same high standards of strength and sacrifice that we shall ask of you. With a good conscience our only sure reward, with history the final judge of our deeds, let us go forth to lead the land we love, asking His blessing and His help, but knowing that here on earth God's work must truly be our own.

At age forty-three, John Kennedy was the youngest man who had ever been elected president, and less than three years after his inauguration the shots of an assassin stunned and bereaved the entire nation. Kennedy was the first president to face tragic death since the beginnings of television. He had been a loyal member of the Roman Catholic Church as well as a spokesman for the public religious tradition, and millions of Americans viewed his solemn requiem mass and somber funeral cortege with its riderless horse. Public and ecclesial ritual traditions coalesced in the minds of Americans as they participated in one profound ceremony of public mourning. The Roman Catholic Mass became a public religious ritual. Americans, it seems, are able to make the ritual traditions of churches their own when the occasion calls for it, when their public life must draw upon many resources to express its religious needs.

Not quite five years later, the public participated in the funeral of Senator Robert F. Kennedy, the late president's brother. As Conrad Cherry has put it: "In the funeral Robert Kennedy was vested with meaning that derived from his 'American dream' or his vision of American destiny. The funeral was another sacred ceremony in which the dilemma of death was met corporately, religious differences were transcended, and death was construed in terms of America's destiny under God. The day of the funeral, unlike Memorial Day, was altogether a holy day."[4] Again, a Roman Catholic mass became a public religious ceremony.

A few weeks prior to Senator Kennedy's assassination, many Americans had been called together for the public funeral of a man who had made great strides toward the freedom of the black people in this country. "I have a dream," said Dr. Martin Luther King Jr. in a now famous sermon delivered in the shadows of the Lincoln Memorial,

> . . . that one day this nation will rise up and live out the true meaning of its creed: "We hold these truths to be self-evident. . . ." I have a dream that one day on the red hills of Georgia the sons of former

slaves and the sons of former slaveowners will be able to sit down together at the table of brotherhood. I have a dream that even the state of Mississippi, a desert state sweltering with the heat of injustice and oppression, will be transformed into an oasis of freedom and justice. I have a dream today that my four children will one day live in a nation where they will not be judged by the color of their skin but by the content of their character. I have a dream today . . . that one day every valley shall be exalted, every hill and mountain shall be made low, the rough place will be made plains, and the crooked place will be made straight, and the glory of the Lord shall be revealed, and all flesh shall see it together.

Dr. King was a prophet of the United States' public religious tradition. He demonstrated how white America fell short of keeping its covenant with God, and he showed blacks that they belonged to the same "nation with the soul of a church" as the white population. King combined the rich imagery and rhetoric of black religious experience with the public tradition. In the same way that the Roman Catholic Mass had been used for public ritual in the case of the Kennedys, the African American sermon and distinctive worship of blacks became part of the practical religious expression of our public religious tradition.

Malcolm X, another American cut down by assassination, used the public religious tradition even more prophetically than King. For X, who converted to Islam partly because of his disillusionment with Christianity and the public tradition, the latter tradition had failed to live up to its creed. "I'm one of the 22 million black people who are the victims of Americanism," he said, "one of the . . . victims of democracy, nothing but disguised hypocrisy. So, I'm not standing here speaking to you as an American, or a patriot, or a flag-saluter, or a flag-waver—no, not I! I'm speaking as a victim of this American system. And I see America through the eyes of the victim. I don't see any American dream; I see an American nightmare!"[5] But before his death in 1965, he lamented: "It is a time for martyrs now, and if I am to be one, it will be for the cause of brotherhood. That's the only thing that can save this country."[6] At the end of his life his concern was for his country and for the souls of white folks as well as for those of black folks.

The reader has probably noticed the absence of women among America's saints. Certainly Frances Willard, Elizabeth Cady Stanton, Sojourner Truth, and Rosa Parks (among others) may be considered candidates for consideration. Meanwhile, their exclusion makes it difficult for many women to take the public religious tradition seriously—to find it a significant reference for their own sense of meaning and identity.

There are many ways in which the public religious tradition finds practical expression. As we have seen time and again, to be human is to discover ourselves involved in ritual—actions that have no apparent utilitarian function. These actions do not create food, clothing, shelter, or children. They are necessary to our lives in a different way. They express our need to acknowledge the fact that ultimate order and meaning are a given. Life is something to which we belong. Its meaning is discovered in our ability to belong, to know who we are in relation to everything that is. The meaning of life is more than our ability to create that meaning. Saluting the flag and reciting a pledge of allegiance are actions that express the fact that Americans are a people who share a special destiny. Life has meaning for us because this republic is "one nation [under God] indivisible" where "liberty and justice" are a rule of existence. Some Americans, such as the Jehovah's Witnesses, refuse to pledge allegiance to the flag. In an act of conscience, they remind the rest of us that to make the pledge is a ritual act, a practical religious expression of our faith as Americans. To the Witnesses, this is a pledge that can only be given to God and otherwise represents a form of idolatry.

"Holy days," "saints," and "saints' days," special days of fasting, prayer, thanksgiving, and mourning—these are a large measure of the practical expression of our American public tradition. And, of course, many public events use the service of clergy to provide a sacred canopy of prayer and benediction. Commencements, inaugurations, athletic events, and the dedications of buildings still retain a measure of public religion. After all, events that celebrate and represent the American values of success, competition, courage, and perseverance are certainly quasi-religious, if not recognizably so.

Social Expression

The social expression of our public religious tradition is, of course, the nation itself. To say, "I am an American," is to suggest much more than the fact of living in a certain geographical space in which the people share a common polity. To be an American signifies something. In the past, at least, it meant that we were a nation with the soul of a church. Several decades ago we worried about being "ugly Americans," people who entered foreign countries and acted patronizingly and condescendingly toward the inhabitants. The "ugly American" was a tourist from the greatest nation on earth, a successful person from a successful nation, who came to help those who did not want to be helped and to demonstrate superiority by a display of wealth, power, and generosity. The "ugly American" was a true believer in the public religious tradition in one sense, a mark of national self-righteousness in another. Those Americans who were concerned about the antics of the "ugly American" really believed, "That's no way for an American to act!" Implicit in our criticism of such deplorable behavior is a prophetic standard of judgment derived from the belief that good Americans do not act that way. Accordingly, both the "ugly American" and his or her critics derive their behavior simply from an understanding that they are Americans. To be an American is to find one's identity in relationship to a people, a place, and a way of life—all of it in some sense sacred, sharing a mode of ultimate order and meaning with us.

The land itself has been sacred to Americans. People of many traditions assumed it was the Garden of Eden. The lushness of its landscape, the untouched beauty and bounty of its rivers and forests, the naked innocence and comeliness of its native inhabitants could only mean that paradise itself had been regained. America was the garden of plenty and rebirth. And today many Americans still believe that this is "God's land, God's country." The land itself is holy.

There have always been some Americans who discerned the alter ego of the landscape. To them, it has been a sinister wilderness, a place where forces of darkness and evil lay in ambush. In such a perception of the world, the land is something to be vanquished or subdued. The natives are demonic creatures who must be conquered or converted before the land can truly become God's country. Those who thought in this manner about the American landscape assumed that its conquest was an important step in the preparation of the world for the consummation of God's kingdom on earth. To the more secularly minded, this kingdom was to be of our own making, since we are the gods who decide the future of all things.

It appears that the image of the land as a paradise of good has been more popular in the American imagination than the image of the dark and sinister wilderness. In this fascination, we have been somewhat schizoid, inasmuch as we have *acted liked* those who believe in the image of the land-to-be subdued. Nevertheless, the American landscape is idealized and romanticized in our collective mind. It is a place of beauty, goodness, and plenty even in our darkest hours. It shelters, comforts, and succors us like a mother. Gaston Lachaise's sculpture "Standing Woman," done in the first third of the twentieth century, is an image of America itself. This is a nude figure, ample, mature. The effect is at once overwhelming, yet alluring, erotic. In spite of her massive proportions, she is smooth and taut of body. Standing on small arched feet, she seems to glide above the earth she represents. In the social expression of our public religious tradition, the American land gives itself to us as mother and lover. Life has order and meaning received from America the beautiful. For much of our history and for many Americans, it has been enough to live in worship of our fruited plains, our amber waves of grain, and the majesty of our purple mountains.

In the paintings of Thomas Cole, Asher Durand, and Albert Bierstadt, we see an American landscape both mystical and awesome. Winslow Homer's paintings link the ordinariness of human existence with the passion and sensitivity of the land. "The land was ours before we were the land's," wrote the poet Robert Frost in "The Gift Outright":

> Possessing what we still were unpossessed by,
> Possessed by what we now no more possessed.
> Something we were withholding made us weak
> Until we found out that it was ourselves
> We were withholding from our land of living.
> And forthwith found salvation in surrender.
> Such as we were we gave ourselves outright
> (The deed of gift was many deeds of war)
> To the land vaguely realizing westward
> But still unstoried, artless, unenhanced,
> Such as she was, such as she would become.[7]

The public religious tradition is not without its polity. Historian Daniel Boorstin has argued that America has never had a full-blown ideology. We have had no fully developed American philosophy, no system of thought, that lies at the foundation of our society. We have not been constituted out of a system of principles and ideas as was, for example, the Soviet Union before 1989. A carefully devised Marxist ideology was the basis of the latter nation, as it has been for China. In those nations, life had been judged by the orthodoxy of its Marxism.

However, America has a distinctive polity shaped by a Constitution and developed in the laboratory of practical necessity. Our polity is difficult to label: it is republican; it is democratic. There is no ideology by which to define it or evaluate its orthodoxy. There are only certain rules of fair play, certain general principles that are part of the verbal expression of our tradition. We speak of freedom, of equality, without knowing what they mean until we work them out in response to some particular challenge or crisis. We have no republican or democratic system of thought, no ideology that determines our polity or divines what we must believe and how we shall interpret our faith. Our faith is endowed by a Creator, with special responsibility for the problems of each moment of our history. The First Amendment contains no absolute law, only a set of images that must be interpreted again and again in new situations. We do not *know* absolutely what "no establishment of religion" means; it means different things in different times and crises.

We have been republican to the extent that we have been a *res publica,* a public order—a people who are joined together by a constitution of values, ideas, and commitments. A republic depends for its continued existence upon this constitution. The constitution must be nurtured because it guarantees that the society will be controlled and ordered internally by the people themselves, committed to the notion of community with diversity. In the case of the United States, it was the existence of this constitution that led to the establishment of a legal document called the Constitution, now the frame of reference for our communal life. The constitution is the living soul of the "nation with the soul of a church." It was this constitution that made a republic possible.

As our republic becomes more and more a democratic republic, however, it demonstrates the gradual loss of its constitutional soul. A democracy is the rule of the people; that is, the people as the state or nation are the origin and source of all authority and all law. Eventually such social control becomes external, no longer dependent upon a constitution of belief and value, upon commitments nurtured by a natural law that is an endowment of the Creator. Instead, the "rule of the people" responds to whatever external authority appeals to its meanest desires. A radical democracy is usually controlled externally—that is, held together by an agency such as technology or a corporation. A radical democracy is a republic that has lost its constitution. A radical democracy can be considered a form of socialism—in our own day there is a corporate socialism, a society controlled externally by an alliance of politics, corporation, and technology, with an appeal to consumer interests.

American polity has been a republican polity, our democracy a republican democracy. We have governed ourselves as a nation that allows no single authority to gain an upper hand. Our system of checks and balances recognizes the biblical truth that no individual, no group, no office is absolutely sovereign. In the public religious tradition sovereignty is reserved for God. All human agencies, no matter how knowledgeable, wise, or seemingly righteous, are self-centered. Their power must always be balanced by other powers, under the mandate that the "sacred and undeniable" truths are endowed by God.

A Typically American Problem

A problem inherent in our public religious tradition has been pluralism. Our original pluralism was a Christian and biblical diversity, comprised of many Protestant denominations, the Roman Catholic Church, Anglicanism, and a small contingent of Judaism. The diversity was first of all a Protestant diversity, eventually a Christian pluralism, and then one that shared certain biblical ideas, metaphors, and beliefs. Our religious diversity in the twentieth century became radically pluralistic, representing the plural paths of the world's nonliterate and literate traditions. There is little to integrate this radical pluralism. The most that can be managed is a kind of Americanization that converts the Buddhist sects into forms of American Buddhism and leads Muslims to treat their mosques like the "little church around the corner."

In the earlier days, the constitution of our republic was fed by the common resources of the Christian and Jewish traditions. The many denominations were able to support their own enterprises while contributing to the public religious tradition, providing the republic with the nurture essential to its constitutional soul. As early as 1782, Thomas Jefferson noted the role of the denominations in relation to the public tradition. "Our sister State of Pennsylvania and New York," he wrote in his *Notes on the State of Virginia*, ". . . have long subsisted without any establishment at all. The experiment was new and doubtful when they made it. It has answered beyond conception. They flourish infinitely. Religion is well supported; of various kinds, indeed, but all good enough; all sufficient to preserve peace and order. . . ." By the late twentieth century the public religion and the constitutional soul were threatened by secularization and radical pluralism. The denominations that had assumed a certain responsibility for the common essentials of religion "sufficient to preserve peace and order" have lost their authority for the American mind. They are a weakened voice, fading into insignificance in a society bent upon self-interest and self-determination. The message and program of the churches have become a matter of private psychological preference for believers. Their "religion" is an item in the marketplace, which some may "buy" if what they see appeals to them. But the main business of the world is conducted with little reference to what the religious traditions offer.

Meanwhile, of course, values are being taught. A sense of order and worth, of meaning for existence, is advocated by the electronic media, by slick journalism, and by pressure groups that seek to rationalize society according to their own visions of rights and demands. Educational institutions become agencies concerned with facilitating the demands of the public for ready access to the true and abundant life. Instead of serving humankind by standing somewhat outside the mainstream of the present order of value and meaning in order to exercise critical judgment, our colleges and universities do little more than reflect the lowest common denominator of values in contemporary life. Nevertheless, human religiousness is at work. Technology, business, and education play the role of religion. Functioning in quasi-religious fashion, they fashion a perception of the world for us to live in. Perhaps we must ask ourselves whether what they are fashioning is the United States' new public tradition. Historians, anthropologists, and sociologists have told us that, thus far in human history, no society exists without a commonly shared set of values and beliefs. Religion is the foundation of human society. What is the form of public religious tradition essential to American society? Have we arrived at the point where external control has eliminated any need for the internal nurture of commitments within a community that is a republican democracy?

chapter 13

The Restorationist Traditions:
Christians to Latter-Day Saints

What then is the American, this new man? . . . He is an American, who, leaving behind him all his ancient prejudices and manners, receives new ones from the new mode of life he has embraced, the new government he obeys, and the new rank he holds. He becomes an American by being received in the broad lap of our great *Alma Mater*. . . . The Americans were once scattered all over Europe; here they are incorporated into one of the finest systems of population which has ever appeared, and which will hereafter become distinct. . . . The American is a new man, who acts upon new principles; he must therefore entertain new ideas, and form new opinions.

J. Hector St. Jean de Crevecoeur published his *Letters from an American Farmer* in 1782, a year before the end of the War for Independence. He returned permanently to his native France in 1790, but his book is an early and distinctive contribution to American self-understanding. Crevecoeur described the character of the "new American" in the making, especially during those crucial years between 1775 and 1820. To him it seemed apparent that the American was a new being, a creature of the American Eden, a new "Adam" sprung with new manners, morals, and perceptions of the world from "the broad lap of our great *Alma Mater*."

Crevecoeur's description of this "new man," this American, rightly belongs to the early "theology" of the public religious tradition. It speaks of new birth and world perception. These are always religious expressions. However, the idea of this "new man, who acts upon new principle" is a basic assumption behind a distinctive set of American religious traditions often referred to under the heading of restorationism.

We turn now to those traditions that have been conceived in the womb of a new "Alma Mater." It is, of course, true that the "new" religions of the nineteenth century usually have some relationship to what has been before. In a Christian America, the marks of a Christian past will have their effect upon those religions that consciously reject much of the history of Christendom.

The Restorationist Position

Restorationism is a form of religion that rejects the immediate past in order to restore an original one. Sometimes the word *repristination* is used, indicating an attempt to return to an earlier period, an earlier form of the religion. American restorationism refers to those religious movements that emerged in the "broad lap of our great *Alma Mater*" just after the War for Independence and during the National Period of American history. These movements are all ventures in the restoration or repristination of an "original" or primitive Christianity. The American, "[this] new man, who acts upon new principles" was no longer enamored of the results of the sixteenth-century Reformation, nor interested in just reforming what existed, because what existed seemed to many a jumbled mess of competing claims. Reformation had been attempted and had failed, according to the restorationist mentality. Reformation had produced all sorts of "man-made doctrines" that had departed from pristine Christianity. Reformation had not made Christians; instead, it had fashioned Presbyterians, Methodists, Roman Catholics, Congregationalists, Universalists, and all kinds of Baptists.

A new nation, comprised of new humanity, seemed to be the place where the errors of more than a thousand years of church history could be transcended. This past was a distortion of the truth, but now God had fashioned a new humanity in a new nation where the truth could be restored. A land of new beginnings, where humans perceive of themselves as new and different from those who have come before, is a world where the answers to the human dilemma seem simple and very reasonable. Even the Transcendentalists comprised a kind of restorationist movement. They were a group of American intellectuals, an elite body, who felt the urgency of the divine in the midst of the American landscape. Their title is misleading inasmuch as they are not essentially believers in a Wholly Other, a God Beyond, or a Transcendent Being. (In the latter sense, John Calvin was the transcendentalist *par excellence*.) Instead, the Transcendentalists believed that the divine was present in nature but that nature was more than our ordinary senses made of it. The truth of religion is to be found in the individual soul, which needs no authority other than its own intuition to break through the ordinary senses and find its oneness with the transcendent soul of all being. To the Transcendentalist, the "American, this new man" was free of the past with its tradition, its history, authoritarianism—free to take up the transcendental enterprise.

"Why should we not . . . enjoy an original relation to the universe?" asked Ralph Waldo Emerson. "Why should not we have a poetry and philosophy of insight and not of tradition, and *a religion of revelation to us* . . . why should we grope among the dry bones of the past? . . . In the woods is perpetual youth. Within these plantations of God, a decorum and sanctity reign, a perennial festival is dressed, and the guest sees not how he should tire of them in a thousand years. In the woods, we return to reason and faith." Emerson's contemporary, Henry David Thoreau, did not agree on all points with other Transcendentalists, but he shared their sympathy for the new beginnings in an American Eden. "God himself culminates in the present moment," he wrote, "and will never be more divine in the lapse of all the ages. . . . Be a Columbus to whole new continents and worlds within you. . . . Every man is the lord of a realm beside which the earthly empire of the Czar is but a petty state."

Of course, Transcendentalism was not a restoration of pristine Christianity, at least not in any sense of some biblical model that previously existed. However, the Transcendentalists assumed that in the American setting they were privileged to break through all historical authority and return to the original state in which humans are truly religious. They believed that Jesus himself was a pioneer in such transcendental experiencing. In that sense they, too, were restoring an original model.

Nevertheless, the Transcendentalists were an elite, an intellectual fraternity of the poetic, the aesthetic, and the artistic. There were other restorationist movements that arose from the democratic masses of the emergent nation. These people assumed that history had been waiting for the founding of America in order to prepare for the millennium, the new age of Christ's reign on earth. Even Jonathan Edwards earlier in the eighteenth century had thought of the Great Awakening as a sign of the dawning of the millennium:

> 'Tis not unlikely that this work of God's Spirit [the "awakening"] . . . is the dawning, or at least a prelude, of the glorious work of God, so often foretold in scripture, which . . . shall renew the world of mankind. If we consider how long since the thing foretold, as what should precede this great event has been accomplished; and how long this event has been expected by the church of God . . . and withal

consider what the state of things now is . . . we can't reasonably think otherwise, than that the beginning of this great work of God must be near. And there are many things that make it probable that this work will begin in America.[1]

By the end of the century there were many who believed that the new age had indeed dawned in the United States and that it was a return to a relatively simple state of nature.

Alfred Thomas DeGroot, a historian of restorationism, reveals his own restorationist assumptions when he writes, "This is the gift religion seeks: the restoration of the Founder's vital faith, his rapturous identification with the very heartbeat of the Creator so that the prosaic world is seen to be verily the substance of the kingdom of God, and its events and histories are bathed in color and meaning emanating from the gallery of eternity."[2] There are those thinkers who would question both the necessity and the possibility of "the restoration of the Founder's vital faith." In Christianity, for example, is it the founder's vital faith that is to be recovered, or is it the mode of perceiving the world that the founder made possible? In addition, the historian wants to know whether it is possible to leap across the centuries and find oneself in the world of the Founder. Do not our own questions and assumptions always accompany us? Must we not settle, in the matter of the world religions, for the teachings and institutions that the Founder's life and work have called into being through the centuries? It is the responsibility of the student of religion to get inside the circumstances of what we call "the past." Nevertheless, it is a task greatly affected by our concern for the present and the future.

Christian restorationism believes that it is possible to return to the origins. The return may be to the simple faith of Jesus, to the model of a New Testament church, or to a lost original hidden since the dawn of Christian history. Restorationism purports to leap over history to another world of time and space. Let us turn now to three types of restoration movements that appeared on the American scene in our National Period. They are what I've chosen to call democratic Christianism, biblicist and rationalist Christianism, and radical dispensationalism.

Democratic Christianism

Democratic Christianism is the attempt to restore a simple Christianity, the polity of which reflects the rule of the membership. Crevecoeur's "new American" was a person with a voice that wished to be taken seriously. The Great Awakening had given increased recognition to the experience of the people in American religion. We have already seen (see chap. 11) that clergy such as Gilbert Tennent had begun to question the traditional leadership role of the churches. What good are education and ordination if they are not accompanied by conversion? he had asked. Evidence of saving faith is the only real qualification for ministry, said Tennent. He merely expressed a point of view that was to be shared by many on the eve of the Revolution. Democracy was in the process of formation, although it was called republicanism at the time. People began to assume that the usual standards of leadership, inherited from centuries of European Christendom, no longer applied to this new Adam, this American in the making. In politics as well as religious and ecclesiastical matters, the old was giving way to the new. A new constitution of values and beliefs was being formed.

Of course, the American wilderness from the first had not been hospitable to the models of European Christendom. In places such as Pennsylvania, the people had frequently gathered as faithful Reformed and Lutheran Christians without benefit of clergy. There was no adequate supply of pastors. Yet the artisans and farmers sought to remain true to the Heidelberg Catechism and to Luther's Catechism. They worshiped on the Lord's Day when they could and read the Bible and prayed together in their homes. Religious democracy was an actual experience for them. They had to assume responsibility for their own spiritual well-being. This experience of self-reliance made democracy a reality even before it became a popular theory. The United States became a constitutional republic because the constitution of the American people was one of self-determination, equality, and liberty. No other mode of governance, either civil or ecclesiastical, was appropriate to this constitution.

Among the churches, the denominational concept had shown early on the democratic formation of American religion. A denomination is different from a sect. A sect assumes that it is the "true religion," exclusive of others. A denomination acknowledges that it is one expression of a larger whole, a greater unity that is shared by others. Denominationalism gives rise to the notion that one is as good as another, that a principle of equality and freedom exists among competing societies. In the United States no church, no religious body, could manage any abiding hegemony. No establishment could function in a land with so much space and so great a diversity of claims. Denominationalism became a functional necessity—a practical, democratic necessity.

As John Wesley's perfectionism and emphasis upon the spiritual needs of the common person made their way within the Church of England, they created a set of values in keeping with Wesley's own assumption about ecclesiastical governance. As we have seen, Wesley remained a priest of the Church of England. His Methodism was at home in his Anglican heritage. He had hoped that it would serve as an Anglican religious order, used to renew the church and propagate the gospel, to evangelize. He continued loyal to the Church's basic hierarchical structure and was by no means a democrat. A new denomination took shape in the nation after the War of Independence because the Anglican church was incapable of adjusting to "methodist" hopes. And so the Methodist Episcopal church was born in the 1780s. However, Wesley was astounded at the authority assumed by the preachers who had gathered for the Christmas Conference of 1784, even though they had pledged themselves to be his "sons in the gospel, ready in matters of church government to obey his commands." This reverential statement turned out to be little more than a deference to the great founder of the Methodist way. Methodism became not only a new denomination, but a particularly American one, asserting principles of self-determination.

Among those who opposed John Wesley's hierarchical and authoritarian ways was a man named James O'Kelly. He represented a new mode of thinking. He was a man of the "circuits and forests and swollen streams and bare preaching houses." He was a new American Christian, very much aware of the kind of world in which he lived, a world of equality and self-determination. Wesley was a stranger in O'Kelly's world.

As Sweet has said, the Methodists preached a democratic gospel while under a monarchical form of government. Perhaps the Methodist Episcopal church was not entirely monarchical, but as we noted earlier (see chap. 10), it was certainly connectional and somewhat autocratic. Its success in the American scene was partially due to its carefully supervised missionary activity. But it was the American "bishop" Francis Asbury who guided the direction of the church through its formative years. Not accustomed to consultation in such matters, he made all preaching appointments until near the time of his death in 1816. It was this authoritarianism of Asbury's that distressed James O'Kelly. Agitating for reform that called for the abolition of arbitrary authority, O'Kelly sought to inaugurate democratic and representative principles into the system of Methodist polity. When he was unsuccessful, he walked out of the meeting of the general conference and eventually organized his followers into the Republican Methodist Church. Initially this new denomination might have lured away as much as one-fifth of the membership of the Methodist Episcopal church. O'Kelly's schismatic church gave the laity significant rights and created a preachers' democracy. His ideas had special appeal among the people of the frontier and for a time there was considerable controversy, disrupting families and friendships. At stake was a question of the need for law and wise use of authority on behalf of the gospel. However, O'Kelly's ways were part of the developing spirit of the emergent nation. Eventually O'Kelly and his followers changed the name of their movement to the Christian Church. They assumed that those who followed the claims of the gospel should be known simply as Christians, not by any denominational designation. Being a Christian was an individual matter and no outward use of authority was proper. The new movement was democratic to the point of little or no organization and a reliance upon the "pure Word of God" as the basis of spiritual discipline. We may remember that this notion is similar to Roger Williams's decision that the true church is known only to God and no attempt at regulation by state or visible church can be justified.

O'Kelly's democratic Christianism led to a very small organization. The Christian Church merged with the Congregationalists in 1931, forming the denomination that finally united with the Evangelical and Reformed Church in 1957 to form the United Church of Christ. However, democratic Christianism is greater than the sum of its statistics. It partakes of the spirit of the United States and is an attempt at the restoration of what is assumed to be the simple and democratic character of the Christian gospel. Beneath the surface of much American denominational and confessional devotion is the conviction that we should all be simply and merely Christians, and that all of our spiritual qualifications are privately equal, with no deference to any authority beyond our own experience in relation to sincere use of Scriptures.

Biblicist and Rationalist Christianism

When we turn to biblicist and rationalist Christianism, we are faced with a more complex and institutionally successful account. Two denominational groups, each with a membership in excess of two million adherents, are representative of this form of American restorationism. They are the Christian Church (Disciples of Christ) and the Churches of Christ (not to be confused with the United Church of Christ). There are also several smaller denominations, most of which have splintered from the earlier Disciples and Christian movements. This form of Christianism is called rationalistic because it assumes that belief in the lordship of Jesus Christ is an entirely rational assignment. It requires no great emotional or intuitional qualifications; instead, it is perfectly reasonable. The individual has only to examine the evidence of Scripture and his or her own existence to arrive at the point where a reasonable commitment to the truth may be made. This Christianity is biblicist because it also assumes that the Scriptures themselves (especially the New Testament) are a self-contained rational repository of the divine truth. The Bible is consistent and reasonable for those who are prepared to examine the fullness of its evidence and commit themselves to its way.

Any notion of divine truth in a tradition complementary to the Bible is rejected. According to this form of Christianity the process of church history from earliest times to the present age in the United States has been a story of priestcraft, superstition, and false authoritarianism in doctrine. What is true and necessary is available to each individual, who must be the judge of its worth. No creeds, confessions, or theological tomes must stand between the believer and the rationality of his or her commitments. It is *reasonable* to discover that Jesus Christ is Savior and Lord. Any doctrine not found in the Bible is suspect and unnecessary. This form of Christianity set itself in reaction against Calvinistic theology, opposing such doctrines as original sin and predestination as unscriptural and unreasonable. However, its uniquely American spirit can also be seen in its denial of excesses, its pragmatic struggle to believe and practice only what works. Even though this restorationist movement was born in the revivalistic fervor of the frontier in the early nineteenth century, it tended to decry many of the excesses of "enthusiasm," along with the sectarian competition and conflict that often accompanied revivalism. Even Baptists were attacked as judgmental, rigid, and unreasonable.

The Disciples' movement sought to be liberal in its outlook, understanding doctrinal dispute as but the haranguing of sinful humanity. Like all such Christianist traditions, it hoped to be the basis for the reunion of Christianity by returning to the presumed simple Christianity of the New Testament. All restorationist movements began with unsatisfactory experiences with denominational proliferation and discovered what they hoped would be the truth beyond factionalism. Restorationists are those who consider true religion to be the gathering of perfect people in a perfect society.

An important figure in the restorationist movement was Barton Warren Stone, a native of Maryland who made his way into Kentucky at the time of the great camp-meeting revivals. Disturbed by the disputations that took place among his fellow Presbyterians, he was instrumental in the framing of "The Last Will and Testament of Springfield Presbytery." Signed in 1804, it served as one of the early manifestos of restorationist theory, asserting the necessary death of what Stone and others claimed were human-made teachings and polities. Stone was no longer a Presbyterian, and there was to be no more presbytery. All distinctions brought about by ordination were to be removed, "that there be but one Lord and one God's heritage, and his name one." All people following Stone and his associates were to have "free course to the Bible," which was to be the sole guide of the Christian life. Creeds and doctrinal definitions such as the Westminster Confession were to have no authority. Taking the name "Christian," the group adopted what they hoped would be a democratic congregationalist style of governance. The congregations were to be designated, simply and solely, Churches of Christ.

A few years after the publication of Stone's "Last Will and Testament" appeared two more important statements of restorationist principles. "The Declaration and Address" of 1809 followed the formation of "The Christian Association of Washington [Pennsylvania]" by another group of restorationists who seceded from the Presbyterian Church. The documents were primarily the work of Thomas Campbell, an Irish native of Scottish descent. Campbell had come to America in 1807 where he encountered what he considered to be unnecessary party spirit within his denomination. He was a man impatient with rigid and exclusivist attitudes and had labored on behalf of unity in his native Ireland. "Where the Scriptures speak, we speak; where they are silent, we are silent" became the watchword of Campbell's position as he moved toward the restoration of an ideally united and simple primitive Christianity. This principle means that the Scriptures are assumed to be a manual of faith and practice. What the Scriptures do not specifically prescribe cannot be considered essential in doctrine or polity. The question remains, of course, as to whether a certain teaching or practice should be accepted as useful or helpful even if it is unessential. The watchword, if taken literally, would seem to indicate that one should say or do nothing as a Christian (in worship, teaching, or governance) about which the Scriptures are silent.

The "Declaration" asserted the intention of Campbell and his sympathizers to avoid "the bitter jarrings and janglings of a party spirit." It reveals much of the same viewpoint as that of the Stoneites. What was being formed was not a church, "but a voluntary movement seeking to promote 'a pure evangelical reformation.'" In this same turn of mind the "Address" was directed to all who "love our Lord . . . *throughout all the Churches*" (emphasis mine). It was obvious that Campbell assumed that the harvest of his hope for a simple and unified Christianity was to take place in the fields of a Christianity that was already defined by its many walls and fences. In other words, he did not intend to create another denomination, but to call for the gathering of all true and simple "Christians" from out of the existent denominations. Another task at hand was that of converting those sinners who did not know the liberation of the gospel, but the evangelical task was hindered by a divided Christianity. How, asked the restorationist, can you present the claims of the gospel, when the evidence suggested that there might be different Christs, different gospels—insofar as those who presumed to be purely Christian actually did so in such groups as Presbyterians, Methodists, Baptists, Seceders, and Anti-Burghers?

To Thomas Campbell the restoration of simple, New Testament Christianity was a means of achieving Christian unity as a necessary prelude to the conversion of the world. This point was made even more clearly by Campbell's son, Alexander, who became the more articulate architect of the movement. In 1835 he published *The Christian System, in Reference to the Union of Christians, and the Restoration of Primitive Christianity.* The only means of uniting all Christians is the testimony of the apostles found in the New Testament, wrote Alexander Campbell, and only the union of Christians can attend to the conversion of the world: "Neither truth alone nor union alone is sufficient to subdue the unbelieving nations; but truth and union combined are omnipotent. They are *omnipotent,* for God is in them and with them, and has consecrated and blessed them for this very purpose."

Together the Campbells launched their repristination. The Bible they read was silent about the practice of infant baptism. Accordingly, they renounced their baptism as infant Presbyterians and were immersed as adult believers. Joined by another Scottish Presbyterian named Walter Scott, who arrived in Pittsburgh in 1819, the "Campbellite" movement grew in numbers. Scott was a gifted revival preacher who was able to appeal to the expectations of those who gathered on the frontier to hear good and simple preaching, carefully done up to make sense to common folk.

The practical expression of Campbellite restoration emphasized adult baptism. They were "baptists" who for a time found themselves in union with various Baptist societies and associations. Of course, their views on baptism tended to defeat their strong desire for openness and unity among Christians. After all, to a Presbyterian, a Congregationalist, and many Methodists, infant baptism was a sign of belonging to God's covenant of grace. But Campbellites had come to the conclusion that scriptural silence about infant baptism made it invalid. Unity among Christians is not an easy matter. Eventually the Campbellites found themselves in disagreement with fellow "baptists" as well. They began separating from Baptists and forming congregations of their own. By 1826 these congregations of simple "Christians" or "Disciples" comprised a sizeable movement. Thus, as Sweet reminds us, what "had begun as a protest against the numerous sects of Christians, instead of uniting them, had only succeeded in adding one more to the number."[3] This seems to be the fate of religion in a radically pluralistic society. What begins as an affirmation of truth becomes the whole truth, and sectarianism takes over. What might well be an important testimony of faith within the catholic or universal church becomes the occasion for a new and separate body that assumes that it proclaims the fullness of faith. "On the American frontier," writes Edwin S. Gaustad, "restoring the primitive church of the apostolic age seemed so alluring: it proved so difficult."[4] What began in a "nondenominational" gesture to restore an original unity readily became a new denomination.

The followers of Barton W. Stone and Alexander Campbell eventually discovered they had much in common. They were congregationalist in polity, baptist in theory and practice, and shared the theoretical assumptions of biblicist Christianism. The Campbells tended to be more rationalist and less revivalistic than Stone, but there was sufficient agreement to lead to the formation of the Disciples of Christ—what is today called the Christian Church (Disciples of Christ). This denomination tends to be open and democratic in its membership. As a form of Christianism it professes no doctrine or dogma beyond belief in Jesus Christ as it is set forth in the primitive documents of the New Testament. Creeds and dogma are divisive, according to the Disciples. Clergy are trained laity. The Lord's Supper is celebrated weekly and is presided over by lay elders. The supper and the communion of the people are not understood sacramentally, but as a simple memorial rite mandated by Jesus in the New Testament. The church is a voluntary association of those who are able to make a simple statement of faith. If we compare the Disciples movement to the Puritan tradition, we note that Disciples make no attempt to test the evidence of saving faith. No extraordinary revelatory or conversion experience is necessary. Faith is a voluntary, rational act of commitment. The Disciples of Christ were in the forefront of the ecumenical movement of the twentieth century and are often quite liberal in theological interpretation.

In the early decades of the Disciples movement there were those who opposed the use of organ music in worship and the formation of missionary societies. The Scriptures were silent about these matters, leading some people to conclude that *what was not instituted or advocated* was inappropriate. They opposed organs because the Scriptures made no mention of them. They disapproved of the use of the adjective "Reverend" as a form of address because they found no record of it in Scripture. Missionary societies were human institutions that become bureaucratic and fostered unscriptural habits. The work of evangelization and mission had to be done without societies. The New Testament proposed no such institutions. The people who held these views eventually separated from the Disciples movement and formed themselves into Churches of Christ, which today represent a sizeable membership in what we must call a separate restorationist denomination.

Radical Dispensationalism: Mormonism

American restorationism reached the pinnacle of conception and success in the radical dispensationalism of the Book of Mormon and the Latter-day Saints. Mormonism, as it is often called because of the significance of the Book of Mormon, is a uniquely American religious tradition. It is a new religion because of its radical departure from the theology and practice of eighteen hundred years of Christian history, and because its present institutional history began little more than a hundred and seventy years ago—a brief period in the comparative history of the world's religions.

The story of Mormonism is a fascinating one. No survey of the shaping of American religious traditions is complete without it, and any attempt to understand American society and culture must come to terms with this distinctively American tradition. Mormonism is a form of restorationism because it is one more attempt to restore a primitive Christianity in an American setting, where the immediate past is considered obsolete and the land sacred. As restorationism it is radical dispensationalism because it proposes a restored Christianity that has little or no connection with the Christianity represented in Protestantism, Anglicanism, and Roman Catholicism. Mormonism is indeed a new dispensation—a new dispensing of the truth of Jesus Christ. It is also dispensationalism because of its view of the history of salvation. According to the Church of Jesus Christ of Latter-day Saints (Mormons) there are distinct periods of history during which God reveals or dispenses the teachings that are necessary for salvation in that time. In this way, human beings do not need to rely upon the past for saving knowledge. God issues a new dispensation. This also means that whenever people neglect the necessary priesthood and keys to salvation, God does not permit the truth to be obscured but confers it upon humanity again. For example, the first dispensation was Adamic, meaning that saving knowledge was first revealed to Adam, considered as a historical personage. Mormon doctrine speaks of Enoch, Noah, Abraham, Moses, John the Baptist, the Jaredites, and the Nephites, among others, as having received dispensations of the truth of salvation in their times.

Another aspect of Mormon theory (that is, verbal expression) that is unique is the understanding that the saving knowledge revealed in each dispensation is the gospel. That is to say, the gospel is not confined to the New Testament period, to the times of Jesus of Nazareth and the beginning of the Common Era. The gospel is the plan of salvation, comprised of principles that were made known in preexistence. Here the word *gospel* moves beyond the ordinary conception of it in the rest of Christianity. Traditionally the gospel has been "good news," the glad tidings of what God demonstrated in the life of Jesus the Christ. Gospel has been generally understood as being supplementary to the Law, that is, the commandments of God. In other words, the good news is that God accepts us even though we fall short of keeping the Law. In Jesus Christ, the Law is fulfilled even though we personally fall short of its fulfillment. In Jesus Christ, God takes on the death that our sinfulness inflicts. That, presumably, is good news—"gospel."

However, in Mormonism the gospel acquires the character of newly dispensed Law. The gospel becomes a set of truths, principles, sealing practices, and a restored priesthood. The gospel in Mormonism is a system administered by two levels of priesthood—"the gospel is concerned with those particular religious truths *by conformity to which men can sanctify and cleanse their own souls,* thus *gaining for themselves salvation* in the eternal worlds." We can know authentic representation of the gospel via the presence of revelations, visions, miracles, signs, apostles, prophets, and "all the gifts of the Spirit." The gospel had been lost but was restored in the latter days through Joseph Smith, first prophet of the restored church. In him the presence of the gospel again became evident—a gospel lost in the American wilderness almost sixteen hundred years ago.

The restoration of the gospel and of the true Christian church takes place through agents specially chosen by God. Mormonism projects a gospel that is bestowed through a chosen priesthood. Now, of course, Mormonism as a distinctively American religion has no professional clergy, no priesthood dependent for its livelihood upon the support of the people, no process of special education and ordination that sets anyone apart except by way of conferring upon certain people the "keys" by which they may unlock the secrets of heaven. God holds all of Creation together by the power of God's own priesthood and delegates to humanity a priesthood through which all things necessary to salvation are administered. "There are, in the Church, two priesthoods," states a document of Mormon scripture, The Doctrine and Covenants, "namely, the Melchizedek and Aaronic, including Levitical Priesthood." It is taught that the Melchizedek is the grand head, the comprehensive priesthood of which all other priesthoods are part. Indeed, all authorities or offices in the church are expressions of (or representative of) the Melchizedek Priesthood. The world is to become a kingdom of priests, and to this end the Melchizedek order is directed.

However, in order for the Melchizedek order to take effect, a period of preparation or schooling is necessary; a lesser priesthood is called into being. The Aaronic Priesthood had been restored through Joseph Smith and the Book of Mormon. Through this priesthood the functions of teaching and administration of the restored church are shared. The power of salvation is through the priesthood. Certain sacred ordinances are channels for the gospel. Ordinances are rites and ceremonies, but also laws and commandments. Any male member of the church is eligible to receive the Aaronic Priesthood by "the laying on of hands, by those who are in authority to preach the gospel and administer in the ordinances thereof." Only those already belonging to the priesthood may ordain those who are "called of God, as was Aaron."[5] The offices in this priesthood are deacon, teacher, priest, and bishop, in that order of responsibility. A boy who has been baptized and confirmed and is considered "worthy" may be ordained to the office of deacon at age twelve, thereby taking the first step into the Aaronic Priesthood.

The Melchizedek Priesthood consists of the offices of elder, seventy, high priest, patriarch, and apostle. Here the fullness of the priesthood is expressed, although special functions and duties are reserved for each particular office. It is from this priesthood that the senior apostle is chosen as president of the church. The president is also the "Prophet of the Church," with supreme authority to speak for the Lord for the welfare of the entire church and the salvation of the world. In spite of the detailed definition of doctrine and office that one finds in Mormonism, there is always a certain equivocality. For example, it is frequently said that anyone may be a prophet, for a prophet is a spokesperson chosen by God. Presumably every member of the church may be God's spokesperson. However, the spokesperson's prophecy is applicable only to personal circumstance and status in the church. Only the president exercises the *fullness* of prophecy. "We have a prophet living on the earth today. This prophet is the President of The Church of Jesus Christ of Latter-Day Saints. He has the right to revelation for the entire Church. He holds the 'keys of the kingdom,' meaning that he has the right to control the administration of the ordinances."

It is very difficult to isolate the verbal expression of Mormonism from the practical expression. More than most other American religions, this tradition emphasizes function and practice. It is a tradition of rites and ceremonies, of undergoing various stages of initiation into a priesthood that is salvation itself. As we have seen, the process of transformation is one of ordinances; that is, the individual is transformed into the being desired by God through participation in certain ritual events that only the Melchizedek Priesthood can administer. "The kingdom" is protected and opened by certain "keys" possessed by some and not by others. The keys are frequently secret but always essential to the process by which we may be transformed into eternal life. As some critics have put it, being a Mormon is like belonging to a Masonic order that holds the key to one's ultimate destiny at various degrees or levels of one's pilgrimage.

Another aspect of the verbal expression of Mormonism is the emphasis upon continuing revelation. As we have seen in previous chapters, revelation is special knowledge of divine things. The idea of revelation is necessary because divinity is of another order than humanity. In order to know the divine, the will of the divine must be revealed. Our natural, ordinary reason is able to provide us with ordinary knowledge of the ordinary things of nature. Revelation is the superordinary knowledge of superordinary realities. Throughout the history of traditional Christianity, revelation has been assumed to be the special truth of God's salvation, delivered once and for all to Israel of old and then to the "New Israel" of the Church of Jesus Christ. This has not meant that God has no more truth to reveal. Rather it means that all subsequent truth for human well-being will be a clarification and interpretation of the original revelation. It is the task of theology and the teaching authority of the church to make the truth of revelation accessible to people in all times and places. The reality of God's salvation can become present to us today, in meaningful and exciting fashion, through the original revelation. No new revelation is essential.

However, the "new American" described by Crevecoeur did not care for the notion that the past was necessary to the present. And Emerson, when he asked, "Why should not we have a poetry and philosophy of insight and not of tradition, and a religion of *revelation* to us . . .?" was expressing a dissatisfaction with groping in the past. Instead, he sought "experiences." Revelation, for Emerson, was an experience, a subjective encounter with the divine. This was a new meaning of revelation, and it was certainly close to the meaning of revelation accepted by Joseph Smith and his Mormon restorationists. To traditional Christianity, revelation was the special knowledge and truth of God's salvation, offered once and for all. To Transcendentalists and Mormons, revelation was the visitation of new truth or the experience of new insight. The Articles of Faith (Joseph Smith's summation of the basic doctrines) tell us that "revelation signifies the making known of divine truth by communication from the heavens." In Mormon understanding, the Lord[6] appears personally to certain perceptive and chosen persons. He speaks audibly so that the person may *experience* his message through the senses, and he has various other means of direct encounter and communication of whatever truth is necessary for us in our particular circumstances.

Revelation is therefore a continuing and personal affair. To the head of a Mormon household, a revelation may come that is important to the conduct of his family. To the wife, whose role is extremely important even though she is not a member of the priesthood, a revelation may occur that clarifies the truth of the gospel for her special responsibilities. A revelation may come to the stake president, helping him in his spiritual oversight, and the bishop of a ward may be visited with special truth for his own assignments. Only the president of the church, the prophet in the tradition of Joseph Smith, can have the revelations necessary to the welfare and direction of the whole church.

This theory of continuing revelation is closely related to the dispensational view of history, the theology of priesthood, and the Mormon understanding of the gospel. The Lord renews and restores his priesthood in successive historical dispensations. He brings the ordinances of the gospel to light for people in their particular time and circumstance. It therefore stands to reason that revelation cannot be a once-for-all matter of special knowledge. Rather, it becomes a personal message from the Lord, revealing his will for the Saints of the Latter-day and showing the way for the resolution of personal and social problems. The Lord reveals to his prophet, the president of the church, whatever doctrines are important for his people. A revelation that is binding on the members of the church will always be identified as such. That is to say, the Lord makes it evident that a revelation is a revelation. "No one shall be appointed to receive commandments and revelations in the church excepting my servant Joseph Smith, Jun.," says the Doctrine and Covenants, a book of scriptural authority based upon revelation, "for he receiveth them even as most. . . . For I have given him the keys of the mysteries, and the revelations which are sealed, *until I shall appoint unto them another in his stead*" (emphasis mine).

Revelation authorized the practice of plural marriage during the early days of the restoration of the church in the nineteenth century. Plural marriage was openly taught and directed in practice by the presidency until 1890. At that time President Wilford Woodruff issued a manifesto, based upon revelation, which set aside the command to continue the practice. However, a reading of Isaiah 4 of the Bible is used to indicate that plural marriage will be restored at the time of Christ's second coming: "And seven women shall take hold of one man in that day, saying, 'We will eat our own bread and wear our own clothes, only let us be called by your name; take away our reproach'" (v. 1).

In the same manner, it is Mormon belief that the priesthood was not available to blacks in the dispensation until 1978. At that time President Spencer W. Kimball received a revelation directing that all men, regardless of race or color, were eligible to share the ordinances of the gospel and its priesthood.

Mormonism represents a radical departure from traditional Christianity. Because of our religious pluralism, Americans tend to harmonize the diversity of theologies in our midst. A certain ritual piety pervades our public life. We find it necessary for commercial and political reasons to be civil to each other. Often we hear messages on television beckoning us to deepen our spiritual lives, our faith, "by whatever understanding of God we may have." Little do we realize that this notion itself advocates a theology, a doctrine of God. In order for this harmonizing to take place, it is necessary to believe, either that there are many gods/Gods, or that there is a God beyond gods/Gods who is patient with our ineptitude. Mormonism's doctrine of God is not one that harmonizes readily with the God of traditional Christianity. To Mormonism God is a material being. "God himself was once as we are now," wrote the Prophet Joseph, "and is an exalted man, and sits enthroned in yonder heavens! . . . I am going to tell you how God came to be God. We have imagined and supposed that God was God from all eternity." Not so, says Smith; God dwelt on earth just as Jesus did. God was a man who managed to perfect himself and achieve the same kind of exaltation that is possible for us ("you have got to learn how to be gods yourselves"). God does not create *ex nihilo* (out of nothing), but uses eternal elements. God is a creature in his own creation; he is not being as such, or the ground of being.

Everything has bodily existence, including God. Everything is in some sense preexistent, including God. God was a man on the earth just as we are because it is necessary for all preexistent beings to come to earth in order to undergo the process of perfection. "There is no such thing as immaterial matter," writes Smith in the Doctrine and Covenants. "All spirit is matter, but it is more fine or pure, and can only be discerned by purer eyes; but when our bodies are purified we shall see that it is all matter." Anyone who has looked at a copy of the Book of Mormon, glanced at other Mormon literature, or been to a visitors' center associated with a Mormon temple, becomes aware of an unusual form of art. Pictures are highly representational, very literal renderings of preexistence and of events in the history of the saints. This is because even spirit is matter. This also leads to what some critics have called *tritheism,* meaning three Gods. Mormonism makes no attempt to harmonize the notion of the Trinity in traditional Christianity. The latter doctrine maintains that there is one God, known as Father, Son, Holy Spirit—hence a "tri-unity." To Mormonism the three are separate beings united in purpose and in perfection. The three divine beings represent the different modes and stages in which we also exist. We also are fathers, sons, and spirits, and we are required to achieve harmony and perfection in whatever role we find ourselves, and always in relation to the other two. This is the path to perfection and exaltation as God.

Mormon theology is quite complicated and difficult to understand partly because, as a new and radical dispensation of Christianity, it departs so markedly from our common heritage of understanding. It is impossible to do justice to Mormon tradition in the scope of this volume. We are simply calling attention to certain distinguishing features of this uniquely American religion and must highlight one remaining aspect of the verbal expression. We may ask what it is that is being restored in this form of restorationism. It is not primitive, New Testament Christianity. For one thing, it was assumed that the church of the Christian era had so distorted the Scriptures themselves that further revelation was required in order to provide Joseph Smith with the key to translate a true and inspired version. And so he did. What is being restored in Mormonism is the people Israel, the patriarchal society in which the gospel principles and ordinances were first revealed. It was Israel's society that first demonstrated the way of special ordinances and laws, which in Mormon understanding make up the gospel. It was in Israel that God revealed the necessity for procreative activity, the primary purpose of which was to make it possible for preexistent beings to be born on earth to begin their initiation into gospel perfection.

Mormonism teaches that salvation is universal because of the mercy of God shown in Jesus Christ. However, there are three different levels on which that salvation is ultimately realized. Again, the teaching is based on the Inspired Version of the Bible, which corrects the losses and distortions of previous translations of holy scriptures. First Corinthians 15:40 of the Inspired Version tells us that there are "celestial bodies, and bodies terrestrial, and bodies telestial; but the glory of the celestial, one; and the terrestrial, another; and the telestial, another." The telestial is the lowest level of God's merciful provision for all life. The telestial kingdom is reserved for those who live a law of carnality, worldliness, and wickedness. Most of the adults who have ever lived will go to the telestial kingdom. Those people who are lukewarm in their devotion to the gospel ordinances of the Church of Jesus Christ of Latter-day Saints will go to the terrestrial kingdom. They will be joined there by just and decent folk who do not accept the gospel and by those who accept the gospel in the spirit world after having rejected it on earth. The celestial kingdom is a state of exaltation shared by those who have been faithful to the gospel law. Even this celestial realm has degrees through which the faithful may pass on the way to exaltation in the highest heavens. It is important to note that life on earth *and* life in the spirit world make provision for decision and growth on the way to that perfection in which we become gods.

Many people in early nineteenth-century America were lost in a vast sea of religious chaos. They found themselves historyless and meaningless, adrift and suffering vertigo in a world that was big and promising, but without roots, without a firm foundation. They sought escape; they sought relief from their poverty and hardship by whatever means available, including treasure hunting by seer stones. And they sought a sense of community, of belonging to each other and to the great American landscape. The significance of the Book of Mormon is an unsettled issue in the history of the Latter-day Saints. There is little doubt that it plays an important role in missionary efforts, providing, as it does, a salvation-history that is a profound alternative to the traditional Christian understanding of America, while at the same time answering questions about the origin of the American

Indian and the failure of denominational Christianity. Brigham Young, successor to Joseph Smith as prophet and president, is reported to have begun his conversion with the reading of the book. However, he said that he "wished sufficient time to prove all things for myself," that he wanted to become acquainted with those "who professed to believe that book . . . I watched to see whether good common sense was manifest."

It would seem that much of the appeal of Mormonism has always been the strength of its community, its disciplined personal and family life, and its lay-priesthood. It is in the context of that common sense appeal that people turn to the book that belongs to this common-sense community and provides a rationale for its existence. The origins of the Book of Mormon remain controversial in the minds of scholars of religion who wish to apply the same principles of literary and historical criticism that have influenced contemporary understanding of the origins of the Bible. At the time of its publication in 1830, the Book of Mormon excited considerable hostility among those who were offended by its presumption to be a "gold bible," holy scriptures in competition with the Bible. Some considered it "the gibberish of a crazy boy," originating in the fertile mind of a disturbed youth in nineteenth-century western New York, rather than in ancient America. Whatever the scholarly verdict about its origins may be, it remains an ingenious document central to the idea of radical dispensationalism.

The Book of Mormon became "another testament of Jesus Christ." It answered puzzling questions for many people. The Book predicted the emergence of a great seer whose name would be Joseph like that of his father and who would be God's agent in the restoration of Israel. The story deals with a thousand-year period from 600 B.C.E. to 421 C.E. In it we learn of the people of Lehi, a Jew who led some of his family and friends to the promised land of America six hundred years before the birth of Christ. Lehi's exodus preceded the time of the Babylonian captivity. Lehi was of the house and lineage of Joseph, son of Jacob and heir of the promises to Abraham. Laman and Lemuel were sons of Lehi who could not depart from their wicked ways. They came to be known as Lamanites, the dark-skinned ancestors of the American Indians. Their wars against the more righteous followers of Nephi, another son of Lehi, led to almost total destruction of the Nephites. One of the surviving Nephites was Mormon, who, with his son Moroni, managed to hide the documents containing the great record of the true gospel ordinances. These documents were the gold plates from which the Book of Mormon was supposedly translated.

One of the important aspects of the story recorded in the Book of Mormon is the postresurrection appearance of Jesus Christ on the American continent. In this visitation he offers his message to those children of Israel who had not heard him in Palestine. The gospel is thus offered in a new dispensation that will one day lead to a restoration that will gather all of Israel—establishing the house of Joseph in America, the house of Judah in Palestine, and eventually gathering the Lost Tribes to the house of Ephraim in America.

The story is complex but fascinating. The student is encouraged to piece together the details of the account by reading the Book of Mormon. We "believe the Book of Mormon to be the word of God," says the eighth article of faith. This Book is believed by Mormons to present the doctrines of the gospel with greater clarity than the Bible. Many of its writings are presented as a more ancient record than the Bible, having been brought to this continent for safekeeping during the days of destruction and exile in Palestine. The revelation given in this scriptural document provided America with a biblical past heretofore unknown. It answered questions about the origins and conditions of Native Americans and gave America a unique role in the unfolding of salvation history. "This great American nation the Almighty raised up by the power of his omnipotent hand," wrote president Joseph Fielding Smith, "that it might be possible in the latter days for the kingdom of God to be established in the earth. If the Lord had not prepared the way by laying the foundations of this glorious nation, it would have been impossible . . . to have laid the foundations for the coming of his great kingdom." Mormons are engaged in kingdom-building, and America is a chosen land for the restoration of Israel as a people of the gospel.

The practical expressions of Mormon tradition are almost as interesting as their complex theoretical life. However, in the scope of this chapter we shall confine ourselves to a few observations. First of all, much of the ritual life of Mormonism is secret practice. We have already pointed out that Mormonism is itself a religion of following detailed directions. The gospel of Jesus Christ is for Mormons a set of ordinances—living out the behavioral style of patriarchal Israel. The Word of Wisdom is a revelation received by Joseph Smith on February 27, 1833, and contains laws of dietary practice prohibiting tobacco, strong drinks, and hot drinks. For a time this revealed law of health was only modestly regarded. It was not until the church officially gave up the practice of plural marriage that the Word of Wisdom was taken more seriously as a way of distinguishing "restored Israel" from the rest of society. There is so much of Mormon life that is the practical expression of a religion that is a new dispensation, with practices meant to discipline the Latter-day saints as a people set apart.

However, it is probably the temple ordinances that are of greatest significance in an attempt to understand the radical departure from traditional Christianity. Certain gospel practices are so sacred that the Lord has authorized their performance only in temples, which are holy places—houses of the Lord erected by his revelation. Baptism for the dead, along with what are called washings, anointings, endowments, and sealings are performed in the temples according to careful direction. It is assumed that there were temples in all previous dispensations of the gospel, that these temples were the site of these ordinances of exaltation—the marks of the celestial kingdom. Baptism for the dead is an ordinance that permits the entrance into the celestial kingdom of worthy persons who died before being given the opportunity to receive schooling in the ways of gospel principles. Inasmuch as baptism is essential for entrance to the celestial realms, baptism for the dead makes such an inheritance possible. This secret rite of baptism, performed in the temples, is a central feature of Mormon practice. Mormon interest in genealogy is related to baptism for the dead, as well as other vicarious ordinances of salvation.

Much of the practical expression of the religious life of the Latter-day Saints takes place in the family and the local "churches." The family gives body and nurture to the preexistent spirits waiting for the opportunity to use the gospel ordinances as keys to the celestial kingdom. Families are sacred units, reflective of the patriarchal order of Israel. It is there that the prayer life of the Saints is focused. Prayer is basic conversation with the Lord: "Pray in your families unto the Father, always in my name," reads 3 Nephi 18:21 (Book of Mormon), "that your wives and your children may be blessed." Families are eternal, with members continuing in the highest heaven of the celestial world, "where they have *eternal increase.*" Procreation is a continuing and sacred reality.

When the faithful gather as a congregation of the Saints on a Sunday, their worship includes the celebration of the Lord's Supper. They are thereby following the Lord's commandment. A priest or elder breaks bread, kneels, blesses it, and passes it to the members. Water is then blessed and distributed. Although the ancient Scriptures refer to the use of wine, a more recent revelation recorded in the Doctrine and Covenants indicates that it does not matter what is eaten or drunk, so long as it is in remembrance of the Lord. In this way, the reception of water instead of wine conforms to the Word of

Wisdom, with its admonition against the use of "strong drink," meaning alcoholic beverage. Worship in the congregation tends to follow a simple and informal pattern. There are readings, prayers, testimonies, addresses (what might be called sermons), and other forms of instruction. However, the tone of these services is in contrast to the special rites that occur in the solemn secrecy of the Mormon temple.

The concept of continuing revelation makes it difficult for a significant theory of scripture to emerge in Mormonism. In practice, this means that the revelations and inspired words of the living prophets (presidents) of the church become scripture. Nevertheless, there are four books with special scriptural authority. They are the Bible, the Book of Mormon, the Doctrine and Covenants, and the Pearl of Great Price.

The social expression of Mormonism rests upon the concept of the new dispensation, the idea of the restored church. Through Joseph Smith, God has restored the true church after centuries of apostasy that followed the ascension of Christ into heaven. According to the Doctrine and Covenants, the church is to be called the Church of Jesus Christ of Latter-day Saints. Thus began the gathering of Israel from out of all nations and all parts of the earth. The true measure of society for Mormonism is the ideal family, gathered to keep the gospel ordinances and become members of the celestial kingdom.

In polity, Mormonism again seeks to be a repristination of the apostolic church and the patriarchal society of Israel. Living on this earth as a faithful member of the Church of Jesus Christ of Latter-day Saints is already a participation in the celestial kingdom. This is especially true when we consider that keeping the gospel ordinances, sharing the priesthood, and receiving the sealings of marriage and family are themselves marks of the perfection of celestial reality.

Mormons maintain that the polity of the church is always the same when God calls a new dispensation of the gospel into being. In other words, whenever the true church is established, whether in Abraham's, Nephi's, or Jesus' time, there are prophets, evangelists, pastors, and teachers. However, in true Mormon fashion since the days of Joseph Smith, there are always provisions for necessary change. In the complex world of these latter days, church organization is itself likely to be intricate and must have those administrative units essential to the promotion of the gospel. Changes in ecclesiastical organization will follow the dictates of revelation. Little that the church does takes place without revelation. Only revelation can provide the dependable solutions to the church's ministry in today's world. Nothing is left to chance; bureaucracy and social ethics (solutions to various social, economic, and political problems) are affairs of revelation.

The First Presidency, a quorum of three presidents belonging to the Melchizedek Priesthood, presides over the whole Church. The Lord selects and the body of the saints "sustains" or affirms the presidency. One of these three serves as president of the Church and is therefore High Priest and Prophet. Upon the death of the president, the First Presidency is dissolved until a new president is chosen. The president is a senior apostle selected from the Council, or Quorum, of the Twelve. Here we observe a theory of apostolic succession at work. It is the apostles who are the earthly manifestations of the authority and power of the church. They are given the keys of the kingdom. Whenever the First Presidency is dissolved, the Council of the Twelve is supreme in governing authority until a new presidency is instituted and sustained.

In keeping with patriarchal practice and the New Testament reference to Jesus' appointment of seventy as missioners, the Latter-day Saints maintain a Council of Seventy who share the central authority of the Council of Twelve and the First Presidency. However, as Joseph Fielding Smith put it, all is under direction of the president: "There is never at the same time two equal heads in the Church—never. . . . There is always a head in the Church, and if the presidency of the Church is removed by death or other cause, then the next head of the Church is the Twelve Apostles, until a Presidency is again organized."

The church is divided into stakes and missions. The *stake* takes its name from the notion of Zion as a great tent, a tabernacle held firmly in place by stakes. Depending upon such factors as membership in the Church, stakes range widely in geographical area. The Saints are gathered metaphorically in tabernacles. Stakes are divided into smaller units called wards. Members of the church in a ward are the congregation (assembly, gathering) of the Saints. It is on this level that the work of the gospel is conducted under the care of quorums and presidencies.

Although there are many republican principles at work in the constitution of Mormonism, it is fundamentally a hierarchical order in keeping with its notions of patriarchy, apostolic succession, and headship. Today this new American religion must be considered among the major world religions. It is a tradition reporting constant growth at a time when the membership of many of the heirs of sixteenth-century European Christianity is at a standstill.

The study of Mormonism is essential to an understanding of America and the changing culture of the early twenty-first century.

Mormonism has been a carefully organized tradition, maintaining a discipline that permits little digression from its doctrinal and ritual standards. However, the tradition does exist in a secular and pluralistic America, and one of the characteristics of religion in America is the need to respond to shifting values and ideas. There have been signs that some Mormons are trying to re-think their tradition in relationship to such issues as the role of women. Feminist concerns are also encouraging the tradition to explore more deeply the concept of the Divine Mother that is hidden in the Mormon idea of the Godhead as involving male and female counterparts. After all, if the family and eternal procreation are paradigmatic to the tradition, then the Godhead must of necessity be centered in a Mother-Father divinity. Needless to say, many of these issues threaten the authority and solidarity of the patriarchal hierarchy in Mormon practice. Many of those who advocate radical departure from traditional authority have been censured or excommunicated. Margaret and Paul Toscano are two such pioneering thinkers. In their book, *Strangers in Paradox: Explorations in Mormon Theology,* they are bold to write: "For us, Joseph Smith's teachings, like those of every other prophet, constitute not the final word but a point of departure."[7]

In this chapter we have explored the traditions of restorationism that have been an important element in American religious history. Restorationism came into its own in the national period of our history. With typical American impatience with history, the advocates of restoration had sought to put an end to divisions, to differences of opinion and theology. By the middle of the nineteenth century it had become evident that the movement had instead contributed several new "denominations" to the diversity of American religion. These were to be traditions not directly linked to the sixteenth-century Reformation. They partook of the spirit of Crevecoeur's "American, this new man." Whether by rationalist assumptions or dependent upon new and continuing revelation, they were most definitely "made in the USA."

chapter 14

The Jewish Tradition in America

Judaism is one of the oldest of religious traditions; however, it did not come into its own in the United States until after the middle of the nineteenth century. Although Jewish traditions were present during the Colonial and early National Periods, they remained relatively unnoticed until the German Jewish immigrations of the 1830s and 1840s began to alter the religious landscape of America. Accordingly, the study of Jewish traditions has been heretofore delayed in this book.

A plural reference to "traditions" is necessary because it is important to understand that diversity exists within Judaism as within Christianity. It may be inaccurate to speak of Jewish denominations, inasmuch as Judaism tends to deny any doctrinal precision. In addition, the history of the Jewish people in dispersion throughout the world has nurtured a vigorous individualism and congregationalism. This is in spite of the fact that Jewish traditions generally emphasize the solidarity of the people Israel (not to be totally identified with the state of Israel). God has made a covenant with Israel. Salvation is a social affair, a matter of community.

Centuries of living amid the cultures of North Africa and the Arabian Peninsula have forged traditions of keeping God's covenant with Abraham that are quite different from those fashioned in central and eastern Europe, or even in Italy and the Iberian Peninsula. The more we probe into the depths of Jewish history and religion, the more we discover a complex fabric of ideas and practice. For the sake of convenience and brevity, singular Jewish tradition will be referred to as if there were one. Certainly it is possible to discern some unity to Jewish religiousness, even though there is no uniformity of faith and practice. On the other hand, the mysticism of the kabala (a medieval source of Jewish mystical thought) and the eccentricities of certain forms of Orthodox Judaism and Hasidism defy all attempts at generalization.

When the waves of Jewish immigrants from Eastern Europe hit the American shore after the 1880s, they were an embarrassment to those Jews who had established themselves earlier in St. Brendan's Land Promised to the Saints. Of course, to the Eastern Europeans these Americans were not Jews at all. The Eastern Europeans were Jews who had lived for generations in the shtetls[1] and ghettoes of such countries as Poland, Russia, Romania, and Ukraine. Isolated and often persecuted, they lived an existence in which their religious and civil responsibilities were all interwoven forms of keeping the covenant. The rabbi was the teacher and judge at the center of the community. In those circumstances, a form of Jewish tradition developed quite in contrast to the ways of the Jews who had accommodated themselves into the social and religious life of the United States, where any isolation was voluntary and little oppression existed.

The earliest Jews in America were *Sephardim*, which is a Hebrew word designating the Jews of Spain and Portugal. Many of them came to America by way of Brazil, Holland, England, and the Caribbean islands. Around the time of Columbus's voyages of American exploration, Spain was seeking to unify its culture and centralize its political authority. The prosperous Jewish community was seen as an aberration, a threat to the religious solidarity essential to cultural unity. Accordingly, there began a policy of conversion, expulsion, or execution. The Jews were expelled form Portugal in 1497. Many of those who converted to Christianity remained secretly Jewish; they were called *Maranos*. When this was discovered by the authorities, a program of inquisition began that was designed to hunt down and eliminate phony converts. Some of the Maranos sailed with Columbus; others found their way to South America and the Caribbean. Many of the exiled Sephardim ended up in Holland, where they enjoyed the hospitality of the Dutch. Secret Jews were already living in eastern Brazil when the Dutch conquered it. However, the Portuguese conquered this region in 1654, sending the Jews in flight to New Amsterdam (later to become known as New York) and the Caribbean. Newport, Rhode Island, also received a small community of Sephardim shortly thereafter. The American poet Henry Wadsworth Longfellow visited their synagogue in 1852 and wrote his poem "The Jewish Cemetery of Newport," from which the following is excerpted:

> Closed are the portals of their Synagogue,
>   No Psalms of David now the silence break,
> No Rabbi reads the ancient Decalogue
>   In the grand dialect the Prophets spake.

Gone are the living, but the dead remain,
    and not neglected; for a hand unseen,
Scattering its bounty, like a summer rain,
    Still keeps their graves and their remembrance green.

The early Sephardim were prosperous and influential people. Many of them were shareholders in the companies that regulated the commercial development of the New World. They were an aristocracy whose ritual life differed from that of other Jews. In Europe they avoided their "poorer and more uncouth coreligionists," the *Ashkenazim,* that is, the Jews of central and northern Europe, or Germanic Jews. During the American Colonial Period most Ashkenazim lived in Poland; however, small communities existed in Amsterdam, London, and other cities of Europe. By the middle of the eighteenth century they had begun to outnumber the Sephardim in the American colonies. By this time, of course, the Sephardic ritual life had been established in the few synagogues that existed. As Joseph L. Blau tells us, "So the Ashkenazim joined the Sephardic synagogues, sometimes married into Sephardic families, were elected to office in the synagogue, and learned to tolerate and in some cases to love the strange sound of the sephardic *minhag.*"[2] Most of the Jewish settlers during the Colonial Period were merchants, not scholars. There were no rabbis, and Jewish congregational life depended upon the minyan of ten adult males required to form a synagogue. The services were led by the *hazan,* a prayer-chanter or cantor. Jewish religious life tended to be primarily ritualistic, with little scholarly reflection upon the profundities of Judaism and little discussion of the intricacies of ethics and decision making.

We must remember, of course, that the total number of Jews in America before the nineteenth century was little more than three thousand. "Obviously," writes Nathan Glazer, "we deal with a very miniature history, so miniature that it has been possible to track down every Jew who set foot on these shores."[3]

Origins of the Jewish Way

We turn now to an examination of the basic meaning of Judaism, in an effort to discover the tradition that accounts for the diversity of Jewish traditions. What we know as Judaism today is partly the result of the Diaspora, the dispersion of Jews throughout the world after the destruction of the Temple in Jerusalem in 70 C.E.

From that time on the rabbis sought to direct the survival of the Jewish way by devising a program of studying Torah (see pages 260–63), carrying on the commandments, and doing *mitzvoth*—deeds of loving kindness. In other words, the Jewish way became the way of the rabbis, the teachers. Less attention was given to apocalyptic notions of coming punishment and destruction. The rabbis sought to teach a way of regeneration that would be pleasing to God, rather than to focus on a messianic future. What we know as Judaism today is primarily the result of the work of those rabbis of the Diaspora.

We must understand that Christianity and Rabbinic Judaism are products of the same period of history. They are both initially manifestations of the religious life of the Hebrews. We should not think of Judaism as a settled and well-defined tradition, out of which Christianity emerged as a kind of aberration or sectarian offshoot. Instead both are forms of Jewish religiousness that emerged out of a common background, in response to the circumstances of a world in turmoil. The first century of the Common Era was not only a traumatic time for the Jews, who had lost the very focus of their religious life—the temple—but also a time of cosmic pathology, a time somewhat like our own, in which the sense of being part of a meaningful universe, a cosmos, was lost. We live in an age in which so much of our thinking is centered on the isolated individual that we tend to assume that pathology[4] is a subjective problem, therefore psychological. We fail to understand that much of human anxiety is the loss of cosmos, the sense that one is lost without a story, without anything meaningful to which one belongs. The first century was just such a period of upheaval. The options facing the people were: (1) cling to the ways of the fathers; (2) restore what seems to have been lost; and (3) try to discover a new answer to the dilemma of existence. There were numerous variations to each of the three options. The times were filled with curious cults, civic rituals designed to promote peace and solidarity, and diverse attempts to preserve tradition or explore its relationship to the new age. Christianity and Rabbinic Judaism are variations on the same theme, the same religious heritage.

The Jewish way is the way of tradition. Joseph Stein's "Fiddler on the Roof" portrays the lives of Hasidic Jews in Eastern Europe at the beginning of the twentieth century. It takes us inside the lives of simple people who eke out their existence in the shtetl of Anatevka. The central character, Tevye the milkman, provides us with insight into the nature of tradition and its importance to the Jewish way:

A fiddler on the roof. Sounds crazy, no? But in our little village of Anatevka, you might say every one of us is a fiddler on the roof, trying to scratch out a pleasant, simple tune without breaking his neck. It isn't easy. You may ask, why do we stay up here if it's so dangerous? We stay because Anatevka is our home. And how do we keep our balance? That I can tell you in a word—tradition! . . . Because of our traditions, we've kept our balance for many, many years. Here in Anatevka we have traditions for everything—how to eat, how to sleep, how to wear clothes. For instance, we always keep our heads covered and always wear a little prayer shawl. This shows our constant devotion to God. You may ask, how did this tradition start? I'll tell you—I don't know! But it's a tradition. Because of our tradition, everyone knows who he is and what God expects him to do.[5]

As we saw previously (chaps. 1 and 2), tradition is the storehouse of human knowledge and wisdom. It is what we draw on for ideas, actions, and consolation. Many of the creatures of the earth live by instinct, a kind of mechanical response to certain stimuli. Among human beings tradition is the surrogate for instinct. Perhaps tradition is the form of our instinct. We cannot think out each situation, consider each action as if it had no precedent. We have neither the time nor the ability. We must rely upon what we have learned, even if we devise new methods, new interpretations. Humans are social beings; reality itself is social. Tradition is the social mind at work. Tradition is always a living, creative business. Tradition is people transmitting, receiving, revising, and supplementing what they have learned.

The Jewish people are very consciously a people of tradition. Tradition has it that this people was called into being from out of the multitudes of ancient people who lived in the cradle of civilization, the Middle East, the lands of Sumer and Palestine. It seemed that most people were content to live in the captivity of gods. They believed that nothing ever changes, that humans exist in an immobile world where they must conform to the powers that maintain everything in an order of eternal return. However, goes the story, there were those who believed they were free of this kind of immobility and changelessness. They had experienced liberation from the gods, at the call of the very life of Being itself. They had been removed from captivity at the call of God beyond gods. They were challenged to live a life of risk and change, on behalf of a world that presses ever onward, mobile, and very real. This consciousness of liberation from captivity was linked in their minds to a historical event called the exodus.

These Hebrew people, the liberated ones, thought of themselves as the children of Abraham, who long ago had also left the gods of captivity and immobility in the Tigris and Euphrates River Valley far to the east. And so they told the stories of Abraham and his progeny, the fathers of this exodus people. The stories recounted the promises of the God beyond gods. This god was not really a god. This one had no name, but was Being Itself and could only be called "the Lord." "Now the Lord said to Abram [Abraham], 'Go from your country and your kindred and your father's house to the land that I will show you. And I will make of you a great nation, and I will bless you, and make your name great, so that you will be a blessing. I will bless those who bless you, and him who curses you I will curse; and by you all the families of the earth shall bless themselves'" (Genesis 12:1-3, Hebrew Bible).

The many generations of the children of Abraham were like most human beings. Sometimes they were obedient to the Lord who beckoned them onward; at other times they preferred the comfort and security of the risk-free life lived in the captivity of the gods. The story is one of struggle, of faithfulness and disloyalty. It is not easy to live a life where one is available to the needs of others because he is not captive to the gods. Eventually these people found themselves in a situation of captivity from which there seemed no exit. They were in Egypt where they lived a secure existence as second-class citizens of a people who worshiped the gods of security. It was out of that captivity they were finally led by Moses, one of their own people who had been given a glimpse of the power of the God who is no god, the Lord of Being itself.

There followed a period of testing and preparation in which there emerged a tradition of how to live without captivity, how to live the liberated life that was free to serve the needs of humankind. The tradition was the way of covenant in which the Lord of Being revealed to the children of Abraham the secrets of living. This was in the days before much writing was done, and so the way of the covenant was taught and preserved orally by the elders of the tribes of the generations of Abraham. At the heart of the covenant way was the idea that the Lord of Being can only be known in history. That is to say, the Lord is not known as a metaphysical concept or by way of speculative reason, but is known by those who have no gods before the Lord; the Lord is not known as a principle of nature, but as the truth that we encounter when we act responsibly, remaining mobile, risking security for the right decisions. In other words, the Lord of Being is known in history and responded to by ethical decision, not by speculation or incantation.

After all, it is decision-making that constitutes history; at least it is human action, whether by way of deliberation, accident, or impulse.

This means that the Jewish tradition will be strongly historical and ethical in perspective, in contrast with traditions that may be more concerned with techniques of meditation or ritual participation in the cycles of nature and rites of passage from birth through death. This is not to say that these other forms of religious expression are absent from Judaism. It is a matter of emphasis, a matter of degree.

Torah

The way of the covenant became known as *Torah*. This is a word that may be translated as Law, Path, Way, Revelation. As Law it is to be understood not merely as a set of legal regulations. Rather it is Law in the sense of base principle, the basic order of reality. Laws are reflections of Torah; they are like sparks and flames that come from the fire, that together make up the fire. Were it not for the fact that human beings assert their own selfhood as being worthy of center stage, there would be no need for the development of particular laws, norms, and regulations. Where Torah exists in its purity, there no Torah is necessary. The Lord of Being made a covenant with the children of Abraham because he sought to bring people back to the basic order of things. And so the Torah became those principles by means of which the covenant between God and humanity is restored and maintained. The Torah became a tradition of commandments—*mitzvoth* (plural of *mitzvah*).

The Hebrew religious way was a rich tradition of ethical and ritual principles that are necessary to the way of the covenant. As might be expected, this tradition gradually included not just the principles themselves, not just the commandments of the Lord of Being, but also commentary, interpretation, and case studies. People began to ask whether a certain law must be kept in the same way in all circumstances. Do not circumstances alter the way in which a commandment is interpreted and kept? Soon there was a tradition of interpretation and practice that accompanied the commandments themselves. The laws had to become specific, particular. And there emerged a group of teachers and scholars who preserved the tradition and became its authoritative interpreters. The Jewish way is a continuing tradition. The commentaries and interpretations of our time became a part of the way of Torah—they are the way in which the revelation of the Lord of Being continues to be understood.

The story of Abraham and his progeny, the narrative of the exodus, and the history of the Hebrew people and their struggle with God's covenant were all part of the Torah. Eventually, with the birth of writing, much of this material was recorded. It became Scripture, written Torah. The sacred writings of the Torah form the Hebrew Bible, which includes the revelation of truth found in the Five Books of Moses (Genesis, Exodus, Leviticus, Numbers, Deuteronomy), the *Nevi'im* (Books of the Prophets), and the *Ketuvim,* which are "writings" found in the books like the Psalms, Proverbs, Job, Ruth, and Esther. This Hebrew Bible is called *Tanakh,* a word derived from supplying vowels to the three Hebrew Characters, T, N, and K (Torah, Nevi'im, and Ketuvim). It is this Tanakh that Christians call the Old Testament.

A great deal of the revelation of God's ways with the children of Abraham remained an oral tradition. Along with the written Torah there continued the tradition of oral Torah. The Lord of Being was understood as revealed in the ways of the people, in their struggle to be faithful to the Lord in a world that made the captivity of the gods such a desirable affair. The oral Torah was a tradition of narratives and laws that underwent the same process of constant interpretation as the written Torah. The way of interpretation of oral Torah is known as midrash, a way of reading between the lines, asking questions, and preaching. Eventually much of the early corpus of oral tradition itself became a matter of record called the *Mishnah.* By the beginning of the third century of the Common Era, the work of the rabbis had succeeded in compiling an intricate code of laws. Divided into six major parts, called *Seders* or Orders, the Mishnah dealt with virtually every aspect of human existence from regulation of the economy to proper modes of prayer at stated times.

It is noteworthy that this formation of the Mishnah took place at the same time that the tradition of Christianity was also taking shape, out of the common heritage of Hebrew religion. Of course, Christianity was gradually being weaned of that Hebraic dependence as it made its way deeper into the life of the Greek and Roman world. The formation of the Mishnah was the work of the rabbis and formed its own unique religious tradition—what we call Judaism, meaning, in effect, Rabbinic Judaism. Rabbinic Judaism is a religious tradition that works out the meaning of life by reflecting on the things that human beings need to do day by day. In other words, whether we are cooking a meal, planting a crop, remembering the dead, trying to survive in the desert, or conceiving a child, we are performing certain actions. The good and responsible life is one that knows why and how these things are done; it explores what is and what ought to be. It wonders whether there are different prayers or no prayers for one who takes his own life. It is concerned with whether a man who dies before he fathers children shall leave a childless family, or whether his brother should take upon himself the responsibility for conceiving children with his deceased brother's wife. This is the way of Rabbinic Judaism, the way that is called *Halakha*.

As you may suspect from all that has been said thus far, the Jewish religious tradition is a dynamic one. The way of Torah never ends. The rabbinic struggle to find the appropriate way to live in a particular situation and particular time necessitates an ongoing development of tradition. In order to decide what is the best decision to make, the rabbis consult what other rabbis have said and done, then proceed to evaluate the new and specific ingredients they face in their own circumstances.

The ink was barely dry on the Mishnah before the commentary and discussion of its cases began. *Gemara* is the name given to this commentary, a compilation of derived material that is relevant to the understanding of each portion of Mishnah. Together Gemara and Mishnah form the *Talmud*. "In point of fact," writes Jacob Neusner, "two Talmuds exist for the same Mishnah, one edited in Palestine, called the Palestinian or Jerusalem Talmud, the other edited in Babylonia, and called (naturally) the Babylonian Talmud. It is the latter that is widely studied to this day and which supplies the authoritative interpretation of Mishnah."[6]

Jews exist as Jews by virtue of belonging to the children of Abraham. However, this is not primarily a racial matter. It means that a people exists by virtue of its special calling to live a life of liberation from the captivity of gods. The children of Abraham are to be people of the covenant, living the way of Torah, and by so doing, bring a blessing to all the people of the earth. However, Jews exist as Jews whether they are faithful to the covenant or not. They are Jews because they belong to a people who has been "called out"; they are Jews because the Lord of Being is faithful to the Torah even if the people are not. Like Tevye, the Jew lives in conversation with God. Sometimes the conversation is an argument. Sometimes the argument is a standoff, and the Jew goes off angry, deciding to forget the Lord, to let the Lord have his own way—the Jew will do so, too. The tradition is richly human and humane.

At the heart of Jewish life is study. The faithful Jew studies Tanakh and Talmud as a student of Torah. All of existence is regulated by Torah. And the good and serious scholar will know the commentaries and the arguments of rabbis since the days of the compilation of the Talmud. The process of studying all points of view and arguing with others is the way in which the Torah becomes alive and manifest. Study and argument are themselves sacred actions.

The Jew takes this life very seriously. The Jew wants to learn and be a good citizen because that is what the Lord of Being expects of us. Torah is for the living of these days. If in a Jew's struggle for success, he or she forgets the poor or runs slipshod over the lives of others, the Prophets and the rabbis are there to offer reminders that he or she is becoming captive to the gods, that God beyond gods requires justice.

Like many other religious traditions, Judaism is not simply a matter of belief. We cannot ask, What do Jews believe? and gain an authentic insight into the Jewish tradition. Jews have seldom talked about beliefs or doctrines. The Orthodox Jew has often maintained that there is no Jewish theology. The Conservative and Reform Jews may belie that claim by virtue of the publication of many books of Jewish teaching and philosophy. Judaism has indeed produced Jewish theology. This may be due to the fact that Jewish traditions have had to make their way in a world that has been strongly influenced by the history of Western philosophy out of its Hellenic past, and also by two thousand years of the development of Christian theology.

In order that the way of Torah and Talmud should be understood in such a world, a kind of Jewish theological tradition emerged. However, we must be sensitive to the fact that a concentration on belief and doctrine obscures the fact that no religion can be reduced to mere belief. The study of religion is not the "study of different beliefs." Not all religious thinking is belief-thinking, and there are many things said and practiced by the representatives of a religious tradition that are not matters of belief. Often we can learn more about a religion by analyzing what the people do than by examining their doctrine.

Practical Expression

In Chaim Potok's novel *The Promise* there is a Jewish philosophy professor who considers himself an atheist. Nevertheless, this Professor Gordon observes the high holy days of the Jewish calendar. He says the prayers of his people on *Shabbat* (Sabbath) and other appropriate times. Some of us may be quick to accuse him of hypocrisy, but perhaps he is more honest than such accusers might be. What his story suggests is that the full meaning of a religious tradition is not always reducible to the individual's ability to believe, to reason, or to explain. The prayers and practice of the Jewish tradition have a way of communicating meaning for Professor Gordon in spite of his inability as a private subject to say that he believes in God. In a way, "belief in God" may be a proposition he cannot rationally accept. Perhaps he can find no reason to believe that there is a God, but he may very well live his life in conversation with the Lord of Being. The point is that Professor Gordon knows he is a Jew and that Jewish people do certain things, say certain prayers, keep certain times holy. Life is given ultimate order and meaning in a very special way. That is what we mean by religion. It is a curious business, much greater than an affair of "beliefs."

What do Jews do? What practices are unique to their traditions? They study Torah; they strive to live by Halakha. Halakha deals with the concretization of Torah; it strives to apply the 613 mitzvoth (commandments) to every circumstance of existence. Halakha is concerned with responsibilities and obligations to others and to the Lord. In other words, Halakha is both ethics and ritual. Jewish religious tradition is most definitely a comprehensive path. Jews who claim not to be religious usually mean that they are not observant—they do not observe the ritual commandments. However, as we know, that is a misuse of the term *religious*—especially for the Jew. For Jewish religiousness expresses itself in everything people do—from politics and occupation to keeping the Sabbath. Sexuality, dining, social activity, art, music—all fall within the scope of the mitzvoth.

It should be stated that doing a mitzvah is not primarily a matter of smug self-righteousness. That notion is the result of certain Christian misreadings of New Testament references to people called Pharisees, some of the forerunners of Rabbinic Judaism, who seemed to be fastidious exponents of ritual purity. However, the doing of a mitzvah is being a Jew, a child of Abraham. The doing of a mitzvah tunes one in to a true understanding of the Lord of Being who constantly calls us into divine service by serving our brothers and sisters. One knows who the Lord is and why the Lord is by doing mitzvoth—living the halakhic way. Twice a day, morning and evening, the Jew recites *Shema:* "Hear, O Israel, the Lord is our God, the Lord is One. Blessed be the name of his glorious majesty forever and ever." This is a Jew's confession of faith, drawn from Torah itself, where the people are instructed to teach these words "diligently to your children, and . . . speak of them when you are sitting at home and when you go on a journey, when you lie down and when you rise up." As a matter of fact, these words are to be worn on the hands and the forehead, and inscribed on doorposts and gates. This explains the Orthodox practice of wearing leather prayer containers called *tefillin* and placing a little prayer box called a *mezuza* on the doorpost.

One of the distinguishing features of halakhic practice is *kashrut,* the dietary law. Known as keeping kosher, it is a practice concerned with the holiness of the person. The book of Leviticus in the Hebrew Bible is a work filled with many references to *mitzvoth*. But behind the commandments is the notion expressed in the words: "Speak to the whole Israelite community and say to them: you shall be holy, for I the Lord your God am holy" (Leviticus 19:2). One follows dietary laws because the Lord asks it of the Jews. He asks it because the children of Abraham, who are to be a blessing to all the nations of the world, must be a holy example in their eating habits. *Kosher* means fit, proper, or in accordance with the Halakha. It is not a style of cooking or cuisine. Food that is not prepared in accordance with *kashrut* is not kosher and is called *trefah.* In a sense, the faithful Jew keeps *kashrut* because it is a joy to know that he or she belongs to a people who obeys the Torah. He or she communes with the Lord by keeping the Law. Accordingly, it is not primarily a matter of good health, but a matter of good faith. The pig may indeed wallow in the mud and have been the bearer of a disease such as trichinosis, but the faithful Jew does not refrain from eating pork for those reasons. It may very well be the case that *kashrut* has become so powerful a factor in Jewish tradition because their enemies sought to get them to deny their faith by eating nonkosher animals. The Jews are a people set apart. They are the world's monastics, the monks for the world, those who withdraw from the world's ways for God's sake and the world's. Perhaps being a set-apart people is sufficient reason to keep *kashrut*.

The Sabbath is another distinguishing feature of Jewish practice. "The meaning of the Sabbath," writes Abraham Joshua Heschel, "is to celebrate time rather than space. Six days a week we live under the tyranny of things of space; on the Sabbath we try to become attuned to *holiness in time.* It is a day on which we are called upon to share in what is eternal in time, to turn from the *results* of creation to the *mystery* of creation; from the world of creation to the creation of the world."[7] What does this mean? Again, as in our earlier discussion, it means that life is ordinarily lived by attachment to things. They exist in space. We exist in space. We are to some extent like other things that exist in space. We are part of creation. In the ordinary world of nature, everything has a function. The Sabbath is not an ordinary day in time. It is a day without function. It reminds us that we are more than nature, than space. To be human is to live in time, not as captives to space and place. The Jewish tradition of the Sabbath is a unique reminder that time is important. Time is history—events. An event is what happens—the result of some kind of action, a decision or an accident. The Sabbath is holy. It is the presence of wholeness in the midst of fragmentation. Things—nature, creation—are only important to the extent that they do not define our existence and make us captive. The Sabbath is the visitation of freedom from captivity to space. "To Israel," writes Heschel, "the unique events of historic time were spiritually more significant than the repetitive process in the cycle of nature, even though physical sustenance depended on the latter."[8]

The Jewish practice of *Shabbat* (keeping Sabbath) is another instance of doing what God tells us to do. It may be a day of rest, relaxation, or recuperation, but that is not its real meaning. Shabbat is something lovely that happens. The tradition says that Sabbath is like a bride who comes to us graciously, elegantly, waiting for our affection. Shabbat is feminine, a queen, a majestic and royal visitor, whom we welcome and enjoy. Shabbat is God coming into creation, hallowing it. This is eternity in time. Six days a week there is little mind for beauty, for the likeness of God. We work under stress, are driven by anxiety and immersed in worry. But the Sabbath will come on the seventh day, like a lover, to remind us that we are more than all this concern with things.

The faithful Jew anticipates the Sabbath and busies himself or herself with preparations. "This was the practice of Rabbi Judah ben Ilai—on the eve of the Sabbath a basin filled with hot water was brought to him, and he washed his face, hands and feet, and he wrapped himself and sat in fringed linen robes, and was like an angel of the Lord of hosts."[9] The image of the eternal paradise, the world to come, is that of the loveliness of an eternal Sabbath. The Sabbath is not a restrictive occasion: "A precious jewel have I in my possession, which I wish to give to Israel, and Sabbath is its name."[10] A person who does not keep the Sabbath forgets who she or he is. The whole fabric of the Jewish religious tradition is woven out of Shabbat, and the neglect of Shabbat causes the understanding of the tradition to deteriorate.

Orthodox Judaism recommends the importance of preparation. The people must bathe and dress, like Rabbi Judah. Work clothes or play clothes do not honor the spirit of Shabbat. The house should be clean and the dinner prepared in advance. The meal is festive. Shabbat begins with the lighting of candles by the wife of the household approximately twenty minutes before sundown. "Blessed art Thou, Lord our God, King of the Universe who has sanctified us with his commandments and commanded us to kindle the Sabbath lights." After this benediction is recited, the people greet each other with *"Shabbat Shalom."* On the table are loaves of challah, the braided white bread that is baked especially for Sabbath and other holidays. A cup of wine accompanies the recitation of kiddush, the declaration of the special holiness of Shabbat. The keeping of Sabbath is a mitzvah, and the reverent Jewish family dresses up the occasion in a joyful and festive manner.

The synagogues, or gatherings of Jews for study and prayer, also take place on the Sabbath, when many Jews assemble in a synagogue building for *Kabbalat Shabbat,* the service of welcoming the Sabbath. These Friday evening services begin prior to sundown. Late services, after the family observance, have become an important part of synagogue Shabbat in the United States.

Traditionally the primary activity for the Sabbath is the studying of Torah. Whether in the morning service of the synagogue or the leisure of the home, the Jewish people read from the scroll of the written Torah and seek opportunity to enhance their understanding of the Halakha. The Sabbath is kept holy by the study of Torah. Of course, it is also a day for leisure—for games and singing, for folk dancing.

Sabbath ends when at least three stars are visible in the gathering darkness. *Havdalah* (division or separation) is the special benediction that ends the day with a blessing to the Lord of Being for the creation of wine, spices, and light. It should be noted that Jewish religious traditions tend to direct prayers as blessings to the Lord. There appears to be less concern expressed for what the individual wants or needs. Instead there is a gratitude for being the people of God, for having been given the Torah and the earthly means to study it.

Certain things are forbidden on the Sabbath. It is recognized that a human being has an inclination to want to do those things that will detract from the holiness of Shabbat and the Torah, things that she or he has not finished as an accountant, a salesperson, a broker, or a farmer. These activities are functional, utilitarian. They have a "use" and are meant to benefit the individual. But Torah is the way of a people who have been shown that they are more than a bundle of tasks or struggles for livelihood and wealth. Therefore, the oral Torah defines certain activities as *melakha,* tasks that are forbidden on Shabbat.

The Sabbath, according to Rabbi Heschel, is not dependent upon any event in history or any part of nature's cycle. Shabbat is detached from "the world of space" and is a celebration of what is eternal in the world of time. There are other festivals in the practical or ritual tradition of Jewish religion that are determined by nature. Although they may be occasions for remembering certain events in the history of the children of Abraham, the dates of observance are dependent upon the natural order. "Passover and the Feast of Booths," writes Heschel, "coincide with the full moon, and the date of all festivals is a day in the month, and the month is a reflection of what goes on periodically in the realm of nature, since the Jewish month begins with the new moon, with the appearance of the lunar crescent in the evening sky."[11]

"On the first day [the commemoration of the day when the Lord "passed over" the house of children before their exodus from Egypt] you shall hold a sacred convocation," says the book of Exodus (12:16), "and on the seventh day a sacred convocation; no work [melakha] at all shall be done on them, only what every person is to eat, that only may be done by you." From this passage of written Torah we gain insight on the observance of sacred seasons that are Sabbathlike. The Exodus passage refers to Pesach (Passover), the festival that commemorates the liberation of the Hebrews from Egyptian captivity. The Lord of Being had promised to "pass over" the children of Israel even as the angel of death fell upon the children of their Egyptian oppressors. The blood of a lamb on the doorpost was the sign of the presence of a child of the covenant, and death passed over.

Pesach occurs in the spring of the year of the common calendar and is usually close to the time of the Christian celebration of the resurrection of Christ. During the seven days of Passover no hametz (food containing leaven) is to be eaten. The dutiful Jewish family prepares for this festival by cleaning the house in such a way that no leaven should be found anywhere, not even a crumb. Not only must it not be eaten, but it must not be on the premises. It is assumed that any of the five major grains—oats, barley, wheat, rye, and spelt—that comes into contact with water will begin the leavening process. Even matzo, the unleavened bread used during Passover, may become hametz if necessary precautions are not taken to avoid leavening.

The celebration of Pesach calls for special preparation, since it involves a week of avoiding hametz. There is even a ceremony, which consists of a ritual search for hametz on the night before Passover, the eve of the fourteenth of Nisan.[12] "Blessed art Thou, Lord our God, King of the Universe who has Commanded us concerning the destruction of the hametz." The significance of this blessing comes home to us when we know that Torah tells us that the precepts were given prior to the liberation journey out of Egypt. "For seven days no leaven shall be found in your house; for if any one eats what is leavened, that person shall be cut off from the congregation of Israel, whether he is a sojourner or a native of the land" (Exodus 12:19). The people are to commemorate their liberation and the "passing over" regularly. The exodus had to be made quickly; there was no time for the luxury of leavening. The Lord of Being liberates the people *now,* not according to their own agenda. In many of the world's great traditions there is the teaching that true liberation (enlightenment, salvation, and so on) occurs only when individuals have learned the inadequacies of their own demands and expectations.

The Seder is a ritual meal that takes place during the first days of Pesach. It begins with a telling of the story of the exodus in such a way that it includes the Jews of the present day. Special foods remind the people of the many hardships that accompanied the escape from captivity and the joy of deliverance. During the remainder of the week, and continuing for seven full weeks, the Jews are to count the days until the festival of *Shavuot,* which celebrates the giving of the Torah and Israel's acceptance of the Law as the covenant way. Shavuot is sometimes called Pentecost (fiftieth day) and marks the birthday of the people of the Torah. It is on this Jewish festival day that the early Christians celebrated their beginnings as people of the gospel, or the new covenant.

One of the most important ritual occasions of the Jewish tradition is the period of Rosh Hashanah and the Days of Awe. Although Nisan is the first month of the year according to Torah, the first day of *Tishrai,* the seventh month, has become known as Rosh Hashanah, the New Year. This is partly because tradition began to think of creation as beginning on the first of Tishrai, and began to be the time reference for the counting of years.

Rosh Hashanah is a day like a Sabbath, a day of remembrance and the Day of Sounding the *shofar* (ram's horn). With its blast the people begin a ten-day period of self-examination and repentance for the many ways in which they have been involved in breaking the covenant during the past year. It is important on Rosh Hashanah to listen to the tones of the shofar, because the Torah says so and perhaps because its plaintive sounds come forth out of the eternal soul of the Jewish people. "The Lord spoke to Moses, 'on the tenth day of this seventh month is the Day of Atonement; it shall be for a time of holy convocation, and you shall afflict yourselves . . . and you shall do no work on this same day; for it is a day . . . to make atonement for you before the Lord your God. For whoever is not afflicted on this same day shall be cut off from his people'" (Leviticus 23:26). The period from Rosh Hashanah is the Ten Days of Repentance leading to Yom Kippur, the Day of Atonement. As for all such Shabbat-like practical expressions of Jewish tradition, Yom Kippur is preceded by a day of great preparation for the fast. Charity money is set aside, people make last-minute attempts to find reconciliation with those they have wronged, and the synagogue becomes the setting for shared blessings. Yom Kippur itself is a fast day—a time for "afflicting the soul." Eating and drinking are prohibited, and it is best not to wash or bathe, have sexual relations, wear shoes made of leather, or anoint the body.

The recitation of *Kol Nidre* begins the services of Yom Kippur. This is a prayer that is somehow the essence of all Jewish prayer and sets the tone for the entire observance. Traditionally the people wear white as a sign of purity and of respect for those no longer living. The Day of Atonement ends with a single blast of the shofar. Four days later is the festival of *Succoth* (Feast of Booths) in which the people remember the forty-year period of wandering in the desert after the Exodus from Egypt. During that time the Jews lived in tabernacles or booths—temporary dwellings. And so the Jewish family constructs a *succah* and spends some time in it. To do so is a mitzvah of remembrance.

In addition to the major festivals and fast days, there are ritual occasions like Hanukkah, Purim, and *Tishah b'Ab*. These are primarily postbiblical in origin and meaning and are not Sabbathlike in demeanor. It is important to understand that the Jewish tradition finds meaning in events in history, inasmuch as history is the arena of meaningful action by the Lord of Being who is indeed Lord of history. Of course, nature also belongs to the Lord of Being, but it is in history that he has fashioned a special people who knows his ways. Jewish ritual expression may relate its special days to the cycles of nature, but it is in order to celebrate the giving of Torah to a people called out of captivity to be a blessing to all the nations of the earth.

Social Expression

It is rather obvious by this time that the social expression of Jewish tradition is Israel itself, the people of God. Regardless of how serious one is in keeping the covenant, in performing the mitzvoth of the halakhic way of Torah, one is always a child of the covenant. It is possible to find ultimate order and meaning in one's life just by being a Jew. Like Professor Gordon, the philosopher in *The Promise*, the modern Jew knows that even if it is difficult to believe in God, there is a kind of assurance to life that makes it livable. Perhaps the Lord of Being understands how difficult it is sometimes to believe in him. There is a story about the Hasidic Rabbi Barukh of Medzebozh. His grandson, Yehiel, came running into his study, all in tears. "My friend cheats when we play hide-and-seek. It was my turn to hide, and I hid so well that he couldn't find me right away. So he stopped looking; he gave up. That's not fair!"

"Ah," said Rabbi Barukh as he dried his grandson's tears, "God too, Yehiel. God, too, is unhappy. He is hiding and the people have stopped looking for him. Do you understand, Yehiel?" The old man whispered softly as he held his grandson's head to his breast, "God is hiding and the people are not even searching for him."

In some ways the Jew goes on as a Jew even when belief is at a low ebb. Again, in the words of Tevye: "Because of our traditions, we've kept our balance for many, many years. . . . Because of our tradition, everyone knows who he is and what God expects him to do." To be a Jew is to be religious. There is little other reason for being a Jew. It is certainly not a matter of race, politics, or nationality. After all, Jews are Americans, Australians, British, Israelis, or Italians. Jews are Democrat and Republican, communist and capitalist. Some will say being a Jew is a sociological matter. If that is so, it is basically because this people exists as a social entity only by virtue of its being a liberated people, a people called to keep a covenant.

Orthodox, Reform, and Conservative Jews

The measure we have taken of Jewish religious tradition in order to understand it is only a glimpse of one of the greatest and richest of all traditions; there is still much to be said and studied. Also, the measure we have taken is an Orthodox measure, that is, we have examined Judaism using the fullest development of Jewish concern for the keeping of Torah. To be orthodox about anything is to be concerned for the most complete manifestation of it. Orthodox is generally assumed to be right *(ortho)* thinking *(doxos)*. However, the thinking is an orthodoxy of a mind that seeks to show something for what it really is—"to give glory." And the rightness of the thinking has to do with its fullness or completeness, not its narrowness. The orthodox way is in reality a way that seeks to rise above ways of judging and thinking that try to focus in upon a partial truth and make it into the whole truth.

In the modern world, orthodoxy is faced with assumptions about human knowledge that challenge its traditions, its accumulated heritage of thought and practice. The modern mind is usually convinced that no one has ever been quite so intelligent or knowledgeable. The modern mind frequently lives with the "belief" that newer is truer. One of the assumptions of the modern age (1500–circa 1950) has been that thinking is done by an autonomous individual, a mind that is centered upon itself. The result has often been that insights gained are thought to be exclusive of other insights. Be all this as it may, the Jewish religious tradition began to respond to the modern age long before its first Ashkenazic immigrants came to America. There were those Jews in France and Germany during the eighteenth century who began to question the traditional authority of the halakhic way.

Earlier in the chapter, attention was paid to the fact that living the Halakha was a kind of end in itself. That is to say, one kept *kashrut,* for example, because it was the way of the fathers and the commandment of the Lord. Presumably one learned the truth of the practice by doing it. One did not keep *kashrut* for reasons of health or anything else. Those who questioned the authority of the Halakha were asking for reasons. They wanted to participate fully in the "enlightened, reasonable" world they saw taking shape. They wanted to know whether it was necessary for the Jewish way to be so "ascetic," so withdrawn from the world. Their efforts resulted in a weakening of the traditional Jewish society. Many of these Jews became *maskilim*— enlightened ones. They sought to be full citizens of modernity, yet remain somehow Jews. To the maskilim it was possible to peel away unnecessary tradition and be proponents of some "essential" Jewish values.

In Germany in particular, the tendencies of *Haskalah*[13] led to the formation of what has been called Reform Judaism. By the early nineteenth century, more and more Jews were convinced that there was much to be gained by living in and among Gentiles instead of in traditional separate Jewish society. They sought major adjustments in the verbal and practical expression of the Jewish way in order that they might fit in with the modern gentile world. Why should Jewish ritual and ceremonial practice be so different from the church life of Protestant Christianity? they asked. Why should Jews dress like survivors of the Middle Ages? Why should their synagogue services be so informal and undignified? Why was it necessary to hang onto certain notions of Jewish "chosenness," which always offended the "chosen" of Christianity? These questions and others led to a major reform of Judaism, a movement away from the tradition associated with Orthodoxy.

By the 1840s, large numbers of Jews from Bavaria and other parts of the German states were coming to the United States. Many of these people were of the trading classes. They were not wealthy entrepreneurs, but quickly adapted themselves to the economy of a growing nation with its need for clothing, dry goods, and general merchandise. They became peddlers, tradespersons, owners of general stores. Although they were not of the educated elite—careful students of Torah and Talmud—they hoped to remain Jews in a world that was changing before their eyes. Among their leaders were those who tried to reinterpret the Jewish tradition as the way of a people concerned with social justice under the rule of the one living God. These Jewish thinkers believed that many of the beliefs and practices of earlier Judaism were the result of years of exile, suffering, and isolation. Earlier tradition represented a defensiveness that was no longer necessary in the United States. Change was in the air, and a new form of Judaism was being born, very much concerned with being streamlined enough to make a contribution to the emergence of the modern world.

The United States was a natural habitat for people who were much concerned with fitting in and getting their share of the good things of the modern world. As Jacob Neusner has pointed out, many of those who were not students of Torah were not very serious about their status as a people of Halakha. They were more interested in being Jews like one Protestant group seems like another—by belonging to a denomination that exists comfortably alongside others, without lingering on the margins of society. The United States was for these people a promised land. It was the place where Jews could belong, where they could take their place as productive members of the larger society. It was a promised land as it had been for the Christians who had come before. It promised "milk and honey," but it also was the place for the realization of a new and true Judaism, one not slavishly linked to the fortunes of a return to Palestine.

And so the United States was also a promised land for the thinkers who helped to form the mode of thought and practice that became Reform Judaism. Isaac Mayer Wise emigrated from Bohemia in 1846 and served as rabbi for congregations in Albany, New York, and Cincinnati, Ohio. Wise understood the congeniality of the American setting for the program of reforming Judaism into a modern religion that would not be hampered by the drag of tradition. He was eager to fashion a *minhag* America—a new Halakha, a set of Jewish practices that reflected life in the promised land of North America. His work eventually led to the development of a new prayer book, the organization of Reform rabbis and congregations, and the founding of Hebrew Union College in Cincinnati as an institution for the education of rabbis and the promotion of the way of Reform.

There were other leaders such as David Einhorn who helped to fashion Reform Judaism. Their work eventually led to the publication of the Pittsburgh Platform of 1885, which set forth the principles of the Reform movement in its formative American period. One has only to read these declarations to understand the direction of the Reform Jewish tradition in its departure from Orthodox moorings. The first principle reads, "We recognize in every religion an attempt to grasp the Infinite One, and in every mode, source or book of revelation held sacred in any religious system the consciousness of the indwelling of God in man." This assertion places the Jewish way alongside other traditions and makes it a "religion" rather than a comprehensive life system that sets the children of Abraham apart from those who worship "gods." "We recognize in the Mosaic legislation a system of training the Jewish people for its mission during its national life in Palestine, and today we accept as binding only its moral laws and maintain only such ceremonials as elevate and sanctify our lives, but reject all such as are not accepted to the views and habits of modern civilization." This is a far cry from Tevye's assertion: "Because of our tradition everyone knows who he is and what God expects him to do."

We see in the Pittsburgh Platform the rise of modernism, the formation of certain assumptions that become items of conviction and belief. It is one thing to be aware of the fact that the present age is different from past ages. It is quite another to believe that what the present age presumes to know is superior to the past and is the basis on which the truth of religious tradition is to be judged. Perhaps we may excuse the Jewish people for their desire for full participation in the society of the modern world. However, we must be cautious of their religious embrace of "the views and habits of modern civilization."

Reform Judaism did not begin in the United States, but its fruition was dependent upon the modernity of the New World. Here the Reform rabbi became a minister, like the clergy of Methodist and Presbyterian churches. Formerly the rabbi had been the teacher and judge for the Jewish community, teaching and interpreting Torah in relationship to life's many passages and problems. The synagogue was a house of prayer and study, but the rabbi's duties were not tied to the synagogue. The synagogue in America began to play the same kind of institutional role as the churches of American Christian denominations. And so the rabbi became pastor, worship leader (along with the *chazzan*), and preacher, like his Protestant Christian counterparts. The existent American religious situation was a powerful shaping force in the formation of Reform Judaism and its rabbis. The Jewish prayer book was revised, the English language instituted in place of the sacred Hebrew of the fathers. Sermons, mixed choirs, organs, family pews, and a Calvinist sense

of decorum in worship became characteristics of life in the Reform synagogue. It has been said that, at one stage in the history of Reform Jewish history in the United States, if one entered a synagogue one might have
difficulty in distinguishing it from the local Congregational church; one
might find its rabbi robed in the black Genevan gown of the Reformed[14]
clergy.

Of course, the history of Jewish tradition in the United States is very complex. Beginning in the 1880s, thousands of Jews arrived from the Eastern
European ghettoes and shtetls where Orthodox Jewry was the rule. In dress,
habit, belief, and tradition, they were distinctively Jewish. Some were Hasidic
Jews, charismatics whose leader (the rabbi) is thought of as *tzaddik,* the just
and moral person who is a Torah model and whose role is hereditary, passed
on from father to son. In many ways a departure from the venerable tradition
of rabbinic Judaism, Hasidism owes much to the Orthodoxy nourished in the
world of the Diaspora and offers a rich and colorful contribution to the history of religions.

The Orthodox and Hasidic Jews of Eastern Europe were an embarrassment to the assimilated people of the United States. On the other hand, to the
Orthodox, the Reform Jews were not Jews at all. So they initially went their
separate ways in the vast and diverse seas of American religious denominationalism. Gradually there emerged a third party to the Jewish scene. Under
the influence of ideas born in Europe, Conservative Judaism developed. This
form of the Jewish way represents an attempt to bridge the gap, provide a
middle way, between Orthodox and Reform traditions. Conservative Jews
were motivated by the desire to fit into the religious and social scene of a
nation that does not justify religious persecution, and they also wished to
conserve those aspects of the tradition they considered essential and distinctive. The Hebrew language was retained in services; the practice of *kashrut*
was maintained. Most Conservative Jews regarded the Reform movement as
too radical a departure from the truth of Torah, perhaps too much of a sell-
out to modernity. The services of Reform synagogues seemed lacking in
warmth and passion, in the soulful power of the children of Abraham in
prayer and blessing.

The Conservative movement hoped to become the basis of a Judaism that
would be distinctively American but not modernist. Out of this struggle to
find an American Judaism there emerged numerous other movements, the
most prominent of which is perhaps the Reconstructionist way of Mordecai
Kaplan. A professor at the Jewish Theological Seminary in New York City (a

Conservative institution), Rabbi Kaplan understood the Jewish way to be a civilization rather than a religion. Thus the Jewish way becomes not a system of beliefs, rituals, and ethical teachings, but a way of living together in a civil manner as a society of mutual enrichment. Both religion and civilization are expressions of human religiousness. Both find it necessary to subscribe to certain assumptions and practices that express the ultimate order and meaning of existence. Kaplan sought to retain the richness of Jewish tradition as a meaningful way of life. To him it was possible to do so without requiring any test of belief or conforming to accepted practice. To Kaplan Judaism had to be reconstructed as the preservation of an ethos, a special way of living. One was justified in living as a Jew in the same way that one lived as a member of a family or a particular nationality. It was the civilized way to live.

By the late nineteenth century Theodor Hergl issued his call for the creation of a Jewish state for the Jewish people. Partly a reaction to rising anti-Jewish sentiments in Europe, the movement known as Zionism was opposed by many American Jews who feared the possibility that their American loyalties might be questioned. Although Zionist advocates eventually decided that Palestine was the logical location of Zion as Jewish homeland, there were those who had entertained other sites. Zionism began gathering momentum in the twentieth century, leading to the gradual settlement of Palestine and the creation of the state of Israel after World War II. Many proponents of Zionism thought of themselves as secularists, giving up on those religious particularities that made them a "peculiar" people and seemed to frustrate the advance of modernity. It is not difficult for the historian of religion to point to the continuing religiousness of modern secular-minded Jews, clinging as they do to a unique identity as a source of ultimate order and meaning.

Jewish thinkers, like Elie Wiesel, winner of the Nobel Peace Prize in 1986, demonstrate the ambivalence of Jewish religious life since the formation of Israel. As a survivor of the Holocaust, in which millions of Jews were exterminated by the policies of Nazi Germany, Wiesel took comfort in the notion that the creation of Israel meant "never again"—pogroms, persecutions, and extermination were at an end: the Jews had a power-base from which to respond to anti-Jewish thought and action. On the other hand, Wiesel has been much troubled by the patronizing attitude of Israeli leadership toward Jews of the Diaspora and their frequent lack of compassion for the suffering of non-Jewish Palestinians.

There are interesting developments in present-day Judaism. It is possible to observe a revival of interest in tradition that cuts across the lines that once separated Reform, Conservative, and Orthodox Jewry. People are discovering the value of *kashrut,* Sabbath and holy day observance, and study as spiritual discipline for the living of these days. Of course, modernity keeps asserting its urgent claims, forcing many into attempts to find a "new Halakha" that goes beyond Reform Judaism in its devotion to "the views and habits of modern civilization." Today there are new developments in American Jewish life. Experimental forms of synagogue life have emerged in harmony with the democratic and psychological demands of contemporary culture, and women have become rabbis. Habad Lubavitch Hasidism has become a prominent movement in the attempt to revise Jewish identity and also to persuade outsiders to consider the Jewish Way. Meanwhile, Jewish thought and spirituality have entered into rigorous dialogue with Christianity and others of the world's religious traditions. And the Jewish tradition continues to wrestle with the significance of the Holocaust—Hitler's calculated extermination of millions of Jews during World War II—and with the emergence of political Israel in *eretz yisroel,* the ancient land of the people. The Jew always faces the need to resolve the relationship of his or her peoplehood to that nation that exists so precariously off the shores of the eastern Mediterranean Sea.

chapter 15

The Eastern Orthodox Tradition

Eastern Orthodoxy is a tradition of Christianity quite far removed from the understanding of most Americans, in spite of the fact that several million Americans belong to the churches of this tradition. Somehow the theology and practice of Orthodoxy have remained inside the churches and among the people of Greek, Russian, Romanian, Serbian, and Bulgarian extraction who live as members of the tradition. Orthodox priests and theologians have long been involved in ecumenical discussions, yet the richness of the Orthodox way remains unknown to many. This is partly because American evangelicalism tends to reduce Christianity to a simple pattern of belief in Jesus Christ. Americans in general have been influenced by evangelical assumptions and by the public religious notion that there are "common essentials" to religion. The result of this way of thinking is the belief that all Christianity is essentially the same and that the exotic liturgy and theology of Orthodoxy are external matters of little real consequence.

Nevertheless, the more the student of religion ventures into the Orthodox world, the more he or she will discover a way of thought, practice, and spirituality that are quite unique. Orthodoxy has much to offer the scholar of religions. Perhaps it has even more to offer those who search for meaning and self-understanding. As with the study of all traditions, we should not assume that we know what Orthodox Christianity is before we enter into its inner sanctum. There have been many Christianities throughout two thousand years of history, all of them placing their faith on the fact that something profound entered into human history through the life of Jesus the Christ. However, that "something profound" has been expressed and interpreted very differently at different times and places.

When we read the novels of Tolstoy, Dostoevsky, Pasternak, and Solzhenitsyn, we become aware of a pervasive spirit that has shaped their way of life. The officially atheistic dogma of Soviet communism apparently never eliminated the religious sensibilities of the people. Russian Orthodoxy lives and breathes in resistance to anything that seeks to make captive the human spirit. Orthodoxy reminds the people that they are more than what secular and Marxist thought and "sloganizing" have made of them. It helps them to celebrate the truth that they are children of God, that there has been given to them a divinity that makes them free of all lesser claims to authority. To attempt to understand the Russian and Greek people and their culture without recourse to the Orthodox spirit of their history is to make a grievous error of judgment.

Definition of Eastern Orthodoxy

Orthodoxy is the name given to that form of ancient Christianity centered in Asia Minor, northeastern Africa, and Eastern Europe. It is Christianity basically untouched (though not entirely) by the sixteenth-century Reformation in Western Europe. Orthodoxy is Eastern Christianity, that form of Christianity that was isolated from the Western Christian world after the Great Schism of the eleventh century. Of course, the schism was never absolute. There have been cultural and theological encounters across the East-West divide all through the Christian centuries down to the present. Nevertheless, the passion for the risen Christ, along with other ideas and practices at the heart of Orthodoxy, has been largely neglected in the West—certainly in America.

The Christianity of the East was nurtured in four ancient centers—Jerusalem, Antioch, Alexandria, and Constantinople. Tradition preserves the notion that these centers were established by the apostles Peter and James, Paul, Mark, and Andrew, respectively. These churches, therefore, are patriarchal centers—they form the original authoritative heart of Christianity. It is from those centers of "fathering" (patriarchy) that Christianity permeated the ancient world. The historical assumption at work is this: the small Jewish sect out of which Christianity emerged very early on found its way into the wider Greek culture of the times. In the eastern Mediterranean world this Greek influence continued to shape the liturgy and thought of the churches. This is why the term *Greek Orthodox* is frequently used synonymously with the name of Eastern Orthodox. Technically speaking, of course, orthodoxy tended to follow a pattern of what are called *autocephalic* national churches. Therefore, we tend to speak of Russian Orthodoxy, Greek Orthodoxy, Rumanian Orthodoxy, Albanian Orthodoxy, and so forth. To be autocephalic is to have one's own "head" or patriarchy, to be a national or ethnic self-governing and independent church.

Eastern Orthodoxy thinks that it has preserved the original catholicity of Christianity. It has been true to the *ortho-doxy* (right faith and practice) of the "one, holy, catholic, and apostolic church." Although there may not be a great deal of doctrinal distinction between Orthodoxy and Roman Catholicism, there is a great difference in spirituality and liturgical practice. Both churches consider themselves to be orthodox, both catholic; however, the circumstances of history have helped to shape two different religious systems or worlds. In some parts of Eastern Europe, the differences are of degree. Perhaps the proximity of that part of the world to the Orient has helped to fashion an Eastern Christianity that shares certain perceptions with Hindu and Buddhist mentality. There are Eastern churches that remain loyal to the bishop of Rome as pope (therefore, Roman Catholic) while continuing a liturgical and spiritual life in harmony with Eastern Orthodoxy. From this fact we may conclude that it is the doctrine of papal primacy that is at the heart of the division between Orthodoxy and Roman Catholicism.

Verbal Expression

It is not always easy to clarify what is distinctive about Eastern Orthodox Christianity. Turning to the verbal or theoretical expression of the tradition, we discover that theology itself carries a unique meaning in Orthodoxy. There is no great summation of systematic doctrine. Doctrine is important, but it points to the essential "mystery" of God and God's relationship to creation. Neither God nor the profundity of the creation are susceptible to religious definition. A theology that becomes a system tends to imprison the reality to which it offers testimony, but to Orthodoxy God is a mystery to which our minds must be opened. In contrast, "system" operates with a rational method that is primarily concerned with its success. Therefore, theology in Orthodox Christianity is more literally the "Word of God." That is, one does not do theology unless a relationship with God makes it possible. Theology is openness to God's becoming one with us. Theology is the capacity to use words that testify intelligently to the mystery of God-with-us (which is what Jesus Christ means). Theology does not exist without faith. Faith, of course, is not a psychological attitude or a willingness to believe. Faith is like realizing that one is more than one knows, a realization that is the spark that begins all true thinking. Christian faith begins with discipleship. It says: I realize that I am more than I know because the image of Christ has awakened that realization; now I wish to think as one who has the mind of Christ. The thinking that takes place is called theology.

We have already called attention to a central aspect of Orthodox thought. In this form of Christian tradition emphasis is upon the fact that God is essentially unknowable to us. We might say that inasmuch as God is always more than we can know, the *essence* of God is always beyond our knowing. After all, the Lord of Being of the Hebraic world out of which Christianity emerges makes a covenant with those who are to have "no other gods" before him. In spite of the inaccessibility of God's "essence," Orthodoxy reminds us that God is known in God's "energies." "He is outside all things according to his essence," wrote St. Athanasius in the fourth century, "but he is in all things through his acts of power." The *energies* are the manifestations of power and insight we encounter in the world. However, to become aware of the energies of God is to be aware of God's essence. Energies are not part of God; they are the whole of God who is always more than we know. "Every visible or invisible creature," wrote John Scotus Erigena, "is a theophany or appearance of God." There is always an "otherness" to God, yet it is an otherness that we encounter in our own selfhood, in nature, and in our human relationships. Reality is social. The essence of God points to God's otherness; the energies of God point to the presence of that otherness. "We know the essence through the energy," says St. Basil. "No one has ever seen the essence of God, but we believe in the essence because we experience the energy."

Orthodoxy, like Anglicanism, places great emphasis upon the incarnation as a means of understanding Christianity. God becomes human. This does not mean that *a* person becomes *a* god. Rather, it tells us that God in essence identifies fully with our humanity. In Jesus the Christ we become intensely aware of the fact that this "more than" in the midst of our existence is a very personal affair. We discover that our understanding of God begins with our acknowledgment of the fact that we only know who God is to the extent that we encounter God in the real circumstances of personal existence. In other words, it is not as if we knew who and what God is, then are faced with the task of having Jesus Christ fit into our already formed demands and expectations. Rather, in Jesus Christ, the reality of God becomes centered in the midst of existence as it is actually lived, with all of its suffering and evil. This is what is meant by incarnation. This incarnation is now known through the activity of God as Holy Spirit. Therefore, the heart of orthodoxy focuses upon the Spirit rather than Christ and what is called Christology.

Orthodoxy would maintain that ordinary human existence is inclined toward self-centered ends. It accepts the captivity of its own myopic vision and comes to the conclusion that life is no more than we can make of it. This myopic vision is another name for sin, the alienation of our lives from the "more than," from that ought to be, from God. Sin is alienation from true relationship to God, our fellow humans, and nature. "Since man could not come to God, God has come to man, identifying himself with man in the most direct way," writes the Orthodox theologian Kallistos Ware.[1] And Eastern thinkers like St. Isaac the Syrian (seventh century) urge upon us the notion that this action of incarnation proceeds out of the fullness of love that is at the heart of the universe. Even if there were no alienation—or perhaps, especially because there was no alienation—God's love would identify itself fully with humanity.

The incarnation introduces a new creation into the world. It begins a new stage of human history. Everything is changed, a point that leads to another emphasis in the verbal expression of Orthodoxy. God becomes humanity in order that humanity may become God. This statement sets the tone for the Orthodox teaching about "deification." Inasmuch as we are created "in the image of God," it is the intention of the Creator that we should also be "in the likeness of God." Being "in the image" implies that something of what God is in and of himself is also characteristic of us. As humans we are creatures of body, soul, and spirit. We are conscious, decision-making beings, with a measure of freedom that makes us agents of creation itself. We are "more than" animality, more than physicality—more than we know, more than what seems to be. Therein is our being in the image of God. It means that our very being is always related to others. We have the potential for full and loving mutuality. We ordinarily reject that image in favor of the illusory life of self-aggrandizement. We opt for becoming self-contained gods.

God becomes human in order that we may overcome this impediment that stands in the way of our being "like God." By living in close communion with the risen Christ in his body, the church, we undergo deification. We are made into the *likeness* of God. Obviously, the wholeness and essence of God is inaccessible—God is always "more than." We become like God as God is in divine energies, not as God is in his essence.

Orthodoxy also emphasizes the joy that is at the heart of the Christian life. God has participated in the suffering and death of this life and overcome it. We have only to do with the risen Christ in his body, the church. The risen Christ has restored and reconciled the whole created order. It is a new creation, a glorious creation, known by the power of the Holy Spirit. The Christian life must be thankful and joyful for God's victory. Of course, this does not mean that we ignore the continuation of suffering and evil in the world. These things are still with us. Human existence is still free; it has not been reconstituted into computerized goodness. To the extent, however, that we can focus upon God's victory, we transcend our own expectations. We learn to see the world with the eyes of the risen Christ. We become Christs, who do not try to reshape the world into our own narrow and self-centered understanding.

To enter an Orthodox church building is to find oneself as part of a brilliant tapestry. There are colors and lights, the glow of candles. There are ornate paintings of saints, of Mary as *theotokos* (bearer of God), of Christ. The aroma of incense and the deep, rich sounds of Orthodox music (quite unlike the hymns or gospel songs of Western Christianity) help to transport us with all of our senses into a glorious world, a new creation in which victory over death is the dominant perspective. Orthodox people perceive the world with a very different sensorium[2] from many of us. For Orthodoxy the world, including nature, is the domain of the glorious, risen Christ.

Orthodox thought also focuses upon the classical reality of the Trinity. Any Western rationalist, for whom the Trinity poses a mathematical problem (for example, How can God be three, yet one?), should begin a careful study of Orthodox Trinitarian theology. Essentially, for Orthodoxy, God is Trinity; God is mystery revealed. The assumption is that, in our individual self-centeredness, we require God to be a single identity, even as we suppose we are self-contained singularities. However, the Heart of the universe is not that kind of reality. The Heart of the universe is revealed as social reality. God is not single identity, but interpersonal identity. God is the mystery of the interdependence, the coinherence, of reality. When we have "eyes to see and ears to hear," we will suddenly be illuminated by the truth of this revelation. The result will be that we will begin to understand ourselves in the same way. We will discover that we are created in the image of Trinitarian reality. In other words, we too are more than we wish to be in our pretense to be self-contained singularity. We are part of a mysterious co-dependent and social reality.

God is Father, Son, and Holy Spirit. The doctrine of the Trinity is shared by all of Christianity, East and West. However, Orthodoxy takes this mystery "seriously." Its verbal and practical expressions alike show forth the Trinity. The modern West tends to ignore the Trinity as a doctrine too difficult to understand, or as a teaching no longer as important as it may have been in the past. If we probe the richness of Orthodox concern for the Trinity, we may find insights into the nature of God and humanity that are missing in Western understanding.

For Orthodoxy the incarnate, risen Christ leads us into an understanding of reality as Trinitarian. This understanding is the beginning of reasoning about such matters. The discovery that the Heart of the universe itself is dynamic, social, interpersonal is a revolutionary discovery. "God is not stillness, repose, unchanging perfection."[3] God is not the immovable singularity that I project him to be. He is not even "he" as I am he in the illusion of my unmovable singularity. God is Father, Son, and Holy Spirit, but not in some sense of self-centered maleness. Rather, these are the given symbols by means of which we learn of God and consequently learn to live our own lives.

God the Father refers to the fact that the Heart of the universe is a source and a cause from which everything originates. However, God is more than that. God is the personal mystery that serves as the inner principle by means of which everything exists in order, and reflects the source and cause of everything. In other words, God is Son. But God is also Holy Spirit, that sense of being "more than" which is in each of us and draws us to the point where we may see the Son, the inner principle of purpose and order. Accordingly, there is an inner connectedness, says Orthodoxy, that makes each "person" of the Trinity the fullness of God *in energies,* while at the same time being a unity. However, an understanding of the paradox that God is one, yet three, demonstrates the fact that that is precisely where truth lies—in paradox.

Orthodoxy has been careful to maintain a loyalty to this essential mystery of existence. It worships God as Trinity and it thinks carefully about what that means. One of the factors, in addition to the papacy, that separates Orthodoxy from Roman Catholicism and from the rest of Christianity is what has been called the *filioque* clause in the Nicene Creed. This creed emerged in the fourth century in order to protect the integrity of Christian understanding of the real meaning and significance of Jesus Christ. There had been those who wished to remove the paradox of Christ's persons: either he is a man or he is God, they said. But the conservers rejected this "either/or." In an effort to distinguish carefully the three persons of the Trinity, while maintaining their essential unity as One God, the third table of the creed stated: "We believe in the Holy Spirit, the Lord, the giver of Life, who proceeds from the Father. With the Father and the Son he is worshiped and glorified."

The Western church, especially from the ninth century on, began to insert the *filioque* (Latin for "and the Son") into its chanting of the creed: "We believe in the Holy Spirit, the Lord, the giver of life, who proceeds from the Father *and the Son.*" To the unsophisticated ear this may seem a harmless interpolation. To the Orthodox theological mind, the phrase asserts what is called a doctrine of "double procession"—it has the Spirit proceeding from both Father and Son, which to Orthodoxy is theologically inept and spiritually detrimental. The *filioque* confuses the relationship of the three persons of the One God. "According to the Greek Fathers of the fourth century," writes Kallistos Ware, "whom the Orthodox Church follows to this day, the Father is the sole source and ground of unity in the Godhead. To make the Son a source as well as the Father, or in combination with him, is to risk confusing the distinctive characteristics of the persons."[4] This is important because it is the Father who must be the source, the bond of unity, from whom and into whom the order of persons runs its course. The "Son" is begotten of the Father; the Spirit proceeds from the Father. Obviously, the subtleties of this theological controversy are beyond the scope of this chapter, but their existence and the significance of the entire matter should be appreciated.

Practical Expression

A consideration of the practical expressions of Orthodox tradition must include a discussion of the Divine Liturgy, the holy mysteries, icons, and Orthodox spirituality. The Divine Liturgy is the name given to the central observance of the Eucharist in Orthodox worship. This is what the Roman church came to call the Mass, although in recent decades the Eucharist has come to be a more commonly accepted name for this act of worship for much of Christianity. For Orthodoxy, as for the other more catholic traditions of Anglicanism and Roman Catholicism, the liturgical life of the church is a very concrete and objective event; that is, the Divine Liturgy of Orthodoxy is a happening. Its value is centered in *what takes place* rather than in the private subjective attitudes of the assembly of worshipers. The divine mystery of God-in-Christ is a definite presence. Inasmuch as God is a communion of persons (Trinity), there is an objective encounter with God in the communion of the people. The Divine Liturgy of the Eastern church is somewhat different from the eucharistic services of Western Christianity. However, the shape of the liturgies is similar. "The liturgy of the Eucharist," wrote Orthodox theologian Alexander Schmemann, "is best understood as a journey or procession. It is the journey of the Church into the dimension of the Kingdom. We use this word 'dimension' because it seems the best way to indicate the manner of our sacramental entrance into the risen life of Christ."[5]

The building itself is part of this liturgical action; the worshiper leaves the ordinary world and enters into another. Everything about the design and appointment of the Orthodox church building enhances the nature of journey, of "entrance into the risen life of Christ." The floor plan is usually in the shape of a Greek cross, with arms of equal length. A large dome covers the crossing,[6] on which in brilliant colors and gold finish will be an image of the holy face of Christ or of the *theotokos*. An individual entering the building may pause before an icon of a saint or holy person, kiss the icon, light a candle, make the sign of the cross, and say a prayer. By these actions one symbolizes one's entrance into a holy world where realities that the outside world ignores become the substance of one's experience. Across the eastern front of the building stretches a large screen called an iconostasis, separating the sanctuary from the nave. The icons on this screen are another reminder that holiness is a journey guided by Father, Son, and Holy Spirit. Only clergy and laity with special assignments are permitted in the space behind the iconostasis, for it is in this sanctuary where the holiest aspects of God's love are reenacted. To the north and south of the sanctuary with its altar are the places for the offering and preparation of the elements of the Eucharist, and for the use of the deacons who serve with the priests at the altar. These areas are called the *prothesis* and *diaconicon*.

The Divine Liturgy begins with the prayers and rituals attendant to the preparation of bread and wine for consecration. The Little Entrance includes traditional prayers (some of which are inaudible to the congregation), reading from the epistles, the chanting of the Gospel of the day, and the sermon by the preacher of the day. At an appropriate point in the liturgy, the priest, preceded by altar boys bearing candles, comes forth out of the sanctuary, symbolizing the coming of Christ. "O Master and Lord our God," says the priest silently, "who hast appointed in heaven order and hosts of angels, and archangels for the service of thy glory, grant that with our entrance there may be an entrance of holy angels, serving with us and glorifying thy goodness. For unto thee belong all glory, honor and worship, to the Father and to the Son, and to the Holy Spirit, now and for ever and from all ages to all ages." The priest re-enters the sanctuary, where preparation for the Great Entrance begins.

The altar is censed by the priest and the gifts of bread and wine are brought into the sanctuary. After an exchange of Christian greetings, the words "The doors, the doors, with wisdom let us attend" are heard, and the priest emerges from the altar carrying in each hand a square veil called an *aer*.

These veils have been removed from the paten and chalice[7] and symbolize the holy gifts contained therein. The Creed of Nicaea is chanted and the great prayer of thanksgiving *(eucharistia)* begins. After the consecration, the priest censes the gifts, pours boiling water into the chalice, and intones, "The ardor of faith, full of the Holy Spirit." The communion itself includes a prayer for worthiness, and the people receive the Holy Eucharist. A benediction accompanies the reception of the elements by the people, during which the priest says, "With fear of God, with faith and love draw near. O God, save thy people and bless thine inheritance." The choir replies, "We have seen the true Light, we have received the Heavenly Spirit, we have found the true Faith worshiping the undivided Trinity; for He hath saved us." The Dismissal includes a prayer of thanksgiving and a prayer recited before the icon of Christ.

Reflection upon what has taken place will confirm the notion of the liturgy as a pilgrimage to a holy center where the Trinity and the whole company of the sacred are encountered. The people make entrance into a world where God and God's reconciling love for creation have entered. The beauty and profound majesty of the Divine Liturgy cannot be adequately described here, and the interested reader is urged to examine these matters.

Although there are five liturgical orders in Orthodoxy, the one used most widely is the Divine Liturgy of St. John Chrysostom, a fourth-century bishop who became patriarch of Constantinople in 398, nine years before his death while in exile. There are in Orthodoxy the seven sacraments of Baptism, Chrismation, Holy Eucharist, Confession, Ordination, Marriage, and Holy Unction. Chrismation, the anointing with holy oil, takes place immediately following baptism. Orthodoxy prefers the word *mysteria*—mysteries—instead of sacraments to refer to these ritual actions that accompany the people in the various stages of their lives. The faithful participate in holy mysteries. This term helps us to understand the perception of the world in the Orthodox tradition. One of the reasons for the grandeur of the Divine Liturgy is that it is a reminder that human existence is a mystery to the core. Orthodoxy celebrates the fact that the Trinity makes the whole of being so much more than we can conceive or imagine. Mysteries are evidence of this presence of the "more than" quality of reality. One participates in a holy mystery, knowing that grace abounds, which is not the outcome of human effort or comprehension. Mystery also reminds us that there is a certain "secrecy" about the truth of our salvation. The truth is not open to our control either by definition or by some attitude of simplicity. Orthodoxy is not puritanical in its emphasis upon beauty and elegance. That is because the truth of the gospel is a known mystery that does not submit to our puritanizing illusions. The Puritan must always be reminded that salvation does not come from personal simplicity or humility, even though these qualities may be the expression or "fruit" of salvation.

The use of icons has always been a key element in the Orthodox tradition, in contrast to its recent introduction into the spirituality of Anglicanism and Roman Catholicism as a result of the ecumenical encounter and the recovery of tradition. As a practical expression of human religiousness, the icon is similar to the *mandala* of Oriental traditions such as Buddhism. Professor Okamura Keishin of Kochi University in Shikoku, Japan, has said that a mandala is an image or design that represents a way of perceiving the world.[8] The mandala focuses upon an image or images that are an important aspect of religious experience. The design is in some manner symbolic of the whole world. In Japan the image may be a *kami,* that mysterious life force that is sometimes thought of as a spirit, a god, or divine being. The most important mandalas of Japan are those that reflect the oneness and manyness of Buddha. Accordingly, a given mandala may have many faces and portraits all held together by an intricate design that mysteriously shows the whole world encompassed in its space. The Buddhist monk learns to meditate by way of the mandala; in so doing its secrets are revealed.

It is interesting to note Keishin's comment in an essay on the philosophy of Kukai, ninth-century founder of the Shingon school of Buddhism, that "it would be very difficult to develop a mandala with a Christian world view."[9] Keishin believes that monotheistic traditions are repulsed by images of God's activity and consider such things idolatrous. Yet close observation of the use of icons in Orthodoxy reveals a mode of design and experience not radically different from the mode of the mandala. Of course, it is true that the veneration of icons sparked a controversy that agitated the church from around 725 to 842 C.E. and centered on accusations of idolatry. However, icons remain a distinguishing characteristic of Orthodox practice, and a sophisticated theology denies the charges of idolatry.

Icons are flat pictures, usually painted in egg tempera on wood. They usually represent the Trinity, Christ, the Virgin Mary *(theotokos)*, or a saint of the church. These images are not three-dimensional, not sculptured or "graven" (carved); therefore they are in keeping with the second commandment of the Jewish and Christian traditions. The icon is also not really a likeness of anything or anyone. For example, although an icon of Christ is a face, it is not like a face in nature. We can tell that it has human qualities, but it is more than a human face, naturally considered. The painting of icons is carefully regulated by certain iconographical canons maintained by the church. The icon is a highly stylized symbol. Again, a careful observation of an icon reveals that it functions like a mandala. It is a way of perceiving the whole world through the image of Christ or Virgin or saint. The design of the icon, like the mandala, has various facets in addition to the central image. It is meant to be a means of directing the veneration of the masses, a means of communion with the triune God and the holy church. As such it is a kind of transparency into the divine reality. But it is also a focus for meditation that can bring the individual into understandings of the Christian gospel that are often hidden from ordinary observation. There is a certain sternness in the faces of icons, which often arouses negative responses from the unfamiliar observer. However, it is necessary to remember that the work is not a resemblance, and many of the images were nurtured in a world of pain and suffering, which reminds us that compassionate existence emerges from an encounter with the reality of suffering. In Christian understanding, the world is redeemed through God's own suffering. God suffers in energies, not in essence. God suffers in a world that favors the illusion of self-sufficiency.

Orthodox practice is profoundly shaped by the monastic experience in the soul of its history. The monastic ideal provides the norm for all of the Christian pilgrimage. Monastic virtues are the aspiration of all Christians. In this way, there is no great distinction between what is expected of monks and what is expected of the rest of the body of Christ. Presumably every Christian can find a way of doing what the monk does, that is, follow Jesus the Christ as he was "led up of the Spirit into the wilderness" (Matthew 4:11). A certain discipline of *ascesis*—withdrawal from the "world"—is normative for all Christians. The monk withdraws into the monastery in order to seek himself as he really is, rather than to live as his own desires and the "world's" seductions tell him he is. He serves "God with fasting and prayers night and day" (Luke 2:37). The monk is in warfare against the powers of evil and darkness, and he faces those powers in the "wilderness" even more than he would in the centers of civilization. In Christian monasticism the monk's withdrawal is not primarily for his own sake. He wishes to benefit the "world" by his prayer and contemplation. He prays for the church and the "world." He gains a way of perceiving the world that comes from being able to "see the forest" rather than merely to see his own limbs or the other "trees." The virtues of monasticism are summed up in the word *compassion*.

The monk becomes compassionate as he participates in God's suffering for the world. He does not strive to be compassionate, which would create a false piety; he simply becomes compassionate. Humility, prudence, temperance, fortitude, and justice are related to the virtues of faith, hope, and love that constitute compassion.

The Orthodox individual would find it difficult to take seriously the salvation she or he shares in the body of Christ without a certain monastic withdrawal from the world. Going to Divine Liturgy, saying the daily offices and prayers, keeping the life of Christ ever in mind by observing a liturgical year—these are forms of ascesis. The monastic virtues are the virtues by which every Christian must be measured.

Related to monasticism as a factor in understanding the practical expression of Orthodoxy is the tradition of the *hesychasts*. A student of Oriental spirituality and modes of contemplation will recognize an affinity with Orthodox *hesychasm*. The word *hesychia* means "quiet" and alludes to a special discipline of contemplation. There are four elements to *hesychasm*. First, there is a striving for total repose and silence during which time all formal modalities such as meditation, reading, singing, or articulate prayer are excluded. Second, techniques designed to assist in the centering of the mind are used. Control of breathing and body is developed, and a fixation of perception upon the heart, the navel, or the stomach is practiced in order that the mind may move back into the true center of one's being (the "heart"). A third aspect of the *hesychasm* method is the repetition of the "Jesus-prayer." Both this practice and the mind-centering techniques are related to the striving for a state of quiet. The Jesus-prayer eventually becomes a quiet resident in the very soul of the person. The fourth element is the perception of "divine light" or "light of Tabor," a physical perception of illumination like no other light—the glory of God, or the Shekinah of God in Judaism.

Hesychasm originated in a distinctively monastic environment within Orthodoxy, but its methods have since been adopted by many. A classic nineteenth-century work by an anonymous author, *The Way of a Pilgrim*, tells the story of a simple wayfarer who practices the Jesus-prayer. And J. D. Salinger, in his novel *Franny and Zooey,* provides us with insight into certain implications of the use of this prayer. Also called the prayer of the heart, it is a spiritual technique that, like many such methods, should probably be used with the guidance of a spiritual director. Essentially it is a response to an injunction of the apostle Paul in 1 Thessalonians 5:17: "pray without ceasing." The individual who uses the prayer faithfully discovers that he or she is praying without knowing it. As the above-mentioned "Pilgrim" tells us:

> I felt the prayer stirring strongly in my heart, so wishing to be alone as soon as I could and not hinder the prayer, I said to the lady as soon as we rose from the table, "No doubt you will rest for a while after dinner, and I am so used to walking that I will go for a stroll in the garden."
> "No, I don't rest," she replied. "I will come into the garden with you, and you shall talk to me about something instructive."[10]

In this delightful little episode, we are provided with an interesting account of how the Jesus-prayer works. But we are shown that it is not considered to be an "escape" from the pressures of life, as we sometimes want it to be (witness the pilgrim's desire to be alone with the prayer). Rather, it affects the life of the pilgrim in the midst of human interaction, the routine of social existence.

Prayer is a central aspect of Orthodox practice. "There is no life without prayer," writes Vasilii Rozanov, "Without prayer there is only madness and horror. The soul of Orthodoxy consists in the gift of prayer."[11] It is obvious from Orthodox writing that prayer is much more than a natural inclination to call upon a higher power for help, or to "say some words to the close and holy darkness." Although Rozanov speaks of prayer as a gift, it is also a work. It is a discipline and it must be learned under spiritual direction. In Orthodoxy there are degrees of prayer. Prayer is a continuous and repeated process, the ultimate stage of which is contemplation. This is a stage in which the individual waits upon God in quietness and silence, a stage in which the person is overwhelmed by the realization that God is the very Presence of God in ultimate absence. That is, God is the very real "more than" in the midst of personal existence. The prayer of the heart begins on an oral level, grows inwardly into the intellect of direct apprehension, then descends into the very center of one's being—the "heart." The pilgrim in prayer is one whose thoughts and words are directed less to wants and needs of the self, more toward a sharing of God's compassion for all of being.

Orthodoxy has also fostered the tradition of the spiritual director in ways that lie undeveloped in much of the rest of Christianity. The spirit of America tends toward privacy and self-sufficiency, making it difficult for Americans to understand this central principle of Orthodox spirituality—that one needs a guide, a teacher in the spiritual life. Called a *staretz* in the Russian tradition, this spiritual director need not be a priest of the church. Quite often a layperson emerges whose human and spiritual qualities are such that he or she will be sought out to assist other "pilgrims" along the way. The staretz is the spirit's physician, who assists in diagnosing the progress of the pilgrim, helping the latter to discern whether his or her progress is of God or of personal projections and fantasies. The staretz may hear a confession, may cajole or admonish, may direct or may remain silent. Often she or he gives "a word," avoiding any detailed or overly didactic addresses, leaving the pilgrim with a new focus for his or her own meditation or contemplation. "A staretz," says the Russian novelist Dostoevsky, "is one who takes your soul, your will into his soul and his will."

Social Expression

It is not necessary to say very much about the social expression of Orthodoxy. For Eastern Christianity, the church is the great mystery of the risen Christ in the life of the world. Salvation is a sharing of the Trinity. Each social unit—family, school, work—is to become the likeness of the triune God. As Ware puts it, God is a circle of love. Presumably, love must be a circle; if God is love, then God is a Trinity: "three equal persons, each one dwelling in the other two by virtue of an unceasing movement of mutual love."[12] There is diversity and unity in God. This circle of love is victorious over death and exists in the world, for the world, as the church, the body of Christ. In the sacramental life of the church the Holy Spirit works to unite us to the circle of love by way of the love of the risen Christ. The individual lives in the body of Christ, and Christ resides in the individual, who through him is helped to become the likeness of God. In this sense, Orthodoxy reminds us, we become Christs.

The polity of the Orthodox tradition is episcopal. That is to say, the bishop (episkopos) is successor to the apostles and chief pastor of the body of Christ in a certain vicinity. The bishop's care for the people of the body is shared with priests, deacons, and laity. Orthodox churches tend to be the Orthodox Christians of a nation or ethnic body within a nation such as the United States. Each such Orthodox church (for example, Greek, Rumanian, or Russian) is autocephalic, independently administered by a council of bishops, which is called a synod. Although the "Archbishop of Constantinople, the New Rome, and Ecumenical Patriarch," is a first among equals, he does not command an authority parallel to the pope as bishop of Rome in Roman Catholicism.

In keeping with a Catholic sense of order, there are the usual three orders of ministerial priesthood: deacon, priest, and bishop. However, Orthodoxy acknowledges three ranks among bishops. Archbishops are chief pastors of the church in a large and outstanding city where the church is strong. A metropolitan is a bishop with jurisdiction over a large province of an autocephalic church or of one of the original chief sees of the Christian church. These bishops seldom wear modern dress, confining themselves to the use of full-length black cassocks. Orthodox priests may marry before ordination, but unmarried priests may attain the rank of archimandrite. Married clergy may not be selected as bishops; most bishops have been chosen from the archimandrites. The tradition does not include the ordination of women in the priesthood. However, women have been prominent members of Orthodox monastic orders and leaders in the devotional and spiritual disciplines.

History in the United States

Orthodoxy in the United States had its beginnings in the cold northern lands of Alaska and the Aleutian Islands, where the Asian and North American continents strain to touch. On October 6, 1977, the Holy Synod of the Church of Russia added the name of Innocent to its calendar of saints. The man was originally the Reverend John Veniaminov, one of the first Russian Orthodox priests assigned to Alaska, a man who was later to become Metropolitan of Moscow. When Father John arrived in the archipelago in the early nineteenth century, he was greeted by the general manager of the Russian-American Company for the entire Unalaskan region, as follows:

> O merciful Pastor, Father John! Through the Providence of our Creator Most-High, this region is made glad by the arrival of Your Blessing to teach in these parts the Orthodox Christian faith. After short periods of time spent here by reverend individuals preaching the Word of God—beginning with the arrival of our venerable Father Macarius in 1795; then by Fr. Gideon, hieromonk of the Trinity Lavra's Cathedral, who visited in 1809; and then in 1820–21 by the Priest Michael—you are established here as a *permanent* presence to convert through your assignment and lawful ministry our earth chapel into a Church of God and to set us by active sacramental and liturgical ministrations and soul-saving exhortations on the true path of the Orthodox religion.

When Alaska became a territory of the United States in 1867, there was considerable anxiety among the Russian residents. Many returned to their native lands. The Orthodox church was faced with problems of reorganization and reconception. It could no longer be the Russian Orthodox church. It had to adjust to its pluralistic status in a nation without an establishment. Although it maintained an evangelical and missionary policy with regard to the inhabitants of its new American homeland, it gradually acquired the status of an ethnic enclave in a society dominated by Western Christian, even Protestant, thought and practice. A diocese formed in Alaska after the Purchase of 1867, transferring its episcopal seat to San Francisco in 1872, then to New York in 1905.

Eastern Orthodoxy did not become a significant presence in the United States until around the turn of the twentieth century, when large numbers of Slavs and other Eastern Europeans began to work in the steel mills, cement mills, and mines of northeastern and western Pennsylvania. Many of these people were Orthodox. Their churches altered the landscape with the curious onion-shaped domes of their buildings. Small numbers of Greek Orthodox had been in the country prior to the influx of the Slavs. However, the Greeks were seldom among the laboring classes; along with their Orthodox brothers and sisters from Asia Minor, they tended to be restaurateurs and merchants. Often these people found themselves in parts of the United States where they lived as solitary families. There were no ethnic enclaves such as those of the Slavs. In these solitary circumstances many Greeks found themselves attending Anglican (Episcopal) churches, where they discovered a certain liturgical congeniality. As the American population increased and became more urbanized, the automobile made it possible for Greek Orthodox churches to be established, drawing from a wide radius within a given metropolitan area.

Orthodoxy in America continues to be somewhat clannish, ethnic, and often isolated from the mainstream of American religion and culture. Some people who discover a certain intellectual and liturgical affinity with Orthodox Christianity have reported feelings of frustration in their attempts to find a church home because Orthodoxy is so "ethnic." In the words of one such person, "How can I become Orthodox when that means I must try to become Russian, Greek, or Serbian?"

Orthodox churches still tend to be organized along ethnic lines, although there have been numerous efforts to create an autocephalic American Orthodox church. There exists an Orthodox Church in America, alongside the various ethnic jurisdictions. Orthodoxy has been a participant in the ecumenical movement of the twentieth century, working in close association with the National and World Councils of Churches. There are thriving theological seminaries in Scarsdale, New York, and Brookline, Massachusetts. The faculties of these institutions are made up of leading church historians and theologians, whose scholarly work contributes significantly to a reconstruction of Christian understanding in the postmodern era. In addition, special negotiating commissions charged with exploration of unity among Orthodox, Anglican, and Roman Catholic Christians have been in existence since the nineteenth century.

Eastern Orthodoxy has been the Christian tradition least shaped by the circumstances and conceptions of the American setting. It has begun to come of age in the United States since World War II. It will probably be shaped by the pragmatic and theological necessity of a united Orthodox church required by the American situation. Perhaps its earlier isolation places it in a position where it can make a unique contribution to a reconstruction of Christian thought and practice. Orthodoxy has been least affected by the individualistic assumptions of the revivalistic evangelicalism that has so shaped American religion since the nineteenth century. The verbal and practical expressions of Orthodoxy are unique. As we have seen, the average American must not assume that he or she knows what Christianity is all about before coming to terms with the Orthodox tradition.

chapter 16

The African American Traditions

It is important to remember that Africans have been a presence in the American religious and cultural landscape for almost as long as European Americans. The first slaves were brought to Virginia as early as 1619, therefore even prior to the founding of Plymouth and Massachusetts Bay Colonies. Along with Native Americans, they constitute an influence in the thinking of Americans that has not yet been carefully explored. We must ask ourselves: How have our self-understanding and religious behavior been shaped by the presence of African Americans and their traditions?

It is difficult to generalize about the religious traditions of Americans of African descent. Many black Americans are participants in the traditions discussed in other chapters of this book. These Presbyterians, Roman Catholics, Anglicans, and Jews, to name a few, have either become party to the ethos of predominantly white congregations or denominations, or they have transformed inherited Christian traditions into unique versions of their own religiosity. It is also true, however, that the African presence in American history is a special one; rather distinctive religious ideas, practices, and institutions have emerged from the particularity of their circumstances. After all, African Americans are the descendants of largely involuntary hordes of immigrants. The circumstances of slavery and decades of second-class citizenship have shaped unique traditions. For the most part these traditions have been forged from the resources of African tribal heritage and Christianity in the crucible of suffering and oppression.

The blending of African tradition and slave Christianity into a unique religious sensibility shared by many African Americans of varied institutional commitments is the topic of this chapter. An understanding of this black religiousness will help us to explore the character of the black churches, the "sects and cults" of Afro-Americana, and the special political nature of black religion.

Indigenous Heritage

The African heritage of the United States' blacks was a tribal culture very similar to that of the Native Americans. Human existence in such cultures tends to be a drama of nature. Life is highly traditional, with the role of the individual closely ordered by the character of the tribe itself. Of course, these cultures are shaped by the oral-aural modes of thought and communication. The figure of Kacou Ananzé, the trickster, is a favorite of the Ashanti and other African peoples. The trickster appears in many cultures and is a reminder of the sophisticated manner in which the folk comprehend the precarious order of existence. A figure who "upsets the applecart," the trickster does not operate by the rules but reveals the surprises that lie at the heart of all that people think and do. Bernard Binlin Dadié is an African writer who has preserved many of the tales of Ananzé, or Spider. One such story follows.

One day Ananzé decided to visit the High God because he had heard that the High God kept a box of stories near his throne. All the stories of the world were in that box.

And so Ananzé spun a web and climbed up to visit Nyami, Lord of the Sky. "I must have that box of stories!" said Spider.

"Oh really?" said Nyami as the other gods roared in laughter at the audacious request. "Well, well! That is not an easy matter. The price is high."

Ananzé assured the High God that he would do whatever was necessary. He was told that he must bring four creatures: Onini the python, Osebo the leopard, Moboro the hornet, and Mmoatia the fairy that no one can see. "Then you may have the stories." Again the gods shook with laughter as Spider scurried down the web.

Ananzé had to consult his wife Aso, who was always patient with her husband's schemes. "I have to catch Onini the python and take him to Nyami." Aso continued with her work as she replied, "Well, cut some vine." Spider thought for a moment. "Excellent! I understand!" And away he went to find a long piece of vine, which he coiled up as he walked through the jungle, saying: "I think it's longer than he is. Well, maybe shorter. No, longer. It's hard to say!"

Now, Onini heard this imaginary conversation and asked, "What are you talking about?" "I've been arguing with my wife Aso," said Ananzé. "She says this vine is longer than you; I say it's shorter. Oh, I know. If you will stretch out along the river bank I can measure you."

And so Onini stretched himself out and Spider laid the vine alongside him. *Nya-a-ang, nya-a-ang* was the sound made as Spider quickly wound the vine around Onini. "Now," said Ananzé, "I will take you to Nyami!" The High God stretched out his hand and touched Onini. "What my fingers feel, my fingers feel," said Nyami. "However, what they have not yet felt is still to come." And so Spider hurried down his web to find Osebo the leopard.

"Aso, Aso," said Spider to his wife, "I must take Osebo the leopard to Nyami." Aso replied, "Dig a hole." Spider thought for a moment. "Excellent! I understand!" And off he ran into the jungle, where he dug a big hole in the middle of the trail that Osebo used when he went to the river for a drink. Ananzé waited in the bushes. Along came Osebo, on his way to the water. *Zer-unk!* He fell into the hole. Spider looked in. "My, my, Osebo! What are you doing down there?" "Don't ask questions," begged Osebo, "Just help me out!" "Oh, but if I did that you'd eat me!" said Spider. "That would be very unkind of me," replied Osebo, "To repay a good deed in that fashion!" "Okay!" said Ananzé, as he threw a vine across a branch that hung over the hole. "Hold up your front legs. I'll tie the vine around them and pull you out." Down came Spider's knife on Osebo's head. *Z-zlap!* was the sound of it. "Now," said Ananzé, "I will take you to Nyami!"

The High God stretched out his hand and touched Osebo. "What my fingers feel, my fingers feel," said Nyami. "However, what they have not yet felt is still to come." And so Spider hurried down his web to get Moboro the hornet. "Aso, Aso," said Spider to his wife. "I must take Moboro the hornet to Nyami." Aso replied, "Get a calabash!" Spider thought for a moment. "Excellent! I understand!" And away he went to find a calabash.

Spider took the gourd, hollowed it out, and made a stopper for it. He filled the calabash with water and went to Moboro's nest. He watched the hornets coming and going, their sirens screaming and their stingers sharp and ominous. Then Spider quickly sprinkled water from the calabash on the hornets' nest and on his own head. "Moboro, Moboro!" he called, "The great rains have come! I am already soaked. Quickly! Save yourself. Fly into this calabash. It will keep you dry." *Pflug!* was the sound of the stopper as Spider closed it on Moboro in the calabash. "Now," said Ananzé, "I will take you to Nyami."

The High God stretched out his hand and held the calabash. He could hear Moboro inside. "What my fingers feel, my fingers feel," said Nyami. "However, what they have not yet felt is still to come." And so

Spider hurried down the web to find Mmoatia the fairy that no one can see. "Aso, Aso!" said Spider to his wife, "I must take Mmoatia the fairy that no one can see to Nyami." Aso replied, "Make a doll." Spider thought for a moment. "Excellent! I understand!" And he began to make a small baby-doll. He made it so that its head would move up and down. Then he tied a vine to it and put it under a tree with some sweet yams in its lap. Spider covered the doll from head to toe with sticky honey. Then he hid in the bushes and watched.

It was not long before the leaves began to flutter as if the wind had stirred them. But there was no wind. Spider knew it was Mmoatia. She came up to the doll. "Little one," she said, "I see yams. Are they for me?" Ananzé pulled on the vine and the baby nodded. "Thank you, little one," said Mmoatia, as she ate the yams. But the doll did not move its head. "I said, 'Thank you, little one.' It is polite to answer me." But Spider did not pull on the vine and the doll did not move.

"Little one," said Mmoatia, "answer me or I will spank your crying place." The doll made no move and Mmoatia got angry. *Pow!* was the sound as she slapped the doll's crying place. Her hand stuck to the honey. "Little one! Let go of my hand or I will slap your crying place again!" The doll made no move, and Mmoatia slapped it again. Now that both her hands were stuck, she became furious. She kicked with her left foot, then her right foot, and pushed against it with her stomach. "O-ho!" cried Spider, as he jumped out of the bushes. "Now I will take you to Nyami."

The High God stretched out his hand. "What my fingers feel, my fingers feel!" said Nyami. "You have paid the price, Ananzé. The box of stories is yours." Nyami gave Spider a beautiful carved box, and Spider hurried down the web as fast as he could go.

"Aso, Aso!" cried Spider. "Come see! Nyami has sold me the box of stories!" Aso came, and all the people of the village gathered around. Ananzé set the box down in the middle of the village and began to dance. Then he told the people the story of the price of the box of stories. After everyone heard the story, Spider opened the box. *Psssh!* was the sound as all of the stories flew out of the box. Spider caught some. So did Aso and some of the villagers. But there were so many that they flew away to all the corners of the world. You can catch one or two, if you wish. You may even catch this one.

This has been a long story, taking up a large section of what must be a short chapter in the story of religion in the United States. If only all books could simply be storybooks. But we no longer live as simply and profoundly as the Africans from whom we got the story of the box of stories. It is a truth of African religion that stories are the source of wisdom. The truth can best be told in a story, and the stories themselves originate in a story. There is no better way to say something meaningful. But, of course, we have also learned to set down abstract principles and rules. We speak of concepts and work at logical and technical reasoning. We analyze. And so we have already left out storytelling in order to discuss what it means. The best way to remember what is important in life is to tell a story, says the story of Ananzé and his beautiful carved box. Africans are storytellers. They think by means of story and communicate by story. They inhabit a world that is full of surprise and trickery, but it is not a disorderly world. The gods, the High God, and the creatures live in community. There is easy intercourse among them.

When we attempt to describe the African religious heritage, we are faced with many of the same problems encountered in our general discussion of American Indian traditions. These traditions are tribal traditions, which means that the social expression of religiousness is paramount. That is to say, the ultimate order and meaning of life are expressed in belongingness—in being part of a special people, a community that has special relationship to the trees, rocks, mountains, and streams of a particular place. Many spirits, powerful energies, and deities reside with a unique people who live in a special place.

In a certain sense this means that each tribe has its own religious tradition. This fact obviously makes generalizations difficult. American blacks who are descendants of the involuntary immigrants of the early centuries are predominantly West African in origin. This simplifies the task of generalization somewhat. However, the reader is cautioned that a thorough understanding of African religious heritage requires a close examination of particular history.

The West Africans lived in a world perceived as a community of spirits. Tribes were closely knit communities, extended families in which a certain hierarchy prevails. There is equality and democracy, but they function according to an accepted pattern of order and levels of authority. The world of the tribe is united by a High God (or Sky God) who often exists in deistic aloofness from the world. While the High God is a court of last resort, the world itself is carefully regulated by a great variety of deities, spirits, or life-forces. Life-forces are relatively free agents—certainly within their proper sphere of authority. "The belief that a person's spirit wanders while the body sleeps," writes Albert Raboteau, "was . . . a part of the lore of African black folk. 'Pepul's sperrits wander at night an' effen dey's woke too sudden like de sperrit is likely tu be left out walkin.'"

Nyami, the High God in the story of Kacou-Ananzé, lived in council with the other gods. But even Nyami was accessible. In African tradition, death is a veil, a curtain between different modes of being. The dead are living dead; they just do not live as we do on this side of the veil. The dead are often present in some way, and there continues to be communication between the different modes of being. The family and the tribe are made up of an "innumerable company" that extends beyond the grave. Existence in such a world is a highly ritual existence. After all, rituals are those actions, forms of behavior, that are important to communication. A gesture, a special movement such as a kiss or a handshake, are traditional modes of communication. They rely upon memory and recognition. They may be accompanied by words or stand by themselves. Sometimes a movement is an expression of emotion—joy, pain, expectation, passion. It may also be the result of being overcome, overwhelmed—possessed. In this latter sense, the person's own ordinary mind and will are emptied, taken over by other forces. In a world where there is easy intercourse between various levels of being and power, possession is readily comprehensible. The people begin to develop a treasure house of ritual behavior. They learn how to respond when the ancestors make an annual visit, or when the spirits of the earth open their hearts to the sun and the rain. Whether they dance, or sing, or rock to the rhythm of the drums, each move is important, as important and natural as a handshake or a kiss.

The forebears of African Americans lived in a world that was alive with power and energy. In addition to the High God and the other deities, there were spirits that inhabited rivers, trees, rocks, and animals. It is difficult to discern any clear distinction between some of these spirits and the gods themselves. Although the world was unified and supervised by gods and deities, the secrets of the control and manipulation of the mysterious power had been revealed to the tribe. Each tribe had its own tradition of stories and special instructions that were carefully preserved and passed on by specialists. Sometimes the means whereby power is controlled and directed for good or ill is not accompanied by any attempt to honor the gods. Instead, it is religiousness expressed by magic. Healing and certain kinds of possession took place according to the secret recipes of the "root doctor" who was well versed in magical formulas and the use of "herbs, barks, leaves, and roots."

Frequently the root doctor was also a priest who was charged with preserving and directing the ceremonial life of the tribe.

An important activity of the realms of magic was the business of divination. In a world so alive it seems natural that the line between the known and the unknown should be very thin indeed. Divination seeks to "divine" the proper answer to a person's problems. As Albert Raboteau tells us in his book *Slave Religion,*

> If people want to determine guilt or innocence or to seek the answer to any important question in West Africa they will turn to priest-diviners, who are skilled in reading the fate of individuals and the wills of ancestors or gods by means of simple or elaborate systems of divination. Simpler methods include interpreting omens, reading the entrails of a fowl, or water gazing. More elaborate is the Yoruba. In the Ifa system . . . [in which] a *baba-lawo,* "father of mysteries," casts a chain of eight halves of palm nuts or else sixteen separate nuts, and then, reading the pattern of the cast, he marks the permutation on a tray covered with wood dust. Each permutation corresponds to an *odu,* or saying, of which there are two hundred and sixty-six. To each *odu* is attached a number of verses conveying a myth or story that points to the answer of the client's problem.[1]

The art or science of divination is a belief and practice that is written deep within the folk memory of most people. Tribal traditions have clearer and continuing evidence of its use. However, many of us are aware of those moments when we seek "signs" that will help us to sort out a solution in time of crisis. The use of astrology, palm-reading, biblical texts, and to some extent "channeling," crystal gazing, and séance are evidence of folk religion in the most modern of societies.

African religions are danced religions. Songs, drumming, and ritual movement are essential to these traditions. Often the dance is designed to produce trance and other modes of transnormal mentality during which the gods take possession. On such occasions the god may "mount" the individual as a rider mounts a horse. In this way, the individual is "ridden" in whatever direction or manner the god decides. The one possessed by the god may also become the deity's mouthpiece, the one in whom the god expresses himself in shouting, dancing, or convulsive behavior.

Just how much of African religious heritage has survived under the institution of slavery and subsequent Americanization is a controversial question.

Some scholars have maintained that slavery in North America was a cruel institution that disrupted the familial and tribal structure of human relationships that is essential to the preservation of traditional religion. Husbands were taken from wives and children; children were sold or resold to slaveholders often hundreds of miles away. In North America (as contrasted with the Caribbean and South America) slaveowning tended to be confined to relatively small numbers of Africans who helped in the household and labored in the fields. Only rarely did a single slaveowner hold a hundred or more bondspersons. Where the Africans existed in large numbers, they were able to preserve their stories and religious practices. Storytellers, priests, and root doctors were likely to be present among a large group, and there were ways to communicate the essentials of ultimate order and meaning.

Tribal traditions are generally eclectic. Tribes are accustomed to adopting new stories, new deities, and new rituals as a result of their encounter with other ways, other tribes. That is because a certain pragmatism becomes the rule when existence is assumed to be an arena of power and energy. In such a perception of the world it is necessary to learn the ways of whatever gods and spirits there may be. To encounter another tribe with other stories, other forms of magic, is to face the problem of adaptation. In the Caribbean and South America, the Africans found themselves in the presence of new powers. Their African ways adapted these powers into their own systems, sometimes creating new religions, at other times reshaping their own traditions. The eclecticism is what accounts for the many African American cults such as *Santeria, shango,* and *candomble,* that have recently become part of the North American religious scene—the result of Latin American immigrations into our metropolitan areas. It was in Latin America that traditional syncretism[2] adapted to a religious landscape in which Roman Catholicism, revivalistic Protestantism, and native religions were forms of power to which the tribal mind responded, for a variety of reasons.

During most of the history of the United States, the African slaves lived in small numbers among a slave-owning populace that was predominantly evangelical Protestant, a form of Christianity centered upon personal morality and the experience of conversion, all of it guided by the principles of the Bible and private judgment. The primary exception to this observation was Louisiana, where Roman Catholic influence permitted African syncretism to express itself. Voodoo, as a worshiping cult and also as a separate system of magic, flourished under these circumstances. Voodoo practices often existed as folk-religious expression even among converts to Catholicism, who attended Mass and prayed the rosary.

For most of African America, the tribal heritage declined. Perhaps only the eclecticism remained, for the slave was quick to discern the power of the language of the Protestant Bible. And although the slave may have forgotten many native stories and the names of the gods, he or she did not lose entirely the memory of danced religion. It became relatively easy for him or her to apply the theme of salvation found in the Bible (and preached in the pulpit) to personal conditions. And the keen power of memory and intellect developed in those who are part of oral-aural (nonliterate) societies provided assistance in remembering and retelling the stories and texts of a Bible that most slaves could not read; nonetheless they knew the power of the spoken word in ways the oppressors had often forgotten. The rhythm and music of words and the divine poetry of speech were deep within their souls. And so suffering and joy that transcended pain found natural expression in the use of the body and the voice; it was the African way.

Practical Expression

Native heritage is present in the practical expression of African American religiousness. Theoretical considerations may have been lost, but ritual ways linger. Of course, there is some evidence to suggest that black American Christians also think of their Christianity in different modes than do whites. For example, black Christians are seldom fundamentalists. They are not rigid and fiery-eyed debaters about the literal meaning of a text, because they seem to know intuitively that the meaning of words is more than our ability to comprehend at any single moment. Words carry the whole person through the experience of meaning; they do not bear some kind of mechanical precision. Words are discourse; they set up a relationship in which meaning is communicated. Words are not exchanged as coins are traded. This the African American knows by virtue of an oral heritage. Words are like songs and rhythms that embrace us with meaning. To hear the stories and texts of the Scriptures is to be in the presence of God; it is not a matter of hearing definitions of doctrine. That is why the texts are more than words; they are the Word of God—communication, encounter, with the divine Reality. Africans feel God's loneliness at the moment of creation. As storytellers, they read between the lines and create a "midrash"—they sense that God must have been lonely before deciding to create humanity in the divine image. Without humankind, the world was empty, even with all the birds of the air and beasts of the field. And as storytellers, African Americans hear the cry from the great cross of Golgotha, feel its pulsations in the spasms of their own flesh.

In an essay dealing specifically with African American thought, I would have to pursue very carefully this idea of the "Africanness" of much Christian theology among blacks. In this volume, however, we must be somewhat satisfied with Raboteau's observation that "it is in the context of action, the patterns of motor behavior preceding and following the ecstatic experience, that there may be continuity between African and American forms" of religious expression. Although certain forms of ritual behavior may have been forbidden among North American slaves (for example, the rhythm of drums), "hand-clapping, foot-tapping, rhythmic preaching, hyperventilation, antiphonal (call-and-response) singing, and dancing are styles of behavior"[3] associated with religious expression both in Africa and America.

In order to understand the character of this African influence on black American religion, we must turn to a consideration of the slave encounter with Christianity. American Christianity, as we have said, was predominantly Protestant and Anglican, with a strong evangelical emphasis upon the Bible and the private judgment of individuals. But among Lutheran, Reformed, and Anglican churches, there was also a continuing emphasis upon the importance of catechetical learning. *Catechism* refers to an ancient style of oral instruction in matters of religion that, by the Middle Ages, had been formalized in manuals. These books contained such basic items as the Lord's Prayer, the Apostles' and Nicene Creeds, and sometimes lists of mortal sins. Questions and answers were prescribed in order to understand the fundamental doctrines and texts of Christianity. The magisterial, loyalist, and Anglican reformations of the sixteenth century continued the use of catechisms in the preparation of people for baptism and the pastoral life. That is to say, pastors frequently met with people in their homes and churches to review certain sections of a catechism. Catechetical education was thus a pastoral nurturing as well as a mode of initiation into the Christian life.

The question faced by many slaveholders in America was whether the Africans should be exposed to the worship of the churches and to catechetical activity. The rural style of much of American life made it conducive to the revivalistic evangelicalism of the frontier, with its camp meetings, protracted meetings, sacramental meetings, and baptismal assemblies near rivers and streams in the countryside. Although many slaveholders took the position that slaves were less than human and were not worthy of the message of the Christian gospel, the great majority of whites assumed that a certain amount of worship experience and catechesis would be "good" for the blacks and keep them in order. Certainly a knowledge of the Ten Commandments and the Lord's Prayer would tend to raise these creatures above the level of animals and provide a foundation for responsible behavior as slaves. And so numbers of Africans attended services in churches, where they usually sat in segregated fashion. They listened to the preaching, sang the hymns, and learned the Ten Commandments. Some of them were taught from the catechism. And even when they were not invited, they could hear the singing and excitement of the revivals. It was difficult to shut out the sounds and activities of the informal religious life of frontier revivalism. Whether the white slaveholder intended it or not, the Africans were exposed to the ideas and practices of white people's religion.

No great religion is one thing. If it is a world religion and has persisted through many centuries and in many parts of the world, it is because its fundamental teachings and practices are capable of being incarnate in many different settings. Christianity has been dressed in many languages, among people in distinct times and places. In a very real sense, there is not one Christianity, but many. The rich man hears a different message than the poor. The Russian expresses the gospel differently from the Spaniard or the woman from Atlanta. This is not to say that the religion is whatever one wishes to make of it; it is, rather, to realize that a message is always heard in a specific situation. Liberation or salvation or reconciliation is one thing to the laborer in the mines; it is quite another thing to the mine owner. The followers of the Hebrew patriarch Abraham knew of God's liberation in a different way than it was known by those who were to follow Moses out of the captivity in Egypt.

The black American heard the words of the Christian gospel with quite a different agenda of experience from his white oppressors. Some Christians will want to say that it is the same gospel, and so it may be. However, as students of religion in America, we may observe the shaping of a distinctive Christian tradition out of the experience of African American slavery. The powerful rhythms of the literature of the King James Version of the Bible communicated profound meaning to the lives of the slaves. They could feel its words pulsating in their souls—souls accustomed to the power of spoken words. They heard of God's promises, justice, and mercy. They felt God's loneliness and frustration, and they knew about suffering. The crucifixion of Jesus was very real because they knew that any hope of reconciliation or for meaningful existence is encountered in suffering. They could understand a story that spoke of God's suffering as a way to compassionate living. And their souls trembled at the proclamation that God can raise us from death into life.

To African Americans the gospel spoke of liberation, and persons had to recognize their captivity before they would understand liberation. The agenda of African Americans emphasized a great need for liberation, hope, forbearance, and compassion. This agenda shaped a black religious tradition that is uniquely American and expresses itself in the many institutional forms of black religion. The African American listened to the Word of God with different ears than his or her oppressors. Theirs were the ears of an oral-aural culture living in a land of oppression.

Some of the slaves knew the Christian Scriptures better than their oppressors. They learned the cadences, remembered the stories, and could repeat text after text. The groom and manservant to Methodist Bishop Francis Asbury was Harry Hosier, who became known as "Black Harry." He often accompanied Asbury on his rounds. "Small, utterly black, keen of eye, and quick of speech, the inspired groom caught the ear of every audience," writes Methodist historian Charles W. Ferguson. "Many were the times he preached for Asbury, who said that he would rather hear Harry preach than to hear himself. In time the preaching of the black became a legend." Dr. Benjamin Rush, Philadelphia physician and statesman of the early National Period, called Black Harry "the greatest orator in America," and Asbury's colleague Bishop Coke suggested that Harry was "one of the best preachers in the world." It is quite evident that black Americans were very successful in understanding the essential themes of the Christian tradition. These themes were often very meaningful to a people who had lost most of their own tradition and lived in a world that robbed them of much of their humanity.

Not only did the slaves participate in the catechetical and congregational life of white Christianity, but they also devised their own form of Christianity. Raboteau has shown how the "invisible institution" of black Christianity emerged out of the clandestine meetings of slaves in the brush arbors late at night. Although the blacks were forbidden any right of assembly on their own, those who lived in the larger plantations soon discovered ways of meeting after hours in secluded and remote forest clearings where they posted watch and proceeded to pray, sing, dance, and listen to the liberating oratory of their own folk preachers.

The black experience in America was shaped into a diversity of institutional forms, all of which shared the need for liberation from the dire circumstances of slavery and the later segregated, second-class citizenship. Most of these institutional forms were expressive of some interpretation of Christianity. That is, most black American religion is black Christianity—in some form or other. There has been a special affinity for revivalistic evangelicalism. Most black people are Baptist or Methodist, even though the uniqueness of the black experience has transformed those traditions into special manifestations of black Baptist and black Methodist piety and practice. The evangelical emphasis upon subjective experience, combined with the revivalistic styles of free and expressive worship, provided a congenial vehicle for African American religious expression. The African heritage often continued to manifest itself in the way black Americans worshiped. They adapted Christianity to their need for antiphonal expression, shouting, singing, and rhythmic movement.

Institutional History in the United States

The first institutional forms of black religion were the congregations and denominations that separated from predominantly white churches. In parts of the South there eventually developed congregations of Africans that remained linked to the Methodist or Baptist denominational structures and conventions. In Mississippi "black members outnumbered whites by a five-to-one margin in the Union Baptist Association"—this in the antebellum years. The story of these congregations comprises a fascinating history yet to be told. It is interesting to reflect upon the fact that the congregational polity of the Baptists and the freedom of their ritual practice were conducive to a great deal of independent religious development among blacks.

In Philadelphia, African members of St. George Methodist Church withdrew to form the Free African Society. Their separation occurred because they were disturbed in the midst of prayer, having sat in the "wrong seats" after the building had been remodeled. For a time the Free African Society served as a church until Richard Henry Allen organized it into a Methodist congregation. "Notwithstanding we had been so violently persecuted by the elder, we were in favor of being attached to the Methodist connection," wrote Allen, "for I was confident that there was no religious sect or denomination that would suit the capacity of colored people as well as the Methodist; for the plain and simple gospel suits best for any people; for the unleashed can understand, and the learned are sure to understand; and the reason that the Methodist is so successful in the awakening and conversion of the colored people, the plain doctrine and having a good discipline."[4]

By 1816 Allen's pioneering work had led to the formation of an independent denomination of Methodists, the African Methodist Episcopal Church

(AME). Allen's early colleague, Absalom Jones, had meanwhile been ordained by Bishop William White and chosen in 1796 to serve the African Episcopal Church of St. Thomas in Philadelphia, a congregation that remained part of the Episcopal Church. In New York City Peter Williams had also established a congregation of blacks who had left a white Methodist church in protest. Named Zion Church, it became the basis for the establishment of another national denomination, the African Methodist Episcopal Church Zion. The independent and competitive nature of American church life had begun to express itself in the lives of African Americans.

In 1895 black Baptist churches were aligned as part of the National Baptist Convention of the U.S.A., which remains the largest of black Baptist denominations and came to be the affiliation of one of the twentieth century's most outstanding religious and political leaders, the Reverend Martin Luther King Jr. There are several other black Baptist denominations, all of them smaller than the National Baptist Convention. A schism in 1915 formed the National Baptist Convention of America, and in 1961 King supported a further division in the organization of the Progressive National Baptist Convention. In addition, some few predominantly black congregations continue to be aligned with such essentially white denominational bodies as the Southern Baptist Convention and the American Baptist Churches (a primarily northern denomination).

Other black Methodist denominations, such as the Christian Methodist Episcopal Church, joined the ranks of American denominationalism. For some years after the War between the States there was a rather fierce competition among these denominations as they sought to claim constituencies and retain a measure of control of their own destiny. Some black leaders became totally disillusioned with the possibility of ever achieving any kind of equality in the American religious and cultural scene. They concluded that white Christianity was a corruption of the gospel and true faith, and they sought to establish their own missions to Africa and other parts of the world. Bishop Henry McNeal Turner of the AME Church in Georgia began to lead a movement espousing black migrations to Africa. He preached a form of black superiority but realized that many African Americans had been reduced to aimless rabble and servile minions of whites. Such useless creatures as these were not wanted on the African pilgrimage.

Bishop Turner's increased commitment to the superiority of African spirituality serves as a foundation for other developments in African American religion. Not only did the blacks create their own Christian denominations,

modeled in the fashion of white Protestantism, but they established many
new forms of Christianity. Often they blended Christian ideas and practices
with those of other religions and of ancient cultic origins. Many of these
"new" religions reveal a strain of black consciousness and uniqueness.

Joseph Washington, in his study *Black Sects and Cults,* tells us that "poor
Blacks were nearly brushed aside in black independent churches just as black
independents had been left without dignity in white churches."[5] Many of
these blacks found a home in the holiness and Pentecostal movement that was
emerging at the end of the nineteenth century. Holiness churches emphasize
the need for experiencing the sanctification that floods the individual after he
or she has given the soul to Christ and experienced justification in the eyes of
God. John Wesley had emphasized the necessity for the experience of holiness—sanctification. As Methodism became more and more institutionalized
and part of the ordinary fabric of society, it often lost the heat of holiness and
became satisfied with the presence of perfection—usually in an undramatic,
matter-of-fact sense. The poor, less formally educated elements of society
were often left out of such staid institutional Christianity. Their experience of
disinheritance and alienation from the ranks of power and affluence called for
a religion that would be a catharsis and an affirmation of their personal worth
in spite of their trying circumstances. From the impoverished sections of large
cities and the remote areas of the Ozarks and Appalachia came reports of religious meetings of great excitement, where the heat of holiness came as a second blessing to folks in desperate need of the blessings of God. Holiness
churches were born of this movement. And many blacks found themselves
attracted to leaders who gathered their followers in simple surroundings to
share the life of holiness. Holiness meant not only the reception of the second
blessing of sanctification; it meant initiation into a new lifestyle. Holiness
meant living the life of perfection. It meant no drinking, no dancing, no card-
playing, thus calling for separation from the often slovenly existence of
impoverishment, which may seek solace in cheap alcoholic beverage and
undisciplined sexual activity.

However, the combination of "holiness" with the gift of the Holy Spirit in
the speaking of tongues also appealed to many blacks. There were those people who focused their attention in what they felt was the predictive prophecy
of the book of Joel in the Hebrew Bible: "Be glad, O sons of Zion, and rejoice
in the Lord, your God; for he has given the early rain for your vindication, he
has poured down for you abundant rain, the early and the latter rain, as
before" (2:23). This passage was interpreted to mean that the "early rain" was

the gift of speaking in tongues reported on the first Pentecost (Acts 2:4) and the "latter rain" the descent of the Holy Spirit prior to the premillennial return of Christ. Out of this folk interpretation of the Scriptures emerged the Pentecostal movement in the early twentieth century. W. J. Seymour, a black preacher, spearheaded the famous Azusa Street revival in Los Angeles in 1906, which gave the pentecostal movement the momentum it has since carried among whites and blacks. Amanda Berry Smith (1837–1915) was a preacher in the African Methodist Episcopal Church who joined the holiness movement because of her denomination's inflexibility with regard to women's ordination. She became a prominent itinerant holiness preacher in the last quarter of the nineteenth century.

We have observed that the antislavery movement gave rise to the strengthening of feminism in American religion and culture. It provided a channel for African American women to exercise freedom of expression and influence in the practice of their faith. Harriet Tubman (1823–1913) and Sojourner Truth (1797–1883) were members of the Zion congregation in New York City who became early feminist leaders, expressing ideas that later became important to the woman's liberation movements of the twentieth century.

Today fewer than 10 percent of the clergy in historic black denominations are women. Nevertheless, "according to theologian Jacqueline Grant, womanist theology not only proceeds from the particular context of the suffering and experience of African American women, but that context, which brings together the issues of race, sex, and class, provides the broadest and most comprehensive base for liberation theology."[6]

There are various differences of interpretation among members of the pentecostal and holiness movements. The result has been a proliferation of denominations and independent congregations. However, some churches emphasized both pentecostal and holiness themes, especially among blacks. "Some sects are anti-trinitarian," writes Washington, "baptizing in the name of the 'Father only' and others in the name of 'Jesus only,' the latter including the Apostolic Church of Jesus Christ, 1915, Indianapolis, and the Church of Our Lord Jesus Christ of the Apostolic Faith, Incorporated, New York City, 1919. But such distinctions are not theologically or sociologically significant, based as they are on exegesis[7] carried forward in the oral tradition or created out of vivid imaginations."[8] From this we may understand the folk nature of much black Christianity. That is to say, economically and socially depressed folk interpret Scripture with the authority of their own experience and insight. The conclusions to which they come frequently serve as the basis for denominational difference. Denominations such as the Church of God in Christ; the Church of Christ, Holiness U.S.A.; and the Church of the Living God, Christian Workers for Fellowship, are among the prominent black holiness and pentecostal churches that "broke out like wild fire among the masses."

There were many blacks whose search for ultimate order and meaning in their lives led them farther away from Christianity. They formed black cults that blended Christian motifs with ideas borrowed from other religions and from the tribal history out of which blacks had been seized many centuries before. Cults tend to focus on the power and charisma of a single individual whose life is shared vicariously with his people. Usually the cult leader is divine or semi-divine and, like a shaman, communicates with another world deriving secrets to be shared with loyal followers. Frequently these movements serve as little "kingdoms" or "nations" in which the people may live a special existence in the midst of an otherwise drab and oppressive world. The United House of Prayer of Daddy Grace and his successors and the Peace Mission of Father Divine have been examples of this kind of black religious tradition.

In the twentieth century this tendency to the formation of unique African American religion has led to the formation of groups that began to stress black separateness and superiority. They were to draw upon the earlier work of Bishop Turner and Marcus Garvey, whose Universal Negro Improvement Association in the 1920s sought to remove his people to the land where the "God of Africa" ruled. Increased black consciousness resulted in the emergence of several black Jewish movements. However, most significant of those groups that turned their backs on Christian America was the Black Muslim tradition. Now known as the Nation of Islam, this movement traces its beginnings to 1913 and the founding of the Moorish Science Temple of America by Timothy Drew. Drew had produced his own version of the Qur'an (sacred texts of Islam), blending a Christian and separatist message with Islamic teachings. Drew's *Holy Koran* attempted to provide a distinct sense of peoplehood for American blacks by providing Moorish origins. By the time of his death in 1929, he was known as Noble Drew Ali.

Drew's principal successor was Wallace D. Fard, who gathered his followers into a "temple" and began teaching black supremacy and explaining that Allah had used white oppression to prepare blacks for their future unique role in history. Fard's successor was Elijah Poole, a Georgian who became known as Elijah Muhammad. Under Elijah's leadership the movement prospered and refined its doctrine. The Nation of Islam advocated the establishment of black self-sufficiency. The man who became known as Malcolm X discovered the more universal teachings of orthodox Islam and began to modify the supremacist claims of the parent body. Malcolm's activities led to his assassination in 1965. However, his ideas continued to agitate change within the movement. After the death of Elijah Muhammad in 1975, his son Wallace D. Muhammad restructured the teaching and organization of America's Black Muslims, bringing them closer to traditional Islam. In 1980 the name was changed to the American Muslim Mission, in which title we can observe the American coming-of-age of a new religion. Initially shaped into a black separatist and supremacist movement by the circumstances of white oppression, the Black Muslim establishment was transformed by the circumstances of American pluralism and freedom of religion. Some 20,000 or so black Muslims continue to follow the nationalist teachings of Master Fard and Elijah Muhammad, now under the leadership of Minister Louis Farrakhan. In a pluralistic society it is necessary to live civilly among those who differ in doctrine and behavior. Civility reshapes religious traditions, forces them into functioning on a basis of equality with other groups. This necessity, along with the discovery of the more universal teachings of traditional Sunni Islam, reshaped much of African American Islam into a mission in the midst of American religious diversity.

Phenomenon of the Preacher

It is important for us to make one further observation in this introduction to African American religion. In his classic American study of *The Souls of Black Folk,* the sociologist W. E. B. DuBois writes, "The 'preacher' is the most unique personality developed by the Negro on American soil. A leader, a politician, an orator, a 'boss,' an intriguer, an idealist—all these he is."[9] It is a mistake to assume that the black "preacher" is a simple counterpart to the white clergyman. The circumstances of American history have fashioned the black preacher into a "unique personality." In the world of black America there is no neat, rigid, and legalistic separation of religion and politics—as we at least assume to be the case in the rest of the country. Black Americans tend generally to live in a perception of the world that is organic, much like their ancestral existence in tribal Africa. The black church and religious institution is not merely a "religious" organization as it is for most whites. It is a symbolic and sacred center around which all thinking and doing takes place. It is a political realm because a truly sacred center shapes all human activity. It is, of course, a temple as well, because the ideas and symbols necessary to life's order and meaning are celebrated there.

The black preacher functions according to this perception of the world; knowing almost intuitively that the human polis must be governed according to the sacred and redeeming love of God, the preacher cannot separate something called "religion" from politics. The black preacher is, as DuBois says, leader, politician, orator, boss, intriguer, and idealist—all things for the people. This may turn the black preacher into a demagogue or a scam artist, or into a Martin Luther King Jr., a Jesse Jackson, a Malcolm X, or an Andrew Young. Or, as is most frequently the case, it creates a form of leadership that has provided hope and security for millions of black Americans caught in the dilemmas of a modern techno-corporate society dominated by whites.

chapter 17

New Traditions for the Common People: Millenarian, Holiness, and Pentecostal Traditions

Winthrop Hudson, in an essay titled "A Time of Religious Ferment," reminds us that the election of Andrew Jackson to the office of President of the United States in 1829 ushered in an era of great foreboding. It was to be "the age of the common man," in which the redemption offered by evangelical Christianity would be accompanied by a political redemption in which the common folk would be elevated, the institutional life of the new nation would be perfected, and the voice of the people would become the voice of God. "In terms of the broad religious ferment of the time," writes Hudson, "this was the period when popular enthusiastic evangelical religion was the dominant force that supplied the major impetus for the new forms of religious life and expression, which were so characteristic of 'the restless thirties and forties' of the nineteenth century."[1]

However, the "time of religious ferment" was an occasion of ambivalence. The optimism of the Jacksonian common man was tempered by uncertainty: were these not both the best of times and the worst of times? Failure and the collapse of everything sacred, stable, and secure was an equal possibility. The religious sensibilities of nineteenth-century Americans were both optimistic and pessimistic. In either case American religion was becoming more democratized. The "common people" more and more included the intellectual and social elite as well as the forgotten farmers and the new shop workers of the industrial age. Thomas Jefferson's agrarian and yeomen's values were giving way to individual initiative in almost every cranny of society, including religion.

The democratic impulse in religion meant that some people sought to withdraw from the frantic and evil material world. They prepared for the end of the faithless age and the coming of Christ and his millennial kingdom. By the end of the century the same impulse gave rise to religious movements that separated people from the world either by personal holiness or by a sharing of enthusiastic "gifts" (speaking in tongues, healing, snake handling). These movements were examples of people's religion, in which personal experience and raw talent were of greater consequence than the education and ordination that had been required by the traditions with roots in European Christianity.

By the mid-twentieth century the religions of the common people were thought of as a third-force Christianity, to be distinguished from Catholic and Protestant Christianity. Pentecostal, holiness, and adventist groups— Assemblies of God, Seventh-day Adventists, Church of the Nazarene, Jehovah's Witnesses, Church of God in Christ, and others were growing in membership at a much greater rate than traditional Protestant denominations and Roman Catholicism. They were indeed a third-force type of Christianity, generated by freedom of religion and the democratic impulse.

The numerical strength of the third force is difficult to measure because millenarian, holiness, and pentecostal themes and experiences have led to the formation of many independent institutions for which statistics are not available. All of us are familiar with the many churches that occupy storefronts or use vacant warehouses, meeting halls, and abandoned church buildings. Most of these congregations are the result of the leadership of self-styled clergy whose qualifications are an experience, a "call," or a vision of opportunity.

The third force may very well be the largest representation of American Christianity. Along with fundamentalism (see chap. 19), it has commanded the attention of great numbers of Americans. The third force has been successful—in the American sense of it. Its members are great, and its influence is increasing. The news media give it greater audience than any other form of religion. In an increasingly secular age, when religious illiteracy is at an all-time high and people are susceptible to "every wind of doctrine," many journalists assume that the third force speaks for all of Christianity. Obviously, that is not so. Yet it is equally obvious that fundamentalism and the third force have been triumphant in America. It is possible for a historian to speculate and conclude that third-force Christianity is typically American, that it is a product of the modern age and shares many attitudes with those who claim no religious identity at all. Perhaps mainline Protestantism and Roman Catholicism are old-world traditions that lingered into the twentieth century, already having been superseded or altered by the millenarian, holiness, and pentecostal religiosity of the modern age, which has been centuries in the making.

Origins

New
Traditions
for the
Common
People

317

These traditions are not really part of Protestantism. They do not have their origins in the sixteenth-century magisterial and separationist branches of the Reformation. They are very much the product of the nineteenth- and twentieth-century United States. Even though many spokespersons for these third-force groups would claim to be reaffirming primitive Christianity or Reformation principles, it is not difficult to describe the uniquely modern character of their teachings and practices. These traditions may be called a third force because they align themselves in separation from traditional, mainline Protestantism and Roman Catholicism. They are distinct from Anglicanism and Eastern Orthodoxy as well. In 1972 Dean M. Kelley published *Why Are Conservative Churches Growing?*, a study that sought to demonstrate that churches outside the old mainstream were growing because they had clearly defined doctrinal positions and made certain demands of morality and commitment. Kelley claimed that by 1970 the mainstream had become an "ecumenical" fellowship in which the attendant denominations played down differences and directed their efforts toward social reform and accommodation with modern knowledge. In other words, the mainstream had been "converted" by the religion of civility into an ineffective and harmless religious caucus. The winners in the struggle for souls were the "conservative" churches, which include the groups discussed in this chapter, along with fundamentalist and what are called neo-evangelical movements.

Conservative and third-force Christianity continued to grow as the twentieth century came to a close. Historian George Marsden informs us that the remarkable resurgence of American evangelicalism arose out of a public dissatisfaction with the prevailing culture. Like other religious trends, it views the struggle to rescue Christianity from modernism's tendency to eliminate the authority of the Bible as a common-sense resource for the religious needs of a democratic people.[2] Factors affecting the resurgence include the charismatic movement, dissatisfaction with materialistic and rationalistic society, effective organization and use of the media, and the reemergence of a conservative and evangelical South as a full participant in national life. These reasons help us to understand the significance of millenarian, holiness, and pentecostal traditions.

Millenarianism

The verbal expression of the adventist and millenarian wing of the third force has been dominated by a concern for the end of the age and the second coming of Jesus Christ. Mainline Christianity has tended to interpret the second coming in a very postmillennialist manner. Strongly influenced by theological liberalism, the ecumenical mainstream does not expect a return of Christ on the clouds of heaven (as, indeed, Orthodox Judaism's Messiah/Christ is also expected). It understands Christ's "second advent" as a coming of the kingdom, an idealistic age, or assumes that Christ's second return has already occurred. The emphasis is upon a symbolic second coming, a "Christification" that is subtle, hidden, or mysterious.

Human history is replete with millenarian sects and cults. In trying times or stressful circumstance, the religious need to discern order and meaning in a world that is disordered and meaningless often asserts itself in commitments to an alternative reality, another world. An age that is chaotic and meaningless is assumed to be on the verge of cataclysmic destruction. A new age is anticipated in which something or someone from another realm introduces a way of life not of this world. This kind of millenarianism is found in all parts of the world, in all cultures. Some readers may be familiar with the Cargo cults that emerged in the South Pacific during World War II. The basic pattern of these movements is that the oppression and ignorance of the native peoples is the result of evil and deception. All this mode of existence must be destroyed; the people must prepare themselves for the impending destruction in order to await the cargo ships that will be the divine instruments of justice and well-being—the dawn of a new age. Most of the world's religions have some form of thinking about ages and eons. Such notions lend themselves either to literal interpretation or to symbolic and philosophical speculation.

In the case of Christianity, millenarianism uses the apocalyptic literature of the Bible for its source of interpretation. The word *apocalypse* means an "uncovering" or "revealing," so that apocalyptic literature is what people commonly (perhaps incorrectly) call prophecy. That is to say, it claims to reveal what is normally hidden; it reveals the future. Usually, the literature is of a highly symbolic and exotic nature—its ideas and characters are exceptionally imaginative. There are books and sections of books in the Bible that are of an apocalyptic nature. There are other works of apocalypse that are not included in the Hebrew Bible and New Testament. Canonical books such as Daniel and the Revelation to John are apocalyptic. Sections of works by Ezekiel, Isaiah, and the other prophets may also be considered in the same light.

The arcane nature of apocalypse lends itself to a variety of interpretations and entices many readers into ardent attempts at finding and deciphering

NEW
TRADITIONS
FOR THE
COMMON
PEOPLE

319

some presumed code that holds the secret to future events and a future age. Many people throughout the history of Christianity have sought to use apocalyptic literature to calculate the signs of the times in order to prepare for the second coming of Christ. We must remember that the Christian church was born in times of great anxiety and unrest—times somewhat like our own—during which an old order was passing away. Jesus of Nazareth, according to gospel accounts, was constantly contending with those who were "seeking signs." He often spoke of the kingdom of God as a present relationship among peoples and nature, while also offering a paradoxical note that "there shall be signs in the sun, and in the moon, and in the stars; and upon the earth distress of nations, with perplexity; the sea and the waves roaring; men's hearts failing them for fear . . . and then shall they see the Son of Man coming in a cloud with power and great glory. And when these things begin to pass . . . your redemption draweth nigh . . . when ye see these things come to pass, know ye that the Kingdom of God is at hand" (Luke 21:25-28, 31).

Many biblical scholars point out that the Jesus of history was a child of his times. He understood history in apocalyptical terms, as indeed was common particularly among many Jewish leaders. Jesus, therefore, expected the end of the age to come soon. The early church likewise assumed that Jesus' death, resurrection, and ascension were evidence of a final preparation for the end times that would be inaugurated by the second advent of Christ. This great expectation was intense during the first generation of Christianity. However, St. Paul and others had already begun alternative interpretations of the future age. The Revelation to John, written probably toward the end of the first century, heightened apocalyptical fervor because of its hostile attitude toward the Roman emperor in the midst of persecution. This book has aroused millenarian notions again and again throughout Christian history.

Until the latter twentieth century, millenarian Christianity seems to have surfaced among members of the dispossessed and despairing elements of society. It has emerged among the poor and those generally powerless in this midst of wealth, education, and prestige. During the sixteenth-century continental Reformation and the somewhat later Puritan Reformation in England, there arose numerous sects that sought to find solace in the end of the age and the second coming of Christ. Sometimes millenarian movements became militant, revolutionary factions warring against the forces of evil and darkness, thereby in their own minds hastening the end of the present reign.

Millenarianism was present in American history from its beginnings. In Pennsylvania during the eighteenth century there were several such groups; one of them was the Ephrata Community, a cloistered order separating men and women. However, it was not until the middle of the nineteenth century that millenarianism found bold and successful expression among the Latter-day Saints and the followers of William Miller.

Miller (1782–1849) was a New England Baptist, typical of many Americans of his time. He lived by the principle that each individual had total and free access to the truth of salvation. The Bible and private judgment were all that were necessary. Miller was a farmer and preacher who became fascinated with the possibilities of interpreting the course of history by calculation of the numerology contained in apocalyptic passages of the Bible. After years of study and figuring, he came to the conclusion that the year 1843 was the date for the end of the present age and the imminent return of Christ.

Miller especially examined certain texts in the book of Daniel and the Revelation to John. Daniel 8:14 reads: "Unto two thousand and three hundred days; then shall the sanctuary be cleansed." The cleansing, according to Miller's speculation, referred to a grand cataclysmic event, a preparation for true and holy worship—to Miller, the second advent. "The time or length of the vision," wrote Miller,

> The 2,300 days. What must we understand by days? In the prophecy of Daniel it is invariably to be reckoned years; for God hath so ordered the prophets to reckon days. Numb. XIV. 34, "After the number of days in which ye searched the land, even forty days, each day for a year, shall you bear your iniquities, even forty years." Ezek. IV. 5, 6, "For I have laid upon thee the years of their iniquity, according to the numbers of the days, three hundred and ninety days, so shall thou bear the iniquity of the house of Israel. And when thou has accomplished them, lie again on thy right side, and thou shalt bear the iniquity of the house of Judah forty days; I have appointed thee each day for a year."[3]

Using this idea as the basis of his computations, Miller assumed that the 2,300 years had begun in 457 B.C.E., during the time of Artaxerxes and the rebuilding of holy Zion, Jerusalem. Therefore, the end would come in 1843.

Miller attracted considerable attention with his predictions. He began lecturing on his theories in 1831, refining his calculations to a date somewhere between March 21, 1843 and March 21, 1844. As the world continued on its indigent course beyond March of 1844, Miller was convinced that differences in the old Jewish calendar required a revised date of October 22, 1844. The *New York Tribune* of March 2, 1843, carried Miller's story and the nature of his interpretations and calculations. People from many denominations were enchanted by Millerite doctrine, and there were approximately fifty thousand followers at the height of its significance in 1844.

From the standpoint of ordinary observation, no "cleansing of the sanctuary" took place in October of 1844. Many Millerites were disillusioned with the apparent failure of their expectations. Apparently some had given away their savings, planted no crops, and settled all accounts in anticipation of the appointed time. The movement tried to provide for those believers who faced the ravages of an approaching winter. The ranks of Millerites were soon depleted by defection. However, there were those leaders and followers who remained faithful. From our study of religious traditions we have observed that religion is not merely a matter of belief. There is more than the verbal or ideational expression to it. Human religiousness expressed itself in the sense of belonging and identity. The ultimate order and meaning of existence are expressed in community. There were Millerites disillusioned by the failure of predictive prophecy who nevertheless found eternal comfort and courage in belonging to the movement. They sought explanations for the fact that Christ had not returned on the clouds.

What were the options? First, there could have been some miscalculation. However, after careful study of the sources, the leadership concluded there was no error in computation. Second, God may have altered the scheme of things or not have revealed all things. This seemed unlikely to millenarian thinkers. What was more likely was that humans had failed to recognize the mode of Christ's return. Perhaps his tarrying was due to the fact that the sanctuary to be cleansed was not on earth, but in the heavenly realms. The cleansing had not been a "cataclysmic destruction on this earth, as Millerites had predicted, but a new phase of Christ's ministry in heaven that placed the earth under judgment."[4] Christ had entered the "heavenly sanctuary" on October 22, 1844, in a preliminary move prior to his coming to the earth in judgment. He cleanses the sanctuary of heaven and makes a careful investigation of the sins of the earth. From there he blots out the sins of those who accept his sacrifice. When that work is finished, Christ will return to the earth to bring proper judgment.

Many Millerites discovered the comfort of such interpretations of the second coming of Christ. They separated from Baptist, Methodist, and Presbyterian congregations and formed associations of their own that nurtured their need for community and for assurance that the injustices of this life would be rectified with the second advent. However, it is very likely that these

Adventists, as they became known (especially after the death of William Miller), would not have been the center of an important American religious tradition had it not been for the visioning of Ellen Gould White. As Ellen Harmon she had been converted in an Adventist meeting two years before the year of fateful predictions. Immediately she began to receive messages and insights through dreams and trance-like experience. Ellen White was a Christian shaman whose visions consolidated the Adventist movement and set it on a course that produced the unique tradition of Seventh-day Adventism.

There is a passage in the Revelation to John (14:9-12) in which an angel brings a message that anyone who "worships the beast in its image . . . shall drink the wine of God's wrath." This became the basis for observance of the seventh-day Sabbath. Presumably, the "worship of the beast" referred to the day of the Sun so important to the Roman Empire—"the beast." One of White's visions of the heavenly sanctuary (where Christ was performing his cleansing actions) revealed the tablets of stone containing the Ten Commandments. A halo of light surrounded the fourth commandment and an angel announced, "When the foundations of the earth were laid, then was also laid the foundation of the Sabbath." Saturday observance became a fundamental element in Adventist religion.

Another distinctive feature of Seventh-day Adventism is its emphasis upon dietary matters as a moral imperative. Of course, many religious movements of the nineteenth century were concerned to develop a moral style that prohibited use of alcohol and tobacco. These prohibitions often were extended to deny the use of stimulants and the eating of meat, especially pork. The Adventist tradition began to promote a special concern for proper dress, diet, and medicine. Towns like Loma Linda, California, and Battle Creek, Michigan, became the sites of Adventist settlements where health could be maintained in preparation of the Adventist saints for the imminent return of Christ. Like Mormonism and Christian Science, Seventh-day Adventism was a movement with an identity that separated it from the mainstream of American religion and culture. Like the other two traditions, it also relied very heavily upon the principle of continuing revelation, with Ellen White as the leader who received divine and essential insights that supplemented the normative Christian revelation. However, with White and the subsequent maturity of Seventh-day Adventism, the tradition had become less millenarian and more concerned to provide a community of nurture, emphasizing the necessity for prophetic judgment upon a society too complacent about the injustices of slavery and emerging American imperialism.

America had lost its soul and the community of the Advent was a pre-vision of the kingdom of God in America.

There are numerous other adventist and millenarian movements that owe their origins to the modern religious climate of the late nineteenth and early twentieth centuries. Perhaps none is so important as the Jehovah's Witnesses. These people are not "Christians" but "witnesses," according to their own interpretation. In the book of Isaiah in the Hebrew Bible there is a passage that reads: "'You are my *witnesses*,' says the Lord, 'and my servants I have chosen, that you may know and believe me and understand that I am He. Before me no god was formed, nor shall there be any after me. I, I am the Lord, and besides me there is no savior. I declared and saved and proclaimed, when there was no strange god among you; and you are my *witnesses*,' says the Lord" (43:10-12). To the followers of Charles Taze Russell (1852–1916) and Joseph Franklin Rutherford (1869–1942), these words are a mandate against pretending to be a church. The text also clarifies what the true students of God's way should be called. They are members of a Bible society and witnesses to the works of almighty God, called "Jehovah" by the ancient prophets.

Russell, the founder of this movement, had been reared in Congregationalism, but early came under the influence of adventist doctrine. He was convinced of the verbal inspiration and inerrancy of Scriptures, but concluded that the churches throughout history had made incorrect translations. Churches, like all human institutions, were the playground of Satan. The churches were part of the corruption and sin of human society and, like all institutions, must be avoided in order to preserve the truth and purity of "witness" to the deeds of Jehovah. Russell decided that Christ had indeed returned in an invisible, spiritual manner in 1874. This advent had begun a process of gathering God's true witnesses, which would continue until 1914, when the Battle of Armageddon[5] would establish the millennial reign.

Zion's Watch Tower Bible and Tract Society was incorporated in 1884, the result of about a decade of lecturing and Bible study on Russell's part. He dominated the movement until his death, shaping it with his insights, organizational skills, and the publishing venture that had begun with *Zion's Watch Tower*. The members of the Watch Tower Society quickly developed a profound missionary zeal that has distinguished the religion ever since. Jehovah's Witnesses form a network of lay-missionary activity rivaled only by the Latter-day Saints and characterized by the distribution and sale of books and pamphlets that promote millenarian doctrine.

NEW
TRADITIONS
FOR THE
COMMON
PEOPLE

323

It is interesting to note that the role of the media in the evangelistic, educational, and formational character of religion in America comes into its own in the nineteenth century and that movements like the Seventh-day Adventists and Jehovah's Witnesses have been pioneers in the fostering of this religious phenomenon. There is little doubt that the manner in which people think *of* and *about* religion has been shaped by the iconography and ideas of periodical literature.

After Russell's death on October 31, 1916, the members of the Watch Tower Society chose Rutherford as the second president. It was Rutherford who emphasized the importance of the name of God and made reference to God's faithful as "witnesses." The world had indeed ended in 1914, but not quite in the manner of Russell's predictions. The year marked the eruption of World War I, and the progressive optimism of the nineteenth century came to an end. If we live not so much in a world as in a perception of the world, 1914 was a time of altered perception. One world ended, and a certain realism furrowed the brows of Europeans and Americans. It was the beginning of what the poet T. S. Eliot saw as an age of "The Waste Land" and "The Hollow Men." Rutherford revised Russell's predictions so that 1914 was not the time of the Battle of Armageddon, but the year in which the "wars in heaven" began that finally resulted in Satan's expulsion from the heaven in 1918 and his banishment to the earth. This was also the year in which Jehovah placed Christ on the throne from which he observes Satan's reign on earth until the coming of the millennium.

The Witnesses have been an iconoclastic religious society in a nation that was built on dissent and iconoclasm. However, as we have observed in the case of the Latter-day Saints, the United States has tolerated only that dissent that does not run counter to the common sense and mores of the culture. As in ancient Rome, we have tended to permit dissent from the mainstream of American Christianity only so long as the public religious tradition is supported. The Witnesses were the creators of a theocracy that required full loyalty and understood the political order as primarily the domain of Satan. They refused to vote, hold office, serve in the armed forces, or salute the flag. Their evangelistic enterprises were aggressive and offended the sensitivities of Americans who accept the belief in the "common essentials" of every religion and live by a religion of civility that avoids giving offense to others.

After years of persecution, disdain, and ridicule in relation to the larger American society, Witnesses have entered a phase in which they have attempted greater accommodation to the value of civility. Their own theology and practice may very well be moving through a new phase of adjustment to the modern world. Certainly the rank and file of Witnesses are no longer representative entirely of lower socioeconomic and educational levels. They are no longer the disinherited of the earth who find justice only in a heavenly vengeance. It is not yet clear what they are becoming.

At the heart of their distinctive verbal expression is the idea that the "number of the sealed, a hundred and forty-four thousand sealed, out of every tribe of the sons of Israel" (Revelation 7:4) makes explicit reference to those who will inherit heaven. Jehovah will reveal to this select number that they are of the elect. They will be given spiritual bodies and join Christ in ruling the universe. Others who are judged worthy will inherit the earth after it has been restored to Jehovah's original intent.

The Witnesses are a movement with carefully calculated and distinctive beliefs. Their doctrine pays attention to a great number of interpretations based upon their apocalyptic approach to the Bible. The "kingdom halls" of the Witnesses replace the "churches" of Christendom. Although the practical expression of the tradition resembles that of most evangelical and free-worship forms of Christianity, there are variations. Baptism is not performed in a baptistry or font as in traditional Christianity. Instead, as in many of the folk churches of Appalachia and other parts of rural America, it takes place in rivers, streams, or lakes, and is understood as a form of dedication to Jehovah's invitation to be a witness. The Lord's Supper is shared only by those who belong to the 144,000. Others may attend and observe this occasional event, which takes place annually on the day corresponding to Nisan 14 of the Jewish calendar.

Jehovah's Witnesses live also by the moralistic modes of the evangelicalism of nineteenth-century America. The use of tobacco and alcohol is considered sinful, and they refrain from gambling. Such holidays as Christmas and Easter are not celebrated because such activities are not biblical; they are part of the frivolity of this world during the reign of Satan.

Many of the new religions that emerged in the nineteenth-century United States may be termed reactionary movements. That is, they share with restorationism the hope for the restitution of some past and presumed ideal. They are reactions against the forces of modernization and attempt to reclaim a previous teaching and thereby revitalize a moribund institution. Millenarian doctrine is not new teaching; however, the emphasis given to these ideas, along with the rather literal calculation of biblical numerology, have led to the formation of distinctively modern American religions.

The Holiness Movement

Turning to the holiness movement, we encounter traditions that combine the moralistic values of nineteenth-century revivalistic evangelicalism with an attempt to restore the Wesleyan doctrine of sanctification and perfection. *Holiness* is a term with both moralistic and experiential implication. Those congregations that are part of the movement think of holiness as a direct operation of the Holy Spirit, warming human beings with a "sacred blessing" of being sanctified (made holy). The gift is a definite and certifiable experience. Presumably it is subjectively and psychologically oriented, and occurs to the faithful Christian who has received the "first blessing" of conversion—the discovery of God's justifying grace. The second blessing has the effect of eliminating natural human depravity and sin. From this experience the Christian is "made perfect in love in this life."

At one time this privilege of perfection, of entire sanctification, had been at the heart of Methodism, tracing its origins to the work of John and Charles Wesley in the eighteenth century. Official Methodism at one time was divided over this issue, and there was considerable controversy between perfectionist advocates and those who espoused a more sober and orderly Christianity. Eventually, the Methodist denominations lost the fervor of holiness and perfectionism. But Wesleyan holiness was born again in the holiness movement with its advocacy of "second blessing."

Revivalism had generated a longing for holiness. The plea of the revival, the camp meeting, and the class meeting is generally an admonition to leave behind the sordid and indulgent life, to open one's heart to God's saving grace in Jesus Christ. Often the implication is that Christian salvation has to do with the correction of immoral acts. The assumptions of the average person would therefore turn to a longing for a moral life in contrast to the kind of behavior that is characterized by drunkenness, debauchery, and laziness. People assumed and hungered for a holiness that was clean and wholesome living. Revivalism had taught them well. Holiness was propriety, and they waited for an affirmation from the Holy Spirit, an assurance that they could eliminate dancing, alcohol, tobacco, adultery, and card-playing from their lives.

In our examination of Methodism in an earlier chapter, we have seen how such denominations as the Free Methodist Church emerged as sectarian attempts to reclaim the experience of holiness. As Elmer T. Clark informs us, in his somewhat overdrawn account, *The Small Sects in America:*

At the close of the Civil War, as at the close of all great conflicts, including both World Wars, there swept over the country a wave of immorality, secularism, and religious indifference. The spirit naturally affected the churches, bringing about what many believed to be a lowered moral tone, compromise with "the world." . . . Soon those who professed or were "groaning after" sanctification began to seek companionship . . . drawing apart into "bands," establishing holiness periodicals, and sponsoring holiness camp meetings.[6]

The movement eventually led to the formation of denominations like the Church of the Nazarene, the Pilgrim Holiness Church, the Christian and Missionary Alliance, and various other groups, all of which bear the title of "The Church of God." These holiness churches may differ on what to the outsider appear to be minute and irrelevant points of theory or practice. However, they all exist to advance perfectionism in experience and in morality. They tend also to be strong believers in a second advent and often in the millennial reign of Christ. It is interesting to note that the Church of God (Anderson, Indiana) contemplates a personal return of Christ without any connection to an anticipated premillennial age.

The practical expression of the holiness movement exhibits considerable variety. However, these churches were strongly influenced by the heritage of revivalism. They may not all be congregations of excited preachers and animated prayer and praise, but they nevertheless exhibit the fervor and free style of the camp meeting and the revival stage.

Meanwhile, there were some for whom even a second blessing was insufficient. They waited for a third. In their minds resided the conviction that the coming of the Holy Spirit with the fire and wind of the first Christian Pentecost (Acts 2:1-11) would repeat itself for the faithful. They could become the voice of the Holy Spirit—speaking in foreign languages of which they had no prior knowledge, or babbling in unknown tongues. There were other special gifts that might possibly accompany this third blessing. One might receive the gift of healing or the gift of interpretation of glossolalia (tongue speaking). Thus was born, also out of the bosom of Methodism, the pentecostal movement.

Among African Americans it is often difficult to separate pentecostal religion from the holiness movement. As C. Eric Lincoln and Lawrence H. Mamiya have pointed out, "Pentecostals are widely acknowledged to be the fastest-growing segment of the black religious family." Yet, "Some Pentecostal groups have the word 'Holiness' incorporated in their name; a few others reject the Holiness doctrine of sanctification and are strictly Pentecostal."[7] Amanda Berry Smith (1837–1915) was an African Methodist who became a holiness preacher and "helped pave the way for hundreds of black women who also felt the call to preach and founded their own independent, 'sanctified' storefront churches during the great urban migrations of the twentieth century."[8]

Pentecostalism

The beginnings of pentecostalism are found among the rural poor of places such as the Ozarks and Appalachia, and among the disinherited of the burgeoning cities of the United States. Although pentecostalism finds it language in the New Testament, it is a form of religion that has its parallels in other parts of the world, other traditions. Possession by god(s) is a form of practical religious expression among people as diverse as the ancient Greeks and the Polynesian islanders. In pentecostalism we are face-to-face with ecstatic religion and divine possession of a Christian variety. In witnessing some of the phenomena of pentecostal worship, we realize that we are dealing with people who are out of their natural habitat. They are out-of-body, in a trancelike state in which a force or forces greater than they appear to be in control.

Pentecostalism has become virtually synonymous with the spirit-filled activity of those who speak in tongues, engage in dancelike movements and gestures, and sometimes fall to the floor in fits of jerking exercise. There are often cries, shouts, and moans that accompany these events. This activity is in partial emulation of the circumstances recorded in the Acts. To its practitioners it is an occasion of visitation by the Holy Spirit. Pentecostalists tend to assume that such occasions are normative of all Christian worship. A problem emerging from this assumption is that glossolalia and other forms of ecstasy become routinized. What is reasoned to be free and Spirit-initiated becomes a ritual process. Pentecostalists expect to worship in this way when they assemble. All other forms of worship are suspect.

Certain forms of rural American pentecostalism have been removed from the more sobering effects of civilization. In the mountainous hinterlands there has been less of a need to be "civil" according to the manners of more ordered society. Snake-handling churches, often found among the mining and remote farming sections of Appalachia, are pentecostal assemblies whose

New
Traditions
for the
Common
People

329

Spirit-filled ritual life mesmerizes both serpents and people so that poisonous snakes are handled, most often without harmful effects.

Pentecostal congregations and denominations tend to be extremely conservative in their use of Scriptures. They are representatives of American Christian scriptural literalism, subscribing to what is called a "literal" approach to scriptural interpretation and a theory of verbal inerrancy. This is a theological perspective shared by many Americans, including members of mainline denominations. Certainly, most millenarian and holiness traditions are likely to be literalist in outlook. Inasmuch as pentecostalism is also moralistic and frequently millenarian, its distinguishing characteristics lie in the practical expression of religion we have already discussed.

"The seeds of the Pentecostal revival," writes Catherine Albanese, "were planted in Topeka, Kansas, at the turn of the century, after Charles F. Parham (1873–1937) founded Bethel Bible College. In an atmosphere of intense community, students searched the Scriptures under Parham's direction until, beginning with the century on January 1, 1901, Agnez Ozman, one of the Bethel students, had a full experience of speaking in tongues."[9] In 1905 William J. Seymour, a black Baptist holiness preacher, took Parham's message of tongue-speaking to Los Angeles. There Seymour began praying and preaching in an abandoned warehouse until the famous Azusa Street revival was launched in 1906. News of these services spread, catching the attention of the press with stories of the gifts of healing and tongue-speaking. An old form of religious phenomena had been rediscovered and now joined the increasing array of American popular religion that threatened to outdistance the churches of Reformation heritage. Since the Azusa Street revivals of 1906–19, pentecostalism has been a growing form of American religion, its practical expression drawing the interest of people in search of the experience of being possessed by the divine.

Pentecostal ritual life has become almost commonplace. With the increased popularity of television preachers, America has become familiar with the pentecostal fervor of Oral Roberts and Pat Robertson. What Elmer Clark wrote in the late 1950s is no longer accurate, although still somewhat descriptive:

> The congregation is composed of men and women from the lower ranks of culture. The evangelist preaches on the gift of the Holy Spirit, stresses the possibility and privilege of the pentecostal outpouring for present-day believers, relates experiences thereof, perhaps now and

then breaks out in ecstatic jabbering of strange phrases, and points out the barrenness of those who have never been so blessed. The endorsement is held out as God's supreme act of grace. Mixed with such expositions are dissertations upon the familiar and accepted themes so dear to the lowly soul—"mother, home, and hearth"—with denunciations of the conventional churches, educated preachers, worldly manners, and unbelief. . . . All the tricks of rhythm are employed gradually . . . conditions become right. Seekers come forward in anticipation of the gift. Confessions are made. Excitement runs high. . . . Some cry out, others fall in trances. . . . One . . . begins speaking, faster and faster, words fail, there is a muttering in the throat, and the subject breaks out in a flood of words that have no meaning to ordinary individuals. The Pentecostal power has fallen.[10]

The Assemblies of God, the Pentecostal Holiness Church, and Foursquare Gospel Church are the most prominent denominations of the pentecostal tradition. Some are in opposition to Wesleyan sanctification as an instantaneous blessing; they prefer a doctrine of gradual and lifelong growth in holiness. As such, the gift of tongue-speaking is for them a unique and independent visitation of the Holy Spirit.

In recent decades many members of mainline churches, such as the Roman Catholic, Episcopal, Lutheran, and Presbyterian have become practitioners of pentecostal religion. They have introduced glossolalia and other attributes of spirit-filled worship into the Mass and other services of a more sedate Christianity. The result has been termed the charismatic movement. Although this movement has much in common with older, traditional American pentecostalism, it is a phenomenon of recent times and, at this stage in the doing of religious history, cannot be included in the history of the traditions examined in this chapter.

We have observed how the unique circumstances of modern America since the first third of the nineteenth century have served as the crucible in which a third force of Christianity, the new traditions of the common people, have been shaped. Perhaps it will be possible in the future to demonstrate that this stage in the development of Western religion represents a radical transformation of Christian history fully as revolutionary as the sixteenth-century Reformation. Adventist, holiness, and pentecostal traditions are not Protestant; they are a new form of religiousness emerging out of the heritage of revivalistic evangelism and the trauma of a techno-corporate society. They are at once reactionary and modern, for many of these churches have the largest congregations of any American denomination. Many of them are equipped with the latest electronic devices and are staffed with the efficiency and public relations skills of our finest corporations. Their preachers achieve celebrity status and are figures of affluence. They frequently believe that success and wealth are signs of divine favor, that God wants us to have these things, and that such achievements may indicate that God is about to raise his righteous ones to prominence over the children of "this world" (Satan's servants) in preparation for the Second Advent. Many of the members of these traditions are also content with the private comfort of the salvation they have received and prefer to be concerned with a private morality that seeks to avoid sins of the flesh. They have little interest in exploring the social implications of Christian salvation and are seldom advocates of radical social change as an essential part of salvation. For them it is inconceivable that salvation itself may be a "new creation," a change in the order of society and nature. Instead it is an affair of individual souls, a private faith possessed and enjoyed in the public arena of praise-filled, ecstatic worship.

NEW
TRADITIONS
FOR THE
COMMON
PEOPLE

331

chapter 18

Religion and the Crisis of Authority

Religious history since the War between the States is the story of a crisis of authority, during which time the terms *liberal* and *conservative* tend to describe a persistent struggle of ideas and behaviors. The struggle may have been intensified after the Civil War, but it had begun at least three quarters of a century earlier.

What we call the liberal heritage of American religion had begun as an attempt on the part of Anglican theologians to adjust Christian thought to the ideas of Isaac Newton, John Locke, and later the philosophers David Hume and Immanuel Kant. What was called "Latitudinarianism" in English theology in the seventeenth and eighteenth centuries argued that reason is the judge and authority of truth about God and moral life. Latitudinarians like Matthew Tindal insisted that the truth of Christianity is available through reason as it observes nature—that anything not accessible by natural reason is not true Christianity. This way of thinking was to play a role in the formation of the American Enlightenment and the religious ideas of Thomas Paine, Joseph Priestley, and Thomas Jefferson. Doctrines long associated with Christianity, like Trinitarian theology, were considered unreasonable and replaced by unitarian ideas of God. Much of American Unitarianism had its origins in New England Congregationalism in the late eighteenth century. Business and professional men, who enjoyed the prosperity of New England's mercantile success, found the complications of Trinitarian theology and the strictness of Calvin's doctrine distasteful. Along with some of the clergy they began to emphasize the unity of God and the God-given power of reason. They opposed reference to the Trinity in worship, affirmed the humanity of Jesus Christ, and rejected the excesses of the "enthusiastic" religion of revivals and awakenings as sub-rational.

Thus was born the liberal form of American Christianity known as Unitarianism. The numbers of Unitarians in the United States have never been great, but the movement has had a profound effect upon our intellectual life.

When William Ellery Channing, minister of Federal Street Church (Congregational) in Boston preached the ordination sermon of Jared Sparks as minister of a Unitarian Society in Baltimore in 1819, he said, "We believe that Jesus is one mind, one soul, one being, as truly one as we are, and equally distinct from God." The sermon, titled "Unitarian Christianity," is often regarded as the platform statement of the Unitarian movement. By 1825, 125 congregations had established themselves as the American Unitarian Association.

By the 1830s a group of New England intellectuals, predominantly Unitarian clergy, organized the Transcendental Club. Prominent in this new religious movement was Ralph Waldo Emerson (1803–82), a Harvard-educated Congregationalist and Unitarian, who had resigned his ministry at Second Church, Boston, because the congregation refused to discontinue or alter the communion service to remove its mystical and supernatural connotations. Emerson was to become the forerunner of that unique American religiousness in which people believe that each individual must create his own religion and that Jesus is a great moral exemplar who serves as a model for our own spiritual development. Jesus is not the Christ, not a Savior, but an American Everyman. Emerson and the Transcendentalists had moved beyond Unitarianism in an effort to restore the simple faith of Jesus: "Man is the wonder-worker. . . . It is the office of a true teacher to show us that God is, not was; that he speaketh, not spake. The true Christianity—a faith like Christ's in the infinitude of man—is lost."

Another liberal religious movement circulating in the late eighteenth and early nineteenth centuries emerged out of the evangelical tradition, particularly among Baptists. The movement emphasized the universality of salvation, rejecting eternal damnation and punishment. They believed that atonement—the setting "at one" of the relationship between God and humankind—is universal, that God reaches out to accept all those who recognize his love as exemplified in the life of Jesus. Universalists like Hosea Balbou (1771–1852) were in fundamental agreement with Unitarians on matters of doctrine. Since 1961 the two movements have been organized together as the Unitarian Universalist Association, affirming personal experience, conscience, reason, the free search for truth, and engagement in issues of social justice.

The heritage of the American Enlightenment, Unitarianism, and Universalism lingers in our culture. This so-called liberal tradition exercises its influence not only among groups like the Unitarian Universalists but also in the ideas and attitudes of members of more traditional denominations and those with no formal religious association.

Postbellum Modernity

In the spirit of the American Civil War (1860–65), the effects of modernity already visible in the liberal heritage grew in power and significance. The crisis of authority was evident in the many religious movements that rejected, in different degrees, the cultural dominance of Christianity in its traditional forms.

"No sooner had the fighting ended," writes David Shi in his historical study *The Simple Life*, "than the forces of modernity recovered their momentum, and the country resumed its transition from a predominantly rural society and agrarian economy to a highly structured urban-industrial civilization."[1] What, indeed, is modernity? It is a state of the public mind that is preoccupied with the autonomous potential of the present moment. Modernity is born out of the discovery that it is possible to tinker with ideas and mechanisms so as to be a constant inventor. Modernity is convinced of the autonomous power of repeated innovation; it is an attitude that was later shaped by a belief in the self-sufficiency of technology. The anthropologist Loren Eiseley reminded us that although human beings have always been tool users, they have only recently become obsessed with the inevitability and necessity of constant innovation. Earlier and traditional societies were in "marked ecological balance with [their] surroundings, and any drastic innovation from within the group is apt to be rejected as interfering with the will of the divine ancestors."[2]

Modernity encourages tinkering with ideas and mechanisms just because it is possible to do so. Tinkering is self-justifying, but it is also justified because something that "works" is a demonstration of human power and self-sufficiency right now. Modernity allows people to become modernists, often assuming that newer is truer and better. However, whether or not all Americans became modernists after the Civil War, most Americans were convinced that the past was a drag upon the present and that problems could be solved by the invention of new ideas and gadgets. It is in the crucible of the postbellum United States that our modern penchant for salvation-by-acquisition was fired to its present temperature. Already in 1878 William Dean Howells expressed a concern that still rings in our ears more than a hundred years later. After the War, he said, "new *wants* were invented, prudence and simplicity of life went out of fashion, and habits were formed and sentiments adopted which have wrought most important changes" in our way of thinking.

As during most wars in human history, technology advanced because tinkering was necessary to gain advantage in conflict and defray the costs of battle. Industrialization was given a boost. "Technological innovations," writes Shi, "greatly enhanced industrial productivity and personal mobility, migration westward expanded the scale of social activity, and the influx of immigrants from southern and eastern Europe brought growing ethnic, racial, and cultural tensions."[3] With the increased urbanization and industrialization came new ways of thinking and behaving. The simple agrarian values of Thomas Jefferson and the Puritan fathers were no longer applicable. Prudence, frugality, and hard work were essential to the cooperative existence of rural and small-town America. They hardly seemed appropriate to the production lines and teeming neighborhoods of urban America.

However, the tinkering of modernity was not limited to mechanisms; it extended to ideas. Charles Darwin had published his *Origin of Species* in 1859, and after the war these theories had filtered among the educated elements of the society. Humans had long held onto the folk views concerning world origins. Their basis for understanding the formation of the universe was shaped by their own experience of making things. Yet in their most profound thought they had always known that the Creator God, who was more than they were, was more than a cosmic tinkerer. Through much of human history scholars had known that texts about the ultimate order and meaning of existence had to be interpreted on more than one level. Stories of creations were true, of course, but they were true not merely in some kind of literal sense. After all, one still had to sort out what certain words really meant. And words were the means of communicating a truth that was greater than the words themselves.

Darwin's ideas addressed the issue of biological origins. He was concerned to explain the relationship between various species of life and to demonstrate a scale of development. Similar notions about geological formation had been under discussion for some time. We must remember that much of the popular thought in America had been formed out of Protestant emphasis upon the authority of Scripture. America was host to a kind of individualism that extolled private judgment and held it in tandem with the authority of Scripture. This meant that, for most Americans, thinking about fundamental issues relied almost entirely upon their attitude toward the Bible.

Ideas about the evolutionary development of earth and its living species seemed to be in conflict with the common-sense authority of Scripture. Much Protestant thought had long neglected the medieval art of "levels of interpretation." It recognized no authority other than Bible and private judgment. Accordingly, the new scientific theories were understood to be injurious to the only sense of authority most people possessed. Either Darwin's notions were false, or scriptural ideas were false. That was clearly the dilemma for many Americans.

However, it was not only the new natural science that threatened the old order. The art of literary and historical criticism was coming into its own and was being applied to the Scriptures themselves by some scholars. This was partly the result of the emergence of history as an enterprise designed to sort out all kinds of data associated with a particular person or event. History had long been a matter of simple chronology or of antiquarian interest. Often it was concerned with chronicling events as fully as possible. Frequently the historian was guilty of special pleading, seeking to advocate a special belief or point of view. Much history had been done as if God were a datum in the natural world.

The new history did not escape special pleading in any absolute sense. However, it became an honest attempt to research original texts and investigate the relationship of all factors in any event. There was also an effort to understand history as the relationship of past to present. With regard to the Bible, the historian began to ask, When and how did these writings occur? These questions led to philological, archaeological, and philosophical considerations. What are the earliest texts available? What do we know about the language of the earliest texts? What can the study of other ancient literature tell us about the Bible? What can archaeology teach us about the times? Were all the documents in Scripture written at the same time, by the same person? Under what historical circumstances were the writings done?

Soon the literary critic became involved, examining texts for evidence of multiple authorship, editing, and translation problems, and identifying different literary forms. Poetry, philosophy, chronicle, teaching, perhaps even fiction, were all to be discerned in the text. Such varied literary forms were to be read and studied each in its own unique manner.

For many Americans the Bible was not only a sacred text and authority on matters of life and death, but also a sacred object. It was a holy book. It was not to be tampered with even if it was not read. Literary and historical critics, in their effort to study the Bible, hoping to understand it better than before, were tinkering with the most sacred object in Euro-American experience. Even today we recognize the Bible as a holy image. It lies on coffee tables, on special shelves, and in the drawers of bedside tables. Armed-services personnel have been known to carry copies of the New Testament in their breast pockets as a shield against bodily harm. The Bible is revered for itself as an object as much as it is for its contents.

The new physical sciences and critical biblical study were joined by the discovery of world religions as factors in the radical change of America's cultural and intellectual climate. The texts of Oriental traditions had been "discovered" by European scholars in the eighteenth century. In the nineteenth century Ralph Waldo Emerson and Henry David Thoreau had found these texts congenial in the formation of their own versions of that American Puritan tradition known as Transcendentalism. There was a certain fascination with these texts because they spoke of life's meaning in an idiom quite different from the biblical world of much Western thinking. The "newer" seemed both truer and refreshing, especially to the romantic minds of the early nineteenth century, minds that lived heroically and self-confidently in the robust American landscape. Thoreau could stroll about in his primal world with a copy of the *Bhagavad Gita*[4] in his knapsack.

By the latter part of the nineteenth century the American people became increasingly aware of the fact that there were "others" in the world who were motivated and informed by ideas and rituals very different from those of Christianity or Judaism. What was sometimes disconcerting was that these curious paths to ultimate order and meaning were often strangely sophisticated. Even if one considered them to be "pagan" or "heathen" ways, and in some sense inferior to the Christian gospel, one had to respect the integrity of the teachings. There was enough profundity to take notice. The options were clear: oppose the doctrines of other religions; adopt or synthesize some of the ideas and practices into one's own tradition; acknowledge the radical pluralism of human religiousness; reinterpret one's own religion in the light of these discoveries.

The World's Parliament of Religions, held in conjunction with the World's Columbian Exposition ("World's Fair") at Chicago in 1893, is often considered the event symbolizing the radical altering of America's religious and cultural landscape. Religious leaders from many parts of the world participated in the Parliament. Many of them looked very different from America's priests, pastors, preachers, and rabbis. They spoke in foreign tongues and promulgated mysterious concepts. From the moment of this Parliament, Buddhist monks and Hindu gurus became part of American religious geography.

Although there are other factors to consider and the history is much more complex than this introduction permits, enough has been said to help us to understand that new religious thoughts were in the making. America was in the process of becoming something other than the "Christian" nation it had been since the seventeenth century.

The New Liberalism

Liberalism is a term that denotes openness—freedom, liberation from any inordinate bondage to what is or has been. A liberal is one who is open to new possibilities. In some sense, perhaps, liberalism cannot exist without conservatism. After all, the conservative wishes to conserve what has been found to be good, true, and important. No intelligent human being wishes to disregard or forget what has already been learned or expressed that is of value. When new ideas emerge they must be tested in relationship to what has been conserved from the past. The true liberal wishes to accommodate new ideas to what has been conserved. Presumably no new idea that is good and worthy will be in absolute conflict with the truth of what has been known. Of course, some conservatives are fearful of what the "new" will do to their security. They become closed to the new. On the other hand, some liberals are so enamored of the new (often simply *because* it is new) that they are closed to what has been conserved. Therefore, many people become "doctrinaire" liberals or conservatives.

This kind of conflict and one-dimensional thinking seems endemic of the human condition. It happens all the time, and it happens especially in times of great cultural and intellectual stress. The latter nineteenth century was such a time of stress, when the old pathways were threatened by new developments and people were uncertain whether the old ways could still be used, in whole or in part—whether they had to be widened, whether the course had to be altered. Such was the crisis of authority. Christian liberalism was a movement in theology that sought to adjust to and accommodate the ideas of Darwinism and of historical and literary criticism and the awareness of increasing religious pluralism. Theology is an affair of ideas, the intellectual enterprise associated with religion. Theology seeks to make reasonable and understandable a religious perception of the world. It has to do with the clarification and communication of ideas. It is an essential part of the verbal expression of human religiousness. The great change taking place in Ameri-can life was in the realm of thought, of ideas. It is natural that theology should face the brunt of the challenge. To many American Christians and Jews, it was a time for new ideas.

Liberalism was a movement in theology. It has affected and shaped the thinking of many Americans. Its influence has been felt in all of the major denominational families of American Christianity and has also been a deter-mining factor in Reform Judaism. Other than those that will be examined here, there are very few liberal "denominations." The inclinations of thought that became characteristic of late nineteenth-century liberalism were already present in Unitarianism and in the humanist branch of the Reformation (see chap. 3). In addition, the Congregationalist pastor and theologian Horace Bushnell (1802–76) had made certain liberalizing adjustments to Puritan theology earlier in the century. Bushnell is frequently referred to as the "father" of liberal theology among the traditional denominations.

There were essentially two forms of liberal theology, the one evangelical liberalism, the other scientific modernism. Evangelical liberalism was the attempt to adjust Christian thinking to the new science and history while remaining fervently loyal to the primacy of the gospel of Jesus Christ. Evan-gelicals believed that the good news (evangel) of salvation was to be identi-fied with the life and death of Jesus Christ. That was a basic and fundamental fact—there could be no deviation from that truth. However, there were those evangelicals who assumed that there could be no conflict between the truth of the gospel and whatever genuine truth was to be acknowledged in science and history. They began to use scientific principles to discuss the doctrines of Christianity.

There was, however, a certain drift in the theology of evangelical liberal-ism that was to be potentially threatening to the liberals' own position. Liter-ary and historical critics in Europe had discovered what they believed was the "historical" Jesus. In keeping with the Enlightenment and the liberal heritage of the past, many were convinced that the Christian church had so mystified the figure of Jesus that he was no longer a human being. The critics thought they had uncovered the human and historical Jesus beneath the theological "trappings" of Christian doctrine. The personality of Jesus became a fasci-nating subject for romantic discussion. David Friedrich Strauss and Joseph Ernest Renan, the one a German scholar and the other French, both pub-lished books titled *The Life of Jesus,* the former in 1835, the latter in 1863. These works repudiated the supernatural element in the life of Jesus. In their portrayal of an amiable and heroic Galilean teacher, they present the reader with a romantic image of an equally amiable nineteenth-century folk teacher projected onto the screen of the first century of the Common Era. Nevertheless, the "newfound Jesus" was very popular, especially among the intellectually elite. Jesus became for them the moral example and model for all true teaching about life's meaning, a concept already exemplified in the earlier liberal heritage, present in the thinking of Thomas Jefferson, William Ellery Channing, and Ralph Waldo Emerson.

The evangelical liberals frequently were enamored of the human and historical Jesus. It seemed to them that a scientific world had difficulty believing in the merits of a divine Savior who somehow atoned for the sins of the world. But a Jesus whose humanity rose to divine heights seemed an appropriate model for the new age they believed was dawning. Evangelical liberalism understood the evangel to be a commitment to the life and teachings of Jesus. The validity of that commitment could be demonstrated by the findings of science and history and by the idea of evolutionary progress. "Is there anything in Evolution," asked Henry Ward Beecher, influential liberal pastor of Brooklyn's Plymouth Congregational Church, "that would desire to destroy the Church? Is not this influence in the Church itself one of the signs of the diversified unfolding of God's plans on the earth going to show the truthfulness of that philosophy of God's methods which modern philosophers have named Evolution, one of the results of that Providence that inspires growth upon growth, and growth upon growth?"

Evangelical liberals began to explain Christian doctrine by reference to evolution and the new "scientistic" mood. Many people were developing religious attitudes about something called science. They were in awe of the discoveries and the confident claims of scientists. Science became a way of expressing the need for ultimate order and meaning of existence, and so encouraged "scientistic" convictions that were not necessarily scientific.

Scriptures, said the liberals, are written in languages like all human language. They are not verbally inspired; that is, the individual words are not the result of the direct inspiration of God. Words have been translated, and texts of Scriptures share the same fortunes of history as any other text. There are errors in Scriptures, but the truth of Scriptures is dependent upon their ability to communicate the truth of God's word of love for humankind. Those for whom the Bible is some kind of magical document with a "halo enclosing it" raise unnecessary stumbling blocks for the minds of modern human beings.

George A. Gordon, long-time pastor of Boston's Old South Meeting House (Congregationalist), sought to prevent the liberal drift toward a merely human view of Jesus. As an evangelical and christocentric liberal, Gordon cautioned against the liberal inclination to lose the significance of Jesus Christ in the course of exclusive fascination with his "teachings." Although the humanity of Jesus was important to Gordon, there was "the soul of unique and inapproachable distinction" that was the "supreme organ of the Eternal Son of God." Gordon insisted that the "ancient insights into the monumental meaning of the life of Jesus must not be allowed to fade from our faith; they must be kept and adjusted to the modern insights into the divine worth of man as man, insights for which we are indebted to a new appreciation of Christianity in the light of the general progress of society."[5]

In Gordon's comment we may observe the signs of a more radical position than the evangelical liberal intended. Adjustment of the "ancient insights" to "modern insights into the divine worth of man as man" is a very delicate adjustment. At what point do the "modern insights" begin to dominate? When does the idea of the "general progress of society" become a substitute for earlier Christian insight into history as a drama that is alienated from the purpose of the divine playwright, a drama whose resolution may not be at all akin to some notion of the "general progress of society"? Many religious liberals were to adjust their "ancient insights" to a point where they became "modernists" rather than evangelicals. The modernist liberals were satisfied with Jesus as a superior teacher of the values that modern knowledge describes as the "divine worth of man as man." For the modernist, "modern insight" is the standard by which the Christian faith itself is measured.

There has been considerable confusion over the use of the words *liberal* and *modernist*. One of the most prominent of spokespersons for modernism was Shailer Mathews, dean of the Divinity School of the University of Chicago from 1908 to 1933. Mathews defined modernism as "the use of the methods of modern science to find, state and use the permanent and central values of inherited orthodoxy."[6] In so doing he was trying, like Gordon, to dissociate himself from those who compromised their loyalty to "Jesus Christ as the revealer of the saving God." Nevertheless, Mathews was convinced, with most modernists, that "the starting point for religion, as for any other form of behavior, is a relationship with the universe described by the scientists." Mathews was not impressed with theology and doctrine. Such statements were the mere relative reflection of cultural patterns: ideas are born of social experience; therefore sociology and history were the tools of religious understanding.

The issues are complex. The history of American religious thought from 1880 to 1930 is a fascinating one, filled with such interesting figures as Gordon, Mathews, and Harry Emerson Fosdick. Many of these thinkers tried to remain within the tradition of Christianity. Of course, Reform Judaism produced a form of liberal Jewish thought that had much in common with the Christian liberalism of the age. But there were those whose ideas moved well out of the range of Christianity and Judaism. There were naturalists and humanists. Thinkers like John Dewey, Charles W. Eliot, Joseph Wood Krutch, and Henry Nelson Weiman applied their minds and religious sensibilities to the formation of religious ideas that acknowledged no "Transcendent Other" as God and discovered ultimate order and meaning in the observation of natural and human behavior.

The Social Gospel

Meanwhile the evangelical liberals of Christianity turned their attention to the social concerns of the times. This "quickening of social conscience" gave rise to new thoughts about the nature of the gospel. Thus was born the movement known as the Social Gospel. To many liberals the message of Jesus was a social message. His life and teachings had been directed against war and violence. At the heart of Jesus' work was the theme of the kingdom of God. To the liberals, Jesus' message of the kingdom of God was not primarily a matter of private experience or of concern for the afterlife. The kingdom was a rule of righteousness, a new social order in which people lived a life of love and justice. It was the Puritan dream, recast in the mind of modern America—a holy commonwealth, a beloved community.

To refer to the gospel (the good news of Jesus Christ) as a social reality was to imply that most Americans had too long assumed that the gospel was a message directed to the "salvation" of individual souls. The Social Gospel was a recognition of the relevance of Christianity to the social problems of the urban and industrial age. Many of the liberals were pastors like Washington Gladden and Walter Rauschenbusch who sought to minister to the people of such cities as Columbus, Ohio, and New York City. Immigration and industrialization had created teeming cities with squalid tenements, poor people, and considerable injustice. It was difficult for Gladden and Rauschenbusch to minister to people as pastors had done in a more rural America, where it had been possible to be concerned with the spiritual life of individuals and with the moral standards of the town. The gospel had to be rethought. Society had

to be reformed. Jesus' message of love and the kingdom represented principles by means of which justice could be provided for the poor and the dispossessed of America's cities. The gospel was in fact a "social gospel."

Most of the leaders of the Social Gospel movement tended to be theological liberals. It is probably fair to say that it was never a grassroots movement.
Although not terribly complex theologically, liberalism represented ideas
that seemed to be the result of human speculation. They were ideas spun by
the comfortable, by those whose experiences tended to bask in the harmonies
of existence. An Emerson or a Thoreau would have been content with them.
But by and large, the people wanted "a Word from the Lord." Perhaps they
knew innately that disharmony was as common to human experience as harmony, that salvation required rescue from the dilemmas of the human condition. Whatever the reasons, the masses were not engaged by the Social
Gospel model of Jesus as grand exemplar of the teachings of the kingdom of
God. Some of the leaders of the Social Gospel movement were aware of the
weakness of their teachings. They understood that there was a temptation to
fall into a certain romantic idealism as they turned their hearts in the direction of the poor and the downtrodden. Walter Rauschenbusch tried to provide a sound intellectual base for the movement in *The Theology of the Social
Gospel,* a book that in 1917 reflected the sobering effects of World War I.
Rauschenbusch set himself against the views of those who clung too tena-
ciously to evolutionary notions of inevitable human progress. He was too
aware of the sinister and persistent power of the forces of evil.

It is interesting to reflect, however, on the fact that although millions of
Americans denied the liberal agenda of the Social Gospel, many of them at
the same time espoused visions of inevitable progress. It would seem that
Americans must believe that their destiny is an onward and upward sort of
earthly pilgrimage. It is a pilgrimage that they share with nature and that they
use the doctrine of Providence to affirm. Perhaps this is why another new
form of religious thought seemed so acceptable to Americans—poor and
rich alike. When Andrew Carnegie published his famous essay "Wealth" in
the *North American Review* in 1889, he set forth ideas that many people were
prepared to accept. Carnegie was a Scottish immigrant who had become one
of the United States' leading steel company magnates. His was the rags-to-
riches story with which Americans were prepared to identify even if they
were poor. Carnegie had not much patience with the pauper who continued
to live in squalor; after all, he had proven it was possible to rise above one's
circumstances and succeed dramatically. His "gospel of wealth" asserted the

freedom of the individual, open competition, hard work, and frugality as keys to acquiring wealth, and the belief that wealth brought enormous responsibility. There was a divine law like Darwin's "survival of the fittest" that selected the strongest for success. However, the same law assumed that the wealthy person must not live an ostentatious life or die rich. He must help those who are ready to help themselves and use his riches for the cause of peace and justice. Carnegie believed that without the wealthy there would be universal squalor.

The average American citizen still subscribes to Carnegie's "gospel of wealth," at least certain aspects of it. Perhaps we are less concerned than Carnegie was about what Thorstein Veblen was to call "conspicuous consumption," but we tend to believe that hard work brings success and that God helps those who help themselves. This viewpoint is not entirely out of keeping with one of the most popular documents produced by a representative of the Social Gospel movement: Charles M. Sheldon's novel *In His Steps: What Would Jesus Do?* (1897; still in publication, having sold millions of copies since the initial publication) carried the message that the formula "What Would Jesus Do?" was applicable to virtually every situation that required a decision, that the use of the principle would transform society into a harmonious community without poverty or injustice.

Many of the women associated with the reform movements of nineteenth- and twentieth-century America must be considered leaders in the Social Gospel movement, even though many of them were not theological liberals or representatives of traditional Protestant Christianity. Catherine Booth of the Salvation Army was somewhat radical in her advocacy of social reform and ministry to labor and the underprivileged. By 1900 Jane Addams had founded Hull House, a social settlement in Chicago that sought to provide a laboratory in which to work at social improvement and humanize labor so that workers might have a greater sense of worth and fulfillment. For Addams, religion was a pragmatic affair: ultimate order and meaning are expressed in action on behalf of the improvement of life in a techno-corporate world. Addams's religion was a social gospel without evangelical loyalties, a religion of benevolent humanitarianism. A Catholic Women's Congress held in Chicago in 1893 led to a National League concerned with the role of women in assisting the needy who lived on the edges of industrial civilization. And by the 1930s Dorothy Day, a convert to Catholicism in 1927, had founded the Catholic Worker movement as an answer to the inadequacy of religious and political response to the growing displacement of the many victims of a capitalist society.

New Thought

The issue of authority tended to dominate much of the religious thought of postbellum America. How could human beings find a sound foundation for affirmation of life's ultimate meaning in a society undergoing profound intellectual and cultural change? The world of the late nineteenth century was increasingly mobile. Immigration brought new people and ideas into the stronghold of American Protestant culture. From Europe came ancient doctrines that had been obscured by centuries of Christian domination of Western thought. Many of these teachings continued to exist but were often opposed or accommodated into Christian practice. They tended to be esoteric[7] wisdom, such as that attributed to Hermes Trismegistus, an ancient Egyptian source. The collection of Hermetic writings, available in Latin and Greek, probably dates from the mid-first to the late third centuries c.e. This esoteric wisdom emphasizes the practical nature of sacred truth, the essential unity of all knowledge, and the divine character of humanity.

There is a certain affinity of this esotericism with teachings extrapolated from the great traditions of Asia. From Hinduism, Tibetan Buddhism, Taoism, and Confucianism came a wealth of ideas that lent themselves to syncretic adjustment to the needs of many people who had given up on what they assumed were the tired dreams and lost authority of evangelical Protestantism. The time was right for receiving these "new" ideas. The public religious tradition of America had already made a place for the belief that there are common essentials to all religions. Franklin and Jefferson had been early proponents of such a view. It is understandable that the late-nineteenth-century encounter with world religion and radical pluralization should have turned many minds in the direction of teachings that spoke of essential unity. Americans were also concerned with the pragmatic, with that which works and satisfies well-defined needs and desires. Needless to say, divinity also seemed to be flowing in the veins of the young republic taking its seat in the pantheon of powerful nations. The movement known as New Thought emerged in the midst of this concern for religious unity and the idea of hidden ancient truth.

One of the most important of New Thought traditions was the theosophy of Madame Helena P. Blavatsky, an émigré from Russia to New York in 1872. She had claimed that while in Tibet with her husband, a Russian general, she had been instructed by "masters," highly developed spiritual teachers who are heirs to the ancient wisdom of Egypt, India, and China. Robert S. Ellwood informs us that there are two sides to the theosophical movement: "First, there is what amounts to a cult of the marvellous, a delight in wondrous psychic phenomena, and of apparitions of the masters. Second, there is a vast and deep mentalist philosophy." The masters are "great mediating figures who represent individuals more highly evolved than the ordinary person."[8] Contact with the masters is made through psychic techniques that must be learned in study and apprenticeship. Encounter with them is a marvelous communication that leads to "deep wisdom." The "mentalist philosophy" refers to the notion that mind is everything; mind is the basis of everything.

Madame Blavatsky published two major works: *Isis Unveiled: A Master Key to the Mysteries of Ancient and Modern Science and Theology* (1877) and *The Secret Doctrine: The Synthesis of Science, Religion, and Philosophy* (1888). She founded the Theosophical Society in 1875, the object of which was to form a nucleus of the Universal Brotherhood of Humanity, to investigate the hidden mysteries of nature and the psychic powers latent in humanity, to promote study of the world's religions and sciences, and "to vindicate the importance of old Asiatic literature, namely the Brahmanical, Buddhist, and Zoroastrian philosophies." Considered by many to be a misfit and somewhat of a charlatan, Blavatsky was nevertheless a genius in the promotion of certain religious assumptions that are close to the heart of many Americans. Her influence and that of the theosophical movement (of which there are several branches and organizations) range quite beyond the measure of institutional memberships of the various societies. After Blavatsky's death, leadership of the movement passed to the very colorful Annie Besant and C. W. Leadbeater.

There also emerged several movements that have much in common with the theosophical tradition and are part of the New Thought movement. Their emphasis, however, is upon mind-cure or mental healing. Christian Science and other New Thought traditions share a concern for religion as a means of directing the mind away from disease toward health. Phineas Parkhurst Quimby of Portland, Maine, is generally considered to be the father of those ideas and practices that gave rise to Christian Science and New Thought. One of his patients was Mary Baker Eddy, whose own experience led to a kind of revelation of eternal truth, the discovery of the illusory, nonexistence of matter. Only Eternal Mind is real, and our ability to learn its principles can provide us with control over matter, establishing a harmony with the Eternal Mind that overcomes sickness, sin, and death.

Mary Baker Eddy joins Joseph Smith, the founder of Mormonism, and Ellen Gould White, organizer of Seventh-day Adventism, as examples of nineteenth-century religious leaders whose "new religions" were dependent upon the concept of supplementary revelation. That is, all three movements were established by means of revelation of important teaching that supplemented the already existing Scriptures and doctrine of the Christian tradition. In the cases of Mormonism and Christian Science the supplementary revelation led to the publication of books that are of a scriptural or quasi-scriptural nature. Mary Baker Eddy published *Science and Health with Key to the Scriptures* in 1875. The Church of Christ, Scientist, was founded with control over its welfare directed by the "Mother Church" in Boston.

Other variations of mental healing have led to the formation of numerous organizations and publication houses. In 1899 the New Thought Alliance was formed, bringing together in voluntary association representatives of these churches and disciples of mind-cure. The Unity School of Practical Christianity was founded by Charles and Myrtle Fillmore in Kansas City, Missouri. Many Americans of other religious persuasions read the publications of the Unity School, hoping to find the secret of happy, healthy, and successful living in the midst of a complex and seemingly insecure world. Other organizations that are part of the New Thought tradition of mental healing are groups that use names like *divine science* and *religious science* in their titles. The prevalence of the word *science* in much of this tradition indicates a concern to be scientific—to call attention to the fact that principles and laws of nature that make for health are part of the divine plan of the universe. It is just as "scientific," in the thinking of the mind-cure adherents, to learn the elements of divine science as to work with the laws of physics. Metaphysics (thinking that carries us beyond physical nature into concern for the nature of reality) is as scientific as physics.

Positive Thinking

In the literature of the Unity School we encounter a practice that represents a transition to a slightly different emphasis in American religion. Perhaps Americans have always been positive thinkers, but it was the religious climate of the late nineteenth century that gave rise to the positive thinking varieties of American religiosity. "The body is the corporeal record of the mind of its owner," said Charles Fillmore. "The individual may become any type of being that he elects to be. Man selects the mental model and the body images it. . . . You can be an Adam if you choose, or you may be a Christ . . . the choice lies with you."[9] Here was the discovery of the importance of the repetition of a kind of formula of words. Repetition established a positive healing mind through the constant affirmation of a healthy thought. Sometimes texts of Scripture were used, at other times simple statements like, "I am a child of God and, therefore, I do not inherit sickness."

It was assumed that positive thinking could overcome the negativities of existence, so that one could become healthy of body and successful in life. This principle was, of course, very much in keeping with the optimism and notions of human perfection that were prominent in the nineteenth and twentieth centuries. It was a reshaping of Christian doctrine away from sin and redemption into an emphasis on Jesus as divine healer, teacher of divine principles of health and success. Jesus was the very epitome of that power available to all of us—latent forces waiting to be unleashed. Sin, in New Thought and positive thinking perspective, is living as if the corruptible body of flesh and blood were the truth. Sin is failure to affirm the pure and incorruptible Spirit-mind that is the really real.

Positive thinking has become an acceptable religious tradition among Americans of all social, economic, and educational levels. In the twentieth century the preaching in many American pulpits and denominations was influenced by positive thinking and mind-cure. Norman Vincent Peale, a popular preacher, author, and public speaker who championed the principles of positive thinking, is the name most associated with it. Many people have read Peale's *Guide to Confident Living* and *The Power of Positive Thinking*. During the 1950s representatives of Judaism and Roman Catholicism developed their own variations on these themes. The Roman Catholic professor, bishop, and television personality Fulton J. Sheen was a sophisticated spokesperson for many of the ideas. Robert H. Schuller, minister of the famous Crystal Cathedral in Garden Grove, California, and preacher for "The Hour of Power" on American television, is among those in the succession of celebrity preachers and authors who espouse positive thinking and seek to lead people into an affirmation of images and principles that develop happy and successful lives. Schuller espouses a version called possibility thinking, yet he is an ordained minister of the Reformed Church in America, one of the guardians of classical Calvinistic and Reformed theological orthodoxy. He maintains that his teaching on self-esteem is a faithful interpretation of the Christian gospel.

> Oddly enough, in twenty centuries, the church has moved forward without understanding or acknowledging this question: *What is the deepest need of human beings?* The church has survived through these

centuries by assuming that every person's ultimate need was "salvation from sin." It has held out "hope for forgiveness" as the ultimate answer.

What's wrong with this interpretation? Nothing, and yet, every-thing, if in the process of interpreting sin and repentance the gospel is presented in substance or spirit in a way that assaults a person's self-esteem. Not to understand that truth, or be casual or cavalier in responding to every person's need for dignity, will perpetuate the problems.[10]

Schuller believes that "the will to self-love is the deepest of all human desires" and affirms the dignity of every person.

Critics contend that this focus on self-esteem and possibility thinking is naïve and misplaced. It is naïve because the true self is not naturally known—the will to self-love must be transcended; it is misplaced because it is narrowly individualistic in a world of tremendous hunger, suffering, and tragic injustice. Nevertheless, positive thinking is an important religious tradition in the United States. It is impossible to measure its power and influence. Although some individual congregations and preachers may be known for their advocacy of positive thinking, the movement has not led to the founding of any denomination. It is a popular movement partly because it emphasizes those beliefs and values that Americans by nature are prone to affirm. Positive thinking is not overly intellectual. It posits ideas that are relatively easy to contemplate. It promises results and insists on the propriety of the American dream of success and prosperity. Like Mormonism and some forms of theological liberalism, it is offended by the traditional doctrine of human sinfulness. As H. Richard Niebuhr once stated, Americans like the idea of promise without judgment: "A God without wrath brought men without sin into a kingdom without judgment through the ministrations of a Christ without a cross."[11]

There is little doubt that the early liberal heritage, theological liberalism, mind-cure, New Thought, and positive thinking are distinctively American traditions shaped by modernity. They are often creative responses to the crisis of authority that extends into the twenty-first century. They are pragmatic and attached to the notion of progress. Human religiousness seeks to express itself in the altering circumstances of modern life. There is as yet no reliable indication that humans are any less religious than they ever were. The need to affirm ultimate order, meaning, and possibilities for transformation finds itself expressed in new ways as well as in the reactionary modes of a previous time. It is understandable that our fascination with the magical properties of science and technology should express itself in religious fashion. For some this leads to scientism, the religion of science. Others find it necessary to be "scientific" about the ways they practice religions old and new.

chapter 19

The Fundamentalist and Neo-Evangelical Traditions

It is difficult to understand the rise of American fundamentalism and neo-evangelicalism without first coming to terms with the crisis of authority introduced in the preceding chapter. Fundamentalism is a reaction against the currents of modernism and liberalism discussed previously. It has become an unfortunate label, promoted by the media since the 1930s. The predominantly negative connotations associated with fundamentalism are part of an attempt to deny validity to religious movements that seek to preserve traditional teachings and values in response to the onslaught of modern techno-corporate society. It is even more unjustified to export an American term, heavily laden with pejorative implications promoted by the media, to other parts of the globe. For example, not all Muslim resistance to Western secularism and imperialism is unfounded, fanatical, or extremist. As Seyyed Hossein Nasr points out: "If one is going to speak of 'fundamentalism' in religions, then one must include 'secularist fundamentalism,' which is no less virulently proselytizing and aggressive toward anything standing in its way than the most fanatical form of religious 'fundamentalism.'"[1]

What Is Fundamentalism?

Fundamentalism is American in origin, an outgrowth of American Protestantism in reaction against theological liberalism and the increasingly secular world. It is reasonably safe to assert that there was no fundamentalism prior to 1900 and that our use of the term to refer to all forms of religious reaction is an error of judgment and of history. Fundamentalism is a movement in American evangelical Christianity that has sought to preserve the "fundamentals" of Christianity in the face of a presumed threat posed by science and modern philosophy from without and by over-accommodation from within. Fundamentalism is an evangelical Christian enterprise that seeks to define Christian truth by means of inalienable propositions. As part of this venture to defend the faith in the face of sedition and heresy, there were published from 1910 to 1915 twelve paperback volumes titled *The Fundamentals*. The publication was conceived and financed by a southern California oil millionaire and featured the work of conservative Bible teachers and evangelists. As George Marsden informs us, *The Fundamentals* became "a symbolic point of reference for identifying a 'fundamentalist' movement." Their symbolic significance may have been greater than their power as a polemical statement of the propositional truths that were at the heart of the movement as it developed. For, as Marsden tells us, the books "showed remarkable restraint in promoting the more controversial aspects of their views."[2] *The Fundamentals* were out to convince, to state a conservative position without alienating. They wished to demonstrate the respectability of their views against modernism and the assumptions of the Social Gospel.

Nevertheless, the "word" was out—"fundamentals" were being discussed, and the term was to acquire symbolic power as the watchword of a distinctive movement. Concern for the future well-being of America coupled with anxiety over the destruction of fundamental Christian doctrine, and the stage was set for the rapid growth of a crusading spirit. By the summer of 1919, at the end of the devastation of World War I, a new organization, the World's Christian Fundamentals Association, had held its first meeting. And around the same time, Curtis Lee Laws, editor of *The Watchman Examiner,* a well-known Baptist journal, invented the word *fundamentalist.* They are those, he said, who are ready "to do battle for the Fundamentals."

From this brief introduction it is possible to see that fundamentalism is a very specific religious movement with a particular history. It is not merely a term to be used in reference to every conservative attitude in religion. We must also disabuse ourselves of the notion that fundamentalists are fanatics. There is nothing necessarily wrong with the beliefs, the convictions, that are evident in fundamentalism. Nor is it necessarily wrong to be strong and enthusiastic about religion. Such factors do not in themselves comprise fanaticism. Jay Newman has shown us that the dictionary definitions of fanaticism are misleading. Fanaticism, he tells us, is "a perverted mode of commitment."[3] Someone who is martyred for his commitments is not necessarily a fanatic. By the same token, a martyred fundamentalist is not necessarily a fanatic. The fundamentalist is a fanatic if his commitments make him more concerned with identifying his enemies than with loving the world as his doctrines direct him. A fanatic regards his knowledge of the truth as a God-given charter to condemn the truth in any other form. It is certain that many self-proclaimed fundamentalists have maintained a militant attitude on behalf of fundamental Christianity without perverting their commitments into fanaticism. The fanatic, says Newman, "'overvalues' insofar as his obsession prevents him from paying attention to other things that he values or professes to value."[4]

THE
FUNDAMENTALIST
AND
NEO-
EVANGELICAL
TRADITIONS

353

It is important to remember that human beings are social beings, that this sociality extends through both time and space. That is to say, what it means to be human is an affair of interrelationship that includes the living and the dead. Human existence is "otherness"—who and what I am is always in relationship to others, and the "others" are not limited in time or space. This permits us to understand that all thought and action are historical. They take place in history. To examine a set of ideas without references to this fact is to distort our understanding.

Fundamentalism is a twentieth-century form of American religion. It is new religiousness, but it cannot be understood outside of history. It developed in the American saga. Its antecedents are in the American people's religion and in frontier biblicism. Human religiousness is never limited to the expressions defined and authorized by the official courts of a particular religion. History informs us that Christians have always had beliefs, ideas, and practices that have existed alongside of, and not necessarily in harmony with, the official doctrine and practice of the church. Many rituals, artifacts, and beliefs are part of the lives of people, yet have no place in official Christianity. The church may oppose, ignore, tolerate, or eventually "baptize" such elements of people's religion. Frequently, an official religion such as Christianity is significantly transformed by the influences of people's religion.

Perhaps this is the case with Christianity in the United States. Most religions, at their profoundest level, would assert that people do not naturally understand their greatest needs; but unless a religion makes provision for satisfying the needs of the people, as they themselves define those needs, the people will either devise a new religion or engage in extra-moral religious behavior. Citizens of the new and independent thirteen colonies were creatures of independence and dissent. They were levelers by nature, a people who had had to carve an existence out of a resistant wilderness. Qualifications of education, status, and order were irrelevant. What mattered were skill and perseverance, courage and strength. A priest was out of place if unable to demonstrate usefulness.

The people's religious needs were self-defined in this context. Quick comfort in the face of hardship and disaster was paramount. Needed was a ready message providing consolation for suffering and failure, and a firm promise of justice in the life beyond death. Religion must be quickly and easily accessible, its promise immediately available to everyone and anyone regardless of station. There had to be skills and techniques that leveled and equalized the achievements of people. There was little time for nurture or long-range ministry. There was so much space, so little time. It was necessary to provide an experience that would infuse spiritual energy that would last through days of struggle and apprehension, an experience that could transform the individual in a moment, in the twinkling of an eye, and provide promise of eternal reward. Masses of people in the new and independent nation defined their religious needs in this way, devising a people's religion that transformed evangelical Protestantism into its own image.

Although this people's religion was born of the earth and democratizing spirit of the new frontier nation, it maintained its stability, its authority, by reference to a sacred text. The American people interpreted their experience as one of aloneness, of awesome private responsibility, courage, and expectation. They assumed their existence was a kind of raw and conspicuous individualism. In their own minds this condition was God-given, thrusting upon them enormous potential. Alone with their obligation, they looked to the sacred text for answers to the tension between their obvious weakness and their supposed strength. They became confessors of sin and celebrators of salvation—all of it immediate and assisted by a text that infused spiritual power into the individual who turned to it in reverent private judgment. For such people the Bible was the only authority outside of their own individual judgment that they were willing to recognize. This meant that the Bible was invested with inviolate jurisdiction over their lives. It became an oracle to be consulted instead of a collection of writings representing the faith of a community, the one, holy, catholic, and apostolic church. It became an icon, a sacred object to be worshiped and venerated as a bearer of magical powers. It became a manual, an answer-book, instead of a record of the story of God's dealings with his creation. The stage was set for the emergence of fundamentalism.

Verbal Expression

The absolute authority of the biblical text was essential to the American people's religion and the democratic frontier spirit. When word of scholarly

THE
FUNDAMENTALIST
AND
NEO-
EVANGELICAL
TRADITIONS

355

tampering with biblical authority reached the ears of the people, they assumed it was further evidence of the clumsiness and stupidity of educated folk. Such shenanigans were to be ignored if possible, opposed if necessary. Preachers in hundreds and thousands of evangelical pulpits and aloft on the stumps of camp meetings began to condemn the work of Satan, who encouraged intellectuals and scholars as they "destroyed" the Bible with their historical and literary criticism. The critics were the henchmen of the devil, the dupes of the Antichrist. The heritage of people's religion can be traced into our own century. We can hear its sentiments in the harangues against intellectuals, Ph.D.s, and theological professors. The reader should understand that many of the scholars who subscribe to historical and literary criticism of the Bible do not consider their work to be directed at undermining the authority of the Bible. Instead they subscribe to another version of biblical authority than that which is championed by fundamentalism and people's religion.

The heart of the fundamentalist crusade is the issue of the absolute authority of the Bible. The discussion usually takes its leverage from such phrases as verbal inspiration, plenary inspiration, verbal infallibility, biblical inerrancy, and literal interpretation. What is the nature of biblical composition? Is it a collection of books like all other books, or is it somehow the result of God's own fashioning? Presumably, all of Christianity subscribes to an understanding of biblical authority that assumes God's involvement in the process of compilation. God "in-spirited" the process. The theory of plenary inspiration suggests that God wished that divine communication with humankind be a matter of written record. Therefore, God was concerned that there be Scriptures—writings—and inspired the process that produced a full and complete revelation of divine will. The question that rises immediately is: Does this mean that God "inspired" every word, or just the project in its fullness? In other words, does plenary inspiration necessitate verbal inspiration?

This is one way in which the issues of infallibility, inerrancy, and literal interpretation are raised. An English scholar of language, Owen Barfield, has claimed that words began as sound-gestures in the human experience of relationship to the surrounding environment. These words did not express a meaning that could then be written down in a literal fashion. Literalness is a late development in the history of language. We might say that literalness finally comes into its own in the nineteenth century. It represents a yearning for order and stability through deference to a written record that is presumed to be always and everywhere the same. "But," writes F. W. Dillistone, "life goes on, new discoveries are made, the media of communication affecting relationships are transformed and so the application of a set of laws literally, that is by exact correspondence between the written form and the particular situation, becomes increasingly problematic."[5] Earlier societies seem to have been aware of the symbolic character and power of language. Throughout much of Christian history, Scripture was interpreted with a balanced perspective of allegorical, analogical, and literal methods. As Barfield suggests, the history of language begins at a symbolic stage, becomes literal when written record makes it possible to indulge the desire for permanence, and then moves again onto a symbolic level. Literalness is an impossibility, except as one element in the use of language. Literalness cannot exist by itself. By itself it is an illusion because it attempts to "nail down" the meaning of words that are always more than our immediate knowledge of them. If, for example, we try a "literal" interpretation of the word *love,* we suffocate it. Although we can speak intelligently of love, the word communicates a mystery—a meaning that is more than it seems, more than our comprehension of it. Humans are, after all, symbolic creatures. Our grandeur and misery are demonstrated by our symbolic nature, and language is the supreme emblem of that fact.

Although the mind of the fundamentalist seems avidly committed to a literal interpretation of Scripture, which is believed to be plenarily and verbally inspired, it is a mind that probably realizes the futility of its own enterprise. That is why there are always more "fundamentals" than the single affirmation of biblical inerrancy. It is also why it becomes necessary to impose schemes and typologies upon the reading of Scripture. For example, most fundamentalists are convinced that Jesus Christ is prefigured in many passages of the Tanakh, the Hebrew Bible (Christian Old Testament). The fundamentalist finds "types" of references that are assumed to speak of Christ. The words do not "literally" refer to Christ; the reader must therefore be taught to pursue typological studies. In addition, inasmuch as fundamentalists are most often also millenarians, it is necessary to devise some scheme of Scriptural interpretation that helps the reader to understand what passages of the Hebrew Bible and Revelation refer to the second coming of Christ—especially insofar as many of those passages do not "literally" speak of the millennial events.

We have traced the roots of fundamentalism to the American people's religion and frontier biblicism, in relation to which we have discussed the heart of fundamentalist concern for biblical inerrancy. Recently, however, historians such as George Marsden have been careful to point out that fundamentalism is not merely reaction to the threats of theological liberation, biblical criticism, and the increasing secularism of the modern world. To

Marsden, fundamentalism is also an integral movement of its own making. In other words, fundamentalism is a substantive religious tradition with a history of its own. Certainly this is true to a great extent. One of the classic works of fundamentalist theology is J. Gresham Machen's *Christianity and Liberalism,* published in 1923. Machen maintained that liberalism was both un-Christian and unscientific. Liberals abandon biblical doctrine in the interest of peace; they concede Christianity in order to avoid conflict with the forces of "modern materialism," said Machen. A Princeton professor who defected to found Westminster Theological Seminary and the Orthodox Presbyterian church, Machen was an intelligent and reasonable defender of what is in essence the fundamentalist posture.

Indeed, as Ernest Sandeen has pointed out in his earlier and ground-breaking study of *The Roots of Fundamentalism,* the movement was an out-growth of the Reformed theological tradition of Princeton Theological Seminary (a Presbyterian institution), as it made common cause with a form of millenarianism known as dispensationalism (not to be confused with Mormonism). These beginnings must be considered representative of evangelical Protestantism. In other words, fundamentalism is a unique twentieth-century development out of conservative evangelicalism. Harry Emerson Fosdick, the eminent liberal Baptist who served as pastor of New York's First Presbyterian Church, preached a sermon in 1922 titled "Shall the Funda-mentalists Win?" It represented a heightened awareness of the rigidity of the fundamentalist wing of evangelicalism. "Already," said Fosdick, "all of us must have heard about the people who call themselves the Fundamentalists. Their apparent intention is to drive out of evangelical churches men and women of liberal opinion. I speak of them the more freely because there are no two denominations more affected by them than the Baptist and the Pres-byterian. We should not identify the Fundamentalists with the conservatives. All Fundamentalists are conservatives, but not all conservatives are Funda-mentalists. The best conservatives can often give lessons to the liberals in true liberality of spirit, but the Fundamentalist program is essentially illiberal and intolerant."[6] Fosdick's sermon sets the stage; it calls attention to what had happened to a respectable conservative evangelicalism. The fundamentalist wing had become so alienated from the culture and the mainline churches that it began a life of its own, distinctive and growing. "Respectable 'evangel-icals' in the 1870s, by the 1920s they had become a laughingstock, ideological strangers in their land," writes Marsden. We may ask, of course, How strange are the fundamentalists? It would seem they are not strangers at all, but the soul of much that is American. Be that as it may, fundamentalism is the extremist wing of conservative evangelicalism. As Fosdick put it, not all conservatives are fundamentalists; indeed, not all evangelicals are fundamentalists. I frequently remind my students that former President Jimmy Carter is an evangelical—perhaps even a conservative evangelical; he is most definitely not a fundamentalist.

Let us take a brief look at the Princeton tradition and dispensational millenarianism that Sandeen considered to be the intellectual foundation of fundamentalism. Princeton theology combined the Protestant emphasis of *scriptura sola* with the view of common-sense philosophy that basic truths are readily available to the common sense of humankind. Essential truth was always the same and could be understood without deference to any external authority. To the Princeton professors the Bible was itself God's common-sense message. Its truth was plain and unchanging. Its statements were propositions that meant what they said, so that the simplest of people might understand. No ecclesiastical authority, no tradition of interpretation was necessary.

Any person capable of sharing the common sense of the human race will obviously know and believe what the lot of sane unbiased persons perceive to be true. "The Bible is a plain book," said Charles Hodge (1797–1878). "It is intelligible by the people, and they have the right and are bound to read and interpret it for themselves; so that their faith may rest on the testimony of the Scriptures, and not that of the Church." From 1812 on, when the Presbyterian church organized its seminary at Princeton, professors like Archibald Alexander, Charles Hodge, and Archibald Hodge advocated a philosophy of common-sense realism that permitted a literal and inerrant understanding of the nature of Scripture. Scriptures state certain facts in plain words. Only a fool, beyond common sense, would assert that the words do not mean what they say, especially since no amount of reasoning or speculation can deface or deny the obvious sense of the words.

When the Princeton theologians turned to science, their common-sense philosophy again came to their aid. It is the function of science to gather and classify facts about the phenomenal world, hopefully to discern what truths are involved. What the scientist observes is what he or she claims to observe of the facts of the external world. He or she does not merely fondle some notions of ideas about the world of nature, but observes the natural objects themselves. That is common sense. To these thinkers the mind has a direct relationship to the object of its activity. Again, that is common sense that continued speculation only mystifies.

The same scientific and common-sense perspective may be applied to the Bible. God communicates nothing less than clear and accurate facts to the common sense of humanity. The data to be gathered and classified with regard to God's truth are the facts of Scripture, which are precise and accurate. Proper arrangement and systemizing of this data will put the mind in touch with the objects of salvation. The written word of Scripture is the common sense of God. Treated properly the Scriptures will enable us to perceive not ideas of God but the very deity and the saving grace in a real and objective sense. That is *science*; it is common sense. It is easy to see that the powerful theological tradition of Princeton Theological Seminary provided firm intellectual basis for a conservative view of Scripture that would serve faithfully the fundamentalist wing of evangelicalism as it braced to do battle with liberalism and secularism.

Dispensationalism is not as easy to explain. It is less philosophical and theological than the Princeton intellectual tradition. It represents, instead, an attempt to find a scheme for interpreting the many Scriptural texts that are thought to have millenarian allusions. We have seen in chapter 17 that individuals such as William Miller, Ellen Gould White, and Charles Taze Russell were concerned about the interpretation of apocalyptic passages of Scripture that were filled with curious numerology and imagery. Although they tended to assume verbal inerrancy of the text, they were baffled by these enigmatic references. Somehow, it seemed that a "key" was necessary, some calculation that would unlock the literal truth behind these images.

It is generally assumed that dispensationalism began in England in the ideas of John Nelson Darby, an Anglican priest who had resigned his holy orders and joined a group called the Brethren, which rejected all church order and outward forms. Darby's views on interpretation of apocalyptic prophecy became popular in this country toward the end of the nineteenth century. Darby was a staunch and consistent Calvinist, his theology out of harmony with the prevailing mood of American perfectionism. Nevertheless, there was something about the magisterial character of his system that appealed to the popular need for certainty and permanence in times of cultural stress.

Essentially, Darby and his followers were convinced of the faithlessness of the established churches and the modern age. The churches could not be trusted in their interpretation of Scriptures because they had already become the servants of godlessness. However, in this "present age" there lingered a remnant of the faithful whose responsibility it is to proclaim Christ's reign until he comes. The present age is an interim time in which many prophecies

THE
FUNDAMENTALIST
AND
NEO-
EVANGELICAL
TRADITIONS

359

will literally be fulfilled. The present age is a "dispensation" meant to separate the age of prophecies from the millennial time. Dispensationalists do not agree on all aspects of their system. However, they are agreed that history is divided into "dispensations"—eras that are referred to in the Bible. Marsden writes in *Fundamentalism and American Culture* that the whole dispensational system

> is a very ingenious and complex interpretation of a prophecy in Daniel 9 concerning "seventy weeks." . . . The seventy weeks (or seventy "sevens") is interpreted as meaning four hundred ninety years. Four hundred eighty-three of these years (seven weeks and sixty-two weeks) are thought to refer precisely to the period from the rebuilding of Jerusalem recorded in Ezra and Nehemiah to the time of Christ. The startling and ingenious aspect of the interpretation is that it posits that these sixty-nine weeks were not immediately followed by the seventieth week. This leaves a host of prophecies to be fulfilled in this last brief seven-year time, which is the final period before Christ sets up the millennial kingdom.[7]

From this we can see that the method is intricate and calculating. No simple reading of Scripture will offer this perspective. A principle somewhat in conflict with a literal interpretation is at work. In America the work of Reuben A. Torrey and C. I. Scofield have fashioned dispensationalism into a system that features a red-letter edition of Scriptures, with the key to understanding the various dispensations effectively marked. What is important to an understanding of fundamentalism is that the dispensationalists advocated a literal interpretation of Scripture while combining it with their new historical scheme. Dispensationalism appealed to many Americans because it preserved the infallibility of Scripture and explained the inconsistencies that were handled by liberals and secularists in a seemingly destructive manner.

These then are some of the factors that found direction in the cause of fundamentalism early in the twentieth century. We have explored briefly the role of people's religion, frontier biblicism, the theological positivism of Princeton, and dispensationalism. All of these elements came into focus in the attempt to safeguard Christianity from liberals within the Christian camp and from naturalists and humanists outside. By 1920 the factions were rather clearly positioned for open controversy. Only in a democracy could such ideological battles have taken place without bloodshed. Fundamentalism, after

THE
FUNDAMENTALIST
AND
NEO-
EVANGELICAL
TRADITIONS

———

361

all, represents an understandable reaction to the possible demise of a perception of the world. When one's world is threatened, one will be likely to defend it with whatever resources are at one's disposal.

The fundamentalists observed members of mainline churches who spoke no differently from infidels. The liberals questioned the infallibility of Scripture and followed Jesus of Nazareth as a master teacher of the noble and moral life. They sought to take into their own hands the salvation of humankind and the building of the kingdom of God as a kingdom of man (humanity). They seemed to think that the reform of society must be accomplished by tampering with the governments and institutions of the world. Apparently dissatisfied with changing the hearts and souls of individuals, the liberals presumed to force the hand of God into a transformation of the social order. In the early nineteenth century, before the division of evangelical Protestantism into camps of liberals and conservatives, the evangelical way had always directed its contented souls into good works, benevolent action on behalf of peace and education and against the forces that destroyed the American home—alcohol, tobacco, infidelity. Now the conservative wing of evangelicalism began to be suspicious of much social reform because it was associated with the faithlessness of liberalism. As it took shape in the American religious landscape, fundamentalism became an intolerant reaction against all things liberal. It was to become a powerful and uncompromising religious movement, a clearly distinguishable form of evangelical Christianity.

What are the "fundamentals"? They are varied in number but are conveniently reducible to five: (1) the inerrancy of Scripture; (2) the deity and "literal" virgin birth of Jesus; (3) the substitutionary theory of atonement, meaning that Jesus' crucifixion is a saving act because his death substitutes for our own deserving death; (4) the bodily resurrection; and (5) the imminent second coming of Christ in "literal" descent from the clouds of heaven.

Most readers are familiar with the fundamentalist opposition to the teachings of evolutionary theories concerning the origins of the universe and human life. To the fundamentalist, the Genesis (Hebrew Bible) accounts of creation must be understood as "literal" statements of fact. Presumably the authority of the Bible rises or falls on this issue. Little attention is given to the possibility that a greater concern may be at stake. If it is at all true, as Barfield and other historians of language tell us, that the symbolic precedes the literal in the use of words, then the Genesis stories are witness to the fact that being (all that is) is more than our ability to comprehend it—that within and beyond being there is Being. This would mean that all knowledge of being is the result of the revelation of Being itself. Accordingly, "what is" (being) is the result of "what-is-not" yet the evidence of its reality, its Being. Genesis tells this story in terms of a Creator and the mind and work of the Creator.

Of course, the literal mind rejects such reasoning. However, it does not escape the need to interpret further its own "literal" reading of Genesis. The result is a profusion of attempts to allegorize the "days" of creation into periods or eons. We are familiar with discussions of "creationist science," which seeks to interpret Genesis in a manner that offers a "scientific" understanding that rivals the theories of the established sciences. To the creationist, Genesis is science. She or he has no time for the more "liberal" assumption that Genesis and Creation are so much more than science and are not in conflict at all with scientific theory and investigation. The grand and paradigmatic encounter between fundamentalist creationism and evolutionary theory occurred in 1925 in the well-known Scopes trial. John Thomas Scopes had been a biology teacher in Dayton, Tennessee, who taught about evolution in opposition to state laws. Some years before, the populist Democrat, William Jennings Bryan, had begun to champion the cause of fundamentalism. Three times a presidential candidate, Bryan became the unwavering voice of the prosecution in the Scopes trial. Clarence Darrow, famous trial lawyer of Chicago, was attorney for the defense of Scopes. The trial drew nationwide attention.

Historian Edward J. Larson, in his study of the so-called Monkey Trial, points out that Dayton, Tennessee, was a small town on the edge of distinction. When Tennessee enacted a law against the teaching of evolution in the public schools, John Scopes (a football coach and general science teacher) found himself teaching biology and using textual materials with significant references to evolutionary theory. Like any teacher called upon to deal with a subject in which he had little or no expertise, Scopes was a somewhat innocent violator of a law with implications far beyond his understanding. He presented an opportunity for the law to be tested. Urban school officials did not want to test the anti-evolution law, but "enterprising civic boosters in Dayton craved some attention for their struggling community."[8]

The prosecution, including Bryan, sought to base their case upon the issue of majority rule: Should teachers be permitted to use materials that are contrary to the wishes of the people and to a law democratically sanctioned? It must also be remembered that the populist Bryan was a reformer who sought to prepare America for its role in the world as the moral champion of the common people. For Bryan and many others, evolutionary theory provided a "survival-of-the-fittest" explanation for human development that legitimatized the worst in human nature and affirmed the rights of the strong to trod upon the weak. Bryan was apparently not a biblical literalist or an intolerant fundamentalist. His thinking was much more in keeping with the ideas of the more uncontentious essayists who had contributed to *The Fundamentals* (mentioned earlier in this chapter). As a result Americans have thought about fundamentalism as it was incorrectly portrayed by the play and film *Inherit the Wind* and by representatives of the press eager to appeal to the notion that all religionists are rigid literalists who wish to impede scientific progress and destroy individual liberties. Dr. Kirtley F. Mather, Harvard biologist and lay theologian, appeared as a witness for the defense. There is no contradiction between the teachings of Jesus and the facts of evolution, said Mather:

The
Fundamentalist
and
Neo-
Evangelical
Traditions

———

363

> His teachings deal with moral law and spiritual realities. Natural science deals with physical laws and material results. . . . To say that one must choose between evolution and Christianity is exactly like telling the child as he starts to school that he must choose between spelling and arithmetic. Thorough knowledge of each is essential to success. . . . Good religion is founded on facts, even as evolutionary principle. . . . The theories of evolution commonly accepted in the scientific world do not deny any reasonable interpretation of the story of Divine Creation recorded in the Bible. Rather they affirm that story and give it larger and more profound meaning.

Even with all the eloquence of Bryan, the skill of Clarence Darrow succeeded in demonstrating the somewhat ludicrous nature of the trial itself. It seemed that the world was laughing at Bryan and the backwardness of the fundamentalist preoccupation. As such the Monkey Trial represented a time of retreat for the movement. Fundamentalism became so linked with arrested development and cultural senility that the academic and intellectual world assumed that its days were numbered. It could last a little while only among the uneducated boors who tried to live in the security of some primitive enclave of the mind.

Fundamentalism fostered a rigidly separatist spirit. It would have nothing to do with compromise. It opposed liberalism, the Social Gospel, and the new ecumenical movement that sought to encourage cooperation and reunion within Protestantism. In opposition to the Federal Council of Churches (later the National Council of Churches), Carl McIntire founded the American Council of Churches, a fundamentalist alliance that attacked Catholicism and accused mainline Christianity of being Communist dupes.

It has become increasingly evident that fundamentalism is not dead. Perhaps it had gone underground and been ignored, but it has emerged in recent years as a stable and vital element of American religion and culture. It had already begun its resurgence in the mid-1950s as part of an anti-Communist crusade and the workings of the McCarthy era. Fundamentalism has always aligned itself with the well-being of America. It has assumed the necessity for the continuation of Christian maintenance of American ideas and values in politics, economics, and social order. It has opposed all systems such as communism, which it regarded as anti-Christ or inimical to the Christian fabric of America.

By 1980 fundamentalist power had surfaced to the point where it had to be regarded as a significant voice of the American people. Our intellectuals, many of whom have been anti-Christian or indifferent to what they considered to be the private domain of religion, have yet to accept the reality of the public dimension of religion as exemplified by fundamentalist vitality. Fundamentalism must now be accepted as a form of modern religion in its own right, less as a negative reaction, a foot-dragging moment in the course of the inevitable triumph of naturalism and secular humanism. In a 1983 essay titled "Did the Fundamentalists Win?" Edwin S. Gaustad concluded with this insight, which I paraphrase: Did the fundamentalists win? That is, did fundamentalism succeed in its original purpose? Did it succeed in claiming the truth of Christianity by its rigid attempt to exclude all those who denied the fundamentals? Did the fundamentalists succeed in saving Christianity? The question is an allusion to Fosdick's 1922 sermon (already referred to). Gaustad continues:

> If one is still not quite ready to answer that question, then a somewhat easier one may be put: Did liberal Protestantism lose? So phrased, this query permits us to array alongside fundamentalism all the Protestant catechizers and positive thinkers, all the semi-Protestant New Thoughters and prosperity promisers, all the personality cultists and conservative majorities, together with the turned off, dropped out, disenchanted, and otherwise engaged. Now we're ready: Did liberal Protestantism lose? Yes. This round.[9]

The
Fundamentalist
and
Neo-
Evangelical
Traditions

365

Fundamentalism has indeed won a substantial round, and whether we like it or not, we must give it its due. Students of religion must stop prejudging it and regarding it as an aberration. They must treat it as they would a form of Buddhism. They must ask, what do these people think, believe, and do? What is it like being a fundamentalist, a human being who eats, sleeps, loves, and eliminates waste just as I do—who is no more, no less intelligent than I am? The questions of the honest student of religion are always designed to glean understanding. Judgment comes later, if at all, and is a thankful product of love, hate, and sweat.

Since 1980 various fundamentalist institutions have gained in strength. Fundamentalists like Jerry Falwell have become celebrities. Colleges like Liberty Baptist in Lynchburg, Virginia, and Bob Jones University are in the forefront of the fundamentalist educational enterprise. Hundreds of Bible institutes and colleges are purveyors of fundamentalist religious expression. The Southern Baptist Convention, America's largest non-Roman Catholic denomination, has been somewhat strife-torn for some time as a result of controversy between the fundamentalist wing and the more moderate forces of its evangelical community. Thus far the fundamentalists have won there as well.

By this time it should be obvious to the reader that evangelical Christianity is not a monolithic constituency. Essentially, as we have indicated previously, evangelicalism is a form of Christianity that focuses upon the primacy of the proclamation of the gospel and tends to downplay the significance of tradition. It operates with an individualistic emphasis and tends to promote *sola scriptura* and private judgment. However, there are at least three forms of evangelicalism: liberal evangelicals, against whom the fundamentalist reaction asserted itself; the fundamentalist evangelicals; and in recent decades a more moderate form of evangelicalism, which may be designated neo-evangelicalism.

Development of Neo-Evangelicalism

This movement combines a conservative concern for the preservation of distinctive Christian truth with a restoration of the social conscience of early nineteenth-century evangelical Christianity. The roots of the causes may be traced to the theological positivism of the old Princeton tradition as well as to the rediscovery of the truth of classic Reformation teaching beginning in the 1920s. The latter disclosure has been variously dubbed neo-orthodox or neo-Reformation thought. What it represented was an effort to reclaim the

essential teachings of Martin Luther and John Calvin. The famous Swiss theologian Karl Barth, who more than any other person was responsible for the
vitality of neo-Reformation thinking, had discovered that his liberal theological education was in no way adequate to the pastoral responsibility of having
"good news" to proclaim to a congregation. Liberal ideas were human words,
incapable of communicating God's Word, so far as Barth was concerned.
Somewhere, somehow, liberal Christianity had run adrift. Its teachings held
no positive value. Barth soon learned that Luther and Calvin had taught a
more positive gospel, had indeed proclaimed the Word of God, not the word
of "man."

Some evangelical Christians concluded that Barth and his followers in the
neo-Reformation camp were still too enamored of the philosophical and
other conceptual methods of the modern world. They advocated a fidelity to
the confessional claims of Luther and Calvin. The teachings of the latter were
considered classical—the documentary tradition that contained authentic
Christianity and made for "right doctrine" and the "right worship" (orthodoxy) of God. In the United States Lutheran and Calvinist colleges and seminaries became repositories of the classical orthodoxy of Lutheranism and
Calvinism. In Michigan, colleges like Calvin College were especially instrumental in representing a renewed confidence in the theological integrity of
the Reformed tradition.

Meanwhile, theological schools like Fuller Theological Seminary in Pasadena,
California, sought to champion a classical evangelical Christianity that could
appropriate the positive character of Reformation thought without advocating
a narrowly Lutheran or Reformed confessionalism. This new viewpoint was
later espoused by a new weekly Christian journal of opinion, *Christianity Today*
(founded in 1956). Its longtime editor, Carl F. H. Henry, became an articulate
and adroit theological spokesperson for this neo-evangelicalism. Henry has
affirmed the uniqueness of Christianity among the world's religions and has
advocated an aggressive theological posture that is convinced of the essential
truth of orthodox Protestantism and its dedication to the principle of biblical
infallibility. This doctrine of infallibility has required extensive treatment by
Henry and other neo-evangelical theologians, primarily because they are concerned with distinguishing themselves from the fundamentalists.

The Neo-Evangelicalism of Billy Graham

Perhaps the true father of neo-evangelicalism is Billy Graham, the most
prominent evangelist of the second half of the twentieth century. Although

THE
FUNDAMENTALIST
AND
NEO-
EVANGELICAL
TRADITIONS

367

Graham's background is fundamentalist and his view of scriptural infallibility is much in harmony with fundamentalism, he has sought to be less rigid and judgmental than the fundamentalist camp requires. Graham has never dissociated himself completely from the rest of Christianity. His campaigns have commanded the support of mainline Protestantism, Roman Catholicism, and Eastern Orthodoxy. He has preached in churches of virtually every denomination. The strict separationism of the fundamentalist way has been antithetical to Graham's more irenic Christian spirit. In a gesture of opposition to Carl McIntire and the separatist spirit, he was instrumental in founding the National Association of Evangelicals as an alliance of less militant neo-evangelicals.

Billy Graham has been genuinely concerned to shed the cultic and exclusivist aspects of the fundamentalist position. He has sought to serve the church and the world with the life-saving message of the Christian gospel. As Marsden informs us, neo-evangelicalism has also dropped "the innovations of dispensationalism that had set fundamentalists apart from other conservative Protestants." Graham himself has become increasingly sophisticated theologically. His own pilgrimage from a narrow concern for soul-saving to a more profound commitment to social justice has been instrumental in the neo-evangelical move toward a greater social activism, as represented by a journal like *Sojourners*. By 1976 a "born-again" evangelical (by no means a fundamentalist) was elected president of the United States. Jimmy Carter was a political liberal, a kind of conservative evangelical, whose social and political stance was indicative of the fact that a great body of Americans outside of mainline Protestantism and liberal evangelism has acquired a concern for social ethics not shared by the fundamentalists. At least a part of the heritage of revivalistic evangelicalism had reclaimed its social conscience.

Evangelicalism may be a unique form of religion in the history of Christianity. Nothing quite like it has existed before. It was born in the lusty days of the new nation like none the world had ever known before. It was to be expected that the dominant religious life of such a nation as this, such a people-in-the-making, should be filled with turmoil, overconfidence, and a certain oversimplification of existence. Evangelicalism is exemplary of the brashness of the American people, who demand their own "brands" of everything and are content only with what serves them well. Evangelicalism has now come of age. It is time to accept it, to give it its due, and to get on with the task of setting it in relation to the older forms of Christianity and the many "new religions" of the late twentieth century.

Marsden has written that evangelicalism benefited from the social and cultural convulsions of the 1960s. It "capitalized on the decline of prestige of the liberal-scientific-secular establishment, a value system that evangelicals had already proclaimed as illusory and doomed. [It also] gained from the deep reactions against countercultural ideals." Fundamentalism and neo-evangelicalism may both have benefited immensely from the uncertainties of the post-Vietnam era, pointing to the permanence of their own systems. What is not so apparent is the fact that the liberal-scientific-secular establishment has not really declined in prestige. Its strength is greater than ever, bolstered by the sanctification of greed that accompanies the promises of a techno-corporate society based upon the singular values of consumerism. The power of the techno-corporate establishment exists side by side with the growth of evangelical Christianity. Does one influence the other? Or is an explosive confrontation in the making?

chapter 20

The Age of Radical Pluralism

The religious and cultural landscape of America has always presented a skyline of diversity. From the ceremonial fires of Native Americans and the brush arbor meetings of African slaves to the spires of New England meeting houses and the onion-shaped domes of Eastern Orthodox cathedrals, the horizon has exhibited images of ultimate order and meaning that represent the ideas and practices of people struggling to celebrate different perceptions of the world. Many religious traditions, with their origins in Europe, Africa, and distinct sections of North America, have left their mark upon our landscape. The architecture of our republic provides evidence of idiosyncratic religious perceptions. It is possible to analyze the warp in which people perceive reality by observing carefully the silhouettes and furnishings of many kinds of buildings.

However, there is often an interior landscape not always so easy to assess. Ideas and beliefs are not necessarily visible. Behavior is often more significant than systems of ideas or institutions. The actions of people often tell us more about what people really think or believe than do the ideas they explicitly espouse or affirm. People express the ultimate order and meaning of existence as women, Arabs, Rumanians, Serbs, and West Africans as well as in ideas and practices that are officially Roman Catholic, Sunni Muslim, Conservative Jewish, or pentecostal. During the nineteenth and twentieth centuries these unofficial religious notions gained increasing significance in any profound attempt to understand American religious traditions. The pluralistic character of contemporary American religion is both visible and invisible.

The pluralism of colonial America was primarily a Protestant pluralism. Although there were a few Jews and a sizeable Roman Catholic population in the thirteen colonies, the tone of the culture was evangelical Protestant. The diversity of American religion was a Protestant pluralism, an umbrella of denominations to which even American Catholicism had to adjust its institutional life. By the middle of the nineteenth century, American pluralism was being transformed into an acknowledgeable Christian pluralism. The Roman Catholic Church had become our largest "denomination." There were increasing numbers of Jews, but they were Reform Jews, enamored of the United States as the promised land, altering their Judaism to be a "denomination" and to be a version of American values and belief in the common essentials.

A New Pluralism

By the end of the nineteenth century, it was increasingly apparent that our pluralism was breaking out of its earlier demarcations, stretching the word *Christian* to previously unimaginable proportions. Immigrants from Asia had begun to settle in the promised land. Chinese workers and a few Japanese Buddhists made their way to the West Coast, the former as early as the days of the gold rush. However, Asians were still considered marginal to the inner spirit and outer character of the United States. Well into the middle of the twentieth century, American educators and public spokespersons struggled with the Christian modalities of our pluralism. One scholar, for example, a president of the University of Michigan during the 1930s, published works on the purpose of American higher education; it was to prepare people for life in a "Christian" society and culture. President Charles Franklin Thwing qualified his claim by saying, in effect, "by 'Christian' I mean, of course, to include the Jews." The good president was stretching a point, perhaps to the dismay of faithful Jews, but in one sense he was on safe ground. Jews in America had to a certain extent been Christianized—at least Americanized in a somewhat Christian fashion and brought into harmony with the public religious tradition and the denominational patterns of American religion. Nevertheless, Thwing would have been in more honorable standing had he referred to our biblical foundations rather than to our Christian commonality.

However, Thwing was not alone in his dilemma. The religious landscape was changing and the culture being modified accordingly. Two world wars and a worldwide economic crisis had begun to "globalize" the vision of the promised land. The numbers of people from Asia, the Near East, and Eastern Europe transformed the Anglo-Saxon and Western European hegemony. What is more, the circulation of Asian and Near Eastern ideas, literature, and religious practices accelerated at a remarkable pace. In 1955, the sociologist and Jewish theologian Will Herberg published *Protestant-Catholic-Jew*, in

which he demonstrated the manner in which Americans identify themselves.
To be American was to be Protestant, Catholic, or Jew, said Herberg. This was
a sociological recognition of pluralism that was now a bit more than Christian. Yet the ink was barely dry on Herberg's book before we were *On the Road*
with Jack Kerouac and his Dharma Bums, increasingly aware of the fact that
Asian religious perspective had entered the American marketplace much
more aggressively than ever before. Suddenly we realized that Henry David
Thoreau, scouting the New England wilderness with the *Bhagavad Gita* in his
pack, had been a portent of things to come. American religious pluralism had
moved through Protestant, Christian, Protestant-Christian-Jewish phases
into a radical stage that is wide open and that we are still not able to assess
adequately.

Many of the observations and analyses we will make in this chapter are
tentative. We are too close to the "history" to observe it authentically, and we
have only recently begun to do the basic historical scholarship that will serve
as the foundation for our observations. That is, without careful study of the
many movements, incidents, places, and persons related to the new and radical pluralism, we are not in a position to do more than suggest trends and
point to certain interesting phenomena. Our primary concern is religion in
the United States—American religion. We have already called attention to the
fact that even prior to its European settlement, America was a promised land,
a place of new birth for Europeans. In their thought and imagination, it was
the restoration of paradise, a return to Eden. It was the place of ultimate pilgrimage, a land with the spirit of a shrine. Powerful religious sentiments were
attached to America and its destiny. The social expression of human religiousness took unique form in the American saga—to be American was
somehow to possess an identity, a sense of belonging that invested one with
the power of ultimate order and meaning. There is a kind of tribal religiosity
associated with this country. To be a Navajo or Akamba is itself a form of religious meaning; in a similar fashion, to be American is to reside in an ordered
cosmos, a divine realm.

This American religiousness has shaped and transformed many traditions
that have come to our shores from Europe and Asia. It has also been the
womb of our own conceptions, which have given birth to uniquely American
traditions (as, for example, Mormonism). The religious situation of a radically pluralistic United States is certainly much different from that of the days
of Protestant pluralism. Traditions with their origins in East Asia, Africa,
South and Southeast Asia, the Near and Middle East, and Latin America are

increasingly represented among the immigrant population of our republic. Native Americans have begun to reassert their traditional identity. In the midst of it all there has emerged a search for what is often called "spirituality." Many people make inquiry into ideas and practices outside the traditions with which they may have some affiliation. They combine these religious experiences in new and interesting ways. Since the end of the Christian and biblical era of religious pluralism, the culture has become an open bazaar, a free market for religious exploration. There is often no recognized authority other than individual desire and expectation. Much of the religious life of our time is unacknowledged—those who do some form of yoga do not think of its religious nature; those who promote self-esteem and positive thinking do not often understand these ways as forms of religious expression.

From Asia have come an interesting array of teachers, charismatic leaders, and sacred texts. Many Americans who would not consider themselves either catechumens or devotees of Asian traditions are intrigued by the ideas of the *Bhagavad Gita*, the *Tao Te Ching*, and certain of the sutras. The *Gita* is basically Hindu, the *Tao Te Ching* is Taoist, and the sutras are special collections of Buddhist writings. We are also familiar with the fact that Americans practice various forms of meditation and bodily disciplines that are part of the traditions of Hinduism. Some religious entrepreneurs, responding to the American propensity for consuming new products, have tried to market Asian religious techniques while claiming that they are "not religious"; that is, they have nothing to do with religion. It remains to be seen, of course, whether it is possible to abstract ideas and techniques from a tradition without understanding the intricate relationship of all these matters within the context of a specific Asian tradition.

The Ways of the Hindus

Hinduism is an umbrella concept. Hindus are people of great diversity. There is probably no one pattern or system that may be defined as Hindu. And yet we are certainly aware of the fact that the home of Hinduism has been India and that the social expression of religiousness finds a strong embodiment in Hindu identity. After all, Hindus are in conflict with Sikhs and Muslims in various parts of the Indian subcontinent, and in Sri Lanka Hindus and Buddhists have been estranged. This means that the ultimate order and meaning of existence is expressed in being identified as Hindu. There is a Hindu perception of the world. There is the highly philosophical (often atheistic) form of Hinduism; there are highly devotional and physiological forms of Hinduism; and there is a Hinduism that seeks order and meaning through morality. And, of course, there are numerous versions of each of these. There is the Hinduism of the masses, with their meticulous worship of deities, their dutiful attention to temple ceremonies, and their ablutions in the sacred rivers. And there is the Hinduism of those who seek careful and devout mystical union with Ultimate Reality. On the one hand, there is the austere asceticism of some Hindus who endure rigorous fasting and other subjugations of the body; on the other hand, there is the wisdom and tranquility of the master teacher who responds only to those who are ready to be taught.

When we think about it deeply enough, we begin to realize that all religious traditions encompass a great deal of diversity. Even Catholic Christianity includes the austerity of certain ascetics; the devotionalism of the masses; the refinements of philosophies, theologians, and mystics; and the humble service of a Mother Teresa. One of the implications of the word *catholic* is comprehensiveness: the inclusion of many within the one, or *e pluribus unum*.

What then is the central character of Hinduism? First, it is a perception of the world that has been shaped by the topography of India. Hinduism is not a religion with a founder. It is an attitude of religious tolerance and inclusiveness that mingled in the very course of Indian history and geography. As early as the third millennium B.C.E., there existed a settled people who made ritual use of water, venerated the holy *lingam* (phallus) as the symbol of divine originality, and worshiped a divinity in trees and animals. Among these agricultural and town-dwelling inhabitants there existed devotion to the Mother-Goddess and to the divine principles of creation, preservation, and destruction. The great gods Shiva and Vishnu (of whom Krishna was an incarnation) became the objects of this devotion.

These dark-skinned peoples of early India became known as the Dravidians. Contemporaneous with ancient Sumerian and other Near Eastern cultures, they fashioned a multilayered perception of the world, rich in beauty and power, and unconcerned with Western notions of consistency and logic. From these ancient peoples, Hinduism was to derive the principle that the ultimate order and meaning of existence is diverse—it is response to the power of being in whatever circumstances people find themselves. To be religious was to sing, dance, and think with the forces of nature and human experience.

Sometime between the first and second millennium B.C.E., the Dravidians were joined by a light-skinned people, the Aryans, who invaded the subcontinent through the Himalayan passes—perhaps around the time of the

Hebrew exodus from Egypt. They brought with them their poet-singers, who transmitted an oral tradition of hymns and prayers that later became the scriptures known as the Vedas. One of these, the *Rig Veda*, is presumably the oldest text among world religions. The Upanishads were a doctrinal interpretation of the Vedas commonly called the Vedanta—"the concluding portions of the Vedas." These sacred texts expressed the religious sensibility of nomadic people, who lived under open skies and venerated the earth, the arch of the heavens, and the four directions. Without temples, their altar fires were set in clearings prepared for sacrificial offerings of melted butter *(ghee)*, soma, grains, and animals from their herds of goats, sheep, cattle, or even horses. There was a kind of reflective spirit at work in the Aryan experience, centered upon the relationship between the human mind and the divine consciousness. Aryan and Dravidian ways mingled to form the spiritual world of Hinduism.

Another distinctive feature of Hinduism is its development of the idea of karma. To the Hindu mind there is a law at work in the essential rhythm of being. In all that is, there is a cause and effect—a kind of interactive energy that is continuously at work. Since time is a cycle and not a linear continuum, conscious existence is merely the centering of the rhythm of cause and effect. What is, is; what will be, will be, because individual existence is merely the consciousness of cause and effect at any particular moment. Of course, this means that one's present thoughts and actions are a result of what has been and will also be determinative of what shall be.

This law of karma relates to a third distinctive feature of Hinduism. At the heart of the Vedantic system, which emerged in India after 200 C.E., is the concept behind the Sanskrit words *tat tvam asi,* which express the notion that reality is one. The self is really ultimate reality. *Tat* (that) *tvam* (thou) *asi* (art) means "that thou art"—you are whatever is. The only thing that really *is* is the rhythm of being. To pretend that you are anything other than the incidence of ultimate reality is to take too seriously your conscious selfhood. To the Hindu, *atman* (self) equals *Brahman* (the Infinite and Absolute Reality behind and beyond all appearances). "You" are identical with that which is ultimate in the universe. That which underlies everything that is, is what "you" really are. This Hindu insight is an illuminating kind of experience, inasmuch as most of us spend a lifetime assuming that the empirical ego is the "real" self.

In order to assist the experience of *tat tvam asi,* the Hindus have devised various disciplines that may lead to a transformation of our selfhood. These disciplines are called *yogas*; they are training methods designed to attain

release from the illusions of reality *(maya)* with which we ordinarily exist.
Hinduism offers more than one pathway or *yoga*. If we seem to be drawn by
a desire to control the functioning of our bodies, as physically active beings,
then the way of *hatha* yoga may be for us. We must seek a teacher *(guru)* who
may guide us in so disciplining our bodies that we find ourselves at one with
the nameless and formless Spirit *(Brahman)*.

Some of us are drawn by a desire to use our intellect, to control the mind
in its quest for knowledge and understanding. We must seek a teacher who
will advise us in *jnana* yoga, a pathway that will help us transcend the self that
wants to possess knowledge so that we may find union with the true Self
(Brahman-atman), which is the truth behind all knowledge. There is karma
yoga for the individual who is inclined toward work, achievement, and good
deeds. Eventually the karma yogi should achieve such control over deeds that
he or she is no longer concerned with the achievements of the empirical self.
Instead, his or her actions for good will flow from the eternal Spirit itself.

Perhaps the most prevalent pathway is that of *bhakti* yoga, the way of love,
adoration, worship. Here we sense a recognition of the fact that many human
beings are well-intentioned, loving creatures who do not have great inclinations for physical, intellectual, or moral discipline. Many of us are immersed
in the struggles of daily existence, yet recognize the need to love and to adore
others. This inclination to love may be directed toward ultimate reality itself.
It may travel through simple rituals performed in temples, adoration given to
various deities, and recitation of prayers and chanting of sacred words—it
may travel in such a way that it finds itself embraced by love itself, by the
heart of the universe that beats in our own hearts. "As the waters of the
Ganges flow incessantly toward the ocean," says the *Bhagavata Purana*, "so do
the minds [of the *bhaktis*] move constantly toward me, the Supreme Person
residing in every heart, immediately they hear about my qualities." In some
ways, *bhakti* yoga is an acknowledgment of the significance of ritual in
human existence. It emphasizes the independent power of the practical mode
of religious expression. We are all ritualists who perform actions that signify
ultimate order and meaning for us. These actions take many forms but are
often directed toward the love of an "other." How, after all, do we express
love? By a gift or offering, by a sacrifice, by words or care or adoration, by a
kiss, by an embrace, or by conjugal sexuality (which represents the union of
selves). Ultimately and religiously speaking, all love actions move "constantly
toward . . . the Supreme Person residing in every heart."

Bhakti yoga is the most universal of paths. In Hindu understanding, all of
us are in some way inclined in this direction, even if we are disciples of other

forms of yoga. We may all make offerings, call upon the name of an "Other," and swoon in the ecstasy of love. Whether it is out of fear or duty, devotion is a universal form of human behavior. We pay our respects to something or someone—we are devoted. The true disciple, the dedicated practitioner of this kind of behavior, seeks to perfect and purify his or her motives and acts of adoration and to be a true lover.

The most discussed form of American Hinduism is, of course, the International Society for Krishna Consciousness, more popularly known as the Hare Krishna movement. This is an Americanization of a *bhakti* tradition that originated in Bengal, India, in the sixteenth century. It emphasized that love and devotional service to Krishna as the supreme manifestation of God could lead to a realization of the true self *(atman)*, which was actually Krishna consciousness. The movement disregarded the importance of caste or station in life and sought to make its teachings available to all people. This Krishna consciousness movement was brought from India to America by Abhay Charan De Prabhupada, who spent most of his later life translating and writing commentaries on scriptural texts such as the *Bhagavad Gita*. Today there are many centers of this movement in the United States, with thousands of devotees.

Central to the raising of Krishna consciousness is the chanting of "Hare Krishna" as part of the practice of *sankirtana,* a form of passionate dance and singing of praises to Lord Krishna. This street dancing has been accompanied by book distribution and a form of preaching that has been shaped by the American propensity for the sharing of "evangelical" messages. Of course, the Hare Krishnas, as they are called, are also known for their distinctive Indian costumes of *dhotis* and *saris,* their shaven heads and sacred neck beads, and their vegetarian food.

The influence of Hinduism in the United States predates the Hare Krishna movement. Joseph Priestley came to America in 1794 from Great Britain. He considered himself a Unitarian and celebrated the "common essentials of all religions" (discussed previously in this chapter). Typical of many representatives of the American Enlightenment, he thought of morality as the sum and substance of religion. Priestley was instrumental in many of the scientific investigations of his era, and his religious thought sought to present a view of Christianity as the culmination of the perennial religious experience. The eighteenth century, as a result of voyages of trade and exploration and the writings of Orientalists like Sir William Jones, was a time of direct discovery of Asian religious traditions. In 1799, Priestley published *A Comparison of the*

Institutions of Moses with Those of the Hindoos and Other Ancient Nations.
Perplexed by many of the beliefs and "austere" practices of Hindus, Priestley
was interested in certain attributes of Hinduism that could be considered
inferior to the greater moral perfection of the biblical traditions.

"As to the natural or moral disposition," he wrote, "there is no intimation
in the Scriptures or the writings of Moses, of women being inferior to men."
In this regard, Priestley was particularly bewildered by the Indian practice of
suttee, in which a woman burned herself with her husband's corpse as a ritual embodiment of her oneness with him in paradise. Priestley may be considered one of the forerunners of the study of comparative religions in the
United States, a form of religious studies prevalent until well into the twentieth century. Those who used this method of study usually sought to compare
other traditions with Christianity, imposing categories like God, creation,
and salvation (all derived from Christian teaching) as standards for evaluat-
ing other cultures and traditions. This concept of comparative religion was
highly suspect after World War II and was succeeded by what has come to be
known as religious studies, which seek to investigate religious phenomena
from the perspective of the cultural contexts in which they occur.

Many Americans had their curiosity roused at the World's Parliament of
Religions in 1893, when Swami Vivekananda began to speak of the ancient
philosophical system called Vedanta, "the concluding portions of the Vedas."
These treatises encouraged an intellectual exploration of the implications of
the basic notion of *Brahman–atman.* Vedantic Hinduism became highly
speculative and philosophical, tending to ignore or downplay the significance
of other forms of religious expression. Many Americans found solace and
excitement in these ideas, joining Vedanta societies. In the 1920s, Parama-
hansa Yogananda arrived from India with an appeal to the American penchant for techniques and results. He was more interested in yogic practices
than in Vedantic speculation. Basing his efforts on the ancient yoga sutras
(texts having to do with principles) of Patanjali, Yogananda advocated ideas
and techniques designed to help direct our lives toward a realization of the
divine joy and power that constitute our true selves. Thus began the work of
the Self Realization Fellowship Centers, which represent another form of
Hindu religiousness in the American setting.

The great Hindu epic *Mahabharata,* of which the *Bhagavad Gita* is a part,
cites 270 places of sacred pilgrimage in ancient India. "Just as certain limbs of
the body are purer than the others," reads the great epic, "so are certain places
on earth more sacred—some on account of their situation, others because of

the association of saintly people with them, or the habitation of sages in them." Pilgrimage became a prominent feature of Hindu life, translated to the United States as temples like the Sri Ganesha in Flushing, New York, and the Sri Venkateswara in Pittsburgh, Pennsylvania, were dedicated in the late 1970s.

There are probably three quarters of a million Hindus in the United States today. Of course, the effect of Hinduism in American religion and culture cannot be measured by a survey of membership, organizations, and movements. Our literature, art, and music have been influenced by Hindu concepts of ultimate reality and self-realization. Even some forms of Christian theology have been influenced by ideas and metaphors drawn from the scriptures and metaphysics of the Hindu world. Americans have always been very utilitarian, seeking schemes, techniques, and systems that will serve their desire for success and achievement. Hindu notions of self-realization are especially open to Americanization. The American is a positive thinker who assumes knowledge of the self is what it needs. To the Americans, self-realization means the acquisition of those qualities and techniques that promise wealth and success as ordinarily understood. The Hindu concept of self-realization, on the other hand, speaks finally of a self that is realized quite beyond our ordinary expectations and desires. Hinduism appeals to the American public religious conviction that there are "common essentials to all religions." There is, after all, in Hinduism a tolerance of all paths that lead to the good. Hinduism is not one tradition, but many. Its unity is found in the conviction that beneath all diversity there is only one reality. Sometimes tolerance is less an affair of honoring another person and more a failure to achieve any perspective from which to discern or discriminate. What remains to be seen is whether the toleration and civility required of us in a radically pluralistic society has sacrificed the integrity necessary to the good life. We may, after all, respect another person, while discerning the error of his or her ideas and judgment.

Buddhism in America

Even more significant than Hinduism to the contemporary American religious landscape is the sister tradition of Buddhism. The origins of this religious system are to be found in India, indeed in Hinduism itself. But Buddhism very soon became as much an emissary as it is an exemplary tradition. It was the missionary ventures of Buddhism into China, Tibet, Korea, and Japan that diversified the system and gave it the energy and provocativeness that make it so powerful an influence in American religion and culture today.

Asian traditions tend not to lend themselves to statistical evaluation. As in the case of Hinduism, the success of Buddhism is not to be observed in the membership roles of the temples and teaching centers. Quantitative and statistical measures are an American affectation. In the nineteenth century the United States was an open and driven society. Competition and the struggles for achievement and success required organization; organization called for membership and support. However, the real success of a religious tradition may well be discerned in the manner in which it affects the social system and the cultural effects of a people. After all, Catholic Christianity's real success is observed in the way in which it shaped the European mind; revivalistic evangelicalism's success is observed in the American social and cultural fabric. In many respects the United States has been Christianized evangelically even though not all Americans are members of evangelical churches. Of course, the success of a religion is also observable in the cultic and ritual habits of the "folk." In places like Japan, for example, people engage in Buddhist rites with little regard to whether they are Buddhists. Many wayside shrines in Taiwan are popularly known as Buddhist even though they are primarily Taoist.

The emissary travels of Buddhism, from India through other parts of Asia, brought it into contact with both the folk religious practices of the local peoples and the great systemic traditions like Taoism and Confucianism. Although Buddhism has its origins in Indian thought and language, its history is rich with other influences. In the United States today, Tibetan and Japanese Buddhism gain considerable attention from intellectuals, academics, and potential devotees.

It is necessary to ask whether it is possible to generalize about Buddhism and especially to try to sum up its Japanese and Tibetan features. To some Americans, Buddhism is a sophisticated system of concepts, of ideas. American intellectuals tend to be fascinated with the apparent freshness and profundity of Buddhist insight—particularly those derived from Japanese Zen and Tibetan tantrism. In one sense this is a rather curious phenomenon when we discover that the heart of Buddhism denies the significance and reality of concepts and ideas. The tradition shares with its Hindu parentage a conviction concerning the illusory character of ordinary rationality. Ordinary rationality is the activity of the empirical ego, which is deluded selfhood.

Of course, the contemporary intellectual tends to ignore the fact that he or she is a ritual being and a social reality as well as a conceptual creature, and he or she is often content to think that ideas are exclusive and self-justifying, far superior to ritual and community. If this is so, he or she will never understand religion, including even Zen Buddhism, and will probably never attain any significant degree of religious maturity. Zen Buddhism, for all of its denial of religion and ordinary rationality, is a tradition that includes ritual and community. As a matter of fact, it is necessary to point out that the success of the Zen master's enterprise is dependent upon ritual activity and process. Both Zen meditation and the use of the *koan,* a nonrational statement meant to break through the rational ego, are themselves rituals and are used ritualistically. However, it is at a much more mundane level that we would observe ritual at work. A visit to many Zen temples in Japan will reveal the use of Buddha images and ritual prayer. The grounds of the temples generally contain special shrines and altars, devoted to certain gods and goddesses of the Buddhist pantheon. Images of Jizo, beloved god and friend of little children, is frequently decorated with prayers to aborted fetuses, offered by women who beg the forgiveness of these souls who were never permitted birth into this stage of the karmic journey.

At the heart of Buddhism is the experience of enlightenment. In the middle of the sixth century B.C.E., a young man named Siddartha Gautama broke away from the sumptuous life of his princely birth, shaved his head, donned the ragged clothes of a monk, and became a "forest-dweller," in search of illumination. This was a custom among his people in northern India. He studied *raja* yoga and philosophy and joined a band of ascetics who mortified the body in hope of enlightenment. He learned the principle of the Middle Way, which moves between the extremes of indulgences and severe asceticism. It was in this state of hopelessness, of disappointment in the established paths, that he began a period of contemplation that included the visitation of great temptations. Then one night in May, his mind suddenly broke through the veil of the universe, perceiving things as they really are. He found himself transformed, seeing into the heart of reality itself the world of nature perceived for the first time. For a total of forty-nine days he was rooted in the bliss of this grand illumination. So goes the story that serves as the paradigm out of which the grand traditions of Buddhism emerge. Gautama becomes the Buddha—the Enlightened One, the *Tathagatha*—the one who has been visited by the Truth.

After his enlightenment, the Buddha began teaching all sorts of conditions of humanity. But first he shared the insights he had gained with some old colleagues in a sermon delivered at Isipatana, near Benares. Known traditionally as the Deer Park Sermon or the Sermon at Benares, the discourse may well be like the Sermon on the Mount of Jesus, a later compilation of teachings that are considered by the faithful to be the beginning and core of the tradition. The Deer Park Sermon shares the Four Noble Truths. First is the Noble Truth of Suffering, the discovery that existence is *dukkha*—the unhappiness of sickness, old age, dying, and the sadness of observing loved ones who experience these conditions. The second Noble Truth is that suffering *(dukkha)* has its origins in desire or selfish craving. This *tanha* (craving) has many manifestations and gives rise to suffering and to continued rebirth on the karmic wheel of being. *Tanha* is due to the illusion that *atman* (self) actually exists, an illusion that the empirical self is a reality worth sustaining. This illusion leads us to ask, to demand, more of the universe than it is prepared to give; hence, our unhappiness. The third Noble Truth is that there is liberation from suffering, from the ongoingness of *dukkha*. When one eliminates *tanha*, one has discerned nirvana; or, more accurately, destruction of *tanha* leads to the cessation of reality as we have known it—inasmuch as reality as we have known it is characterized by an empirical self engaged in craving that leads to suffering. Nirvana in this sense is nothingness, nonbeing, and incapable of definition, inasmuch as all definition is the activity of the illusory empirical self. It should be evident that nirvana is not to be identified with Christian or Muslim images of paradise or heaven.

The fourth Noble Truth is the path of the Middle Way out of the terrible wilderness of *dukkha*. Gautama, the Buddha, discovered this Middle Way between the extreme of hedonistic search for the pleasure of the senses and the other extreme of the search for happiness through painful self-mortification. The Middle Way is an Eightfold Path of Right Understanding, Right Thought, Right Speech, Right Action, Right Livelihood, Right Effort, Right Mindfulness, and Right Concentration. Here we have the heart of the verbal expression of Buddhism. Note that in this theoretical realm Buddhism requires no doctrine of God. One might say it is atheistic in that it does not concern itself with God. In a real sense, to believe in God or not to believe in God is of little or no consequence to the verbal expression of Buddhism. The Eightfold Path, examined as a mere list of doctrinal directives, seems rather trite, even moralistic. To the American mind it may seem like a very ordinary set of admonitions, a rather preachy counsel to "get with it." Here we can say that this would be a faulty understanding of the Eightfold Path. What it adds up to, really, is that the way out, the cessation of *dukkha*, requires discipline— an intense directedness of mind and action. To travel the Eightfold Path is to submit to guidance. There is not only the teaching itself *(dharma)*, but also the Enlightened One (Buddha) and the community of disciples *(sangha)*, to whom the pilgrim must turn for refuge and direction. But, of course, the person who seeks the cessation of *dukkha* eventually discovers that there is no authority (not even the Buddha himself) other than the freedom that is necessary for each person to realize the Truth in himself.

In the history of religions we quickly learn that every religious path is a life of paradox. Essential Truth is free of all texts and priests and teachers and Buddhas, but the texts, priests, teachers, and Buddhas are an inevitable necessity. The tradition of the elders of the Buddhist way soon became part of the history of Buddhism. It prepared many texts and scriptures, usually called sutras, which preserved the wisdom of the Way and even speculated upon the philosophical nuances of the Four Noble Truths and the Eightfold Path. Eventually a question arose as to whether a person should be concerned only with his or her own Buddhahood, or whether the profound mindfulness and compassion that one discovered was to be shared with others. The person who experienced enlightenment knew the end of suffering but at the same time felt compassion for those who were ignorant of the Four Noble Truths.

Those Buddhists who decided they had a mandate from Gautama Buddha himself to postpone their own ultimate realization of nirvana for the sake of a suffering world became known as the disciples of the Mahayana—the Greater Vehicle, the teachings concerning the compassionate sharing of the world's suffering. Followers of Mahayana suffer for the world and hope to lead people to an understanding of the Four Noble Truths. From this Mahayana tradition there emerged a number of Buddha-like figures who became known as bodhisattvas—those whose essence *(sattva)* was perfected wisdom or enlightenment *(bodhi)*.

Meanwhile the tradition of the elders continued to focus upon the perfected wisdom of the disciple, upon a continued renunciation of the world for the sake of nirvana. This was Theravada Buddhism, centered upon monastic existence, and known as the Hinayana (lesser vehicle) by the followers of Mahayana. It was the latter tradition of Buddhism that made its way into China, Tibet, Korea, and eventually Japan. From the Mahayana world of the bodhisattvas have come the teachings that have most affected the climate of American religion in the twentieth century.

Before discussing briefly the forms of Mahayana teaching most prominent in America today, it is necessary to qualify a previous statement that the verbal expression of Buddhism has little concern for the doctrine of God.

Two factors must be considered. First, the late twentieth century was the time for considerable dialogue between Buddhist and Christian thinkers. It is impossible to engage in very profound thought on religious matters East and West without coming upon the question of God. This has resulted in the discovery that much of what certain Christian thinkers mean by God comes close to the theories of *sunyata* (emptiness) and Ground of Being that are part of Buddhist thought. The implications are exciting, but we cannot discuss them here. The atheism of the Buddhist Way is qualified by the fact that no religious tradition functions only on the theoretical level. We are aware by now that the practical expression of our religiousness asserts itself in many ways, even among the most verbal and highly speculative of persons. We express our religiousness in ritual action and direct our senses toward their own transcendence. That is, we express very transcendent and nonrational truths by means of images and other sensory creations like perfume and incense. Masses of people, for whom the time and inclination for understanding the Four Noble Truths are inadequate, will turn to statuary, to physical images of Buddhahood for energy and consolation. And that will likely also be true of those who "drop ashes on the Buddha"—who agree with Buddhist theory about the non-necessity of God and the insignificance of texts and teachers and images. For all of us seem to belong to the masses even if we may be numbered among an elite body *(sangha)* who take seriously the discipline of personal responsibility.

Those individuals who have arrived at an advanced stage of spiritual realization, who become bodhisattvas, eventually become like the gods of old. We revere their images and pray to them for assistance and comfort. They are, after all, the compassionate ones and the fundamental need of human beings is most assuredly that of compassion.

Tibetan Buddhism has fashioned its own version of the teachings of compassion. Each level or facet of sentient reality has a capacity for compassion. The highest *lama* is an incarnation of compassion, but so also is the most menial laborer. Reality consists of a chain of compassion that we must learn to understand and to realize. All of us may learn to respond to the chain. We actually do so by recognizing the presence of compassion in those people who are greater manifestations of this force than most of us. These people are the *tulkus* and lamas, who share compassion and provide opportunity for the greater enlightenment of the rest of us.

It has even been said that Tibetan society is structured in such a way that it is a vehicle of Buddhahood. That is to say, when the *tulku* learns to bring his or her ordinary existence into conformity with his or her position in the chain of compassion, the society itself is a world of salvation, of enlightenment. In that society will be those teachers who assist all levels of people to refine their positions in the scale of Buddhahood. There are forms of knowledge and practice that are appropriate to each level on which an individual moves in his effort to respond to the forces of compassion that are incarnate in him. This means that there are "esoteric" teachings that are a profound recognition of the spiritual truth that some knowledge and practice is not for mass appeal or consumption. In other words, certain teachings and practices remain secret (esoteric) until the individual is ready to receive them.

This esoteric emphasis in Tibetan Buddhism gives it an air of mystery and magic, which is often intriguing to the curious minds of America. Tibet has come to America. Since the Chinese occupation of Tibet there has been a suppression of the Tibetan social structure, and Tibetan society, as we have seen, is a sacred society. The Dalai Lama, highest incarnation of compassion, has traditionally been supreme governor of the holy society. He has been forced to flee his homeland, lives in exile in India, and travels widely, sharing his wisdom and compassion with a troubled world. Only the pope of Roman Catholicism is a more universally respected spiritual leader. Of course, many teachers and thinkers have left Tibet, concerned to preserve the great tradition of their homeland and pass the teachings on to those who are prepared to learn. What concerns many of the teachers is the fact that the Tibetan way is undergoing profound alteration. In Tibet it was an organic way, a tradition expressed in the total structure of society and culture. In traditional Tibet the way of compassion is at once spiritual, political, and economic. In the United States, Tibetan Buddhism is a set of teachings that must be passed on to individuals. In the United States, Tibet must conform to the privatistic state of modern religion, a state in which the public dimensions of our religiousness are left to chance and to the totalitarian power of the techno-corporate order.

There are several schools of Tibetan Buddhism. It is a very complex tradition, too complicated for adequate representation in this chapter. Buddhism is a tradition of many texts. The Tibetan tradition claims to go even beyond the "great" vehicle of Mahayana and to be Vajrayana, the highest and most advanced vehicle. Vajrayana teachings are found in texts called tantras, which deal with esoteric ideas and practices. Such texts, like the sutras (primarily philosophical in content) common to all of Buddhism, contain a tradition believed to have come from the time of Buddha himself. The Venerable Chogyam Trungpa Rinpoche, a teacher of the Kagyu-pa order of Tibetan

Buddhism, came to Boulder, Colorado, in 1970, where he established an emissary program for the conversion of Americans to Buddhism. In 1974 Trungpa Rinpoche founded the Naropa Institute, an accredited university, making Boulder a major American center for the study of Vajrayana teachings.

The other Buddhist tradition that has made an impact on American religion comes from Japan. It has come to the United States under circumstances very different from those that have given access to the Tibetan teachings. Zen Buddhism has delighted American audiences and charmed the minds of many American intellectuals since the early part of the twentieth century. Many Zen thinkers make haste to inform us that Zen is not religion, that its truth and practice may be helpful to any religion or no religion.

Many of the pioneer Zen teachers from Japan thought there was something about the Zen spirit that found a natural home in the pragmatic soil of the United States. Zen is a tradition concerned with eliminating all expectations and attachments that prevent us from getting done what has to be done. We can see how receptive Americans would be to such a conception. We are the nation of positive thinkers, of those who want simple and accessible skills—we seek whatever is essential to success and happiness.

When the history of American Zen is written, we shall be able to determine whether the United States shaped Zen more than Zen shaped the United States. Certainly Zen Buddhism at its most sophisticated level is not to be equated with American pragmatism and positive thinking. To the extent that this nation has become the "happy field" of Zen, it may no longer be true to the essence of Zen. For one thing, there is a certain austerity to Zen. The *Roshi* (master) is a demanding teacher, whose ways are puzzling to the outsider and the new initiate. At times he or she is lighthearted to the point of not taking the disciple seriously. At other times he or she may seem cruel and uncaring. It is the *Roshi*'s responsibility to determine the degree of commitment present in those who come to him or her for guidance. The disciple who truly seeks enlightenment *(satori)* will persist even though he or she has been harassed or told to go home.

Zen is the Japanese translation of the Chinese *Ch'an,* roughly translated as "meditation." *Ch'an* was a form of Chinese Buddhism imported to Japan probably in the late twelfth and early thirteenth centuries. There were elements of Taoism in this Chinese tradition. However, in Japan it developed in such a way that it emphasized the ultimate frivolity and impossibility of all forms of attachment. Zen is meditation that is directed toward breaking through our attachments to ordinary mind, ordinary perception, ordinary sensation. When the disciple finally discerns the reality of constant and cease-less change and sees that "form is emptiness, emptiness is form," his or her ordinary mind is transcended—he or she is one with the emptiness out of which everything emerges. This is the moment of enlightenment. It is equiv-alent to what Gautama Buddha discovered; therefore, it is the discernment of the Buddha-nature that we all share—the reality we resist by our attachment to ordinary mind and sensation.

There are two basic schools of Zen, one called *Soto,* the other *Rinzai.* The former school emphasizes the practice of *zazen*—just sitting. Reading the sutras, listening to lectures, studying, chanting, and participating in certain detailed rituals are all part of the total discipline. But "just sitting," usually in the *zendo* (meditation hall) on small black cushions called *zafus,* is the heart of *Soto* tradition. The rigors of *zazen* may finally lead to experience that is not the experience of something, but the absolute encounter with reality itself. Zen knows that experience *of* something, however noble or seemingly good, is simply another form of possession or attachment that hinders experience itself, preventing us from "seeing" things as they really are.

Rinzai Zen is the way of the *koan,* the use of very puzzling statements or questions that are designed to force the disciple to the point of frustration with ordinary reasoning. The master will insist on resolution of the *koan.* He or she will ask questions of the disciple in order to reveal the ultimate futility of reliance upon the hold of the mind. There is no "answer" to the riddle, no solution to the puzzle, but the discipline of trying to solve the *koan* is essen-tial. At a certain moment there will be *satori,* and the mental exercises will have forced the initiate to see the truth of the co-dependent origination of all that is.

Those who understand the tradition often speak of it as Zen and not as Zen Buddhism. However, by means of this dialectical device they merely wish to remind us that Zen is attached to no "religion," no system, no set of sacred teaching. Yet we must remember that the "enlightened" heart of most of the great traditions would agree that the goal of any religion (all tradition) is the end of religion. However, among the masses of people, religion furnishes things and convictions to cling to, as one clings to a log in the raging river. And many Zen practitioners and devotees who visit the Zen temples of Japan are people for whom the ritual ways of Zen are used as consolations for the living of these days. Historically speaking, of course, it is impossible to understand the formation of Zen teaching and practice without perceiving it in the lineage of Buddhist tradition.

One of the greatest of religious teachers of the twentieth century was Daisetz Teitaro Suzuki, a follower of Soyen Shaku, who influenced the thinking of many Americans with his many lectures and publications. The great Roman Catholic monastic and Trappist hermit Thomas Merton was profoundly affected by Suzuki's genius for interpreting Zen (and other forms of Buddhism) for the United States. Writers Alan Watts and Gary Snyder also became important interpreters of an American Zen, deeply influenced by Suzuki. In the United States today there are centers in most major cities devoted to the nurture of Zen practice. But the effect of Zen on America cannot be measured by the membership of centers, or even by the participation of Americans in Zen workshops and institutes. Many of our intellectuals, including Christian theologians and Jewish thinkers, have taken kindly to Zen. Its assumptions have worked their way into our literature and art. It may be the single most important influence on Christian theology in the latter half of the twentieth century. That is partly because Zen offers philosophical direction and spiritual discipline for Christian thought, which has lost its affinity for Western philosophy but needs some kind of philosophy to clarify and communicate the Christian faith. In addition to Merton's efforts in this direction there are the writings of John Cobb and the popular works *Zen Catholicism* and *Zen Christianity* by Aelred Graham and William Johnston, both members of Roman Catholic religious orders. Many other authors and thinkers could be added to the list of explorers.

What some have called "church" Buddhism came to the United States from Japan at the turn of the twentieth century. It arrived through the efforts of missionaries of a branch of what is called Pure Land Buddhism. This form of Buddhism resembles Christianity and is thought by many to be a Buddhism parallel to Lutheranism. Pure Land doctrine emphasizes a faithful relationship to Amida Buddha, a bodhisattva who established a "Western paradise" known as the Pure Land. Amida makes it possible for people to enter the Pure Land and experience enlightenment through trust in his great compassion. In this form of Mahayana Buddhism no meditational discipline or moral perfection is required of practitioners. Instead, they lead a life of grateful response to Amida's compassion, using a mantra, *"Namu Amida Butsu"* (I put my faith in Amida Buddha), which is chanted in order to direct the person to Amida's gift of salvation. The *nembutsu* practice is the heart of Pure Land Buddhism. The Lotus Sutra, one of the most beloved of Mahayana scriptures, maintains that we are in a period of sin and decay, a time when it is difficult to practice the pure and original *dharma.* Therefore, a latter-day *dharma* permits this path to the Pure Land, where the way of enlightenment is available as it is not in this life. The Jodo-Shin branch of Pure Land Buddhism has taken on many of the characteristics of Protestant Christianity. It is known in this country in a denominational form called the Buddhist Churches of America, where it tends to develop forms of polity similar to its Christian neighbors.

In Japan and the United States, many new religions emerged during the late 1950s and through the decade of the 1960s. They were partly a response to the new pluralism facing the world after World War II, an attempt to discover meaning and community in societies that were disoriented by the effects of modernity. Often these religions sought to restore a sense of peoplehood and national religious significance to a world in which social identity seemed a thing of the past. Many of the new religions are concerned with unifying a fragmented world or providing a renewed sense of the divine significance of certain lands, nations like Korea or Japan. These religions tend not to be entirely "new," rather to focus on the charismatic power of a leader or to represent a new arrangement of eclectic teachings from folk practices and world religions. One of the most important of these new religions is the Holy Spirit Association for the Unification of World Christianity, known more familiarly as the "Moonies" or the Unification Church. This is a tradition that has shown remarkable intellectual power, even as it appears to be a bearer of political and economic conservatism. The Unification movement requires serious study by students of American religion.

However Unificationism does not belong to our survey of Buddhism in America. We close that discussion by calling attention to Nichiren Shoshu, which came to America as a missionary movement after World War II. Nichiren's original teachings go back to the great Kamakura period of Japanese history (1185–1333), in which the Zen, Pure Land, and Nichiren movements were founded. Nichiren advocated praise to the Lotus Sutra, rather than to Amida Buddha. As is the case with the emergence of many new traditions, Nichiren sought to find a way out of the apparent conflict resulting from the claims of competing sects. Eventually the "way out" became an additional sect. However, the monk called Nichiren (1222–82) believed that Japanese Buddhism, particularly in its Pure Land schools, was turning too much to "other power" rather than "self power." Instead it should praise the Lotus Sutra with its teaching of the fundamental law by means of which all that is exists. By revering the Lotus Sutra the individual would discover true selfhood in the Buddha-nature shared by all.

As part of Japan's postwar revival, Nichiren Buddhism was given new vigor in the birth of a lay movement called Soka Gakkai that sought to restore self-esteem within the defeated nation. The movement became militant and intense, and it captured the minds of many young Americans who were seeking a simple message that would enable them to live prosperously and securely in a threatening world. The response to Nichiren Shoshu, with its chant to the Lotus Sutra and use of a Gohozon altar in devotion to the Sutra, is not unlike the response of Americans to a simple evangelical Christian gospel that brings God's favor and a new life of dedication to prosperity and happiness. A schism in Nichiren Shoshu occurred in 1991; Soka Gakkai members were excommunicated for ignoring and slandering the authority of the priesthood. Even so, Soka Gakkai remains strong in the United States, with more than sixty centers and upward of 50,000 followers, making it a small but established and growing institution. Although somewhat foreign to the Christian substance of American religion, Nichiren shares much of our religious spirit—our devotion to positive thinking and immediate democratic religion.

New Thought and the New Age

Since World War II our religious life has been altered by the incursion of Asian ideas and movements. There has also been a rebirth of the New Thought movements discussed previously. The ideas and practices of theosophy, with its return to ancient and Asian texts and occult wisdom, have found new vigor in the postmodern era. These movements are themselves strangely American and very eclectic, drawing from a variety of sources to fashion an experience that will excite the imagination and provide solace to a distressful world. We are familiar with the "channeling" techniques made popular by such persons as the actress and author Shirley MacLaine. Some of MacLaine's books have been bestsellers, selling in supermarkets, drugstores, and airport shops. They belong to the New Thought and positive thinking traditions of American religion, filled as they are with Hindu, spiritualist, and even Native American notions of communication with a vast force of personal and impersonal energy that joins the living and the dead in creative interaction. However, they are primarily concerned with equipping people with the spiritual power to get what they want out of life.

The academic study of religion must begin to take these elements of popular religiousness more seriously. They are part of American spirituality, telling us about ourselves and demonstrating the shaping religious power of the American experience itself. From belief in anything from Scientology to flying saucers to channeling, we are a very religious people in this modern age—no less than in the past.

There are many traditions we must pass by in this introduction to contemporary American religiousness and leave the reader to discover on an individual basis. Many movements and traditions share characteristics; all of them take into themselves the effects of the American religious experience. They will likewise make their contribution to that experience, perpetuating some of our religious idiosyncrasies and altering others.

Islam in America Today

In this age of radical pluralism, we have rather suddenly become aware of the presence of Islam in the American religious landscape. Out of India, Malaysia, Pakistan, Africa, and the Arab nations of what is often called the Middle East have come vast numbers of immigrants and students who share the traditions of the last of God's messengers, the Prophet Muhammad. Although the United States Bureau of the Census does not permit the compilation of religious data on the people of our republic, it is estimated that the number of Muslim immigrants and their descendants ranges between two and four million. However, Seyyed Hossein Nasr in his book *The Heart of Islam* states, "There are . . . some 6 million [Muslims] in America."[1] The Islamic movement, as we may know, began in the arid wilderness of the Arabian peninsula. However, it rather quickly outgrew its desert environment, taking its sacred Arab message first into North Africa, Persia (Iran), Asia Minor, and eventually into southern Europe, the Indian subcontinent, and southeast Asia. Those parts of the world were neither Arab-speaking nor Arabian culture. Nevertheless, the sacred language (Arabic) and culture of Arabia have followed wherever Allah has led the faithful.

At the heart of Islam is the Qur'an, a sacred text revealed to a man known as Muhammad some time after the turn of the seventh century of the Common Era. The sacred text was delivered to him one night by a voice from heaven while he meditated in a cave. It was the angel Gabriel who told Muhammad he must "recite," he must "cry" the power of God. There were two words to "cry," but there were many implications to recognize. *"La Illa'ha Illa'lah!"* (There is no god but the God [Al'lah]!) is the first word. The second is: *"Muhammadar rasulu 'llah!"* (Muhammad is the messenger of Allah!).

Those two elements are the heart of the verbal expression of Islam. They are also at the center of Islamic practice, for together they make up what is known as the *shahada,* the first of the five pillars of Muslim faith and practice. The *shahada* means witness, and the faithful Muslim will witness to the truths regularly. Five times a day the call to prayer is heard from the minarets of Islamic mosques. It begins with the words *"Allahu akbar"*—God is the greatest—then gives witness that there is no God but Allah and Muhammad is Allah's prophet.

In 114 chapters or *surahs,* the Qur'an shares the words that came to the messenger of Allah over twenty-three years, through voices that became identified with the angel Gabriel. There are those who say it is the sound of the words that gives such power to a book that must be sounded, recited, cried, not merely read in meditative silence. Just as Christianity speaks of the miracle of God's self-revelation in the son of a "lowly handmaiden" among the poor, so Muslims marvel that the unschooled Muhammad should have been the vehicle of the revelation of all the words that are necessary to human life. "Ask you a greater miracle than this, O unbelieving people! than to have your vulgar tongue chosen as the language of that incomparable Book, one piece of which puts to shame all your golden poesy and suspended songs?" There is a profound aesthetic and charismatic effect that is conveyed by the rhythm and music of the language of the Qur'an being recited. Muslims insist that the book cannot be translated; the wisdom and power of Allah's revelation lie in the Arabic words delivered to the Prophet.

In Muslim thought, Muhammad is the "Seal of the Prophets." The truth of God had been revealed to Moses, to Jesus, and to other prophets before Muhammad. However, Jews and Christians compromised between the human and the divine—they put the Law and the Incarnation between themselves and the powerful, unified, and invisible God. Accordingly, it became necessary for God to select a prophet who would be the Messenger to put an end to this faithlessness by revealing the dictated words of God himself.

Those elements of the practical expression of religion that hold up the world of Islam are the five pillars. *Shahada* is the first. The second pillar is *Salat,* the performance of the five daily prayers, done while facing in the direction of Mecca. At midday on Fridays the people must assemble at a mosque for these prayers, at which time a sermon is also heard. The Muslim is also required to give thanks to Allah by giving alms *(Zakat)* for the less fortunate of the world; this is the third pillar. The fourth is *Siyam* or fasting. Although this practice may be performed at any time, it is essential that it be done during the ninth month, Ramadan. One fasts each day, refraining from food, drink, and sexual relations from just before sunrise to just after sunset. The fifth pillar is the *Hajj* or pilgrimage to Mecca that should be made by all Muslims at least once in their lifetimes. *Hajj* takes place sometime from the beginning of the tenth month and the middle of the twelfth month. The pilgrimage links together Muslims of many ethnic, national, and racial backgrounds. Upon reaching their holy city, the pilgrims remove their usual clothes and wear white seamless garments. All traces of rank, wealth, and other social distinction are removed. (The American Malcolm X was transformed by the power and drama of this pilgrimage experience and sought to reform the black Islamic movement in the United States by bringing it into harmony with orthodox Islam.)

Pilgrimage is, of course, a very universal human experience. All cultures and religious traditions have discovered the holiness, the sacredness, of special places. There is within us a deeply felt need to visit a place where an unusual event occurred, where a spirited person lived. There are certainly parallels in visits to shrines where the Virgin Mother of Jesus appeared in vision and to Graceland, the mansion of the late twentieth-century pop hero Elvis Presley. To some of us it may seem the height of indecency or sacrilege to mention them in the same sentence, but it is a fact that people derive a sense of ultimate order and meaning for their lives by such visitations. Pilgrimages also offer opportunities to withdraw from the routinality of existence, to do penance, to gain new perspective, to find healing, and to make past events present—all of it perfectly understandable religious behavior.

A person who maintains the five pillars of Islam is a Muslim, knows *Allahu akbar,* that "God is the greatest," and surrenders to that god. In submission the Muslim finds peace. (Islam means "surrender," "peace," "doing what one is supposed to do." He who does so is a "surrenderer," a Muslim.)

The verbal expression of Islam includes doctrines of "the Last Day" and "predestination," which are similar to tenets in certain schools of Christianity. In the case of Calvinist Christianity, we have discovered that a doctrine of God that permits little continuity between the Creator and created—God as absolute Sovereign—requires some notion of election and predestination. Human destiny is entirely in the hands of the sovereign God, who chooses those who are to share the joys of paradise. We can but surrender to God's will.

The verbal and practical expressions of Islam include extra-Qur'anic tradition *(hadith)* that is attributed to the Prophet Muhammad. This tradition is the *Sunna,* and the main body of Islamic following is known by the term *Sunni.* A considerable minority of Muslims are known as *Shiites,* found in Iran, Iraq, parts of other Islamic countries, and recently in the United States. The Shiites are supporters of the spiritual leadership of the descendants of Ali, cousin and son-in-law of Muhammad. Shiite leaders tend to combine their teaching authority with strong social and political authority. To them it is important that the will of Allah be evident in all human affairs. Sunni Muslims would not disagree with the fundamental aims of the Shiites. In basic faith and practice there is little difference. Of course, many centuries of controversy have shaped a different perception of the world for Sunni and Shiite Muslims.

Although the five pillars are the heart of Muslim devotion, the concept of *jihad* has been prominent in the tradition from earliest times. *Jihad* refers to "struggle" and "striving." The Muslim is expected to struggle internally and constantly on behalf of his or her own realization of the *Shariah*—the Islamic Path as revealed in the Qur'an and the hadiths that preserve the ideas and practices of the Messenger of God. Sometimes *jihad* is interpreted as external striving for Islam in order to defend it against its enemies. "Fight in the way of God against those who fight against you," says the Qur'an (2:190), "but begin not hostilities. Verily God loveth not aggressors." This scriptural reference serves as the basis for judging the justification of *jihad* as holy warfare. Traditionally the head of the Islamic state in consultation with the *ulama* (religious scholars) determine the necessity of declaring *jihad* as warfare. However, in the contemporary world, there has emerged considerable tension between Western techno-corporate society and Islamic peoples who find their civilization threatened. In these circumstances a variety of individuals and movements have espoused *jihad* without recourse to the classical search for legitimacy. "Let not hatred of a people cause you to be unjust," reads the Qur'an (5:8). A legitimate external *jihad* is one conducted magnanimously on behalf of the truth and the Islamic faith, never for revenge or out of hatred and anger.

A word should be said about the social expression of Islam. The Islamic community is known as the *umma.* "There is no secret conference of three but He is their fourth, nor of five but He is their sixth, nor of less that or more but He is with them wheresoever they may be" (58:7). Allah is the center of the *umma* as well as of the individual. The truth embodied in the *shahadah* creates community. The intent of Allah's revelation to the Prophet was to form an interdependent body of those who live by the precepts of justice articulated in the Qur'an. Here we may observe a principle learned from the academic study of religion, and previously discussed—the social expression of human religiousness has been inseparable from the verbal and practical expressions. In some sense, the community comes into existence *prior* to the settlement of verbal expressions of belief, doctrines, and ritual practices. In Islam it is the *umma* that receives the revelations given to the Prophet Muhammad—they are his followers even as he receives the words of Allah. The *umma* exists antecedent to the completion of the teaching, although it also exists as a result of the teaching. The individual derives his or her identity and meaning as a part of the *umma*. This means that the social expression of the tradition is important religiously—perhaps as important as beliefs. Life is given ultimate order and meaning by being *part of, belonging to,* the community. It is this insight that assists us in understanding why people engage in external *jihad*—to maintain and preserve the *umma*, which is the foundation of meaningful existence.

The *umma* is a community of those who share certain teachings, commitments, stories, and practices. One may even "become" a Muslim because he observes the richness of the community and its discipline (which has often been the case among African Americans like Malcolm X). It is as religiously significant to find meaning as a part of the community as it is to know and affirm all of the beliefs. The *Shariah* is the straight path, the law of God, followed by the *umma*; it is a path of Divine Law, revealed in Qur'an and hadiths, and interpreted by the *ulama* throughout the course of Islamic history—which is the history of the *umma*.

John L. Esposito, director of the Center for Muslim-Christian Understanding at Georgetown University, reminds us that: "Alongside the exterior path of law *(sharia)* is the interior path or way *(tariqa)* of Sufi mysticism, a major popular religious movement within Sunni and Shii Islam. While the Sharia provided the exoteric way of duties and rights to order the life of the individual and community, Sufism offered an esoteric path or spiritual discipline, a method by which the Sufi sought not only to follow but to know God."[2] There is some scholarly controversy about whether Sufism pre-dates the origins of Islam in the seventh century of the Common Era. Within *dar-al-Islam* (abode of Islam), there are also those who reject Sufism because of its mystical tendencies and its supposed neglect of Sharia. Nevertheless, it is impossible to think of Islam without acknowledging this important element in Muslim history. Many Americans, not themselves officially Muslim, are attracted to Sufi spiritual discipline and the Sufi teaching that there is a tran-

scendent unity beyond all religious differences. Professor Jane I. Smith points
out that "the two most popular Sufi personages in the West in [the twentieth
century], Hazrat Inayat Khan and Idries Shah, have both seen Sufism as a
phenomenon distinguishable from the formal religious structure of Islam."[3]

It is entirely possible that some members of the crew of Christopher
Columbus were Muslims (called Moors) from the Iberian Peninsula. It is
also possible that some Moors found their way into the Caribbean after they
were exiled from Spain in 1492. Quite likely some of the involuntary immigrants to the Americas during the African slave trade were also Muslim or
influenced by Muslim ideas and practices derived from their African home-
lands. It is not difficult to acknowledge a very early Islamic presence in North
America.

Between 1875 and 1912 many refugees of the Ottoman Empire, perhaps
mostly Christian, emigrated from Syria, Jordan, and Lebanon, often to seek
to improve their economic well-being in industrial America. Cedar Rapids,
Iowa, is the site of an early Islamic mosque, completed in 1934. Cities like
New York and Chicago, along with urban areas of California have had sizable
Muslim inhabitants since early in the twentieth century, many of them immigrants from the Indian subcontinent. Although many of these early American Muslims sought to maintain their loyalty to the *Shariah,* they were a
minority in a Christian culture becoming increasingly secular and so were
often assimilated into the American Way. However, after World War II many
Muslims arrived as refugees from India, Pakistan, Eastern Europe, and the
Soviet Union. Islamic presence increased significantly after the elimination of
immigrant quotas in 1965.

It will be interesting to observe the formation of Islam in its American setting. In an open society shaped by two centuries of American denominationalism, we may expect that Islamic life in this republic may find it necessary to
emulate the institutional life of much American religion. Mosques will likely
take on the characteristics of our congregational life, offering programs for
diverse age groups, developing educational and social welfare enterprises in a
materialistic society somewhat inimical to the Islamic commitment to a
social and political order directed by the Divine Law.

Will Islamic feminism influence what Amanda Porterfield calls the "bla-
tant marketing of sexuality of Western culture in general and American culture in particular"?[4] Or will Islamic notions of the character of womanhood
be transformed by the dominant culture? Muslim women tend to assume
that the *Shariah* preserves sexual virtue and distinction by requiring them to

cover the skin and the hair. They point to the spuriousness of a liberation in which women accept their exploitation as sexual objects and have no way of transcending the values of a society that denies respectability and dictates our every thought and action.

The social memory of our nation is filled with images and ideas of Muslims, once called Muhammadans. Muslims, of course, are not Muhammadans, inasmuch as Muhammad does not have the same role in Islam as Christ has in Christianity. Christianity is Christ-centered; it is an encounter with Christ. Islam is Qur'an-centered, an encounter with the recited words of Allah. During much of the time between the eighth and twentieth centuries, the worlds of Christ and Qur'an have been in conflict. However, there have also been periods of creative encounter, and Muslim learning and scholarship during the late Middle Ages contributed much to philosophy, literature, the development of modern science, and even Christian theology. For America the perception of Islam was of a somewhat exotic and infidel world during much of our history.

In the 1960s that perception was altered by the emergence of an African American version of the tradition, known as the Nation of Islam. This movement was very much the product of the black experience in America itself. It combined notions of black separatism and black supremacy with certain Islamic teachings and practices. It was a militant movement, providing a sense of personal worth for many black people and helping them to assume responsibility for their economic and social well-being. The Nation of Islam was instrumental in the regeneration of one of twentieth-century America's most significant leaders, Malcolm X, who later discovered the absence of racism in orthodox Islam and acknowledged its superiority over the eclectic teachings and practices of the separatist African American Muslim movement. Since the days of Malcolm X the black Islamic movement has moved into greater conformity with orthodox Islam, opened its temples to whites, and become known as the World Community of al-Islam in the West.

Muslims from the Sunni and Shiite lands of Africa and the Middle East have been coming to America in large numbers, some to attend our colleges and universities, others to remain as citizens or as corporation and governmental representatives. How much will Islam in America be shaped by the institutional and theoretical characteristics of American religion? Most probably an American Islam will emerge, since America has a profound effect upon the shaping of any religious tradition.

The Reshaping of American Religion

Diana L. Eck, a professor at Harvard University, has subtitled her book, *A New Religious America,* "How a 'Christian Country' Has Become the World's Most Religiously Diverse Nation."[5] Eck asks whether the radical pluralism of contemporary America will somehow bring us together or tear us apart. Will Americans be able to learn from their separate traditions and still find ways of being grateful for the presence of other traditions—indeed, *learn* from these others? That is the essential question that pluralism raises. I have discussed these questions in my book *The Culture of Religious Pluralism,* agreeing with Sidney E. Mead, that "pluralism means . . . not only the division into many different . . . organizations and [religious] points of view, but also a state of mind instinctively defensive of it."[6] That is to say, as Eck suggests, that pluralism becomes either a state of conflict or an opportunity to find good in diversity. Needless to say, it is important that we learn the value of the tradition that has nurtured us, while acknowledging the value of diversity and our own willingness to learn from it. There is no tradition that does not have something to teach us about what it means to be human. As a matter of fact, every tradition in existence has already dealt with the problems of diversity and has something to teach us about our responsibilities to other traditions and their representative peoples.

However, it has also been true that we often conclude that following our own paths, our own shariahs, gospels, or torahs, excludes those of other paths, whom we must oppose or deny. Perhaps an initial stage in the discovery of people of other paths is one of opposition or conflict. That is because, as we have discussed repeatedly in this book, an essential element in the pursuit of ultimate order and meaning is the struggle for identity and belonging. Whatever else our religiousness seeks, it strives *(jihad)* for community and the sense of a meaningful place in the cosmos. Because we live not so much in a world as in a story of the world, we often defend the world whose story we live against all others. It is important to recognize and accept that fact, whether the religious world we inhabit is maintained by scientific, economic, political, or traditionally religious traditions. Human beings are always initially threatened and may rise to conflict with people with other stories, other traditions. However, the sensitive and intellectually astute individual eventually plumbs the depth of his religious world, where he or she reaches out to learn from others.

The story of religion in America is filled with episodes in which the discovery of other pathways resulted in conflict, often violent. No one wants his or her world threatened. Traditional peoples, like Native Americans and Africans, have always eventually learned that every story includes a multiplicity of stories (read again the accounts of the Seneca "storytelling stone" and the African tale of Kacou Ananzé, and remember that these are not "just" stories). Somehow it becomes necessary to be loyal to the particular history and truth of our own stories and traditions, while acknowledging the universal and creative human genius at work in the diverse pursuit *and discovery* of ultimate order and meaning.

American religion, as the heart of American culture, is undergoing a radical reshaping. Yet it is the story of persistent reshaping from the beginning of our history, coincident with the rise of the modern world. It is not only, as Diana Eck reads it, that "America has always been a land of many religions," but that we have often been interested in spirituality rather than "organized religion," even as we have constructed the most unique set of religious institutions in history. Our religious life has existed in a state of restructuring freedom, provided by an isolated continent and an unfenced frontier. Freedom is not a static concept. We are always discovering what freedom means in the changing contexts of our life together as a people. Freedom is constantly being restructured—it obviously does not mean what it meant to Benjamin Franklin, Jonathan Edwards, Mercy Otis Warren, Joseph Priestley, John Adams, and Thomas Jefferson in the times of the birth of the American Republic. Freedom does not mean the same thing for Native Americans, African Americans, Latin Americans, and women as it has meant in the rhetoric of a form of Christianity articulated by Anglo-Saxon and Euro-American males since the early seventh century.

The "Christian country" to which Eck alludes has been Christian primarily in the sense, as Mead put it, "that the Protestant churches *apparently* [my italics] exerted more influence in shaping the mores than did other religious groups."[7] The United States and its antecedent colonies, however, have always been host to a pluralistic society. And it is important to note that our pluralism has not been confined to statistical affiliation with the varieties of "official" religions that have been evident among us. A Muslim is never only a Muslim, as defined by leaders of the diverse orders of a worldwide Islamic civilization—even if Muslim theologians claim "the unity of the Islamic lies . . . within the hearts of the true believers,"[8] as they proclaim *shahada,* the Qur'an, and faithfulness to the five pillars. Every member of a tradition exists in a world in which his or her experiences constantly demand new religious inventiveness. Therefore, the Muslim, like the Christian or the Buddhist, expresses religious ideas and practices that either call for reinterpretation of his or her tradition or exist alongside official religion in a complementary fashion. Whatever else human beings are, they are religious—whether they exist as secularists, aborigines, Christians, or Muslims. This is most emphatically true in the American context.

The pattern of our religious life was established early on by the circumstances of what came to be known as immigration. Whether caught up as individuals, small groups, or members of large scale movements of people, "the tides of immigration assured a religious pluralism quite independent of preconceived theory. Although nearly every religious group may consider itself to be the possessor of the whole religious truth, the theory is innocuous apart from constitutional means of enforcement."[9] Americans have always been seekers and finders, followers and dissenters, advocates of private experience and communal necessity. That has been the pattern. "Every type of religious temperament, as well as all religious ideologies, found opportunity for expression and growth here."[10] However, as Sidney Mead and the theologian Karl Barth have observed, we have never come to terms intellectually with this observation. Mead pointed out that the one word that religion speaks is to remind the sovereign ruler (whoever, whatever that may be), "you, too, are mortal; you are not God."[11] In the 1960s, when many Protestant theologians were either lamenting or celebrating the arrival of the post-Protestant or post-Christian era, Mead suggested that religious freedom has always been in conflict with the distinctive theologies of much of Christianity. Yet each of these groups is dependent upon religious freedom; therefore, if they "cannot learn to digest the theory on which such freedom rests, the prognosis cannot be a happy one."[12] The theology of pluralism, said Mead, has been largely ignored and neglected. About the same time that Mead gave this admonition to the readers of the journal *Religion in Life* in 1964, Barth was reminding Americans and Europeans that a proper theology for the times was not "Thomism, Lutheranism, Calvinism, orthodoxy, religionism, existentialism . . . but what I somewhat cryptically called . . . a 'theology of freedom' that looks ahead and strives forward."[13]

Freedom opens the doors to diversity. When diversity becomes a positive virtue—something to be valued, rather than deplored—it leads to what Mead called a "theology of pluralism" and Barth a "theology of freedom."

That is to say, thinking people must give careful thought to the ultimate order and meaning that diversity represents. That is what we mean by doing theology. The theology of freedom is never static. The past is never abandoned; it provides the insights we may use as we theologize about pluralism in a new time and place. The "new religious America" is new, but not-so-new. Philip Jenkins, in *The Next Christendom*,[14] suggests that the title of Diana Eck's book be adapted to *How Mass Immigration Ensured that a Christian Country Has Become an Even More Christian Country*. That is because immigration is bringing large numbers of third-world Christians to the United States. "The number of adherents of non-Christian religions in the United States is strikingly small"—probably less than "about 4 or 5 percent of the total population."[15] Our diversity is apparently much more limited than what is found in many African and Asian nations, more limited, even, than in Egypt, Syria, and Israel.

For our purposes, it is important to observe that our "radical pluralism" still maintains a substantial Christian flavor, but that the Christianity of the new immigration is itself a new diversity imported from parts of the globe that have been missionized since the nineteenth century. The new diversity does not bear the same relationship to the traditions we have studied in part 1 of this book. The new traditions are much more closely related to those examined in part 2. They are the traditions of the poor, the disinherited, who long for healing, for discipline, for charismatic and pentecostal experience, for promises of salvation to those who read their Bibles and share their prayers and confessions as moments of liberation—of freedom in a world of bondage.

We may assume that the new Christianity will reshape the existing religious life of America, just as it will in turn be shaped by the patterns of long standing. The shifting diversity will call for new attention to a theology of pluralism. The presence of Asians, Africans, and Latinos will certainly transform the face of American Christianity. That presence will also give confidence to people of other traditions who find their home in the United States.

Native Americans have already found the courage of their own religious ancestry. In the nineteenth and early twentieth centuries much Christian missionary activity among the Indians of North America was designed in support of a national attempt to assimilate them into an American mainstream. To the extent that Native American traditions were considered backward, "primitive," and inimical to modernist notions of progress, it was assumed that Christianization and Americanization went hand in hand,

teaching the English language and Western ways and suppressing Native languages and traditions. Nevertheless, as we have observed earlier, evangelization of American Indians has not been overly successful. Even in those
instances where Native Americans have become Christian, the ideas and
practices of ancestral tradition have existed in a somewhat complementary
manner.

In the context of today's religious diversity, we may observe an increased
attention to sweat lodges, dances and assemblies called powwows, pipe ceremonies, and the use of traditional medicine. Using ceremonies and stories,
Native Americans maintain a proper sense of relationship to the earth, the
circles of animal and plant life, and the ancestors. In the Indian perception of
the world, the individual exists only in harmony with the community and the
landscape. Religiousness is expressed in rituals and stories that sustain this
harmony. The separation of verbal, practical, and social expressions of religiousness is an impossibility. It should be noted that this manifestation of the
religious runs counter to the prevalent American notion that religion is a private, subjective matter that we may attend to as solitary individuals, but that
it does not involve sacred mountains, rivers, or canyons.

Many Native Americans seek not only to restore or maintain ancestral tradition but also to express those ideas and practices held in common among
many tribal peoples. This gives rise to a kind of Pan-Indian religiousness and
also provides a foundation for renewed attention to movements like the
Native American Church and the Sun Dance. The revitalization of Native
American traditions contributes significantly to the richness of contemporary pluralism.

In a certain sense radical pluralism opens the doors to the patterns of syncretism and eclecticism that have shaped American religious traditions from
the beginning of our history. Pluralism may lead to the kind of confusion
that serves as the setting for what is called "revelation"—the idea that ultimate truth is revealed, that it is directed by language that points beyond itself,
that what concerns us ultimately may be expressed in words that we recognize but that ultimate truth is not directly available to ordinary rationality.
Muhammad, in his confusion, is visited by the archangel Gabriel (a personage that is recognized) with a message that says essentially, "All these tribal
gods are false! There is *no god* as they are gods; there is no God but the God
beyond God!" The adolescent Joseph Smith, overwhelmed by the confusion
of his personal struggle and the proliferation of denominations in early nineteenth-century America, is visited by personages whom he meekly recognizes

and who tell the young man, "Don't believe any of these confusing nonsensical claims! We will show you the truth!"

However, most of us in the confusion of the human condition receive no such alternative revelation. Instead, we tend to assume that there must be some good, some wisdom, among all these claims that have acquired a certain hoary distinctiveness in the course of history. We may think, "I'll see what I can find in this spiritual marketplace that I can put to use—that will make sense to me and help me in my search for ultimate order and meaning." We choose, we pick out. We become eclectic (Greek *eklektikos* from *eklegein*, to select—*ek*, out, and *legein*, to choose), appropriating a bit of these ideas, those practices that we have heard about here and there in the contemporary pluralistic bazaar. The problem is that when you choose or select, you do so as a person who already has some grounds for selection: you "know" what you are looking for, and *what* you are looking for is conditioned by the traditions that have shaped your expectation, whether positively or negatively. Therefore, it is difficult to be more than a syncretist, one who merges new ideas and practices with what has already shaped our lives. The individual, spawned in a Christian society and culture, will engage Hindu, Buddhist, or Native American practices in ways quite different from a native of northwestern India, Nepal, or Cibecue, Arizona.

It is well to remember that, in our radically pluralistic society, almost all ideas, practices, and movements—both traditionally religious and secular—have religious significance.[16] Whether we observe the nature of athletic and entertainment events, the role of celebrities, or the activities of scientists and politicians, we become aware of the fact that certain assumptions about the order, value, and meaning of life are being celebrated and reflected upon. They are all part of the pluralistic religious scene. They alter the thinking and actions of people and influence existing traditions. In a recent holiday letter, a prominent political scientist and friend of mine shared some observations about terrorism: "The terrorists (or *jihadists*) reject a *modern world* in which they see themselves marginalized and long for the creation of a simple, puritanical life based on the caliphate of the seventh century. *Of course,* this vision is perverse. How to replace it with hope and *modernity* is the basic challenge the world faces." Now, it may well be that modernity and modernism will be ultimately victorious. However, it is the protagonist in the religious wars of our time. It would be revealing to substitute the name of any given religious tradition for the terms *modern world* and *modernity* in the above quotation.

Issues of feminism, ethnicity, race, and gender all have appropriate stalls in the religious bazaar of the twenty-first century. Each of these often plays itself out as a perception of the world, as a set of ideas, practices, and sense of identity and belonging. Each, in turn, affects more established religious traditions, requiring reinterpretation and reshaping of their doctrine, ritual, and communities. Tradition is never a static affair but a dynamic process of remembering and responding to changing times and places. Any religious tradition that has established itself beyond the moments when it existed as a new movement (often either sectarian or cultic) has a history that reveals patterns of adjustment and renewal.

We should not assume that traditions like those discussed in part 1 of this book are merely of antiquarian interest, no longer relevant to contemporary life. Many of these traditions (such as the Lutheran, Reformed, and Anglican) have become part of what sociologists may refer to as the mainstream or mainline denominations that appear to be declining in membership and status. On the institutional level they have been joined by pentecostal and Bible churches and by forms of entrepreneurial Christianity with mega-churches designed to appeal to the American penchant for good feeling, success, entertainment, and special effects. However, the ideas and practices represented by the older traditions are very much part of American culture, and the traditions themselves manage to adapt and perform a continuing religious role among us. Understanding the traditions originally imported from Europe is still an exercise in self-understanding and in comprehending the nature of our society and culture.

Every world religion has led to the formation of a culture or civilization. When we speak of Islamic civilization we acknowledge a network of art, ethics, music, philosophy, jurisprudence, governance, and customs that reflect the verbal, practical, and social expressions of Islam. The same is true of Christianity (as discussed in our earlier reference to the concept of Christendom), Taoism, Buddhism, Judaism, and Hinduism; every religious tradition has contributed significantly to the nurture of the human conscience, both individual and social. Each has a long history of casuistry, the manner in which rules, laws, and principles have been applied in specific cases. The study of law, for example, is impossible without an understanding of religious history.

The American people have been nurtured by our religious traditions. Our sense of morality and social responsibility (ethics) owes considerable tribute to religion. We may wonder, in closing, whether a nation "so conceived and so dedicated, can long endure," living only on the interest accrued by the religious, social, and ethical investments of the past. Perhaps it can only if we ask seriously what we can learn about what it is to be human by a critical, but guileless, investigation of American religious traditions and a renewed attention to the theology of pluralism.

Notes

1. The Study of Religion

1. Thomas Luckmann, *The Invisible Religion* (New York: Macmillan, 1967).

2. Joachim Wach, *The Comparative Study of Religion* (New York: Columbia University Press, 1958).

3. Ralph Waldo Emerson, "Nature," in *Selected Writings of Ralph Waldo Emerson,* ed. William H. Gilman (New York: Penguin, 1965), 186.

4. Wilfred Cantwell Smith, *The Faith of Other Men* (New York: Harper & Row, 1972), 18.

2. Myths, Legends, and the Promised Land

1. Barbara C. Sproul, *Primal Myths: Creating the World* (New York: Harper & Row, 1979), 1.

2. Reference to the Genesis story of Adam and Eve, their exile from Paradise. This is known as the "fall" because it implies that human beings (Adam and Eve) have fallen from their original status as creatures in the image of God. Their nature is now "fallen."

3. The common era, used to designate the commonly accepted way of dating the years. To the Christian, the common era is A.D., the year of the Lord.

3. Christendom and the Heritage of Reformation

1. In the West, the Mass or Eucharist, which represented the communion with Christ.

2. Specially prepared two-dimensional images, which are believed transparent to the divine, the holy.

3. *Orthodox* refers to right and consistent teaching, right and consistent praise or worship, while *catholic* refers to the universality of the church. The church considers itself catholic in space in the sense that its truth is for the entire world. It is catholic in time in the sense that its truth is for all time, extending through past, present, and future.

4. Indulgences arose from the assumption that the church shares the meritorious life of Christ and those saints that have had a special role in its history. This was interpreted to mean that the church was the custodian of these merits. Behind the granting of indulgences was the notion that sin requires a penalty either on earth or

in the afterlife of purgatory, even after one is reconciled to God by penance and absolution. The practice emerged of using the merits of Christ and the saints to "indulge" the penalty of sin. Often the indulgences were sold, the penalties of purgatory eliminated.

6. Isaiah Berlin, *The Hedgehog and the Fox: An Essay on Tolstoy's View of History* (New York: Simon & Schuster, 1986).

7. The theory that the integrity of gospel teaching is protected by a teaching authority preserved from the time of the apostles and shared by their successors, the bishops of the church.

4. The Native American Traditions

1. Vine Deloria Jr., *Red Earth, White Lies* (Golden, Co.: Fulcrum, 1997), 69–70.

2. Ruth M. Underhill, *Red Man's Religion: Beliefs and Practices of the Indians North of Mexico* (Chicago: University of Chicago Press, 1965), 47.

3. Ibid., 120.

4. Ibid., 120–21.

5. Sam D. Gill, "The Trees Stand Deeply Rooted," in *Parabola* II/2:12.

6. Corn represents the most fundamental and life-sustaining power among many Native Americans living in semi-arid lands where game and wild plants are scarce. Corn is especially sacred and powerful.

7. A shaman is a religious figure common to the traditions of people from all parts of the world. A shaman is one who is able, by means of out-of-body experience, to communicate with the realm of invisible spirits in the abode of the living dead. He brings back wisdom from his visits.

8. Underhill, *Red Man's Religion*.

9. From which the word *savage* is derived (people who needed saving, salvation).

5. From Anglicans to Episcopalians

1. That is, it focuses upon the resurrection of Jesus the Christ as a new life that overcomes the death and estrangement of existence.

2. Creeds are verbal symbols that include the substance of faith and teaching, which can never be fully defined. The Apostles' Creed is thought to date from the earliest age of the church, suggesting that it was the Creed of the Twelve Apostles. The Nicene Creed is the statement authorized by a Council of the Church held in Nicaea in Asia Minor in 325 C.E. It was revised at the Council of Constantinople in 381 and reflects the church's loyalty to the apostolic tradition in the face of deviating ideas.

3. The word *office* refers to a special kind of work or service. The idea of prayer or worship being an office or service refers to its special function in the life of the people—it is a service done by and for the community of faith and a service to God.

4. This adjective has been dropped from use and is no longer part of the official title.

5. A miter is the tall, two-peak cap worn by bishops as a sign of office; a scepter is an ornamental staff that symbolizes the sovereignty of a monarch.

6. National Period refers to the years (1783–1828) during which the independent colonies struggled to learn what it meant to become a nation.

7. From the Greek word *oikoumene* (the entire world), it refers to the movement within Christianity toward the visible unity of all Christians. Sometimes this has led to cooperation among churches, at other times to merger.

8. A movement begun in the late nineteenth century, often referred to as the Social Gospel.

6. The Puritan Tradition: Congregationalists, Baptists, and Quakers

1. Iconoclasm refers to the tendency to eliminate images or external forms that one considers idolatrous or deviations from the truth—things that hide the truth.

2. *Anglicanism* is a term that is sometimes used interchangeably with the Church of England. It also comes to mean that distinctive form of Christianity that emerged as a worldwide tradition out of the Church of England heritage.

3. Seekers maintain that only God knows the nature of the true church. Only God can bring the church into being; it is not right to make any attempt to form it.

4. Antinomians are those who believe that the true Christian is set apart from any need to observe the moral law (*anti-*, "against"; *nomos*, "law"). The antinomian is above the law.

5. Edmund S. Morgan, *Visible Saints* (Ithaca, N.Y.: Cornell University Press, 1965), 93.

6. Liberal theology is an intellectual movement that is open to the truth and insights of modern knowledge. It is strongly influenced by modern critical, scientific, and historical studies.

7. Founder of Mormonism, the Church of Jesus Christ of Latter-day Saints.

8. The more radical and separatist Puritans.

9. Here "essential" is used as a derivative from the idea of *essence,* or inner, basic reality.

10. Rufus Jones, *New Studies in Mystical Experience* (New York: Macmillan, 1928), 15.

7. The Reformed Tradition: The Scotch-Irish and English, the Dutch, and the Germans

1. The theory or doctrine of the nature of the church.

2. Philip Schaff, *America: A Sketch of Its Political, Social, and Religious Character* (Cambridge: Harvard University Press, Belknap, 1961), 93–94.

3. A schismatic break within the Dutch church, leading to a new and more conservative denomination. The denomination is strong in Michigan.

4. From *dominus,* meaning "of the Lord"; here referring to Christ the Lord.

5. Dutch Reformed pastor.

6. Pronounced "see-tus" and referring to a presbytery.

7. Here *evangelical* is used in its classic sense, meaning in effect Protestant, those Christians who emphasize the primacy of gospel or evangel rather than the ongoing tradition and teaching of the Catholic church. This distinguishes its use from U.S. evangelicals, who emphasize the revivalistic claims of the gospel on the individual.

8. Martin E. Marty, "The Spirit's Holy Errand: The Search for a Spiritual Style in Secular America," *Daedalus* (winter 1967) 103.

8. The Lutheran Tradition

1. Lennart Pinomaa, *Faith Victorious: An Introduction to Luther's Theology* (Philadelphia: Fortress Press, 1963), 3–4.

2. Martin E. Marty, "The New Face of Southern Evangelicalism," in *Religion and Republic* (Boston: Beacon, 1987), 275.

3. John Dillenberger and Claude Welch, *Protestant Christianity* (New York: Scribner's, 1954), 48.

4. Abdel Ross Wentz, *A Basic History of Lutheranism in America* (Philadelphia: Fortress Press, 1964), 2.

5. Sydney E. Ahlstrom, *A Religious History of the American People* (New Haven: Yale University Press, 1972), 667.

9. The Roman Catholic Tradition

1. Richard P. McBrien, *Catholicism,* vol. 2 (Minneapolis: Winston, 1980).

2. In the modern Roman Catholic Church this is a letter circulated by the pope to all the church. It usually speaks to a given and special theological or ethical issue.

3. A council of the church, called by Pope John XXIII and lasting from 1962 to 1965, the purpose of which was the renewal of the church from within in order to meet the challenges and changes of the modern world.

4. McBrien, *Catholicism,* 1080.

5. The appearance of the sacred/God in all manner of forms.

6. Generally bishops, those high in the ecclesiastical hierarchy, rendered suspect by the Protestant and democratic mentality of the majority.

7. The body of ecclesiastical laws concerning matters of faith, morals, discipline, and polity.

8. This English translation of 1611 was commissioned under the reign of King James I. Its authorization applied to Anglican and Protestant usage.

10. The Methodist Tradition

1. William W. Sweet, *The Story of Religion in America* (Grand Rapids: Baker, 1979), 219.

2. Catherine L. Albanese, *America: Religion and Religions* (Belmont, Calif.: Wadsworth, 1981), 99.

3. The eighteenth-century beginnings of the phenomenon of revivalism, which will be examined in the next chapter.

4. Winthrop S. Hudson, *Religion in America,* 2nd ed. (New York: Scribner's, 1973), 123.

5. See chapter 11.

6. J. Paul Williams, *What Americans Believe and How They Worship* (New York: Harper & Row, 1952), 286.

11. The Revivalist Evangelical Tradition

1. Sidney E. Mead, *The Lively Experiment* (New York: Harper & Row, 1963), 14.

2. A *philosophe* is one who is a believer in certain ideas but usually lacks the discipline of careful philosophical discourse.

3. H. Richard Niebuhr, *The Kingdom of God in America* (New York: Harper, 1959), 125–26.

4. Meaning out-of-body, out-of-place, out-of-form; from *ek stasis.*

5. M. Darrol Bryant, "America as God's Kingdom," in Jürgen Moltmann et al., *Religion and Political Society* (New York: Harper & Row, 1974), 75.

6. A religious movement that practiced celibacy, because it assumed that the end of the age was near; that the founder, Mother Ann Lee, was the second appearance of Christ; and that laws of the millennium were in effect.

12. The Public Religious Tradition

1. T. S. Eliot, "Choruses from 'The Rock,'" in *Complete Poems 1909–1962* (New York: Harcourt Brace Jovanovich, 1963).

2. Robert N. Bellah, "Civil Religion in America," *Daedalus* (winter 1967) 1.

3. Parker J. Palmer, *The Company of Strangers* (New York: Crossroad, 1981), 19.

4. Conrad Cherry, ed., *God's New Israel: Religious Interpretations of American Destiny* (Englewood Cliffs, N. J.: Prentice-Hall, 1971), 4–5.

5. Cited in James H. Cone, *Martin and Malcolm and America* (Maryknoll, N.Y.: Orbis, 1991), 1.

6. Cited in ibid., 315.

7. Robert Frost, "The Gift Outright," from *The Poetry of Robert Frost*, ed. Edward Connery Latham (New York: Holt, Rinehart & Winston, 1969).

13. The Restorationist Traditions: Christians to Latter-Day Saints

1. Jonathan Edwards, "Some Thoughts Concerning the Revival," in *The Great Awakening*, *Works of Jonathan Edwards,* vol. 4, ed. C. C. Goen (New Haven: Yale University Press, 1972).

2. A. T. DeGroot, *The Restoration Principle* (St. Louis: Bethany, 1960), 16.

3. William W. Sweet, *The Story of Religion in America* (Grand Rapids: Baker, 1979), 237.

4. Edwin S. Gaustad, ed., *A Documentary History of Religion in America,* 2 vols. (Grand Rapids: Eerdmans, 1982–83), 1:366.

5. In Hebrew tradition Aaron was the brother of Moses. In the book of Exodus it is reported that the Lord says to Moses, "Then bring near to you Aaron your brother, and his sons with him, from among the people of Israel, to serve me as priests . . . and you shall speak to all who have ability, whom I have endowed with an able mind, that they may make Aaron's garments to consecrate him for my priesthood" (Exodus 28:1, 3).

6. Mormons prefer to speak of "the Lord," after the presumed practice of ancient Israel, avoiding an overuse of and familiarity with the divine name.

7. Margaret Toscano and Paul Toscano, *Strangers in Paradox: Explorations in Mormon Theology* (Salt Lake City: Signature, 1990), xi.

14. The Jewish Tradition in America

1. Literally, little cities and towns, which were essentially Jewish in composition.

2. Refers to the ritual, custom, or practice unique to the Jewish people of a given heritage or cultural background. *Minhag* America will eventually be used to refer to the particularities of American Jewish ritual life. Joseph L. Blau, *Judaism in America: From Curiosity to Third Faith* (Chicago History of American Religion; Chicago: University of Chicago Press, 1976), 26.

3. Nathan Glazer, *American Judaism* (Chicago History of American Religion; Chicago: University of Chicago Press, 1965), 15.

4. The notion that something is not right, that something is diseased, distorted.

5. Joseph Stein, *Fiddler on the Roof* (New York: Simon & Schuster, 1965), 3–4.

6. Jacob Neusner, *Between Time and Eternity: The Essentials of Judaism* (Belmont, Calif.: Wadsworth, 1975), 63.

7. Abraham Joshua Heschel, *The Sabbath: Its Meaning for Modern Man* (New York: Farrar, Straus & Giroux, 1951), 10.

8. Ibid., 7.

9. Ibid., 66.

10. Ibid., 73.

11. Ibid., 10.

12. Seventh month of the Jewish calendar.

13. Enlightenment, meaning the movement of Jewish enlightenment, or the way of the *maskilim*.

14. Note that in Protestant Christianity, there is the Reform*ed* tradition; in Jewish tradition, it is appropriate to speak of *Reform* Judaism.

15. The Eastern Orthodox Tradition

1. Kallistos Ware, *The Orthodox Way* (Crestwood, N.Y.: St. Vladimir's Seminary Press, 1980), 89.

2. The way of perceiving the world, dependent upon which of the senses is dominant. Presumably a society where sound is more important than other senses lives in a different sensorium from a society where sight is dominant.

3. Ware, *The Orthodox Way,* 55.

4. Ibid., 40.

5. Alexander Schmemann, *For the Life of the World: Sacraments and Orthodoxy* (Crestwood, N. Y.: St. Vladimir's Seminary Press, 1973), 26.

6. The center of the building, where the arms of the cross intersect.

7. The paten is a saucer-like dish for the bread, while the chalice is the stemmed cup that holds the wine.

8. Okamura Keishin, "Kukai's Philosophy as a Mandala," *The Eastern Buddhist* 18: 22.

9. Ibid.

10. From *The Way of a Pilgrim,* trans. R. M. French (New York: Seabury, 1965), 80.

11. Quoted in Ware, *The Orthodox Way,* 140.

12. Ware, *The Orthodox Way,* 33.

16. The African American Traditions

1. Albert J. Raboteau, *Slave Religion: The "Invisible Institution" in the Antebellum South* (New York: Oxford University Press, 1978), 15.

2. Syncretism refers to the tendency to accommodate or blend religious expressions from two or more traditions.

3. Raboteau, *Slave Religion,* 64–65.

4. Quoted in Edwin S. Gaustad, ed., *A Documentary History of Religion in America,* 2 vols. (Grand Rapids: Eerdmans, 1982–83), 1:301.

5. Joseph R. Washington Jr., *Black Sects and Cults* (Lanham, Md.: University Press of America, 1984), 60.

6. C. Eric Lincoln and Lawrence H. Mamiya, *The Black Church in the African American Experience* (Durham, N.C.: Duke University Press, 1990), 305.

7. Exegesis is the act of explaining a text, in this case the Bible. Exegesis is concerned with analyzing language, sometimes history and literary form, to find out what a text says. Folk exegesis is done by applying imaginative construction to the text.

8. Washington, *Black Sects and Cults,* 60.

9. W. E. B. DuBois, *The Souls of Black Folk* (New York: New American Library, 1969), 211.

17. New Traditions for the Common People: Millenarian, Holiness, and Pentecostal Traditions

1. Winthrop Hudson, "A Time of Religious Ferment," in *The Rise of Adventism: Religion and Society in Mid-Nineteenth-Century America,* ed. Edwin S. Gaustad (New York: Harper & Row, 1974), 15.

2. George M. Marsden, *Understanding Fundamentalism and Evangelicalism* (Grand Rapids: Eerdmans, 1992). See especially chapter 2.

3. William Miller, quoted in Edwin S. Gaustad, ed., *A Documentary History of Religion in America,* 2 vols. (Grand Rapids: Eerdmans, 1982–83), 1:372.

4. Jonathan M. Butler, "Adventism and the American Experience," in Gaustad, *The Rise of Adventism,* 178.

5. Armageddon, a biblical term that has been used to refer to the decisive battle between the forces of light and darkness, good and evil. Originally the name of a place.

6. Elmer T. Clark, *The Small Sects in America* (Nashville: Abingdon, 1965), 72.

7. C. Eric Lincoln and Lawrence H. Mamiya, *The Black Church in the African American Experience* (Durham, N.C.: Duke University Press, 1990), 77.

8. Ibid., 281.

9. Catherine Albanese, *America: Religions and Religion* (Belmont, Calif.: Wadsworth, 1981), 105.

10. Clark, *Small Sects,* 94.

18. Religion and the Crisis of Authority

1. David E. Shi, *The Simple Life: Plain Living and High Thinking in American Culture* (Athens: University of Georgia Press, 2001), 154.

2. Loren Eiseley, *The Invisible Pyramid* (New York: Scribner's, 1970), 57.

3. Shi, *The Simple Life,* 154.

4. The *Bhagavad Gita* is a Hindu classic reflecting a devotional approach to salvation or liberation.

5. George A. Gordon, quoted in *American Christianity: An Historical Interpretation with Representative Documents,* 2 vols., by H. Shelton Smith, Robert T. Handy, and Lefferts A. Loetscher (New York: Scribner's, 1960–63), 2:281.

6. Shailer Mathews, quoted in Edwin S. Gaustad, ed., *A Documentary History of Religion in America,* 2 vols. (Grand Rapids: Eerdmans, 1982–83), 1:398.

7. Secret teachings, the truths of which are only available to those who are prepared to follow certain disciplinary guidelines for use.

8. Robert S. Ellwood, *Religious and Spiritual Groups in Modern America* (Englewood Cliffs, N.J.: Prentice-Hall, 1973), 90.

9. Charles Fillmore, quoted in Gaustad, *Documentary History of Religion,* 2:247.

10. Robert H. Schuller, *Self-Esteem: The New Reformation* (Waco, Tex.: Word, 1982), 31–32.

11. H. Richard Niebuhr, *The Kingdom of God in America* (New York: Harper, 1959), 193.

19. The Fundamentalist and Neo-Evangelical Traditions

1. Seyyed Hossein Nasr, *The Heart of Islam: Enduring Values for Humanity* (San Francisco: HarperSanFrancisco, 2002), 109.

2. George M. Marsden, *Fundamentalism and American Culture* (New York: Oxford University Press, 1982), 119.

3. Jay Newman, *Fanatics and Hypocrites* (Buffalo: Prometheus, 1986), 41.

4. Ibid., 57.

5. F. W. Dillistone, *The Power of Symbols in Religion and Culture* (New York: Crossroad, 1986), 27.

6. Harry Emerson Fosdick, quoted in *American Christianity*, vol. 2, ed. H. Shelton Smith, Robert T. Handy, and Lefferts A. Loetscher (New York: Scribner's, 1963), 295–96.

7. Marsden, *Fundamentalism*, 52.

8. Edward J. Larson, *Summer for the Gods: The Scopes Trial and America's Continuing Debate over Science and Religion* (Cambridge: Harvard University Press, 1997), 83.

9. Edwin S. Gaustad in *Religion and America: Spiritual Life in a Secular Age,* ed. Mary Douglas and Steven Tipton (Boston: Beacon, 1983), 178.

20. The Age of Radical Pluralism

1. Seyyed Hossein Nasr, *The Heart of Islam: Enduring Values for Humanity* (San Francisco: HarperSanFrancisco, 2002), 97.

2. John L. Esposito, *Islam: The Straight Path* (New York: Oxford University Press, 1998), 100–101.

3. Jane I. Smith, *Islam in America* (New York: Columbia University Press, 1999), 69.

4. Amanda Porterfield, *The Transformation of American Religion: The Story of a Late-Twentieth-Century Awakening* (New York: Oxford University Press, 2001), 184.

5. Diana L. Eck, *A New Religious America: How a "Christian Country" Has Become the World's Most Religiously Diverse Nation* (San Francisco: Harper, 2001).

6. Sidney E. Mead, *The Nation with the Soul of a Church* (New York: Harper & Row, 1995), 38.

7. Ibid., 18.

8. Nasr, *Heart of Islam,* 161.

9. James Ward Smith and A. Leland Jamison, *The Shaping of American Religion* (Princeton, N.J.: Princeton University Press, 1961), 11.

10. Ibid.

11. Mead, *Nation,* 10.

12. Ibid., 27.

13. Karl Barth, *Evangelical Theology* (New York: Anchor, 1964), xi.

14. Philip Jenkins, *The Next Christendom: The Coming of Global Christianity* (New York: Oxford University Press, 2002).

15. Ibid., 104.

16. See David D. Hall, ed., *Lived Religion in America: Toward a History of Practice* (Princeton, N.J.: Princeton University Press, 1997).

For Further Reading

1. The Study of Religion

Berger, Peter L. *The Sacred Canopy: Elements of a Sociological Theory of Religion*. New York: Anchor, 1990.

Capps, Walter H. *Ways of Understanding Religion*. New York: Macmillan, 1972.

———. *Religious Studies: The Making of a Discipline*. Minneapolis: Fortress Press, 1995.

Eliade, Mircea. *The Sacred and the Profane*. New York: Harcourt, Brace & World, 1959.

Livingston, James C. *Anatomy of the Sacred: An Introduction to Religion*. Upper Saddle River, N.J.: Prentice Hall, 1998.

Long, Charles H. *Significations: Signs, Symbols, and Images in the Interpretation of Religion*. Series in Philosophical and Cultural Studies in Religion. Aurora, Colo.: Davies Group, 1999.

Pals, Daniel J. *Seven Theories of Religion*. New York: Oxford University Press, 1996.

Smith, Wilfred C. *The Meaning and End of Religion*. Minneapolis: Fortress Press, 1990.

Streng, Frederick J. *Understanding Religious Life*. Belmont, Calif.: Wadsworth, 1985.

Wach, Joachim. *The Comparative Study of Religion*. New York: Columbia University Press, 1958.

2. Myths, Legends, and the Promised Land

Ashe, Geoffrey. *Land to the West: St. Brendan's Voyage to America*. New York: Viking, 1962.

Dorson, Richard M. *America in Legend: Folklore from the Colonial Period to the Present*. New York: Pantheon, 1973.

Eliade, Mircea. *The Quest: History and Meaning in Religion*. Chicago: University of Chicago Press: 1969.

———. *Myth and Reality*. Translated by Willard R. Trask. New York: Harper & Row, 1975.

Loew, Cornelius R. *Myth, Sacred History and Philosophy: The Pre-Christian Religious Heritage of the West*. New York: Harcourt, Brace & World, 1967.

Niebuhr, Reinhold. *The Self and the Dramas of History*. New York: Scribner's, 1955.

O'Gorman, Edmundo. *The Invention of America: An Inquiry into the Historical Nature of the New World and the Meaning of Its History.* Westport, Conn.: Greenwood, 1972.

Smith, Jonathan Z. *Map Is Not Territory: Studies in the History of Religions.* Chicago: University of Chicago Press, 1993.

Sproul, Barbara C. *Primal Myths: Creating the World.* New York: Harper & Row, 1979.

3. Christendom and the Heritage of Reformation

Bainton, Roland H. *The Reformation of the Sixteenth Century.* Boston: Beacon, 1952.

Brown, Peter. *The Cult of the Saints: Its Rise and Function in Latin Christianity.* Haskell Lectures on History of Religions. Chicago: University of Chicago Press, 1981.

Bruce, Steve. *Religion in the Modern World: From Cathedrals to Cults.* New York: Oxford University Press, 1996.

Cochrane, Charles Norris. *Christianity and Classical Culture: A Study of Thought and Action from Augustus to Augustine.* Reprint. Indianapolis: Liberty Fund, 2003.

Dawson, Christopher. *Religion and the Rise of Western Culture.* Garden City, N.Y.: Doubleday, 1958.

Dillenberger, John, and Claude Welch. *Protestant Christianity Interpreted through Its Development.* New York: Scribner, 1954.

Grant, Robert M. *Augustus to Constantine: The Rise and Triumph of Christianity in the Roman World.* San Francisco: Harper & Row, 1990.

Janz, Dennis R. *A Reformation Reader: Primary Texts with Introductions.* Minneapolis: Fortress Press, 1999.

Pauck, Wilhelm. *The Heritage of the Reformation.* Glencoe, Ill.: Free Press, 1961.

Urban, Linwood. *A Short History of Christian Thought.* New York: Oxford University Press, 1995.

4. The Native American Traditions

Basso, Keith H., *Western Apache Language and Culture: Essays in Linguistic Anthropology.* Tucson: University of Arizona Press, 1990.

Berkhofer, Robert F., Jr. *Salvation and the Savage: An Analysis of Protestant Missions and American Indian Response, 1787–1862.* Westport, Conn.: Greenwood, 1977.

Brown, Joseph Epes, ed. *The Sacred Pipe: Black Elk's Account of the Seven Rites of the Oglala Sioux.* Norman: University of Oklahoma Press, 1953.

Deloria, Vine, Jr. *God Is Red: A Native View of Religion.* Rev. ed. Golden, Colo.: Fulcrum, 2003.

De Mallie, Raymond J., and Douglas R. Parks, eds. *Sioux Indian Religion.* Norman: University of Oklahoma Press, 1987.

Gill, Sam D. *Native American Religions: An Introduction.* Belmont, Calif.: Wadsworth, 1982.

Hultkrantz, Ake. *The Religions of the American Indian.* Berkeley: University of California Press, 1979.

Martin, Joel W. *The Land Looks after Us: A History of Native American Religion.* New York: Oxford University Press, 2001.

Neihardt, John G. *Black Elk Speaks.* New York: MJF, 1996.

Silko, Leslie Marmon. *Ceremony.* New York: Penguin, 1986.

Swann, Brian, ed. *Coming to Light: Contemporary Translations of the Native Literatures of North America.* New York: Vintage, 1994.

Tedlock, Dennis, and Barbara Tedlock. *Teachings from the American Earth: Indian Religion and Philosophy.* New York: Liveright, 1975.

Thompson, Stith. *Tales of the North American Indian.* Bloomington: Indiana University Press, 1929.

Underhill, Ruth M. *Red Man's Religion: Beliefs and Practices of the Indians North of Mexico.* Chicago: University of Chicago Press, 1965.

5. From Anglicans to Episcopalians

Albright, Raymond W. *A History of the Protestant Episcopal Church.* New York: Macmillan, 1964.

Booty, John E. *The Church in History.* Harrisburg, Pa.: Morehouse, 2003.

Hatchett, Marion J. *The Making of the First American Book of Common Prayer, 1776–1789.* New York: Seabury, 1982.

Lake, Peter. *Anglicans and Puritans? Presbyterianism and English Conformist Thought from Whitgift to Hooker.* London: Unwin Hyman, 1988.

Neill, Stephen. *Anglicanism.* New York: Oxford University Press, 1977.

Shepherd, Massey Hamilton. *The Reform of Liturgical Worship.* The 1959 Bohlen Lectures. New York: Oxford University Press, 1961.

Staley, Vernon. *The Catholic Religion: A Manual of Instruction for Members of the Anglican Communion.* Revised by Brian Goodchild. New York: Morehouse-Barlow, 1983.

Sykes, Stephen, John Booty, and Jonathan Knight, eds. *The Study of Anglicanism.* Revised edition. Minneapolis: Fortress Press, 1998.

Wolf, William J., ed. *The Spirit of Anglicanism.* Wilton, Conn.: Morehouse-Barlow, 1979.

6. The Puritan Tradition: Congregationalists, Baptists, and Quakers

Bercovitch, Sacvan. *The Puritan Origins of the American Self.* New Haven: Yale University Press, 1975.

Hall, David D. *World of Wonders, Days of Judgment: Popular Religious Belief in Early New England.* New York: Knopf, 1989.

Haller, William. *The Rise of Puritanism: The Way to the New Jerusalem as Set Forth in Pulpit and Press from Thomas Cartwright to John Lilburne and John Milton, 1570–1643.* New York: Harper, 1957.

McLoughlin, William G. *Isaac Backus and the American Pietist Tradition.* Boston: Little, Brown, 1967.

Miller, Perry. *Roger Williams: His Contribution to the American Tradition.* New York: Atheneum, 1966.

Morgan, Edmund Sears. *The Puritan Dilemma: The Story of John Winthrop.* 2nd ed. New York: Longman, 1999.

Stout, Harry S. *The New England Soul: Preaching and Religious Culture in Colonial New England.* New York: Oxford University Press, 1986.

Torbet, Robert G. *A History of the Baptists.* Valley Forge, Pa.: Judson, 1973.

Trueblood, G. Elton. *The People Called Quakers.* New York: Harper & Row, 1966.

Woolman, John. *The Journal and Major Essays of John Woolman.* Edited by P. P. Moulton. New York: Oxford University Press, 1971.

7. The Reformed Tradition: The Scotch-Irish and English, the Dutch, and the Germans

Armstrong, Maurice W., Lefferts A. Loetscher, and Charles A. Anderson, eds. *The Presbyterian Enterprise: Sources of American Presbyterian History.* Philadelphia: Westminster, 1956.

Good, James I. *The Historical Handbook of the Reformed Church.* Philadelphia: Heidelberg, 1901.

Horstmann, Julius H., and Herbert H. Wernecke. *Through Four Centuries: The Story of the Beginnings of the Evangelical and Reformed Church.* St. Louis: Eden, 1938.

Melton, Julius. *Presbyterian Worship in America: Changing Patterns since 1787.* Richmond, Va.: John Knox, 1967.

Schaff, Philip. *The Principle of Protestantism.* Reprint. Philadelphia: United Church Press, 1965.

Trinterud, Leonard J. *The Forming of an American Tradition: A Re-Examination of Colonial Presbyterianism.* Philadelphia: Westminster, 1949.

Zwaanstra, Henry. *Reformed Thought and Experience in a New World: A Study of the Christian Reformed Church and Its American Environment.* Grand Rapids: Eerdmans, 1974.

8. The Lutheran Tradition

Bainton, Roland H. *Here I Stand: A Life of Martin Luther.* New York: Abingdon, 1950.

Bergendorff, Conrad. *The Church of the Lutheran Reformation: A Historical Study of Lutheranism.* St. Louis: Concordia, 1967.

Ferm, Vergilius. *The Crisis in American Lutheran Theology in America, 1840–1880.* New York: Century, 1927.

Gritsch, Eric W. *Fortress Introduction to Lutheranism.* Minneapolis: Fortress Press, 1994.

———. *A History of Lutheranism.* Minneapolis: Fortress Press, 2002.

Jenson, Robert W. *Unbaptized God: The Basic Flaw in Ecumenical Theology.* Minneapolis: Fortress Press, 1992.

Muhlenberg, Henry Melchior. *The Journals of Henry Melchior Muhlenberg*. Trans. Theodore G. Tappert and John W. Doberstein. Philadelphia: Evangelical Lutheran Ministerium of Pennsylvania, 1942–58.

Pinomaa, Lennart. *Faith Victorious: An Introduction to Luther's Theology*. Philadelphia: Fortress Press, 1963.

Reed, Luther D. *The Lutheran Liturgy*. Philadelphia: Fortress Press, 1947.

Tappert, Theodore G., ed. *Lutheran Confessional Theology in America, 1840–1880*. New York: Oxford University Press, 1972.

Wentz, Abdel Ross. *A Basic History of Lutheranism in America*. Philadelphia: Fortress Press, 1964.

9. The Roman Catholic Tradition

Cunningham, Lawrence S. *The Catholic Experience: Space, Time, Silence, Prayer, Sacraments, Story, Persons, Catholicity, Community, and Expectations*. New York: Crossroad, 1985.

Dulles, Avery. *The Catholicity of the Church*. New York: Clarendon, 1985.

Ellis, John Tracy. *American Catholicism*. Chicago: University of Chicago Press, 1969.

Greeley, Andrew M. *The Catholic Experience: An Interpretation of the History of American Catholicism*. Garden City, N.Y.: Doubleday, 1967.

Hennesey, James J. *American Catholics: A History of the Roman Catholic Community in the United States*. New York: Oxford University Press, 1981.

O'Brien, David J. *The Renewal of American Catholicism*. New York: Oxford University Press, 1972.

Strange, Roderic. *The Catholic Faith*. New York: Oxford University Press, 1986.

10. The Methodist Tradition

Cartwright, Peter. *Autobiography*. Edited by Charles L. Wallis. Nashville: Abingdon, 1956.

Clark, Elmer T. *The Journal and Letters of Francis Asbury*. Nashville: Abingdon, 1958.

Lee, Umphrey. *The Lord's Horseman: John Wesley the Man*. Nashville: Abingdon, 1954.

Mathews, Donald G. *Slavery and Methodism: A Chapter in American Morality, 1780–1845*. Princeton: Princeton University Press, 1965.

Muelder, Walter G. *Methodism and Society in the Twentieth Century*. Nashville: Abingdon, 1961.

Peters, John L. *Christian Perfection and American Methodism*. Grand Rapids: Zondervan, 1985.

Richardson, Harry V. *Dark Salvation: The Story of Methodism As It Developed among Blacks in America*. Garden City, N.Y.: Doubleday, 1976.

Sweet, William Warren. *The Methodists: A Collection of Source Materials*. Vol. 4: Religion on the American Frontier 1783–1840. New York: Cooper Square, 1964.

11. The Revivalist Evangelical Tradition

Butler, Jon. *Awash in a Sea of Faith: Christianizing the American People*. Cambridge: Harvard University Press, 1990.

Edwards, Jonathan. *Religious Affections*. Edited by John E. Smith. New Haven: Yale University Press, 1959.

Finney, Charles G. *Lectures on Revivals of Religion*. Edited by William G. McLoughlin. Cambridge: Belknap Press of Harvard University, 1950.

Gaustad, Edwin S. *The Great Awakening in New England*. New York: Harper & Row, 1957.

Heimert, Alan E. *Religion and the American Mind from the Great Awakening to the Revolution*. Cambridge: Harvard University Press, 1966.

McLoughlin, William G. *Modern Revivalism: Charles Grandison Finney to Billy Graham*. New York: Ronald, 1959.

Nevin, John Williamson. *The Anxious Bench* in *Catholic and Reformed: Selected Theological Writings of John Williamson Nevin*. Edited by Charles Yrigoyen Jr. and George H. Bricker. Pittsburgh: Pickwick, 1978.

Weisberger, Bernard A. *They Gathered at the River: The Story of the Great Revivalists and Their Impact upon Religion in America*. New York: Octagon, 1979.

12. The Public Religious Tradition

Bellah, Robert N. "Civil Religion in America." *Daedalus* (winter 1967) 1–21.

———. *The Broken Covenant: American Civil Religion in a Time of Trial*. 2nd ed. Chicago: University of Chicago Press, 1992.

Gaustad, Edwin S. *Neither King nor Prelate: Religion and the New Nation, 1776–1826*. Rev. ed. Grand Rapids: Eerdmans, 1993.

Handy, Robert T. *A Christian America: Protestant Hopes and Historical Realities*. New York: Oxford University Press, 1983.

Mead, Sidney E. *The Nation with the Soul of a Church*. New York: Harper & Row, 1975.

Miller, William Lee. *The First Liberty: Religion and the American Republic*. New York: Knopf, 1987.

Murray, John Courtney. *We Hold These Truths: Catholic Reflections on American Proposition*. New York: Sheed & Ward, 1960.

Neuhaus, Richard J. *The Naked Public Square: Religion and Democracy in America*. Grand Rapids: Eerdmans, 1984.

Strout, Cushing. *Making American Tradition: Visions and Revisions from Ben Franklin to Alice Walker*. New Brunswick, N.J.: Rutgers University Press, 1990.

Tuveson, Ernest L. *Redeemer Nation: The Idea of America's Millennial Role*. Chicago: University of Chicago Press, 1968.

Wills, Gary. *Under God: Religion and American Politics*. New York: Touchstone, Simon & Schuster, 1990.

Wilson, John F., and Donald L. Drakeman. *Church and State in American History.*
    Boston: Beacon, 1987.
Wolf, William J. *Freedom's Holy Light: American Identity and the Future of Theology.*
    Wakefield, Mass.: Parameter, 1977.

13. The Restorationist Traditions: Christians to Latter-Day Saints

Arrington, Leonard J., and Davis Bitton. *The Mormon Experience: A History of the
    Latter-Day Saints.* 2nd ed. Urbana: University of Illinois Press, 1992.
Bushman, Richard L. *Joseph Smith and the Beginnings of Mormonism.* Urbana: University of Illinois Press, 1984.
DeGroot, A. T. *The Restoration Principle.* St. Louis: Bethany, 1960.
Foster, Lawrence. *Religion and Sexuality: Three American Communal Experiments of
    the Nineteenth Century.* New York: Oxford University Press, 1981.
Garrison, Winfred E., and Alfred T. DeGroot. *The Disciples of Christ: A History.* St.
    Louis: Bethany, 1958.
Hughes, Richard T., ed. *The American Quest for the Primitive Church.* Urbana: University of Illinois Press, 1988.
Moore, R. Laurence. "How To Become a People: The Mormon Scenario," in *Religious
    Outsiders and the Making of Americans.* New York: Oxford University Press, 1986.
Shipps, Jan. *Mormonism: The Story of a New Religious Tradition.* Urbana: University
    of Illinois Press, 1985.
West, William G. *Barton Warren Stone: Early American Advocate of Christian Unity.*
    Nashville: Disciples of Christ Historical Society, 1954.

14. The Jewish Tradition in America

Baum, Charlotte, Paula Hyman, and Sonya Michel. *The Jewish Woman in America.*
    New York: New America Library, 1976.
Blau, Joseph L. *Judaism in America: From Curiosity to Third Faith.* Chicago: University of Chicago Press, 1976.
Heschel, Abraham J. *The Earth Is the Lord's: The Inner World of the Jew in East
    Europe.* New York: Farrar, Straus & Giroux, 1978.
Kaplan, Mordecai. *Judaism as a Civilization.* New York: Jewish Publication Society,
    1981.
Neusner, Jacob. *American Judaism: Adventure in Modernity.* Englewood Cliffs, N.J.:
    Prentice-Hall, 1972.
————. *Between Time and Eternity: The Essentials of Judaism.* Belmont, Calif.:
    Wadsworth, 1975.
Philipson, David, ed. *Reminiscences of Isaac M. Wise.* New York: Central Synagogue
    of New York, 1945.
Silberman, Charles E. *A Certain People: American Jews and Their Lives Today.* New
    York: Simon & Schuster, 1985.

Wouk, Herman. *This Is My God: The Jewish Way of Life.* Rev. ed. New York: Simon & Schuster, 1986.

15. The Eastern Orthodox Tradition

Garrett, Paul D. *St. Innocent: Apostle to America.* Crestwood, N.Y.: St. Vladimir's Seminary Press, 1979.

Lossky, Vladimir. *The Mystical Theology of the Eastern Church.* London: James Clarke, 1957.

Meyendorff, John. *The Orthodox Church: Its Past and Its Role in the World Today.* Translated by John Chapin. New York: Pantheon, 1962.

Serafim, Archimandrite. *The Quest for Orthodox Unity in America.* New York: Saints Boris and Gleb, 1973.

Tarasu, Constance J. *Orthodox America, 1794–1976.* Syosset, N.Y.: Orthodox Church in America, 1975.

Ware, Kallistos. *The Orthodox Way.* Crestwood, N.Y.: St. Vladimir's Seminary Press, 1980.

16. The African American Traditions

Cone, James H. *The Spirituals and the Blues: An Interpretation.* New York: Seabury, 1972.

———. *Martin and Malcolm and America.* Maryknoll, N.Y.: Orbis, 1991.

DuBois, W. E. B. *The Souls of Black Folk.* New York: New American Library, 1969.

Lincoln, Eric C., and Lawrence H. Mamiya. *The Black Church in the African American Experience.* Durham, N.C.: Duke University Press, 1990.

Mays, Benjamin E. *The Negro's God as Reflected in His Literature.* New York: Atheneum, 1968.

Pinn, Anne H., and Anthony B. Pinn. *Fortress Introduction to Black Church History.* Minneapolis: Fortress Press, 2001.

Raboteau, Albert J. *Slave Religion.* New York: Oxford University Press, 1978.

Washington, Joseph R., Jr. *Black Sects and Cults.* Garden City, N.Y.: Doubleday, 1973.

———. *Black Religion: The Negro and Christianity in the United States.* Lanham, Md.: University Press of America, 1984.

Woodson, Carter G. *The History of the Negro Church.* Washington, D.C.: Associated, 1972.

X, Malcolm, with Alex Haley. *The Autobiography of Malcolm X.* New York: Grove, 1966.

17. New Traditions for the Common People: Millenarian, Holiness, and Pentecostal Traditions

Anderson, Robert Mapes. *Vision of the Disinherited: The Making of American Pentecostalism.* Peabody, Mass.: Hendrickson, 1992.

Clebsch, William A. *American Religious Thought: A History.* Chicago History of American Religion. Chicago: University of Chicago Press, 1973.

Harrison, Barbara Grizzuti. *Visions of Glory: A History and a Memory of Jehovah's Witnesses.* New York: Simon & Schuster, 1978.

Hutchison, William R. *The Modernist Impulse in American Protestantism.* New York: Oxford University Press, 1976.

Numbers, Ronald L. *Prophetess of Health: A Study of Ellen G. White.* New York: Harper & Row, 1976.

Quebedeaux, Richard. *The New Charismatics: The Origins, Development, and Significance of Neo-Pentecostalism.* New York: Doubleday, 1975.

Smith, Timothy Lawrence. *Called unto Holiness: The Story of the Nazarenes.* Kansas City, Mo.: Nazarene, 1962.

Synan, Vinson. *The Holiness-Pentecostal Movement in the United States.* Grand Rapids: Eerdmans, 1971.

Weber, Timothy P. *Living in the Shadow of the Second Coming: American Pre-millennialism, 1875–1982.* New York: Oxford University Press, 1982.

18. Religion and the Crisis of Authority

Averill, Lloyd J. *American Theology in the Liberal Tradition.* Philadelphia: Westminster, 1967.

Boyer, Paul. *When Time Shall Be No More: Prophecy Belief in Modern American Culture.* Studies in Cultural History. Cambridge: Belknap Press of Harvard University Press, 1992.

Braden, Charles S. *Spirits in Rebellion: The Rise and Development of New Thought.* Dallas: Southern Methodist University Press, 1963.

Campbell, Bruce F. *Ancient Wisdom Revived: A History of the Theosophical Movement.* Berkeley: University of California Press, 1980.

Cox, Harvey. *Fire from Heaven: The Rise of Pentecostal Spirituality and the Reshaping of Religion in the Twenty-first Century.* Reading, Mass.: Addison-Wesley, 1995.

Cross, Barbara M. *Horace Bushnell: Minister to a Changing America.* Chicago: University of Chicago Press, 1958.

Fosdick, Harry Emerson. *The Living of These Days.* New York: Harper & Brothers, 1956.

Gottschalk, Stephen. *The Emergence of Christian Science in American Religious Life.* Berkeley: University of California Press, 1973.

Meyer, Donald B. *The Positive Thinkers.* New York: Doubleday, 1965.

Olds, Mason. "Unitarian Universalism: An Interpretation through Its History." In *America's Alternative Religions.* Edited by Timothy Miller. Albany: State University of New York Press, 1995.

White, Ronald C., Jr., and C. Howard Hopkins. *The Social Gospel: Religion and Reform in Changing America.* Philadelphia: Temple University Press, 1976.

Wright, Conrad. *The Beginnings of Unitarianism in America.* Boston: Starr King, 1955.

19. The Fundamentalist and Neo-Evangelical Traditions

Carpenter, Joel A. *Revive Us Again: The Reawakening of American Fundamentalists.* New York: Oxford University Press, 1997.

Dayton, Donald W. *Discovering an Evangelical Heritage.* New York: Harper & Row, 1976.

Kelly, Dean. *Why Conservative Churches Are Growing.* New York: Harper & Row, 1972.

Larson, Edward J. *Summer for the Gods: The Scopes Trial and America's Continuing Debate over Science and Religion.* Cambridge, Mass.: Harvard University Press, 1997.

Marsden, George M. *Fundamentalism and American Culture.* New York: Oxford University Press, 1982.

———. *Reforming Fundamentalism: Fuller Seminary and the New Evangelism.* Grand Rapids: Eerdmans, 1987.

Quebedeaux, Richard. *The Worldly Evangelicals.* San Francisco: Harper & Row, 1978.

Smith, Timothy L. *Revivalism and Social Reform in Mid-Nineteenth Century America.* New York: Abingdon, 1957.

Wells, David F., and John D. Woodridge. *The Evangelicals.* Nashville: Abingdon, 1975.

20. The Age of Radical Pluralism

Bromley, David G., and Anson D. Shupe Jr. *Strange Gods: The Great American Cult Scare.* Boston: Beacon, 1981.

Christopher, John B. *The Islamic Tradition.* New York: Harper & Row, 1972.

Eck, Diana L. *A New Religious America: How a "Christian Country" Has Become the World's Most Religiously Diverse Nation.* San Francisco: HarperSanFrancisco, 2002.

Ellwood, Robert S., Jr. *Alternative Altars.* Chicago: University of Chicago Press, 1979.

Haddad, Yvonne Yazbeck, and Adair T. Lummis. *Islamic Values in the United States.* New York: Oxford University Press, 1987.

Hall, David D., ed. *Lived Religion in America.* Princeton: Princeton University Press, 1997.

Jenkins, Philip. *Mystics and Messiahs: Cults and New Religions in American History.* New York: Oxford University Press, 2000.

———. *The Next Christendom: The Coming of Global Christianity.* New York: Oxford University Press, 2002.

Kaltner, John. *Islam: What Non-Muslims Should Know.* Facets. Minneapolis: Fortress Press, 2003.

Moore, R. Laurence. *Religious Outsiders and the Making of Americans.* New York: Oxford University Press, 1986.

Needleman, Jacob. *The New Religions.* Reprint. New York: Crossroad, 1984.

Porterfield, Amanda. *The Transformation of American Religion.* New York: Oxford University Press, 2001.

Prebisch, Charles S. *American Buddhism.* North Scituate, Mass.: Duxbury, 1979.

Rochford, E. Burke, Jr. *Hare Krishna in America.* New Brunswick, N.J.: Rutgers University Press, 1985.

Smith, Jane I. *Islam in America.* New York: Columbia University Press, 1999.

Tweed, Thomas A., and Stephen Prothero. *Asian Religions in America: A Documentary History.* New York: Oxford University Press, 1999.

Wentz, Richard E. *Why People Do Bad Things in the Name of Religion.* Macon, Ga.: Mercer University Press, 1994.

———. *The Culture of Religious Pluralism.* Boulder, Colo.: Westview, 1998.

Wuthnow, Robert. *The Restructuring of American Religion: Society and Faith since World War II.* Studies in Church and State. Princeton: Princeton University Press, 1988.

———. *After Heaven: Spirituality in America since the 1950s.* Berkeley: University of California Press, 1998.

Index